Critical Essays on
SHAKESPEARE'S
The Tempest

CRITICAL ESSAYS
ON
BRITISH LITERATURE

Zack Bowen, General Editor
University of Miami

Critical Essays on
SHAKESPEARE'S
The Tempest

edited by

VIRGINIA MASON VAUGHAN

AND

ALDEN T. VAUGHAN

G. K. Hall & Co.
An Imprint of Simon & Schuster Macmillan
New York

Prentice Hall International
London • Mexico City • New Delhi • Singapore • Sydney • Toronto

G. K. Hall & Co.
An Imprint of Simon & Schuster Macmillan
1633 Broadway
New York, NY 10019

Library of Congress Cataloging-in-Publication Data

Critical essays on Shakespeare's The tempest / edited by Virginia
   Mason Vaughan and Alden T. Vaughan.
         p.   cm. — (Critical essays on British literature)
      Includes bibliographical references and index.
      ISBN 0-7838-0051-7 (acid-free paper)
      1. Shakespeare, William, 1564–1616. Tempest.   2. Shakespeare,
   William, 1564–1616—Stage history.   I. Vaughan, Virginia Mason.
   II. Vaughan, Alden T., 1929–   .   III. Series.
   PR2833.C75   1998
   822.3'3—dc21   97-36737
                                                                        CIP

The paper meets the requirements of ANSI/NISO Z3948–1992 Permanence of Paper.

10 9 8 7 6 5 4 3 2

Printed in the United States of America

For Alice Coonley Higgins,
a nonpareil

Contents

◆

General Editor's Note

◆

The Critical Essays on British Literature series provides a variety of approaches to both classical and contemporary writers of Britain and Ireland. The formats of the volumes in the series vary with the thematic designs of individual editors and with the amount and nature of existing reviews and criticism, augmented, where appropriate, by original essays by recognized authorities. It is hoped that each volume will be unique in developing a new overall perspective on its particular subject.

The Vaughans' introduction covers the history of the play's reception in terms of critical interpretation, production history, thematic variations, appropriations, and applicability to a variety of social and political issues and places including geographical and colonialist interpretations and textual sources related to such diverse locations as Bermuda and the Caribbean islands. Their chronicle of source and interpretive possibilities of the ever-metamorphosing versions of Caliban and, to a lesser extent, Ariel as well as other characters reads like a historical novel in its own right, as the Vaughans describe how various artistic appropriations of theme, character, and meaning have given the play's ambiguities new life.

Their selection of essays covers sources in classical literature and mythology, colonial and dynastic politics, performance history, critical readings, and a discussion of political and social appropriations of the play.

ZACK BOWEN
University of Miami

Publisher's Note

♦

Producing a volume that contains both newly commissioned and reprinted material presents the publisher with the challenge of balancing the desire to achieve stylistic consistency with the need to preserve the integrity of works first published elsewhere. In the Critical Essays series, essays commissioned especially for a particular volume are edited to be consistent with G.K. Hall's house style; reprinted essays appear in the style in which they were first published, with only typographical errors corrected. Consequently, shifts in style from one essay to another are the result of our efforts to be faithful to each text as it was originally published.

Acknowledgments

♦

We are grateful to the staffs of the Robert Hutchings Goddard Library of Clark University and the Folger Shakespeare Library for invaluable assistance in the preparation of this volume. Special thanks are also due to the Alice Coonley Higgins School of Humanities at Clark University for its generous support during the final stages. This book is dedicated to the school's incomparable benefactor and guiding spirit.

Abbreviations

♦

Journals frequently cited throughout this text may be identified by the following abbreviations:

E & S	*Essays and Studies*
ELH	*English Literary History*
ELR	*English Literary Renaissance*
MLN	*Modern Language Notes*
MLQ	*Modern Language Quarterly*
RES	*Review of English Studies*
SAQ	*South Atlantic Quarterly*
SEL	*Studies in English Literature*
SP	*Studies in Philology*
SQ	*Shakespeare Quarterly*
SS	*Shakespeare Survey*

Introduction: The Tempest Transformed

VIRGINIA MASON VAUGHAN AND ALDEN T. VAUGHAN

> What's past is prologue.
> —*The Tempest*, 2.1.251

In four brief hours on a deserted Mediterranean island, Shakespeare's *The Tempest* depicts intersecting journeys and confrontations that transform the participants' lives. Gonzalo sums it up nicely:

> in one voyage
> Did Claribel her husband find at Tunis,
> And Ferdinand, her brother, found a wife
> Where he himself was lost; Prospero his dukedom
> In a poor isle; and all of us ourselves
> When no man was his own.
>
> (5.1.249–55)

Caliban, too, seems to find himself, or at least to recognize Prospero's superiority to the drunken butler Stephano, while Ariel finally attains his longed-for freedom. But the enthusiastic Gonzalo may exaggerate; Antonio and Sebastian never demonstrate any psychological or moral change, and we can't be sure that any of the principals has been truly transformed. Despite the "sea-changes" *The Tempest*'s characters have undergone, the play's finale remains ambiguous.

The history of this magical play since its inception in 1611 parallels the pattern described above: a series of intersecting journeys, transformations, interpretive confrontations, and uncertainties. The critical and theatrical history begins in the Restoration with a major sea change, not toward the sublime but toward the ridiculous. In 1667 William Davenant and John Dryden radically transformed Shakespeare's play into *The Tempest: or, The Enchanted*

1

Island, a combination of ribald comedy and political satire that nearly monopolized popular productions until William Charles Macready restored Shakespeare's text in 1838.[1]

Intrigued by Shakespeare's portrayal of a young woman who had never seen a man, Dryden and Davenant gave *The Tempest*'s Miranda a sister, Dorinda, and Prospero an adopted son, Hippolito, the usurped young Duke of Mantua. Prospero has kept Hippolito hidden in a secluded part of the island away from his daughters because of a prophecy that a woman would cause the youth's downfall. Thus the island fosters two women who have never encountered young men and a young man who has never encountered women. Double entendres abound. When Prospero warns Dorinda that young men run wild within doors, chambers, and closets, Dorinda replies that she would "stroake 'em and make 'em gentle." Prospero responds that "no woman can come / Neer 'em, but she feels a pain full nine months" (27). At the play's conclusion, a still-naive Hippolito inquires how men and women make love, while Miranda and Dorinda speculate as to how children come from their parents' "lying in a bed" (80).

Davenant and Dryden extended their doubling to the play's other characters, giving to Caliban a twin sister, Sycorax (borrowing Shakespeare's name for Caliban's mother), and to Ariel a female companion, Milcha. The comic scenes are greatly expanded with drunken buffoonery that not only satirizes democratic principles reminiscent of the Commonwealth period but also implies that only one born to reign—that is, Charles II—is capable of governing such riffraff. In 1674 Thomas Shadwell enlivened Dryden and Davenant's popular amalgam of sexual intrigue and political spoof with spectacular musical episodes. Except for a brief run of Shakespeare's original text under David Garrick's management in midcentury, the Dryden-DavenantShadwell semiopera was the only *Tempest* that eighteenth-century audiences saw and therefore assumed was essentially Shakespeare's creation.

The pseudo-Shakespearean *Tempest* embodied eighteenth-century expectations that a wise and rational ruler (Prospero) could govern the forces of disorder that undermine the family and the state. Between carefully choreographed dances and operatic arias, the gray-bearded magus pulled the strings, ordered the action, and arranged appropriate marriages and happy endings. Not until the nineteenth century rejected neoclassical rationalism was Prospero's authority challenged.

A major shift in *The Tempest*'s reception accompanied the rise of romanticism. From the early nineteenth century on, cheap editions of Shakespeare's plays enabled *readers* to experience *The Tempest* for the first time; the printed text became a site for literary critics and popular writers to contest ideas that they held passionately and to supplant the stage as the center of Shakespearean interpretation. The romantic poets—Coleridge, Keats, Shelley— eschewed Shakespeare in the public theater in favor of private communion with his poetry; they read Shakespeare for his expression of human passion, for beautiful natural imagery, and for felicity of style and diction. To Coleridge, *The Tempest* seemed a purely romantic drama that "addresse[d] itself to the imaginative faculty."[2] Prospero was the locus of that imaginative faculty: as Shakespeare's alter ego, a creator of illusions and a crafter of magic, he could see into the human soul—an identification of Shakespeare with the magus that continues to the present day.[3] Prospero's "Our revels now are ended" has been cited repeatedly as Shakespeare's paean to his art (as it is at the beginning and end of Al Pacino's 1996 docudrama, *Looking for Richard*), and *The Tempest* itself has often been taken to be Shakespeare's ultimate view of human reality.

Although the romantic poets appreciated Prospero's illusion-making abilities, they were also empathetic with Caliban, responding especially to his description of the natural beauties of the island and to his longings for freedom from bondage. William Hazlitt, for example, concluded that Caliban is "one of the wildest and most abstracted of all Shakespeare's characters, whose deformity whether of body or mind is redeemed by the power and truth of the imagination displayed in it."[4] By the middle of the nineteenth century, *The Tempest* and Caliban were enlisted in more wide-ranging philosophical debates. In the aftermath of Darwin's evolutionary teaching, Caliban was often identified with the "missing link" and Prospero with the artistic and technical achievements of western European civilization. In Browning's dramatic monologue "Caliban upon Setebos," for example, the aquatic monster contemplates his place in the universe, his relationship to Prospero, and the nature of his god, Setebos. For Daniel Wilson, Caliban represented aboriginal humanity before its exposure to the elevating influence of Western civilization. By the end of the nineteenth century, leading British actors such as Frank Benson and Herbert Beerbohm Tree epitomized an anthropoid Caliban by climbing trees, eating bananas, and impersonating hairy apes they had seen at the zoo.[5]

Intersecting with the widespread Darwinian conviction that humankind had progressed from its apish origins was a parallel notion that Shakespeare's career had undergone a similar progression, from early imitation of the ancients to eventual expression of the "highest and best" in wisdom, to quote Matthew Arnold's famous phrase. In 1874 the New Shakespere Society set out to discover the exact chronology of Shakespeare's plays so that it could analyze this progression step by step. Located at the end of Shakespeare's career, *The Tempest,* as Gary Taylor aptly noted, "gradually positioned itself as the valedictory culmination of Shakespeare's life work."[6] *The Tempest* embodied Shakespeare at his ultimate. Small wonder then that the author and the play seemed prescient of Darwinian theory.

The later nineteenth century also witnessed the expansion of Shakespeare enthusiasm from theaters and home libraries to the halls of academe. Scholars increasingly insisted that Shakespeare be studied in the classroom and that scientific methods be central to the analysis of texts. Academics sought the plays' precise chronology, their exact sources, the true meaning of obscure words and phrases, the proper interpretation of each character, and, as faithfully as possible, the author's deepest intentions. These emphases in literary interpretation culminated in 1892 with Howard Horace Furness's New Variorum edition of *The Tempest*. It assembled all the information necessary to understand Shakespeare's play: the folio text, abundant textual apparatuses, glosses, commentaries, sources, and analogues—all in one hefty volume.[7] A decade later, Morton Luce condensed current scholarly methodology in the first Arden Series' *Tempest*.[8] Behind these intellectual efforts lay the assumption that if the reader or playgoer had sufficient information, he or she could recoup Shakespeare's original intentions and thus experience the true *Tempest*. In the words of John Dowden, to understand a Shakespearean work (or any other literary masterpiece), students needed to know "how it came to be what it is."[9]

Despite the best efforts of Furness, Luce, and countless others, no one knows just how *The Tempest* "came to be." Unlike most of Shakespeare's other plays, the romance has no certain source for its plot and characters. Some late-nineteenth-century scholars thought Shakespeare's model was the German comedy *Die Schöne Sidea*—Jacob Ayrer's story of a deposed duke-magician, his daughter's courtship and marriage to his enemy's son, and the eventual reconciliation of the hostile noblemen—although Furness and most of his followers were skeptical of Ayrer's influence. Geoffrey Bullough's magisterial compendium of Shakespeare's sources proposes other literary analogues: romances such as the Spanish *Mirrour of Princely Deedes,* court masques such as Ben Jonson's *Hymenaei,* scenarios of the sixteenth and early seventeenth centuries from the Italian commedia dell'arte, and the Bermuda pamphlets discussed later in this essay.[10] Because links between these texts and Shakespeare's drama are merely suggestive, tenuous at best, late-twentieth-century scholars have largely abandoned the search for definitive connections. Instead, as Donna B. Hamilton and Jonathan Bate demonstrate in the essays reprinted here on Virgil and Ovid, Shakespeareans look to an intertextual framework of early modern and classical texts that were formative in the dramatist's education and foundational to the culture in which he lived and worked.[11]

Today's scholars also locate the genesis of Shakespeare's *Tempest* in the political and imperial context of England at the time of production, circa 1609 to 1611. This, too, is the culmination of a trend that has developed over the centuries, beginning with a reexamination of European adventures in the New World and their implications for Shakespeare's magical island.

That *The Tempest* was to some extent an American play was suggested as early as 1778 when a note by Richard Farmer in the Samuel Johnson–George Steevens edition of Shakespeare's works contended that "the *metathesis* in *Caliban* from *Canibal* is evident."[12] Although Farmer and his early converts to the theory—Johnson and Steevens, for example, and, a bit later, Edmond

Malone—did not insist that the etymological cannibals had to be American natives, the word's evolution from *Carib* has made the connection axiomatic to most readers ever since. Other critics in the late eighteenth and early nineteenth centuries suggested more substantial ties between Shakespeare's text and the colonization of the Americas, especially Antonio Pigafetta's early-sixteenth-century narrative (translated and published in England by Richard Eden in 1555 and 1577) that described a Patagonian giant with some Calibanesque characteristics, portrayed vividly an instance of Saint Elmo's fire, cited a miraculous escape by all hands from a storm-tossed ship, and mentioned a "greate devyll *Setebos*."[13] Surely, the critics argued, Shakespeare drew on Pigafetta and other accounts of European exploration and settlement.

In 1808 Malone supplemented and in some respects supplanted the heretofore exclusively South American sources with texts that focused on North America. Malone's brief pamphlet with a long title, *An Account of the Incidents, from Which the Title and Part of the Story of Shakspeare's Tempest were Derived; and Its True Date Ascertained* (reprinted in his posthumous variorum *Tempest,* 1821), insisted that Shakespeare had read one or more of the several descriptions that appeared in London in 1610 and 1611 of the Gates-Somers expedition's shipwreck on Bermuda in 1609, and subsequent editors and critics generally acknowledged tangential ties between the pamphlets and the play. But not until the end of the nineteenth century did English and American scholars contend that Shakespeare meant *The Tempest* to be substantially about English imperialism, to take place in English America (perhaps even, as Rudyard Kipling insisted, in Bermuda), and to have some of its characters—certainly Caliban, but perhaps other major figures as well—emblemize the participants in England's overseas venture. By then, Morton Luce had given a major push toward the perception of *The Tempest* as an American-centered play by demonstrating that Shakespeare "must surely have seen" in manuscript, in 1610 or soon after, the most relevant of the Bermuda pamphlets—William Strachey's narrative epistle, "A true reportory," that had heretofore been overlooked because it was not published until 1625. Strachey's account of "[a] most dreadful tempest," Luce argued, probably inspired the play's title, opening scene, and numerous items of plot and dialogue.[14]

Led by Sir Sidney Lee and Sir Walter Alexander Raleigh in England and by Charles Mills Gayley and Robert Ralston Cawley in the United States, the Americanization of *The Tempest* dominated interpretive trends through most of the twentieth century.[15] Until the 1960s its focus remained principally on Shakespeare's sources and intentions: From which "colonial" texts did he borrow specific ideas, characters, and details? What aspects of English imperialism and its participants did he mean to represent? Not every commentator was so essentialist, of course, but most agreed tacitly if not overtly with Lee that *The Tempest* is "a veritable document of early Anglo-American history."[16]

In the sixth decade of the twentieth century, a more figurative application of *The Tempest*'s Americanization emerged, especially among scholars in the relatively new field of American studies. While accepting the fundamental influence of English colonialism on *The Tempest*'s genesis, Leo Marx, Leslie Fiedler, and many of their post–World War II contemporaries highlighted the play's prophetic lessons for the Americas, especially the United States, and, more ominously, colonialism's stimulus to American exploitation and racism. Fiedler, for example, found embedded in *The Tempest* "the whole history of imperialist America . . . prophetically revealed to us in brief parable: from the initial act of expropriation through the Indian wars to the setting up of reservations, and from the beginnings of black slavery to the first revolts and evasions."[17]

The "new historicists" of the 1970s and 1980s rejected both the intentionalist and the allegorical approaches and insisted instead that what really mattered about *The Tempest* was its broad historical and literary context—the dominant discourses, both written and oral, from which Shakespeare inevitably drew his inspiration and the play's lineaments, characters, and, ultimately, its literary and political significance. Some critical analyses of *The Tempest* incorporated Jacobean England's simultaneous, and often greater, concern with other places and issues, including events in Ireland, Africa, the Mediterranean, and the Caribbean. Relevant, too, were discourses about events at home (social and political disorder, monarchial succession, and witchcraft, to name a few) and in continental Europe (religious wars, dynastic struggles, territorial expansion). Despite such wide-ranging foci, the core of the new historicist reading of *The Tempest* remained colonialist—or, more accurately, anticolonialist—and often, as Merideth Skura has observed, resulted in the misleading exclusion of other important historical and literary perspectives.[18] More recently, *Tempest* critics have explored significant and perhaps formative contexts that did not directly concern England's colonial venture, as in David Scott Kastan's discovery of parallels among *The Tempest*, the court of King James, and the Habsburg empire.[19]

While scholars in the twentieth century were broadening *The Tempest*'s possible sources and meanings to include Europe and especially America, other writers culled the play for still broader geographic and symbolic applications. To social and political commentators, Shakespeare was no longer exclusively an English poet, nor *The Tempest* simply an Anglo-American play. When appropriated by peoples around the world who had been colonized and educated by the British or who had been threatened, even invaded, by Britain's former colonies in North America, *The Tempest* resonated quite differently. In its modern transformation as a colonial text, *The Tempest*'s origins and Shakespeare's intentions have often been unimportant; what matters to many twentieth-century interpreters are the power relations between colonizer and colonized that seem embedded in the play's plot and characters. During the past century, various *Tempest* figures have been cast as Western imperialism's perpetrators, abettors, or victims.

Latin American emblemizations of *The Tempest* began in the late 1890s with identifications of Caliban as the imperialist; added Ariel at the turn of the century as the monster's cultural antithesis and political antagonist ("Arielism" remains to this day an important Latin American cultural concept); further added Prospero, in lieu of Caliban, as the imperialist emblem in the 1950s, when Caliban, in turn, largely inherited Ariel's earlier role. Since 1950, too, the metaphor's practitioners have emerged on every continent and have expanded *The Tempest*'s relevance to every part of the postcolonial world. The breadth of such identifications, as Alden Vaughan's essay on Third World appropriations suggests, is remarkable evidence of *The Tempest*'s popularity, flexibility, and universality.[20]

In 1987 Rob Nixon speculated in the conclusion to his analysis of postcolonial appropriations of *The Tempest* that "the play's declining pertinence to contemporary Africa and the Caribbean has been exacerbated by the difficulty of wresting from it any role for female defiance or leadership."[21] After all, Miranda is the only female figure who actually appears in the text: Claribel and Sycorax are referred to but never materialize, and Ariel's sex—if spirits *have* sexual identity—is ambiguous. Miranda is the dutiful daughter of the white colonizer; she willingly agrees to marry the man her father has selected for her and embraces her role as the foundress of Prospero's future dynasty. Whatever resistance she offers is fleeting. Whereas in other Shakespearean plays, strong women effectively shape their destinies—Cleopatra, Lady Macbeth, Rosalind, and Viola, to name only four—Miranda merely accepts. As Ann Thompson rightly muses, once the feminist critic has exposed the patriarchal assumptions that underlie *The Tempest*'s superstructure, what else can one do?[22]

The answer for feminist writers is the same as for many postcolonial adapters—revise, adapt, and transform. A brief survey of Miranda appropriations, a topic outside the purview of the essays reprinted here, illustrates the variety of approaches that have been taken in the past half century.

As early as 1949, the imagist poet H. D. (Hilda Doolittle) explored the creative woman's struggle to find a voice within patriarchal culture by adopting Claribel as her spokeswoman in a two-part poem, *By Avon River.* Although Claribel never appears in *The Tempest,* her marriage to the African king of Tunis precipitates the Neapolitans' sea voyage and subsequent adventures. Thus Claribel becomes for H. D. "the figure of the exiled, alienated woman,"[23] the vehicle for a prolonged meditation on the nature of creativity and regeneration.

In Canada, as Diana Brydon has eloquently argued, several novelists have found in Miranda a paradigm for their experiences as Anglophone women. To Brydon, Miranda's plight is Canadian; she is "attempting to create a neo-Europe in an invaded land, torn between Old World fathers and suitors while unable to ignore the just grievances of those her culture is displacing."[24] Morag, the Miranda-like heroine of Margaret Laurence's *The Diviners,* moves from marriage with a white professor of English literature to a love affair with a man who is part American Indian, a "Meti." After exposure to both the English and the native traditions, she finds her own voice, writes her own story, and lives independently.[25] Morag, like Miranda, never openly rebels. Instead, she temporizes and accommodates, biding her time. This, Brydon suggests, is how the British empire worked itself out in New Zealand and Anglophone Canada, rather than in the armed resistance of other formerly colonized countries.

A second paradigm in Canadian appropriative literature is to give Miranda a double, a second self who can speak the words she never utters in Shakespeare's text. In Constance Beresford-Howe's *Prospero's Daughter,* the Canadian-born Prospero figure has two daughters: Paulina is the outgoing, wayward sibling, an actor with a botched personal life; her shy sister Nan acts as a servant, cooking meals and cleaning for her father. When the father's plans to marry Nan off to the suitor he has selected go woefully awry, she retreats into silence. The novel exposes Prospero's patriarchal control for the ego trip it is: wrongheaded, arrogant, and downright destructive.[26]

The resistant Miranda is also central to Sarah Murphy's *The Measure of Miranda.*[27] The novel describes the young Canadian Miranda's sacrifice of her own life in order to blow up a Central American dictator after she discovers photographs of the tortures he has committed. For "Murphy's Miranda," in Brydon's words, "violent rebellion must entail self-destruction, because she is part of the system she rejects."[28] Murphy's Miranda remains in the colonial/patriarchal trap.[29]

Suniti Namjoshi uses *The Tempest* quite differently, confronting the play's phallocentrism by transforming Caliban's masculine resistance into the outspoken voice of a transgressive female. In her introduction to *The Bedside Book of Nightmares,* Namjoshi writes, "I tried to create a female Caliban, with a strong ego and a healthy appetite, who just wanted what she wanted. . . . I found that though its manifestation differed, egoism itself was as central to the voices of Miranda and Prospero as it was to Caliban."[30] In Namjoshi's poem "Snapshots for Caliban" (published in *The Bedside Book*), Miranda and Caliban fight as siblings but eventually unite against Prospero and reject his colonial power to establish their own female community.

Another tactic used successfully by Marina Warner in her novel *Indigo,*[31] which combines feminist and postcolonial perspectives, is to make Ariel female. Raised by the aborigine indigo maker Sycorax, Warner's Ariel is an Arawak who knowingly sleeps with the invading white enemy, Sir Christopher Everard (Warner's Prospero figure), and bears his child. Like Pocahontas, Ariel rescues the white invader from an armed rebellion, though this one is orchestrated by the black slave Caliban. She is thus both sexually and politically complicit with the colonizer. But when Warner shifts 350 years to the future, Ariel and Everard's descendant, Miranda, whose skin bears the signs of her mixed heritage, can finally confront colonialism's painful legacy and find a new multiracial identity.

As this brief survey of feminist appropriations suggests, *The Tempest*'s journey need not be male centered. While Gayle Greene declares that "*The*

Tempest is arguably the most sexist and racist of all Shakespeare's plays,"[32] the broad array of English, Canadian, and American poems, plays, and novels it has inspired—not to mention the many sociopolitical offshoots and appropriations in the Third World—take Shakespeare's text as a starting point for imaginative reconsideration of the role of women and minorities within a dominant, European male culture.

As these appropriations were being written and read, theatrical versions of The Tempest experienced their own several centuries of transformation. Although the romance's stage odyssey has often paralleled its journey in print, technical revolutions in the theater have necessarily affected The Tempest's spectacular staging. In an essay reprinted herein, Keith Sturgess recaptures The Tempest as a Blackfriars play, outlining its visual potential at the moment of production.[33] Trevor Griffiths shows how the realities of colonialism and slavery affected stage renditions in the nineteenth century,[34] and Roger Warren brings Tempest staging to the late twentieth century with his close analysis of Peter Hall's 1988 National Theatre production.[35] Common to all three discussions is an emphasis on what audiences see—how visual spectacle built into the play's text resonates with the language to provide extra layers of meaning.

In Shakespeare's text, Prospero's magic is consistently related to the staging of a spectacle: the storm, a disappearing banquet, the masque of Ceres and Juno, even the clothes stolen from Prospero's line—all signify Prospero's power to affect what people see through illusion. Prospero's magic has been a frequent topic of late-twentieth-century criticism, but as Barbara A. Mowat demonstrates in the essay reprinted here, the magus is the product of several different traditions: conjurer, con man, witch, and wizard.[36] Whatever model we use, Prospero's art transforms the appearance of reality until, by relinquishing his magic, he himself is transformed back into a man and a duke.

From the moment of The Tempest's production in 1611 to the present, the play has mingled spectacle and magic. John Dee attributed reports that he was a conjurer to the impact of the stage spectacle he directed in his early days at Cambridge.[37] Just as magic was conflated with science in the early modern period, magic and technology go hand in hand today. Keith Sturgess observes that The Tempest is a designer's play that "has always been staged in a spectacularly visual way."[38] It is hardly surprising that of all Shakespeare's texts, it should have been the most inspirational to late-twentieth-century filmmakers who privilege the camera's visual potential over the theater's spoken word.

Beginning in 1956 with the science fiction classic Forbidden Planet, cinematic appropriations of The Tempest have used the technological magic of special effects to convey the play's visual qualities, situating the characters in contemporary or, in the case of Forbidden Planet, futuristic contexts. Forbidden Planet was set in A.D. 2257 on planet Altair IV, an interplanetary outpost where space-age scientist Dr. Morbius and his nubile daughter live in isolation from planet Earth. The plot parallels some of Shakespeare's original pattern: a spaceship from Earth lands on Altair IV; its commander falls in love with the scientist's daughter; an Ariel figure (Robby the Robot) gets the cook drunk; and the scientist's superior technology, like Prospero's magic, enables him to control events and people. But the film's stunning visual effects—the sudden appearance of huge footprints in the sand, the ruined vestiges of a seemingly modern city wracked by an overpowering electrical field, and the electromagnetic image of a monstrous man-eating figure—suggest the nuclear age. *Forbidden Planet* highlights the perils of technology, specifically nuclear energy, that has the power to destroy as well as to aid. Within humankind lurks Caliban, the id, who embodies the destructive impulses of the human heart.[39]

Derek Jarman's 1979 counterculture version of *The Tempest* plays with Shakespeare by using blatant sight gags that magnify homoerotic impulses latent in the original play. Filmed in the Palladian Stoneleigh Abbey in Warwickshire, the visually suggestive film presents Prospero as an eighteenth-century protoscientist/magician. Heathcote Williams, a dabbler in magic himself, portrays a young Prospero more at home in his study than in relations with his servants or his daughter. As Kate Chedgzoy notes, "Magic is both the subject and method of Jarman's version of *The Tempest*."[40] The film floats easily from image to image, from Miranda playing in her bath, to the dance of drunken sailors on the beach, to the grotesque flashback of Caliban sucking at Sycorax's rotund breast, to black soul-singer Elisabeth Welch's camp rendition of "Stormy Weather" at the end. Though much of Shakespeare's language is lost, the *jouissance* of Jarman's visual magic compensates.

Paul Mazursky set his 1982 *Tempest* adaptation in the contemporary world of Manhattan's professional class. When Phillip Dimitrious, the Prospero figure, is caught in a midlife crisis, partly inspired by his wife's (Antonia) affair with his boss (Alonso), he flees New York with his teenage daughter (Miranda) to find a simpler life on an abandoned Greek island. There the only native is Kalibanos, who tries to seduce Miranda by inviting her into his cave to see his Sony television set. Phillip learns at last to forgive Kalibanos, Antonia, and Alonso, and the reconciled family returns to New York. There are slight suggestions of a colonial motif in Mazursky's film; as the sailors Stephano and Trinculo comment, Kalibanos, who sells trinkets to the tourists, is attractive "in a Third World sort of a way." The primary focus is not on Caliban, however, but on Phillip/Prospero's emotions: his obsessive control of his daughter's sexuality, his anger at his wife's infidelity, and his disgust with the Manhattan rat race. His eventual recognition of his own shortcomings enables him to forgive those around him.

The most elaborate reenvisioning of *The Tempest* of the late twentieth century is Peter Greenaway's 1991 film, *Prospero's Books*. This lavish tour de force evokes the lushness of Prospero's island by myriads of slowly moving naked figures, who bear fruit and flowers in a human cornucopia. The Neapolitans, by contrast, are overdressed in mammoth hats, tight black velvet doublets, chopines, and gargantuan linen ruffs. Presiding over the island is John Gielgud as Prospero, a magus who relies for his power on the 24 books sent by Gonzalo. Images from books on water, color, mirrors, mythology, geography, biology, botany, love, pornography, and so on, tie the film together; Prospero consults them as he writes the text of *The Tempest* in calligraphy, moving from painful memories of the past to his desire for vengeance in the present. In the film's final scenes, Ariel inspires this all-controlling Prospero to forgiveness; he casts his books into the pool and declares the revels ended.[41] Using repeated images of Prospero's hand, writing Shakespeare's words, Greenaway ties together themes of magic/technology and reproduction crucial to the play since its inception.

These four films are strikingly free adaptations; other film versions of *The Tempest* since the 1950s have rendered Shakespeare's original text as traditionally as possible—as plays recorded on film rather than *The Tempest* interpreted through a modern artistic medium.[42] For many observers (ourselves included), no full-scale filmic *Tempest* has yet successfully wedded the camera's visual power with the potency of Shakespeare's plot and language.

Future directions in *The Tempest*'s continuing odyssey are, of course, uncertain, but surely the words that Shakespeare wrote four centuries ago will remain a dynamic source of interpretation and debate. Appropriations and adaptations have highlighted *The Tempest*'s embodiment of power relations between father and daughter, master and servants, Europeans and natives. It is hardly surprising then that *The Tempest* has figured prominently in the culture wars of the 1980s and 1990s. But critics are also realizing that *The Tempest*'s complex text embodies other topos, such as the proper uses of magic, alchemy, and technology; myth that envisions a more perfect world; and music as the avenue to social harmony. Many readers and critics are taking renewed aesthetic pleasure in Shakespeare's romance without losing sight of its historical and colonial resonances.

The complex metamorphoses and transformations surveyed in this introduction prove that Shakespeare's *Tempest* remains strikingly resilient, a continuing source of artistic appreciation and interpretation. It will remain open to new interpretations; as Russ McDonald contends, the effect of Shakespeare's language is to "promote *un*certainty and to insist upon ambiguity."[43] If Shakespeare's words were transparent to all, we would have no passionate exchanges, interpretations, or appropriations, and neither this book nor many, many others would be necessary.

The essays gathered here provide a provocative but highly selective view of where *The Tempest* has been on its long odyssey and where it is in the late twentieth century. They provide multiple avenues into one of Shakespeare's richest and most engaging dramas, but like the multivalent text they discuss, they offer no definitive closure, no universally acceptable perspective. Nor can they be taken as predictive of *The Tempest*'s future. As recent appropriations by African and Caribbean postcolonial writers, by feminist poets and novelists, and by avant-garde filmmakers demonstrate, *The Tempest* keeps moving in unpredictable but provocative and pleasurable directions.

Notes

1. Quotations from Davenant and Dryden's adaptation, *The Tempest, or, The Enchanted Island,* are taken from the Augustan Society reprint, George Robert Guffey, ed., *After the Tempest,* Special Series, no. 4 (Los Angeles: William Andrews Clark Memorial Library, 1969). Quotations from this edition are hereafter cited by page number.

2. Samuel Taylor Coleridge, *Lectures and Notes on Shakspere* (London: George Bell, 1888), 276.

3. Michael Dobson traces the identification of Prospero with Shakespeare from the middle of the eighteenth century in " 'Remember / First to Possess His Books': The Appropriation of *The Tempest,* 1700–1800," *Shakespeare Survey* 43 (1990): 99–107.

4. William Hazlitt, *Characters of Shakespear's Plays* (London: R. Hunter, 1817), 118–20.

5. For a discussion of Caliban in the nineteenth century, see Alden T. Vaughan and Virginia Mason Vaughan, *Shakespeare's Caliban: A Cultural History* (New York: Cambridge University Press, 1991), 102–14, 183–90; for the Darwinian interpretation of Caliban, see Daniel Wilson, *Caliban: The Missing Link* (London: Macmillan, 1873).

6. Gary Taylor, *Reinventing Shakespeare: A Cultural History from the Restoration to the Present* (New York: Weidenfeld and Nicolson, 1989), 172.

7. H. H. Furness, ed., *The Tempest* (Philadelphia: Lippincott, 1892).

8. Morton Luce, ed., *The Tempest* (London: Methuen, 1902).

9. John Dowden, quoted in Taylor, *Reinventing Shakespeare,* 180.

10. Geoffrey Bullough, *Narrative and Dramatic Sources of Shakespeare,* vol. 8 (London: Routledge and Kegan Paul, 1975), 237–339.

11. Donna B. Hamilton, "Refiguring Virgil in *The Tempest,*" *Style* 23 (1989): 352–73, and Jonathan Bate, "From Myth to Drama," in *Shakespeare and Ovid* (Oxford: Clarendon Press, 1993), 239–63, both reprinted in this volume.

12. Samuel Johnson and George Steevens, eds., *The Plays of William Shakespeare,* 2d ed. (London: printed for C. Bathurst et al., 1778), 1:32. For further discussion of Caliban's etymology, see Vaughan and Vaughan, *Shakespeare's Caliban,* 26–36.

13. Antonio Pigafetta, "A briefe declaration of the voyage of navigation made abowte the worlde," in Pietro Martire d'Anghiera, *The Decades of the Newe Worlde or West India,* trans. Rycharde Eden (London: William Powell, 1555), 218v–19; Eden and Richard Willes, eds., *The History of Travayle in the West and East Indies* (London: Richard Jugge, 1577), 433v; Edmond Malone and James Boswell, eds., *The Plays and Poems of William Shakespeare* (London: printed for F. C. and J. Rivington et al., 1821), 15:15 (Malone added that "[o]f the Canibals a long account is given by Eden," thereby encouraging the American connection); Furness, ed., *The Tempest,* 5. See also Charles Frey, "*The Tempest* and the New World," *Shakespeare Quarterly* 30 (1979): 29–41.

14. Malone and Boswell, eds., *Plays and Poems of Shakespeare,* 15:383–434; Rudyard Kipling, *How Shakespeare Came to Write the "Tempest"* (New York: Dramatic Museum of Columbia University, 1916 [first publ. in *Spectator,* 2 July 1898]), 30; Strachey, "A true reportory of the wracke, and redemption of Sir Thomas Gates, Knight; upon . . . the Ilands of the Bermudas . . . ," in Samuel Purchas, ed., *Hakluytus Posthumous or Purchas His Pilgrimes,* 4 vols. (London: for H. Fetherstone, 1625); Luce, ed., *The Tempest,* 144–76, esp. 154.

15. Sidney Lee expounded on *The Tempest* in the many editions of his biography of Shakespeare, *A Life of William Shakespeare* (first publ. London: Smith, Elder, and Co., 1898) and in his essay on American Indians in Elizabethan England (see note 16); and Walter Alexander Raleigh championed American origins of the play in his essay in the final volume in the major modern edition of Richard Hakluyt's *Principal Navigations,* 12 vols. (Glasgow: James MacLehose and Sons, 1903–1905), 12:111–13. Landmark contributions by American scholars include Charles Mills Gayley, *Shakespeare and the Founders of Liberty in America* (New York: Macmillan, 1917); and Robert Ralston Cawley, "Shakspere's Use of the Voyages in *The Tempest,*" *Publications of the Modern Language Association of America* 41 (1926): 688–726.

16. Sidney Lee, "The Call of the West: America and Elizabethan England," part 3: "The American Indian in Elizabethan England," *Scribner's Magazine* (September 1907), 326.

17. Leo Marx, *The Machine in the Garden: Technology and the Pastoral Ideal in America* (New York: Oxford University Press, 1964), chap. 2; Leslie A. Fiedler, *The Stranger in Shakespeare* (New York: Stein & Day, 1972), 228–41, quotations on 237, 238.

18. Meredith Anne Skura, "Discourse and the Individual: The Case of Colonialism in *The Tempest,*" *Shakespeare Quarterly* 40 (1989): 42–69, and reprinted in this volume.

19. David Scott Kastan, " 'The Duke of Milan / And his Brave Son': Dynastic Politics in *The Tempest,*" published for the first time in this volume.

20. Alden T. Vaughan, "Caliban in the 'Third World': Shakespeare's Savage as Sociopolitical Symbol," *Massachusetts Review* 29 (1988): 289–313, and reprinted in this volume.

21. Rob Nixon, "Caribbean and African Appropriations of *The Tempest,*" *Critical Inquiry* 13 (1987): 557–78; quotation from 577.

22. Ann Thompson, " 'Where's Your Sister, Miranda?': Reading Shakespeare's *The Tempest,*" in *Feminist Criticism: Theory and Practice,* ed. Susan Sellers (London: Harvester, 1991), 45–55, and reprinted in this volume.

23. H. D. [Hilda Doolittle], *By Avon River* (New York: Macmillan, 1949). Quote from Kate Chedgzoy, *Shakespeare's Queer Children: Sexual Politics and Contemporary Culture* (Manchester: Manchester University Press, 1995), 109.

24. Diana Brydon, "Sister Letters: Miranda's *Tempest* in Canada," in *Cross-Cultural Performance: Differences in Women's Re-Visions of Shakespeare,* ed. Marianne Novy (Urbana: University of Illinois Press, 1993), 165–84; quotation from 166. See also Brydon's "Re-writing *The Tempest,*" *World Literature Written in English* 13 (1984): 75–88; and Chantal Zabus, "A Calibanic Tempest in Anglophone and Francophone New World Writing," *Canadian Literature* 104 (1985): 35–50. In the analysis of feminist appropriations that follows, we are also deeply indebted to Chedgzoy's *Shakespeare's Queer Children,* 94–134.

25. Margaret Laurence, *The Diviners* (Toronto: Bantam, 1974). See also Gayle Greene, "Margaret Laurence's *Diviners* and Shakespeare's *Tempest*: The Uses of the Past," in *Women's Re-Visions of Shakespeare,* ed. Marianne Novy (Urbana: University of Illinois Press, 1990), 164–82.

26. Constance Beresford-Howe, *Prospero's Daughter* (Toronto: Macmillan, 1988).

27. Sarah Murphy, *The Measure of Miranda* (Edmonton: Newest, 1987).

28. Brydon, "Sister Letters," 176.

29. See also Lorie Jerrell Leininger, "The Miranda Trap: Sexism and Racism in Shakespeare's *Tempest,*" in *The Woman's Part: Feminist Criticism of Shakespeare,* ed. Carolyn Ruth Swift Lenz, Gayle Greene, and Carol Thomas Neely (Urbana: University of Illinois Press, 1980), 285–94.

30. Suniti Namjoshi, in *Because of India: Selected Poems and Fables* (London: Only Women, 1989), 83–84.

31. Marina Warner, *Indigo, or, Mapping the Waters* (London: Vintage, 1992).

32. Greene, "Margaret Laurence's *Diviners,*" 178 n. 5.

33. Keith Sturgess, " 'A Quaint Device': *The Tempest* at the Blackfriars," in *Jacobean Private Theatre* (London: Routledge and Kegan Paul, 1987), 73–96, and reprinted in this volume.

34. Trevor Griffiths, " 'This Island's Mine': Caliban and Colonialism," *Yearbook of English Studies* 13 (1983): 159–80, and reprinted in this volume.

35. Roger Warren, "Rough Magic and Heavenly Music: *The Tempest,*" in *Staging Shakespeare's Late Plays* (Oxford: Clarendon Press, 1990), 159–207, and reprinted in this volume.

36. Barbara A. Mowat, "Prospero, Agrippa, and Hocus Pocus," *English Literary Renaissance* 11 (1981): 281–303, and reprinted in this volume.

37. See Peter J. French, *John Dee: The World of an Elizabethan Magus* (London: Routledge and Kegan Paul, 1972), 24.

38. Sturgess, " 'Quaint Device,' " 78.

39. Bob Carlton's popular rock musical, *Return to the Forbidden Planet,* is another *Tempest* transformation. Carlton sets words from Shakespeare's plays to popular tunes of the 1950s and 1960s in a plot borrowed from the science fiction film. See Bob Carlton, *Return to the Forbidden Planet* (London: Methuen, 1985).

40. Chedgzoy, *Shakespeare's Queer Children,* 200.

41. See Peter Greenaway's film script, *Prospero's Books* (New York: Four Walls, Eight Windows, 1991) for a scene-by-scene description; and Paul Washington, " 'This Last Tempest': Shakespeare, Postmodernity, and *Prospero's Books,*" in *Shakespeare: World Views* (Cranbury, N.J.: University of Delaware Press, 1996) for critical commentary.

42. For an overview of *Tempest* films and videos, see Vaughan and Vaughan, *Shakespeare's Caliban,* 199–214.

43. Russ McDonald, "Reading *The Tempest,*" *Shakespeare Survey* 43 (1991): 15–28, and reprinted in this volume.

SOURCES AND ANALOGUES
◆

Defiguring Virgil in *The Tempest*

Donna B. Hamilton

The *Tempest* is one of three plays in the Shakespeare canon (the others being *Love's Labors Lost* and *A Midsummer Night's Dream*) that have regularly been referred to as plays for which we lack information about "sources." In these plays, there is no known source that features a narrative line that is a compelling match to the plot Shakespeare offers. Nevertheless, there has been over the years a growing acceptance of the *Aeneid* as a text to which we somehow *must* refer when talking about *The Tempest*.[1] But because the story line of *The Tempest* does not match from beginning to end the story line of the *Aeneid*, it has been difficult for scholars to know how to describe the connection that seems to exist between the two texts.

Clearly, we would have all sorts of problems were we to claim, in the same way such claims have sometimes been made, that the *Aeneid* is the source for *The Tempest*. When J. M. Nosworthy attempted to match the narrative lines of the two works, he concluded that Shakespeare's plot takes its direction from the storm–shipwreck–new love sequence in the *Aeneid,* but only for the first two scenes. Jan Kott found, however, that the play relies on the Dido and Aeneas narrative until midway through act 4. And Colin Still saw the entire play as shaped by the *Aeneid,* but rather than seeing the Dido and Aeneas love story as the chief shaping influence, he assumed that it is Aeneas's journey to the underworld that is at issue. Put another way, Nosworthy and Kott found that *Aeneid* 1–4 are crucial (though to differing degrees), while Still found that *Aeneid* 6 is crucial. It is hard to imagine this degree of contradiction and confusion in any traditional source study. Our options for dealing with it seem to be either to consider that the enterprise of trying to associate the two texts may ultimately be unproductive or to consider that, for this play at least, the method by which we assess the impact of a precursor text on a Shakespeare text needs revision.

I shall argue that we can use what we know about the theory and practice of rhetorical imitation (*imitatio*)[2] to reconsider the question of how *The Tempest* and the *Aeneid* are related. This essay pursues that relationship by con-

"Defiguring Virgil in *The Tempest*" originally appeared in *Style* 23 (fall 1989): 352–73. Reprinted with permission.

sidering *The Tempest* as a work that imitates the first six books of the *Aeneid,* and does so rather rigorously, both in its larger patterns of theme and structure and in its smaller details of vocabulary and syntax. Many steps must be taken before one can feel comfortable either posing or granting that a strong and deep connection exists between these two texts. Clearly not everyone will be persuaded of the kind of genealogical link I am proposing; so much depends not merely on noticing the connections that are easy to see but also on finding that, in Shakespeare's play, the *Aeneid* has been dismantled, reversed, and rewritten. The fundamental obstacle we confront in pursuing such a notion, therefore, is not simply our own habits of expecting Shakespeare's sources to be obvious, but the conditions that inform the practice of imitation, a practice founded on methods for changing and concealing the precursor text.

Among the various conditions that can make recognition possible, one is simply the patience for "quiet meditation" that Petrarch said was necessary if one was to discover the deep similarities between texts that imitation produces (Bishop 199; also qtd. in Greene 95). Another condition, one that is easier to come by, is sufficient understanding of the methods used in imitation. A reader who would recognize an act of imitation must know the possibilities that exist whereby a precursor text can make a reappearance in a new text. For without that knowledge, often the codes that make recognition possible cannot even be seen. When that knowledge is available, however, one can reach the point where it is possible to find, in the very act of concealing, the systems that promote revealing.

In "The Life of Ariosto" that Sir John Harington includes in his translation of *Orlando Furioso,* Harington remarks that Ariosto privileged Boiardo for imitation because Boiardo was so familiar at the time: "he chose *Boyardo* upon whose work he would ground . . . because he said *Boyardos* worke was fresh in everie mans minde" (572).[3] One implication here is, as Michael Riffaterre might express it, that the text "is constructed in such a way that it can control its own decoding" (6),[4] and that the author who uses a very familiar system (as indeed the *Aeneid* also was very familiar), even when his use of it is extraordinarily clever and obscure, offers his audience or reader the opportunity to see that from which the text has been made. Here as everywhere, the fact that something is hidden does not mean that it is lost. The issue is one that Riffaterre addresses in formulating his theories of text production. For Riffaterre, the concealing that occurs in a literary work often exists as a means of calling attention to the genetics of a text and therefore to its artistic ideas. I would suggest that we may be able to say of *The Tempest* what he says about some of the French texts he studies: it is a work that "conceals only in order to reveal," and it "veils" its art "but it always points to where it is hidden and how it can be revealed" (111, 112).

DEFIGURATIONS OF THE TEXT

Imitation in the Renaissance means beginning with the art of another artist and then making of that art something new. This assumption about poetic composition is implicit in Ben Jonson's definition of imitation: the imitative poet, he said, was "to draw forth out of the best, and choisest flowers, with the Bee, and turne all into Honey, worke it into one relish, and savour" (8:639).[5] And it is also the assumption articulated by Petrarch, who, in writing to Boccaccio about the problem of imitating Virgil, used not the familiar bee metaphor but the filial metaphor, which was also common to ancient and Renaissance discussions of imitation:

> A proper imitator should take care that what he writes resembles the original without reproducing it. The resemblance should not be that of a portrait to the sitter—in that case the closer the likeness is the better—but it should be the resemblance of a son to his father. Therein is often the great divergence in particular features, but there is a certain suggestion, what our painters call an "air," most noticeable in the face and eyes, which makes the resemblance. As soon as we see the son, he recalls the father to us although if we should measure every feature we should find them all different. But there is a mysterious something there that has this power. Thus we writers must look to it that with a basis of similarity there should be many dissimilarities. And the similarity should be planted so deep that it can only be extricated by quiet meditation. (Bishop 198–99; also qtd. in Greene 95–96)

To compare the new work to its model as one would compare son to father is to suggest how much the two works hold deeply in common: the new work bears unmistakably the essence of the other. But it is equally important that there should be radical dissimilarities between the two. Just as the son is indisputably an entirely separate individual from his father, the dissimilarities between the parent work and the imitation are so many that the new work stands securely on its own.

In placing the emphasis on the difference between the model and the new work, Petrarch was following Seneca, who, in his well-known "Epistle 84," had answered his own question as to whether or not the model would be obvious: "I think that sometimes it is impossible for it to be seen who is being imitated, if the copy is a true one; for a true copy stamps its own form upon all the features which it has drawn from what we may call the original" (84.9). Clearly, for both Seneca and Petrarch, the poet's object was to change the model so that the genealogical lines disappeared from sight and the parent work became hidden. If Petrarch differed from Seneca, it was in his consideration of the ability to notice resemblances. While Seneca held out the possibility that recognition might never occur, Petrarch assumed that "a certain suggestion," "an 'air'" would be glimpsed. But his emphasis, at the same time, on the "quiet meditation" needed for recognition acknowledged that recognition was not always easy.

It probably is not hard to see that these notions about how texts relate to each other apply in a general way to the relationship between *The Tempest* and the *Aeneid*. The two works are profoundly different from each other, but there is still an "air," easily and frequently sensed, of the *Aeneid* in *The Tempest*. The storm—shipwreck—new love sequence ensures that. But to go farther than this, farther than making statements that sound as though we might just as well use the terms "influence" and "analogue" to describe the relationship of these two texts, and to reach the point where we can see *The Tempest* formally as an imitation of the *Aeneid*, we must also go farther with an understanding of what the object of imitation is. Imitation is not merely building echoes of one work into another or taking the work of another writer and dressing it up for one's own purposes. Imitation involves the poet in the finest subtleties of another's work. It involves the poet in the art, the workmanship, of the parent work, and it is the art that is often a primary object of imitation.

We find this point forcibly made by Johannes Sturm in *Nobilitas Liberata,* published in Germany in 1549 and in English translation in 1570 under the title *A Ritch Storehouse or Treasure for Nobilitye and Gentlemen.* Called "perhaps the most suggestive document in English that we have on the practice of imitation" (Trousdale 165),[6] *A Ritch Storehouse* contains Sturm's instructions to his students on how to write well.

Sturm took the standard Renaissance position that good writing was made by imitating other good writing. While his concern was writing compositions for classroom exercises rather than writing poetry, he proceeded with the same assumptions about models and newness that we have just noted in the statements of Jonson, Petrarch, and Seneca. For models Sturm directed his students to the best authors; if they were to learn to imitate, then they had to follow Virgil, and this included learning how Virgil imitated Theocritus and Homer. But what makes Sturm's book especially helpful for understanding what an act of imitation involved is the emphasis he placed, first, on the process of reading and analyzing the text to be imitated and, second, on the alternative methods available for changing that text into something new.

When Sturm took up the subject of reading, he distinguished the reading one did in preparation for imitation from the reading one did to acquire "knowledge and understanding." The chief distinction was that reading in preparation for imitation required more time and painstaking care; it required "a pawse or stay" (H7) because the object of the reading was to discover "the Arte or workmanship" (E3) that had gone into the text being studied. The students who would become these more pausing and observant readers were encouraged to notice what the text was made out of and how it had been put together. To that end, Sturm instructed them to attend to the arrangement of its various parts; they were to observe "the order and placing of things" (D5v), an exercise that made them pay attention to what came first, what came in the middle, and what came at the end. They were also to analyze the "handling" (D5v). Handling included what was treated briefly, what at length, and what was repeated; it also referred to the "kindes of wordes and formes of sentences" (D5v). Sturm elaborated this last point later in his discussion when he explained that "handeling . . . conteyneth as well the ornaments and figures of speach, as the polishing of sentences and reasons, as also the framing, knitting and numerousnesse both of members and whole Periodes, with the varietie of all those things compared togither" (F8–F8v).

To aid further the process of observation and analysis, Sturm recommended that students perform three different kinds of noting, that is, three different methods of representing on paper the text being studied. One method was the occasion "when we write out whole places": that is, when we take one segment of a text and copy it down word for word. In a second method, which Sturm called "abridgements," "we gather the summe of the same places in fewe words." But it is a third kind of noting that alerts us that Sturm was urging his students to a higher order of thinking than what these first two methods might alone suggest. Sturm wanted to teach them to conceptualize a text and articulate its art; thus he recommended that they cast the patterns they perceived into linear shapes: "drawe out every part in figures." Explaining that this exercise had also been done in Greece and Italy, Sturm first called these drawings "figurative draughts," but, later, in considering that making figurations was what the author did, he suggested the drawings might better be called "defigurations" (D8) instead. The concept of defiguration reflects in yet another way how a precursor text could be conceived of as art and design, a requisite step if the imitator were to be able to proceed from "defiguration" to "figuration." Both of these terms are so rich in their connotations that we will do well to fetch them from the *Ritch Storehouse* for our own critical purposes.

When Sturm left the topic of reading and analyzing behind to take up that of composition, his emphasis throughout was on hiding. To write was to hide. "For he ought to be a hider of his Arte, which would be a good Imitator" (G4), Sturm explained; "an Imitator must hide all similitude and likeness" (G5v). Thus Sturm advised that "we must first endevour that our doing may appeare unlike the patterne" (G4v), and suggested that it might be necessary to get a teacher to help with this step, "to shewe us how we may hide and cover lyke thinges by unlike using and handling" (G4). Being such a teacher himself, Sturm directed his students to try various techniques, such as "addition, ablation, alteration, and chaunging: wherein is contained, conjunction, figuration, commutation, and transformation, both of wordes and sentences, of members, and periodes" (G5v). Sturm clarified this list by giving definitions and illustrations of each term.

His longest example was the familiar comparison of Virgil's first lines in the *Aeneid* to the Homeric lines that he therein imitates: "For as Homer sheweth the wrath and furie of *Achylles,* so Vergill painteth out Aeneas with more words and speciall tokens: so that in the persons there is varietie and in the handling there is likenesse" (H2v). As Sturm proceeded with this example, he cited lines only from Virgil, for it would have been superfluous to have to write down for these students the corresponding lines from Homer. They would have known what he referred to when he observed "what distinction of Genders, numbers, vowels or voyces is there" or that this "doth differ from the invocation of Homer by order and placing," or that "Vergil hath separated the proposition from that invocation, and hath chaunged the persons and matters, and hath recited more plentie of things which is proper to addition" (H3).

So self-assured was Sturm with this type of analysis that it comes as some surprise to find him acknowledging that people might deny the intricate relatedness between texts. He introduced this point while considering one of Virgil's imitations of Theocritus: "But some will say, he useth not the same polishing of his sentence, nor the same wordes that Theocritus doth," and, again, "But peradventure some man will denie that this was done by imitation seeing the thinges be not all one in both writers" (H1v). Sturm answered these objections, as we might expect, by emphasizing the large degree of difference that there had to be between the old text and the new one: "Imitation is not in things that be all one, but in things that be like, and that which is like, must be, not the same, but another thing" (Hv). And he explained, moreover, that the imitator strove to make it impossible for "unskillfull persons" to perceive all of his art: "he would have it known whome he imitateth, although he would not have it spyed, how and after what sort he doth it" (Hv).

We should notice in this last remark both what was given and what was taken away. The imitator wished to be both a concealer and a revealer, Sturm suggested. If the copy was a true one, by Seneca's standards, then the use of the precursor text would be concealed. But if his art was to be discovered, and so appreciated, then he had to do some revealing too. This meant, among other things, that he might decide to advertise that to which he was indebted and yet do so in such a way as not to remove the pleasure of discovering his artistry that the hiding itself promoted.

For mature poets setting out to copy an ancient text, the following of step-by-step instructions like the ones that Sturm gave would not always have been necessary. They would already have learned these habits of composition years earlier and also have acquired through long acquaintance and frequent rereading a knowledge of classical texts that far surpassed what a school child might have. Such surely was the case for Petrarch, who spoke of knowing the classical texts so well as to have completely ingested them intellectually and spiritually:

> I have read Virgil, Horace, Livy, Cicero, not once but a thousand times, not hastily but in repose, and I have pondered them with all the powers of my

mind. I ate in the morning what I would digest in the evening; I swallowed as a boy what I would ruminate upon as a man. These writings I have so thoroughly absorbed and fixed, not only in my memory but in my very marrow, these have become so much a part of myself, that even though I should never read them again they would cling in my spirit, deep-rooted in its inmost recesses. (Bishop 182–83; also qtd. in Greene 99)

Jonson alluded to knowledge of a similar kind when he remarked on the challenge it had been to annotate *The Masque of Queenes* (1609) for Prince Henry: "it hath prov'd a worke of some difficulty to mee to retrive the particular *authorities* to those things, which I writt out of fulnesse and memory of my former readings" (7:281). Greene, thinking about what permits imitation of a high order to occur and guided by Petrarch's remarks about his knowledge of texts, ascribes the capacity to imitate to this very "intimacy of conversation with the ancient text, a habitual interiorization of its letter and essence," "a kind of assimilation [that] must occur if the modern text is truly to recall its paternal model imprecisely but unmistakably" (99).

While we do not have Shakespeare's personal letters, as we have some of Petrarch's, or prefaces and marginal glosses, as we have from Jonson, we do know that Shakespeare was well grounded in the many classical texts that had wide currency in the Renaissance and also that he would have had the same access to the techniques of and assumptions about imitation that his contemporaries had. As far as his knowledge specifically of Virgil goes, we know that most of Shakespeare's explicit allusions to Virgil in the canon as a whole refer to material in the first six books of the *Aeneid* and that of these most are references to the story of Troy's fall, the love story of Dido and Aeneas, and the visit to the underworld. What this information suggested to T. W. Baldwin is that Shakespeare, like many people in his day, knew the first half of the *Aeneid* better than he knew the last half (2:495–96). That is probably so. But the reuse of the same patterns over and over for different purposes suggests something too about how the patterns available in Virgil, and especially in the first six books, had become a part of the permanent but moveable furniture of Shakespeare's mind, intimately interiorized to the point where they were endlessly available for rearrangement and changing in one work after another throughout the entire canon. Frequently, Shakespeare's reuse of Virgil is as simple as an obvious allusion, but very often that reuse is more complex. And occasionally, I shall argue, the Virgilian patterns become the chief means by which Shakespeare accomplishes a large and complex figuration.

Perhaps the most simple and obvious reference to Virgil in all of Shakespeare occurs in *The Tempest* in the conversation in 2.1 where the name Dido or Widow Dido[7] is repeated six times. Also at this point, Gonzalo makes some statements about equivalencies: "This Tunis, sir, was Carthage . . . I assure you, Carthage." It is possible to dismiss this entire conversation as idle chatter or even as another example of the miscellaneous quality of some

Renaissance citation of classical details. It is also possible to wonder, as Kermode did[8] whether the allusions are there to reveal anything. Two lines especially—"You make me study of that" and "What impossible matter can he make easy next?"—offer encouragement to anyone who is inclined to feel that the unusual specificity in the lines is in itself a signal to pay them attention. What that specificity does refer to, I am arguing, is a complicated use of Virgil that Shakespeare, utilizing the procedures of imitation, has concealed. In order to gain access to this use, we need to pay further attention to the methods and principles whereby things can be hidden.

VARIATION AND REVERSAL

Presumably, what Sturm's students were to do upon finishing his little book was to prepare to write something. As we have seen, that would involve, first, reading and analyzing a text and, then, setting out to vary it. Varying being the handmaiden of imitation, syntactical units of one design could be used to replace those of another, one word or image could stand where another one stood, and units of one length could replace those of another length. Something that had come at the beginning now could come in the middle or at the end, and one rhetorical device could stand where a different one had stood; tone, occasion, context, order, and style all could change. And, again, if the art were good, if the copy were true, the originating work would be obscured at least from the superficial view.

When Sturm chose illustrations to show his students how to arrive at such results, the illustrations he used were inevitably short ones. Even though he knew how Virgil's whole work had been imprinted with Homer's, he illustrated that use and others with one or two sentences or a few lines of verse. The changes on which he focused are comparable in size and degree, we might say, to that of changing and rearranging the furniture in the smallest room of a house. What is moved is not moved very far; what is added, even though it fits in perfectly, can be found because, the room being small, there are not many places to look. Moreover, the observer who would understand all the changes can stand at the door and look at the entire room all at once.

In comparison to what is required when one analyzes a few lines or a single passage, analyzing the imitative techniques in a longer work is not only a bigger task but also a different one. There is not only more to do and more places to look, but when the object of imitation is a long work, the art of imitation involves larger and different features of structure than can be contained in a few lines. In a longer work, in addition to all the smaller structures of vocabulary and syntax, there are also the larger structures, within which the smaller ones are contained and which are superimposed on the smaller ones or bridge them or bind them together.

In the following pages, I shall suggest what the range of imitative techniques consists of for *The Tempest*. We shall look at some instances of imitation which give recurrence to smaller segments in Virgil and which also illustrate various degrees of hiding and changing. We shall consider too how Shakespeare has organized his imitation and, in the process, structured his whole play, using some of the larger structures of character, action, and meaning in the *Aeneid* for these ends. These structures, moreover, are not simply those that a modern reader might deduce from the *Aeneid*, but are also those defined by a long tradition of allegorical interpretation with which Shakespeare and his contemporaries were familiar.

A logical place to start is where Shakespeare does, with the tempest that begins the play. The first stage direction reads, "A tempestuous noise of thunder and lightning" (1.1), and the action opens on a ship and its occupants about to be wrecked in a storm. Were Sturm doing this analysis, he would no doubt have first remarked that Shakespeare begins where Virgil begins. But here it is not Virgil's first phrases that Shakespeare copies, as Virgil began by copying Homer's first phrases, but Virgil's first action, his "tempestas" (*Aen.* 1.53, 377), that shipwrecks Aeneas at Carthage. Shakespeare does, of course, move us a bit further into the middle of things by beginning at a point where the storm is already at full force. And he adjusts the ominous and despairing tone of Virgil's opening to something more suitable to comedy. The words near the end of the scene that seal this generic identity are "we split," repeated five times; it is a phrase that tells an audience that knows other stories where ships split, that all will be well, for occupants of ships that split are typically reunited and in sound body.

Still, the presence of a tempest at the beginning of the play is a more complicated matter for a discussion of imitation than it might first appear to be. One could say that Shakespeare, by beginning in the same way Virgil begins, is being quite open and direct about the work that is the parent of his new play. The reuse of the same action in the same place allows his text to be "ostentatiously diachronic," to make an "explicit adoption" (Greene 37, 19) of Virgil's text. What complicates the truth in this statement is that Virgil's tempest had, over the centuries, been reused by writer after writer until it had passed into the literary language as topos, convention, even as cliché. "If the topos has been everywhere, then it derives specifically from nowhere" (Greene 50). No literate audience experiencing this first scene and inclined to relate it to earlier works would think only of the *Aeneid* as a precedent. It would be possible to argue, then, that by beginning *The Tempest* with a tempest, Shakespeare is being explicit about nothing; in itself, the tempest contains no information whatsoever about the genetics of this work. It may not even be Virgil's storm: "the fact that the same descriptive system appears in two texts does not prove influence; nor does it prove that any such influence, if real, is of significance" (Riffaterre 92). The only thing that can make the opening seem to be a compellingly significant, though changed, copy of Virgil's opening is seeing that the *Aeneid* is a constant presence in the rest of the play.

Provided such presence can be established, one option we have in assessing the technique of imitation represented in the tempest is to consider that the familiarity of Virgil's storm as a topos allows Shakespeare to imitate that topos frankly without his ostentatious reuse calling attention to itself as imitation. By being so overt, he is, on the one hand, revealing his art; he offers information that authorizes us to scrutinize his procedure for still more connections to Virgil. But because what he offers is so obvious, so conventional, it is equally effective at deflecting that attention, even at concealing his art. Only after the play has been searched for other traces of Virgil, is it possible to see that the tempest at the beginning, far from being merely conventional, is virtually necessary.

Another imitative technique that Shakespeare uses is that of translation, the technique that played such an important part in the development of the sixteenth-century lyric and sonnet. When Shakespeare translates Virgil for a word or phrase in *The Tempest,* a metamorphosis occurs simply in the act of changing languages. But however much is changed, translation provides a way for there to be citation of the parent work that is sometimes more specific, sometimes more traceable, than what is exemplified by a topos. Moreover, translation provides a means whereby the old text can actually be inserted into the new text. The old text provides the materials out of which the new text is made; the new text becomes the container and the bearer of the old.

One of the best-known uses of Virgil in *The Tempest,* a use that editors have always accurately glossed, happens to be also an example of translation. In the second scene of the play, where Ferdinand first sees Miranda, Shakespeare has him utter the phrase that Aeneas speaks when he sees his mother disguised as a huntress at Carthage. "O dea certe" (*Aen.* 1.328) becomes "Most sure the goddess" (1.2.424). What distinguishes this translation from some others in the play is that it is verbatim translation, that it is a translation of a famous phrase, and that it appears in a context (a man seeing an extraordinary woman) that prompts reader or audience recognition. Like the tempest in the first scene, this line too is an obvious repetition that need cause no stir; it can be, and often has been, taken as merely an incidental allusion by a poet who works eclectically and whose poetry is often randomly intertextual. Nevertheless, both the topos and the translation remain in the text as encoded points of entry for anyone who would recognize that this time Shakespeare is somehow being newly and truly serious about the relationship of a whole play to the *Aeneid.*

In other instances, however, Shakespeare's use of Virgil's topoi and language is obscure. A changed context and a dismantling of Virgil's phrases can make the use of Virgil almost disappear from sight. An example of this more hidden use of Virgil, and one that combines the technique of imitating a topos with that of imitating by translating, occurs in that florid speech by the otherwise nearly speechless Francisco (at 3.3.40 he has three more words), who describes Ferdinand's swimming to shore. In response to Alonso's lament that his son has been drowned, Francisco offers the opinion that Ferdinand must still be alive; certainly when Francisco saw the prince swimming in the sea, he appeared strong enough to make it to shore:

> Sir, he may live:
> I saw him beat the surges under him,
> And ride upon their backs; he trod the water,
> Whose enmity he flung aside, and breasted
> The surge most swoln that met him; his bold head
> 'Bove the contentious waves he kept, and oared
> Himself with his good arms in lusty stroke
> To th' shore, that o'er his wave-worn basis bowed,
> As stooping to relieve him: I not doubt
> He came alive to land.
>
> (2.1.109–18)

Within the large general pattern of the journey-storm-wreck sequence that occurs early in both the *Aeneid* and *The Tempest,* this description of Ferdinand's coming to shore may seem broadly analogous to Virgil's description of the Trojans swimming from their ships to the Carthage shores. But the specific details of the speech about Ferdinand originate elsewhere in the *Aeneid,* specifically in the famed Laocoön episode, where the snakes swim to shore and, after attacking the son of the priest Laocoön, wind themselves around the waist and throat of Laocoön himself.

For comparison with the swimming passage in *The Tempest,* here is the section from Virgil that describes the swimming of the snakes:

> and lo! from Tenedos, over the peaceful depths—I shudder as I tell the tale—a pair of serpents with endless coils are breasting the sea and side by side making for the shore. Their bosoms rise amid the surge, and their crests, blood-red, overtop the waves; the rest of them skims the main behind and their huge backs curve in many a fold.

> ecce autem gemini a Tenedo tranquilla per alto
> (horresco referens) immensis orbibus angues
> incumbunt pelago pariterque and litora tendunt:
> pectora quorum inter fluctus arrecta iubaeque
> sanguineae superant undas; pars cetera pontum
> pone legit sinuatque immensa volumine terga.
>
> (2.203–8)

In constructing the passage that tells of Ferdinand, Shakespeare appropriates for his own use several of the key verbs, nouns, and images that Virgil uses for the snakes and does so with a degree of exactness that leaves no doubt about their origin. Both Virgil and Shakespeare emphasize the power of the swimming by having their swimmers high in the water. Virgil describes the snakes as "breasting [incumbunt] the sea";[9] their "bosoms rise amid the surge [fluctus], and overtop [superant] the waves." Shakespeare follows Virgil in this description when he writes that Ferdinand has been seen to "beat the surges under him," has "trod the water," and having "breasted the surge" has kept "his bold head / 'Bove the . . . waves."

But while Shakespeare retains all of these details from Virgil, he also changes many things. First of all, he makes an alteration in the persons and in the number, as Sturm would say; he changes serpents to one man. He also changes the nature of these swimmers: in Virgil, the serpents come as a death-bringing menace and as ill omen; in Shakespeare, that menace is erased and replaced with a Ferdinand who comes as an heroic victor. To this end, Shakespeare remakes the huge backs (terga) of the snakes into the "backs" of the surges that Ferdinand rides. And he exchanges the association of the serpents with threat and slaughter for Ferdinand's ability to battle with the sea, to defeat the "enmity" of the water and of "the contentious waves." In fact, so welcome is the healing and mediating power that resides in Ferdinand that the shore seems to lean out to help him reach it, "th' shore, that o'er his wave-worn basis bowed, / As stooping to relieve him."

One of the most important points about Shakespeare's imitation here has still not been made, and that has to do with the occurrence of the Lao-coön passage in a different place in Virgil from that of Virgil's description of the tempest and narration of Aeneas and his men swimming to shore. Were we to assume that Shakespeare's use of Virgil depends upon the matching of corresponding parts of narrative lines, then we might anticipate that the only place in Virgil's text where we might find something that corresponds to Ferdinand's swimming is in *Aeneid* 1, where the action of the storm and ship-wreck yields to the action of swimming. But because Shakespeare is imitating Virgil, not using Virgil as the source for plot, he responds to Virgil's text by varying it. What this means is, as always, that a detail that one poet used in one place may be used someplace else by another poet. It also means that things not in the same place before may now be in the same place. Varying causes separation of some things, conflation of others. And while this method may obstruct recognition of the connections between Shakespeare's text and Virgil's, it confirms a sense of what he is doing. He is not borrowing a plot; he is imitating, and this requires handling Virgil's text discontinuously.

It should also be apparent from what little has been said so far that, in this example of varying, one important characteristic of the imitation is that here Shakespeare alters Virgil to the point of reversal. Shakespeare repeats Virgil's words, but the changes he makes in context result in his being able to use Virgil's text for effects and for matter that are opposite from those it orig-inally possessed. This use of Virgil, it should also be noted, differs decidedly from what we see in the "o dea certe" line as well as from the use of the tempest for an opening.

All three of the examples of imitating Virgil that have been noted so far—the tempest, "o dea certe," and the Laocoön passage—can together offer an occasion for considering how much of Virgil would have to recur in any studied imitation of the *Aeneid*. Although even the first six books of the *Aeneid* hold virtually an infinite number of things that could be imitated, it may be taken for granted that anyone considering a rigorous imitation of them would be obliged to copy many of the most well-known things, from some of the very famous lines ("o dea certe" and "Italiam non sponte sequor" perhaps) to many of the most famous narrative kernels. Sturm acknowledged this requirement when he wrote about what one might choose to imitate from Cicero: he recommended going first to the sections of Cicero "which have either some necessarie, or some notable place in them. I call that necessarie that is almost ever to be used" (E7v). The Laocoön episode qualifies as one such "place" in the *Aeneid;* likewise, in *Aeneid* 1, the tempest and the reaction of Aeneas to being shipwrecked; in *Aeneid* 2, the Trojan horse conspiracy; in *Aeneid* 4, the cave episode at Carthage; and, from the underworld episodes of *Aeneid* 6, both hell and Elysium, both the Sibyl and Anchises, both the joyous prophecies and the lamentation.

It can, of course, be argued that all of these notable places on which thousands of readers and hundreds of commentators had previously focused attention do in fact reappear in *The Tempest* and that they do so by way of the different systems used to organize the imitation. One of the most obvious systems of organization is the use of the Dido and Aeneas love story as the model for the love story of Ferdinand and Miranda, a pattern that is present from the moment of their first meeting in act 1 all the way to the conversation they have during the game of chess in act 5. But Shakespeare alters, even reverses, the model so that the Virgilian patterns tell this time a story of true love, not lust, and of right choice, not of delay and diversion.

A somewhat less obvious use of Virgil is that which produces in the play the series of conspiracy plots: Prospero's being thrust out from Milan, Antonio and Sebastian's plotting to overthrow Alonso, and Caliban's plotting to overthrow Prospero. Shakespeare patterns all three episodes on Virgil's tale of how the Greeks overthrew Troy: all three involve victims who will be threatened or attacked while they sleep. In these instances, Troy not only presents an action out of which an action for a play can be made (as the love test Leir gave his daughters in the old play suggested an action for a new one), but it functions also as a cultural premise. Though this premise may be variously stated, it includes both the notion that to attack a sleeping city is to attack order and civility and the notion that, however strong any society is, it is not absolutely strong. These ideas are so embedded in the traditional readings of Virgil's story of Troy's fall that Shakespeare can transfer them to his own new work simply by transplanting the narrative kernel that represents them. Significantly, the Virgilian narrative of the fall of Troy is not treated in *The Tempest* simply as a memory of a past event, but is represented by Shakespeare as a circumstance that is alarmingly recurrent, essentially repeatable.

In a third system of organization, Shakespeare again uses this method of repetition but applies it to character instead of action. Here I refer to the use he makes of Aeneas as the basic pattern for nearly all of the male characters in the play. Both Prospero and Ferdinand are modeled on Aeneas, but so are Alonso, Gonzalo, and Caliban. The differences in these characters are a result of rhetorical varying; in the case of Caliban, Shakespeare reverses the pattern and parodies it until Caliban becomes an anti-Aeneas figure. In other instances, Shakespeare either combines more than one pattern to make a new construct, or he disassembles the parts of a pattern. An example of the latter is his redistributing, among several different characters, the mixed reactions that Aeneas has upon arriving in Carthage. In response to the storm and shipwreck they have experienced, it is Gonzalo who offers comfort to others, Antonio and Sebastian who complain, Alonso who falls into despair, and Ferdinand, whom Shakespeare sets above the others, who feels a calm settle over him. Even as Troy carries a set of ideas that can be transferred to a play by copying the pattern of Troy, so does Aeneas. All of these details help us understand why Nosworthy and Kott could define so differently how the *Aeneid* is in *The Tempest;* it truly is in there in more ways than one (and often at the same time).

IMITATION AND ALLEGORY

In considering the theory and practice of Renaissance imitation as it is applicable to Shakespeare's art, we need to return to Sturm one more time, to address more directly the issue of what is "the duetie of an Imitator" to imitate (G4), what things are "worthy of imitation" (G3v). On this subject Sturm made two points that are especially relevant to *The Tempest*. The first, though long in implication, can be quickly said. According to Sturm, "what is worthy of imitation" was "whatsoever is worthy of prayse" (G3v); because no poet was regarded as more praiseworthy than Virgil, to imitate Virgil was to apply oneself to the most worthy of endeavors. A second point Sturm made was that it was the duty of the imitator to include in the imitation not only what was apparent but also "what is secret, and is not expressed" (G4); he was to imitate the "hidden and secret poyntes," which included "sometime a further meaning than is expressed in wordes" (G3v).

This point is crucial to a study of imitations of Virgil because of the tradition, well-known in the Renaissance, that the *Aeneid* was a text that contained, as both Thomas Phaer and Richard Stanyhurst acknowledged in the prefaces to their translations of Virgil, "many misticall secretes" (Viv), many "hidden secrets" (Aii). Spenser made a like acknowledgment in his "Letter of the Authors" when he declared that he was following the practices of Homer and Virgil by presenting the virtues "clowdily enwrapped in Allegorical devises" (1.168).

What these writers were referring to is the medieval and Renaissance tradition of reading Virgil's text allegorically, a tradition which, as it evolved, treated the allegorical meanings as a constitutive part of Virgil's text and as intended by Virgil, not as added on by his readers. Thus the *Aeneid* text we read today is, in a very particular sense, not the text as Renaissance readers knew it. To Renaissance readers, the *Aeneid* was all of Virgil's text and also all of the philosophical meanings that they understood to be there and that they could read in the various commentaries on Virgil.

This perception that Virgil's text was both open and secret at one and the same time gave rise to different systems of reading that operated simultaneously for any reader. On the one hand, the story of Aeneas was said to be the adventures of an exemplary public hero. In *Defense of Poesie,* Sir Philip Sidney referred implicitly to this system when he recommended Aeneas as the model for virtuous action: "Only let Aeneas be worn in the tablet of your memory" (Smith 1:179). Such a reading is humanistic and educational in its orientation: it considers the adventures and trials of the hero to be the means to a public end, the founding of a new civilization. As William Webbe remarked in *Discourse of English Poetrie,* "Under the person of Aeneas [Virgil] expresseth the valoure of a worthy Captaine and Valiaunt Governour" (Smith 1:237). This reading of Aeneas as an ideal public figure was also what lay behind Tasso's conclusion that, of all the noble actions that a poet composing heroic poetry had ever devised, "the noblest action of all is the coming of Aeneas to Italy" (49). This way of reading Virgil's text is pertinent to a consideration of *The Tempest* because it illuminates by confirming our sense of the play as deeply political and as deeply and importantly tied to the epideictic tradition.

But knowledge of a system wherein the *Aeneid* is read allegorically is also helpful because it furnishes a widely disseminated example of how Virgil's text could be conceptualized, conceptualization being the mental operation on which successful imitation so often depended. Although there is much variety as one moves from one commentator to another—Fulgentius in the fifth century, Bernardus Silvestris in the Middle Ages, and Cristoforo Landino in the fifteenth century[10]—it is possible to make a few careful generalizations about this tradition of reading the hidden or secret story in Virgil. Generally it is true that the commentary was discursive and philosophical in content, that it espoused Platonic doctrine and assumed Virgil was a Platonist (D. C. Allen 149; Schreiber and Maresca xi), and that it addressed itself primarily to the first six books of the *Aeneid,* the same books that are the object of Shakespeare's imitation. Also, the commentators read these six books as a maturation progress of one sort or another. In the case of Fulgentius and Bernardus, the progress related by Virgil in six books was that of the six ages of man, the progress from infancy to the wisdom of old age. Landino, however, read this progress as the journey of the soul toward wisdom. It will be assumed as we proceed that Shakespeare would have worked eclectically with, or would have possessed eclectic knowledge of, these different but still highly complementary readings, as indeed many readers of his time surely did who were used to seeing the *Aeneid* printed in an edition that surrounded Virgil's text with an enormous critical and glossarial apparatus. But whatever eclecticism might have existed and however much all these commentaries overlap, the reading that found in the *Aeneid* an allegory of the soul, rather than an allegory of the ages of man, is always the one more relevant to the art of *The Tempest*.

In considering how Shakespeare might have used or been affected by this commentary tradition, we do well to recall the instructions in conceptualization that Sturm gave his students when he described for them methods of defiguration. When Sturm instructed his students to represent the text through line drawings, he was trying to get them to perceive the form of the text as an abstraction and then represent their perceptions in a nontextual way. What this commentary tradition offered Shakespeare that was similar to Sturm's suggestion was, first of all, a set of ideas and so abstractions, to which the text of Virgil was understood to refer. Even as Sturm's defiguration drawings were suggested by a text but not made out of the pieces of that text, so too the body of meanings in the commentary tradition was not textualized by Virgil but by his followers in the texts that they wrote about his text. Virgil's text might have referred to those meanings, but it did not itself express them.[11] To the extent that it is possible to talk about the *Aeneid* as providing a sequentially ordered pattern of events that corresponds to a sequence in *The Tempest*, we will do better to look for the correspondences in the sequence of philosophical and ethical states of being that the commentary describes than in a plot outline of the *Aeneid* itself. For what Shakespeare seems to have done in composing *The Tempest* is to use that sequence—the organized discourse of this commentary tradition, a discourse which tells of an educational process—as one organizing principle for composition. In other words, for the purposes of the imitation, Shakespeare has treated the commentary tradition as a continuous text, and Virgil's literal narrative as a discontinuous text. And if both the commentary tradition and the *Aeneid* have been utilized in the composing of Shakespeare's text, it is, then, possible to use both of them to trace the transformations that he has wrought on both. Before we can be more specific, it is necessary to have before us a brief summary of Landino's method of reading Virgil.

Called by modern critics "the prince of Virgilian allegorists" and "the most impressive and influential of the fifteenth century Virgil scholars" (Hughes 402; D. C. Allen 142),[12] Landino included his commentary on Virgil's first six books in the *Camaldolese Disputations,* first printed in 1480.[13] Subsequently, these views were summarized, along with those of his predecessors, in many of the Renaissance editions of the *Aeneid* that printed commentary in the margins and in introductory notes and essays.[14] To produce his reading of the soul's progress toward perfection, Landino did not follow the chronology of Virgil's narrative (as had Fulgentius and Bernardus) but the chronology of Aeneas's actions and so discussed the books of the *Aeneid* in the order 2, 3, 1, 4, 5, 6. Thus Landino read in *Aeneid* 2 and the story of the Trojan War a representation of how the soul strives to subdue the passions. The departure from Troy and the subsequent adventures in *Aeneid* 2 and 3 figure the spirit's initial resistance to the passions and its new tendency toward virtue. The progress of the soul is continually threatened by recurrent disruptions of appetite that throw it off course, the most significant of which was represented for Landino in the arrival of Aeneas at Carthage and the experiences he had with Dido (*Aeneid* 1 and 4). But finally, in *Aeneid* 6, the narration of Aeneas's arrival in Italy and journey to the underworld, the soul comes to rest in an intellectual experience that unites the soul with truth.

Landino's commentary is very detailed, but a summary of it reveals the importance he gave to the Carthage experience and to the arrival at Italy in *Aeneid* 6 as representative of two poles between which the soul, struggling toward goodness, must move. Gavin Douglas, whose translation of the *Aeneid* was well known in sixteenth-century England and was used by both Henry Howard, Earl of Surrey, and Thomas Phaer for their own translations (Ridley 43–46), showed in his marginalia that he too understood the significance that Carthage and *Aeneid* 6 had in Landino's system. Of the several references to Landino in Douglas's glosses, the most detailed treatment occurs at the point in the translation where Aeneas arrives at Carthage, at which point Douglas summarized Landino by stating the significance of Carthage in terms of the ultimate goal: "Eneas purposis to Italy, his land of promyssion." Here is this gloss in its entirety:

> Cristoferus Landynus, that writis moraly apon Virgill, says thus: Eneas purposis to Italy, his land of promyssion; that is to say, a iust perfyte man entendis to mast soueran bonte and gudnes, quhilk as witnessyth Plato, is situate in contemplation of godly thyngis or dyvyn warkis. His onmeysabill ennymy Iuno, that is frenzeit queyn of realmys, entendis to dryve him from Italle to Cartage; that is, Avesion, or concupissence to ryng or haf warldly honouris, wald draw him fra contemplation to the actyve lyve; quhilk, quhen scho falis by hir self, tretis scho with Eolus, the neddyr part of raison, quhilk sendis the storm of mony warldly consalis in the iust manis mynd. Bot, quhoubeyt the mynd lang flowis and delitis heirintyll, fynaly by the fre wyll and raison predomynent, that is ondirstand, by Neptun, the storm is cessit, and, as follois in the nyxt c., arryvit in sond havin, quhilk is tranquilite of consciens; and fynaly Venus, in the vi c. following, schawis Ene his feris recouerit again, quhilk is, fervent lufe and cherite schawis the iust man his swete meditationys and feruour of deuotion, quham he tynt by warldly curis, restorit to hym again, and all his schippis obot on, be quham I ondyrstand the tyme lost. (2:29n100)[15]

As important as this gloss is and as suggestive as it is of Landino's influence in England, we know from reading Douglas's accompanying translation that such a reading was for him only half the story. The translation itself is a heavily politicized one, emphasizing not the story of private life that could be read allegorically in the *Aeneid,* but the story of public life that Virgil's narrative tells, the story of Aeneas's founding a new civilization. And in both of these stories, *Aeneid* 6 has great importance, for the arrival in Italy is the occasion on which the goals toward which both stories strive come to fulfillment. What can be found in Douglas that is not apparent in Landino, then, is the more common tradition of reading Virgil as telling at one and the same time at least two stories, one a public story of political commitment and one an allegorical treatment of an intensely private struggle. As Bernardus said, "we treat Virgil both as poet and as philosopher," as one who observed a method of " 'twofold teaching' " (Schreiber and Maresca 3).

One way of explaining how Shakespeare responded to this tradition in his own imitation is to say that he invented a way to tell these two stories— the political story and the story of the soul's progress—as one. He structured the central political action of the play—Prospero's plot for regaining his dukedom in Italy—so that it incorporates a series of educational journeys. There is indeed the sense by the end of the play that all the characters have been on progresses as Gonzalo acknowledges when he remarks on all that has been found "in one voyage," including "all of us ourselves / When no man was his own." Admittedly, some (Prospero, for example) started before others, and some do not get as far as others. Caliban, we might say, does not get much beyond "Carthage." There is as well the more particularly enacted educational progress of Ferdinand, whom Prospero disciplines, tests, and finally rewards.

This story of moral progresses is virtually the same as the story of the soul's progress that Landino read in Virgil. It is, moreover, the continuous "text" that Shakespeare transfers from the medieval and Renaissance Virgilian tradition to *The Tempest,* where he uses *it* (not the chronology of Virgil's narrative) as the frame within which, and on which, to compose the intricate details of his imitation. Because this story is essentially philosophical and moral in content, a discourse that is in every sense of the word "commonplace," it conceivably can be told in or with any number or variety of specific plot structures and narrative kernels. In this instance, however, this discursive chronology becomes the supporting and organizing structure that enables Shakespeare to work freely with the text of the *Aeneid,* to disassemble that literal narrative and rearrange and reverse its bits and pieces as it suits him in order to invent the new speeches and new actions for the play he is now writing.

If Shakespeare's management of the Virgilian text attests to an expert craftsmanship, it also confirms Greene's sense that one effect of imitation is that it "shook [the] absolute status" of the precursor text "by calling attention to the specific circumstances of its production" (47). Grasping some features of Shakespeare's disruption of Virgil, Kott thought that it signaled a rejection of Virgil. A different possibility is that the rewriting was gauged so that the imitation would better suit new circumstances of production. The highly normative plumage of the play is rhetorically gauged to fit the reign of James, a period when masque and romance (not epic) became the genres for epideixus. The presentation of Prospero as father and as godlike ruler repeats the central terms of James's absolutist self-representation. But the foregrounding of the idea of education—together with the many reversals of Virgil that represent the educational norm as one that discards lust for austerity, discipline, and chastity—must be read as a discursive strategy that modifies the king's language, and so offers a modification of his politics. Here the language of transcendent absolutism is adjusted by way of representations that praise and teach retrenchment, self-abnegation, and limit. If Shakespeare changes Virgil, he also works a change on contemporary authoritative symbols (Burke 209), an intervention that constitutes a disruption of more than one kind of absolutism.

Notes

1. See especially Nosworthy; Kott; Still; Schmidgall 70–76, 82n, 83n, 165–73; Bono 220–24; Pitcher; Miola 254–56; Hulme 103–15; Orgel 39–43; Wiltenburg.

2. See Baldwin, Trousdale, Greene, Pigman, Peterson, Braden, Gordon, Javitch, Cave, and Waller.

3. In the marginalia, John Harington occasionally notes the author whom Ariosto is imitating, as, for example, "Virgil hath the like. But this is described with more particulars" (260; bk. 23, canto 90). I am indebted to Marion Trousdale for the references to Harington.

4. Compare Greene: "The relationship to the subtext is deliberately and lucidly written into the poem as a visible and acknowledged construct" (31).

5. For discussion of the standard metaphors for imitation, see Pigman and Greene 98–99, 147.

6. For another discussion of Sturm, one that cites his later work *De imitatione oratoria* (1574), see Pigman 11.

7. Incidentally, despite the explanation by Orgel (40–41), it may not be necessary to go to a non-Virgilian tradition to understand the references to widow Dido. Dido was a widow when Aeneas came to Carthage; upon leaving Carthage after the cave incident, which Virgil says they called a marriage, Aeneas then became in effect a widower because Dido committed suicide. Still, see Lee Patterson (157–59) for an important consideration of Virgil and the Dido tradition, expressed in terms that admittedly are compelling for anyone interested in Shakespeare and Virgil.

8. Frank Kermode, whose edition of the play I cite in this essay, discards the older assumption that the references to Dido and Aeneas are trivial and comments, "*The Tempest* is far from being a loosely built play; and nowhere in Shakespeare, not even in his less intensive work, is there anything resembling the apparent irrelevance of lines 73–97. It is a possible inference that our frame of reference is badly adjusted, or incomplete, and that an understanding of this passage will modify our image of the whole play" (46–47).

9. Thomas Cooper defines *incumbo* as "to leane upon: to fall on a thyng: to sink downe on a thyng: to be inclined to: to geve diligence or studie to: to indevour earnestly" (63). Surrey

incorporates "incumbunt" in his translation by writing "With rered brest lift up above the sea" (63). Knapp also translates "incumbunt" as "are breasting" and, by way of explanation, refers the reader to the appropriate sections on grammar elsewhere in this textbook. I am indebted to Linda Wallace for this reference.

    10.   See D. C. Allen 135–62; Murrin 27–50; Stahel 1–39; Brinton 24–40; Whitbread 105–53; Schreiber and Maresca xix–xxiii; and Stahl 3–65.

    11.   For a discussion of the relationship between a medieval poem and the commentary tradition as one that gives a poem two outlines, see Judson Boyce Allen 117–50. See also Allen's discussion of the commentary on the *Aeneid* by Bernardus Silvestris (89–91, 133–35).

    12.   For further discussion of Landino's currency in the Renaissance, see Craig Kallendorf.

    13.   The *Camaldolese Disputations* are most conveniently available in, from the translation by Stahel, "Landino's Allegorization of the *Aeneid*." For summaries of Landino, see D. C. Allen 146–54; Murrin 197–202; and Kallendorf.

    14.   See, for example, Virgil, *Opera* (Nuremberg, 1492 and Venice, 1532). For a list of some editions of Virgil and the commentaries each includes, see Sears Jayne and Frances R. Johnson.

    15.   For other marginalia on Landino, see Douglas 1:154; 2:31n.49; and 2:35n.28; references to notes to Servius are reproduced in 1:144ff.

Works Cited

Allen, D. C. *Mysteriously Meant*. Baltimore: Johns Hopkins UP, 1970.

Allen, Judson Boyce. *The Ethical Poetic of the Later Middle Ages*. Toronto: U of Toronto P, 1982.

Baldwin, T. W. *William Shakspere's Small Latine and Lesse Greeke*. 2 vols. Urbana: U of Illinois P, 1944.

Bishop, Morris, trans. *Letters from Petrarch*. Bloomington: U of Indiana P, 1966.

Bono, Barbara. *Literary Transvaluation: From Vergilian Epic to Shakespearean Tragicomedy*. Berkeley: U of California P, 1984.

Braden, Gordon. *The Classics and English Renaissance Poetry*. New Haven: Yale UP, 1978.

Brinton, Anna Cox, ed. *Maphaeus Vegius and his Thirteenth Book of the* Aeneid: *A Chapter on Virgil in the Renaissance*. Stanford: Stanford UP, 1930.

Bullough, Geoffrey, ed. *Narrative and Dramatic Sources of Shakespeare*. Vol. 8. London: Routledge, 1975. 8 vol. 1957–75.

Burke, Kenneth. *Attitudes Toward History*. Rev. 2nd ed. Berkeley: U of California P, 1987.

Cave, Terence. *The Cornucopian Text: Problems of Writing in the French Renaissance*. Oxford: Clarendon P, 1979.

Cooper, Thomas. *Thesaurus*. London, 1565.

Douglas, Gavin, trans. *Virgil's* Aeneid. Ed. David F. C. Coldwell. 4 vols. Scottish Text Society. Edinburgh: Blackwood, 1957–64.

Gordon, D. J. "The Renaissance Poet as Classicist: Chapman's *Hero and Leander*." *The Renaissance Imagination*. Ed. Stephen Orgel. Berkeley: U of California P, 1980. 102–33.

Greene, Thomas M. *The Light in Troy: Imitation and Discovery in Renaissance Poetry*. New Haven: Yale UP, 1982.

Harington, Sir John, trans. *Orlando Furioso*. Ed. Robert McNulty. Oxford: Clarendon Press, 1972.

Hulme, Peter. *Colonial Encounters: Europe and the Native Caribbean, 1492–1794*. London: Methuen, 1986.

Hughes, Merritt. *Virgil and Spenser*. Berkeley: U of California P, 1929.

Javitch, Daniel. "The Imitation of Imitations in *Orlando Furioso*." *Renaissance Quarterly* 38 (1985): 215–39.

Jayne, Sears, and Frances R. Johnson. *The Lumley Library: The Catalogue of 1609*. Cambridge: Cambridge UP, 1956.

Jonson, Ben. *Ben Jonson*. Eds. C. H. Herford and Percy and Evelyn Simpson. 11 vols. Oxford: Clarendon P, 1925–52.

Kallendorf, Craig. "Cristoforo Landino's *Aeneid* and the Humanist Critical Tradition." *Renaissance Quarterly* 36 (1983): 519–46.

Kermode, Frank, ed. *The Tempest*. London: Methuen, 1954.

Knapp, Charles, *The* Aeneid *of Virgil*. Chicago: Scott, 1938.

Kott, Jan. "*The Tempest* Or Repetition." *Shakespeare Today*. Ed. Ralph Berry. Spec. issue of *Mosaic* 10 (1977): 9–36.

———. "The *Aeneid* and *The Tempest*." *Arion* ns 3 (1978): 425–51.

Miola, Robert. "Vergilian Shakespeare: From Allusion to Imitation." *Vergil at 2000*. Ed. John D. Bernard. New York: AMS, 1986. 241–58.

Murrin, Michael. *The Allegorical Epic: Essays in Its Rise and Decline*. Chicago: U of Chicago P, 1980.

Nosworthy, J. M. "The Narrative Sources for *The Tempest*." *Review of English Studies* 24 (1948): 281–94.

Orgel, Stephen, ed. *The Tempest*. Oxford: Clarendon, 1987.

Patterson, Lee. *Negotiating the Past: The Historical Understanding of Medieval Literature*. Madison: U of Wisconsin P, 1987.

Peterson, Richard S. *Imitation and Praise in the Poems of Ben Jonson*. New Haven: Yale UP, 1981.

Phaer, Thomas. *The XIII Bookes of* Aeneidos: *The First Twelve Beeinge the Worke of the Divine Poet Virgil Maro, and the Thirteenth the Supplement of Maphaeus Vegius*. London, 1584.

Pigman, G. W., III. "Versions of Imitation in the Renaissance." *Renaissance Quarterly* 33 (1980): 1–32.

Pitcher, John. "A Theatre of the Future: *The Aeneid* and *The Tempest*." *Essays in Criticism* 34 (1984): 193–215.

Ridley, Florence, ed. *The* Aeneid *of Henry Howard Earl of Surrey*. Berkeley: U of California P, 1963.

Riffaterre, Michael. *Text Production*. Trans. Terese Lyons. New York: Columbia UP, 1983.

Schmidgall, Gary S. *Shakespeare and the Courtly Aesthetic*. Berkeley: U of California P, 1981.

Schrieber, Earl G., and Thomas E. Maresca, eds. and trans. *Commentary on the First Six Books of Virgil's* Aeneid. By Bernardus Silvestris. Lincoln: U of Nebraska P, 1979.

Seneca. *Moral Epistles*. Trans. Richard Grummere. 3 vols. London: W. Heineman, 1920.

Smith, G. Gregory, ed. *Elizabethan Critical Essays*. 2 vols. Oxford: Clarendon, 1904.

Spenser, Edmund. *Works*. Eds. Edwin Greenlaw, Charles Grosvenor Osgood, and Frederick Morgan Padelford. Baltimore: Johns Hopkins UP, 1932.

Stahel, T. H., ed. and trans. "Cristoforo Landino's Allegorization of the *Aeneid:* Books III and IV of *Camaldolese Disputations*." Diss. Johns Hopkins U, 1968.

Stahl, William Harris, ed. and trans. *Commentary on the Dream of Scipio*. New York: Columbia UP, 1952.

Stanyhurst, Richard. *The First Foure Bookes of Virgil His* Aeneis *Translated into English Heroical Verse*. Leiden, 1582.

Still, Colin. *The Timeless Theme*. London: Nicolson, 1936.

Sturm, Johannes. *A Ritch Storehouse or Treasure for Nobilitye and Gentlemen*. London, 1570.

Tasso, Torquato. *Discourses on the Heroic Poem*. Trans. and notes Mariella Gavalchine and Irene Samuel. Oxford: Clarendon P, 1973.

Trousdale, Marion. "Recurrence and Renaissance: Rhetorical Imitation in Ascham and Sturm." *English Literary Renaissance* 6 (1976): 156–79.

Virgil. *Opera*. Nuremberg, 1492.

Virgil. *Opera*. Venice, 1532.

Virgil. *Works*. Trans. H. R. Rushton. 2 vols. London: W. Heinemann, 1940.

Waller, Marguerite. *Petrarch's Poetics and Literary History*. Amherst: U of Massachusetts P, 1980.

Whitbread, Leslie George, ed. and trans. *Fulgentius the Mythographer*. Columbus: Ohio State UP, 1971.

Wiltenberg, Robert. "The *Aeneid* in *The Tempest*." *Shakespeare Survey* 39 (1987): 159–68.

From Myth to Drama

Jonathan Bate

III

Ovid told the story of Medea not only in the twelfth letter of his *Heroides* and the seventh book of his *Metamorphoses,* but also in a play. It was praised by Quintilian, but only two lines survive. Ovid's poems are so full of *coups de théâtre,* of supple insights into character, and of gestural precision that one longs for the *Medea* to be found. Euripides was doubtless its model, and it is highly probable that Ovid's tragedy would have been closer in spirit to its Greek original than to the surviving Roman dramatic version of the Medea story traditionally attributed to Seneca. Despite the resemblances between *The Winter's Tale* and *Alcestis, Titus Andronicus* and *Hecuba,* it cannot be proved that Shakespeare knew any of the plays of Euripides.[1] But there is no doubt that he derived a Euripidean spirit from Ovid. Euripides taught Ovid what Ovid taught Shakespeare: an art of tragicomedy, a way of writing about the mind under the stress of extreme passion, a sensitivity to female suffering. It is therefore fitting that *The Tempest* alludes crucially to the story that was the subject of Ovid's only play; Shakespeare ended his career by collaborating with Fletcher, but his last solo performance was a kind of collaboration with Ovid.

The Tempest does not, however, have the kind of sustained relationship with the Medea story that *Titus Andronicus* had with the Philomel narrative. Rather, it moves among a bewildering array of mythic materials, echoing in its shifts of mood and tone the patterns of the *Metamorphoses. Titus* is Shakespeare's metamorphic tragedy, *A Midsummer Night's Dream* his metamorphic comedy, and *The Tempest* his metamorphic romance. All three plays apparently lack a direct source of the sort that Arthur Brooke's translation of Bandello was for *Romeo and Juliet,* Lodge's *Rosalynde* was for *As You Like It,* and Greene's *Pandosto* was for *The Winter's Tale.*[2] But all three are in profound ways shaped by Ovid: they represent progressively more distanced transformations of a matter and manner learnt from the *Metamorphoses.*

To describe *The Tempest* as a metamorphic romance is to beg the question of its generic classification. The compilers of the first folio placed it first

Jonathan Bate, part 3 of "From Myth to Drama," in *Shakespeare and Ovid* (Oxford: Clarendon, 1993), 239–63. © Jonathan Bate 1993. Reprinted by permission of Oxford University Press.

among Shakespeare's comedies, while twentieth-century criticism has grouped it among the so-called late romances. Both generic terms would have been recognizable to a Jacobean audience, although the latter one was not usually applied to the drama. *The Tempest* shares with Shakespeare's earlier comedies a movement towards reconciliation and marriage, together with a sense of disaster averted. As Don John's conspiracy fails in *Much Ado About Nothing,* so the various conspiracies against Prospero fail in *The Tempest;* the play ends, in the traditional fashion of comedy, with the young lovers united, but also, like all Shakespearian comedies, with certain ends left untied—Antonio does not speak to Prospero when the elder brother offers him grudging forgiveness; the sense of exclusion recapitulates the way in which Shakespeare's earlier Antonios stand apart from the resolutions in marriage at the end of *The Merchant of Venice* and *Twelfth Night.* As for romance, *The Tempest* shares with *Pericles* sea-voyages and storm, lost children, magical transformations and revivals—all features of the romance form which may be traced back through medieval figures like Gower, the narrator of *Pericles,* to Hellenistic sources such as the tale of Apollonius of Tyre, which lies distantly behind not only *Pericles* but also the romance element of *The Comedy of Errors.*

Recent critical readers have, however, described the play rather differently, proposing that it is an *imperial* drama. There have been attempts to link *The Tempest* to the Jacobean court: its two earliest recorded performances were at court, one of them during the celebrations for the marriage of the Princess Elizabeth and the Elector Palatine; furthermore, the play includes Shakespeare's most formal masque and may therefore be said to be his nearest approximation to a court drama. Prospero's show manifestly resembles such explicitly courtly and aristocratic works as Ben Jonson's wedding masque of 1606, *Hymenaei.* But Prospero's masque is not the whole play: indeed, it is not even completed and it is a symptom of the vain art that the play as a whole purports to reject. Nor is there any evidence that it was written as an allegory of the betrothal of the king's daughter, just as there is no evidence that *A Midsummer Night's Dream* was written for an aristocratic wedding. And the fact that the play was performed at court does not in any way mean that it was written for the court or about the court.

The external evidence for a reading of *The Tempest* as imperial drama is therefore flimsy. Two kinds of internal evidence have been adduced: first, the play's allusions to the establishment of empire, what may be described as its New World context; and, secondly, its apparent relationship with the exemplary poem about the establishment of empire, Virgil's *Aeneid.* Donna B. Hamilton has recently devoted an entire book to an imperial reading along Virgilian lines; she is of the view that *The Tempest* is "a formal imitation of the first six books of the *Aeneid,* both in its larger patterns of theme and structure and in its smaller details of vocabulary and syntax."[3]

The Virginia Company was established by royal charter in 1606, the Jamestown Colony set up in 1607. In 1609 several hundred potential new colonists ran into a storm near the Virginia coast; the ship of Sir Thomas Gates, the governor, was driven to Bermuda, where it landed safely and the voyagers were able to winter. It has long been recognized that William Strachey's eyewitness account of these events is a likely source for various details in the play, though Shakespeare would have had to see the 'Strachey letter' in manuscript, since it was not published until 1625. Several allusions give the play a New World aura. Few audience members could have missed the resonance of Miranda's "O brave new world," ironic as her wonder is in context. Ariel links the tempest to the New World with his reference to the "still-vexed Bermudas." Caliban's god Setebos is a Patagonian deity, mentioned in Magellan's voyages; the name Caliban itself inevitably suggests "cannibal" and thus a certain image of New World savages. Prospero's enslavement of Caliban seems to be a stage-image of colonial oppression—in particular, his use of language as a method of control is, according to Stephen Greenblatt in his influential essay "Learning to Curse," a classic strategy of colonialism.[4] Trinculo apprehends Caliban as a bizarre creature who may be exploited for financial gain: "Were I in England now, as once I was, and had but this fish painted, not a holiday-fool there but would give a piece of silver. There would this monster make a man—any strange beast there makes a man. When they will not give a doit to relieve a lame beggar, they will lay out ten to see a dead Indian." The idea is explained by Frank Kermode in a laconic footnote: "Such exhibitions were a regular feature of colonial policy under James I. The exhibits rarely survived the experience."[5]

The text also draws on more positive images of the New World: the island is rich in natural produce and may thus be read as a virgin land—a Virginia—ripe with Utopian possibilities. So it is that Gonzalo lifts from Montaigne's essay "Of the Caniballes" a Utopian vision of what he would do if he had the "plantation" (the word denotes the right to colonize) of the isle. Montaigne inverted the normative view of the relationship between "civilized" and "savage," arguing that the inhabitants of the "new world" of the Americas were the truly civilized ones since they were closer to "their originall naturalitie" and "the lawes of nature" than are the Europeans. "It is a nation," he wrote in a sentence closely imitated by Shakespeare,

> that hath no kinde of traffike, no knowledge of Letters, no intelligence of numbers, no name of magistrate, nor of politike superioritie; no use of service, of riches or of povertie; no contracts, no successions, no partitions, no occupation but idle; no respect of kinred, but common, no apparrell but naturall, no manuring of lands, no use of wine, corne, or mettle.[6]

That Shakespeare read Montaigne's wide-ranging critique of European assumptions about the inferiority of "barbarians" prior to writing *The Tempest* is the most compelling piece of evidence in support of the view that the play is a troubled exploration of imperial and colonial strategies. Montaigne and

Shakespeare have thus come to the assistance of post-colonial critics who for good reasons need to work through their own guilt about these matters.

But there are problems with a New World reading. Caliban's god may be of the New World, but his mother, a much more important figure, is from the old world: apparently Prospero considers it necessary to remind Ariel once a month that she was born in Algiers. Caliban himself is not a native inhabitant of the island: he is the child of the Algerian Sycorax who was herself an earlier exile to the island. Prospero is not establishing an empire, he is exiled to a place that is thought to be barren. The play is not at all interested in the things that colonization is primarily interested in: gold, spices, tobacco. And the location of the island is not the New World, but what was for the Elizabethans the centre of the old world, the Mediterranean; Shakespeare is careful to inform his audience that the shipwreck occurs *en route* from Tunis to Naples.

This is where the second imperial strand, Virgil's *Aeneid,* enters. In the first scene in which the victims of the storm appear on the island, there is a lengthy exchange about "widow Dido," "widower Aeneas," and the identity of Carthage with Tunis. One gets the impression of Shakespeare vigorously waving a flag marked *Aeneid.* "This Tunis, sir, was Carthage" (II.i.88). As in the Dido section of *The Aeneid,* there is a broad pattern of storm, shipwreck, and new love. Then again, Naples is close to Cumae, where Aeneas made landfall in Italy. Cumae was the entrance to the underworld: critics have therefore compared the adventures in the enchanted island of *The Tempest* to those of Aeneas in the underworld; in each strange place, both past and future are conjured up, a process of sacrifice and initiation is undergone, and the initiates emerge in some sense redeemed, ready for a fresh start.[7] A number of local borrowings have also been traced: for instance, the appearance of Ariel "like a harpy" during the banquet (III.iii.52sd) echoes an incident in the third book of *The Aeneid* when harpies befoul the Trojans' food on the Strophades; and Ferdinand's reaction to the sight of Miranda, "most sure, the goddess / On whom these airs attend" (I.ii.424–5), is also that of Aeneas to the sight of Venus after the Trojan shipwreck ("O dea certe"—*Aen.* i.328).

But it is extremely difficult to make the pattern fit. An alternative source for the harpy has been found in Sabinus' commentary on Ovid, where it is connected to King Alfonso of Naples.[8] And as for the broader parallel, is it with Dido's Carthage or the Sibyl's underworld? Claribel in Tunis is not a distraction from empire-building, as Dido Queen of Carthage was for Aeneas (or indeed as Cleopatra is for Antony). The dynastic marriage linking Milan with Naples at the end of the play is something very different from Aeneas' founding of a new empire in Rome. Nor is there a generic match: *epic* is the form of imperial narrative, not romance or comedy, the genres of *The Tempest.*

Shakespeare's play could, however, be described as a romance-style reworking of epic material. His precedent for such a reworking was Ovid's *Metamorphoses,* the later books of which cover some of the same ground as *The*

Aeneid, but in a revisionary way. Robert Wiltenburg concludes his essay on "The *Aeneid* in *The Tempest*" with the following claim:

> Just as Virgil subsumed the Homeric stories of men who fight primarily for themselves to the story of a man who fights primarily for his culture, his concept of civilization, so Shakespeare has subsumed the search for law, for justice, the story told so well by Virgil, into his own larger story of the search for "kindness."[9]

I do not find the comparison with Virgil's treatment of Homer at all illuminating. I would say rather that Shakespeare revises—which is to say incorporates but also in important ways sidesteps—Virgil's imperial theme in the same way that Ovid does.[10] In Ovid, Aeneas' journey is a *frame:* the real interest is in the metamorphic encounters along the way. So too in *The Tempest,* the voyage is a frame; the redemption of the three men of sin, Alonso, Antonio, and Sebastian, is not the absolute focal point, indeed it is questionable whether it fully occurs, given Antonio's apparent refusal to acknowledge Prospero at the moment of forgiveness. What the imperial theme is subsumed into is a demonstration of the pervasiveness of change, and in this sense *The Tempest* is Shakespeare's last revision of the *Metamorphoses.*

The earlier Shakespearian play which *The Tempest* comes closest to resembling is that other most Ovidian comedy, *A Midsummer Night's Dream.* Like Puck, the vernacular equivalent of Ovid's Cupid, Ariel both changes form himself and is an agent who brings about change in the mortals on whom he works. We see him as water-nymph, as Harpy, as actor playing Ceres. We hear of him dividing himself like fire aboard the king's ship and of him leading the conspirators a dance so that they prick their ears like unbacked colts and low like calves. Above all, we hear him sing the great song of metamorphosis:

> Full fathom five thy father lies.
> Of his bones are coral made;
> Those are pearls that were his eyes;
> Nothing of him that doth fade
> But doth suffer a sea-change
> Into something rich and strange.
> (I.ii.399–404)

The father is not literally changed into part of the sea, as would happen in Ovid or in Spenser's protean world; instead, the bodily changes are metaphors for the inner changes that Prospero seeks to work. When Alonso is brought to see his wickedness, he inwardly undergoes the voyage to the bottom of the sea that Ariel has evoked in the song to Ferdinand:

> It did bass my trespass.
> Therefore my son i'th' ooze is bedded, and

> I'll seek him deeper than e'er plummet sounded,
> And with him there lie mudded.
>
> (III.iii.99–102)

"Sea-change" is, as Reuben Brower pointed out in an analysis of the play's imagery,[11] this drama's principal motif. To see this is to apprehend Shakespeare's drift away from the stability of *The Aeneid* into the shifting world of the *Metamorphoses*, where nothing fades but everyone suffers water-change, land-change, or god-change into things rich and strange.

The comparison between Prospero's island and Virgil's underworld seems to me hard to sustain. Tonally, there is much more of a resemblance to the islands visited by Ovid's Aeneas and to the pastoral landscapes and language of the narratives framed by the voyage. A favourite Ovidian device was the representation of a landscape *in bono* or *in male* according to the state of mind of the describer. Shakespeare has a very formal imitation of the device in *Titus Andronicus:* when Tamora is making love to Aaron, the wood is a *locus amoenus,* but when she feigns that Bassianus and Lavinia mean to do her mischief the place suddenly becomes "A barren detested vale"—in her first description "The snakes lie rollèd in the cheerful sun," in the second the sun never shines and the snakes are hissing.[12] When Caliban is helping Trinculo and Stephano, the island is fertile and abundant with food:

> I prithee, let me bring thee where crabs grow,
> And I with my long nails will dig thee pig-nuts,
> Show thee a jay's nest, and instruct thee how
> To snare the nimble marmoset. I'll bring thee
> To clust'ring filberts, and sometimes I'll get thee
> Young scamels from the rock.
>
> (II.ii.166–71)

But when he is cursing Prospero and Miranda, it is a barren and unhealthy place:

> As wicked dew as e'er my mother brushed
> With raven's feather from unwholesome fen
> Drop on you both! A south-west blow on ye
> And blister you all o'er!
>
> (I.ii.323–6)

and, again, "All the infections that the sun sucks up / From bogs, fens, flats, on Prosper fall" (II.ii.1–2).

Embedded within the Aeneas narrative in Book Thirteen of the *Metamorphoses* is the tale of Polyphemus the Cyclops. Like Caliban, the Cyclops is perceived as deformed, yet endowed with a vivid poetry of nature. In his courtship of Galatea, he holds out the promise of lush fruits:

Gay Apples weying downe the boughes have I, and Grapes like gold,
And purple Grapes on spreaded Vynes as many as can hold,
Bothe which I doo reserve for thee. Thyself shalt with thy hand
The soft sweete strawbryes gather, which in wooddy shadowe stand.
The Cornell berryes also from the tree thy self shalt pull,
And pleasant plommes, sum yellow lyke new wax, sum blew, sum full
Of ruddy jewce. Of Chestnutts eeke (if my wyfe thou wilt bee)
Thou shalt have store: and frutes all sortes.

(Golding, xiii.956–63)

This speech is heavy with wonder and sensuousness in its feel for the textures of the fruits of the earth; it adumbrates the rich natural language that is given first to Caliban and then to Ceres/Ariel as (s)he sings of "Vines with clust'ring bunches growing, / Plants with goodly burden bowing." But when Galatea refuses to yield to Polyphemus' love, nature is turned around and used as a way of describing her cruelty: she is said to be harder than aged oak, tougher than willow twigs, sharper than thorns, more pitiless than a trodden snake, and so on.[13]

Caliban is a deeply un-Virgilian creation. If we are to think in the characteristically Renaissance way and find a classical precedent for this figure created from more contemporary sources, such as travel literature, it is to Ovid that we must go. In the "Names of the Actors" at the end of the folio text Caliban is described as a "salvage and deformed slave": the *Metamorphoses* constitute classical literature's major depository of deformities; George Sandys, who actually began his translation whilst crossing the Atlantic to take up the post of treasurer of the Virginia Company, described the Cyclops in his commentary as a "salvage people . . . more salvage than are the *West-Indians* at this day," treating them as exemplars of lawlessness and lack of civility.[14]

A second precedent for Caliban might be the semi-human Cercopes, who are encountered early in Ovid's version of Aeneas' travels. They are "an evillfavored kynd of beast: that beeing none, / They myght yit still resemble men," their bodies clad all over with "fallow couloured" hair (Golding, xiv.110–14). They swear and perjure themselves until in punishment they lose their speech and are turned into screeching monkeys; in Golding's translation, Jupiter "did bereeve them of the use of speeche and toong, / Which they too cursed perjurye did use bothe old and yoong" (xiv.116–17). Language raises man above the beasts; when it is debased, man returns to bestiality. Sandys's commentary on the "Circopians" draws a parallel which is illuminating in the light of Coleridge's comparison of Caliban to the man of base language in *Troilus and Cressida:* "From which consideration it was devised by *Plato* that the soule of *Thersites* (of all that came to *Ilium* the basest and most shamelesse) entred into an Ape; still intimating the actions of men, but retaining his old manners agreeable to that creature."[15] By teaching Caliban language, Prospero tries to civilize him, but since the salvage and deformed creature is naturally bestial, since he has a devilish nature on whom nurture can never stick, all he learns is how to curse. Caliban expresses his own affinity with the Cercopes when he recognizes the risk that he and his fellow-conspirators may be turned by Prospero "to apes / With foreheads villainous low" (IV.i.247–8).

But the complexity of the play is such that this is not the whole truth about Caliban. He does not only curse, he also has his language of nature's fertility and his capacity to hear music. As the Cyclops aspires to become a lover and a poet, in a sequence of the *Metamorphoses* that holds the beautiful together with the grotesque, so the play demands that we see pathos, even beauty, in the deformed creature. Both Ovid and Shakespeare have some cruel comedy at the expense of their creations—Polyphemus sees himself reflected in a pool and, not realizing what a fool he is making of himself, tries to convince Galatea that hairy is beautiful—but their writing also expresses extraordinary pity for these articulate beings trapped in ugly bodies.

It is Jove who metamorphoses the Cercopes into apes, Prospero who has the power to do the same to Caliban. This is a crucial difference between *The Tempest* and the *Metamorphoses*. As the play's sea-changes herald inner transformations, so the poem intimates in its first line that it will be characterized by change and strangeness: "In nova fert animus mutatas dicere formas / corpora" (*Met.* i.1–2, translated by Golding as "Of shapes transformde to bodies straunge, I purpose to entreate"). But the second line of the poem ascribes those changes to the gods: "di . . . nam vos mutastis et illas" ("Ye gods . . . for you are they that wrought this wondrous feate"). It is a mark of Prospero's power that he can perform the transformations traditionally enacted by the gods: he can release Ariel from a tree and imprison him there again (there could be no more Ovidian idea than that of birth from and metamorphosis to a tree); he can restrict Caliban ("you sty me / In this hard rock"—I.ii.344–5) and can freeze a group of mortals, imprisoning them in the lime-grove from which they cannot budge till he releases them. But might such actions also be indications that Prospero is usurping powers which should properly belong only to a god?

Mortals may perform transformations by means of magic; in the Renaissance, the changes wrought by witchcraft and alchemy would have been thought of as prime examples. Like language, magic is a mark of man's superiority over the beasts. In his *Magnalia Naturae,* Bacon proposed that the new philosophy would give man the power to raise storms, control the seasons, and hasten the harvest; by studying nature, one could come to understand it and take control of its forces. Sir Walter Ralegh, in his *History of the World,* associated magic with the wise man who connected different natural agents to bring about effects which seem wonderful to those who do not understand them.[16] But there is always the risk of going too far, transgressing upon divine prerogatives, and sliding from white magic to black. The classic case is that of Dr Faustus. Occasionally in Ovid, metamorphosis is carried out by someone other than the gods. But the characters responsible are viewed as transgressive and not to be admired, for they interfere with the natural order. The most notable of them is the witch Medea.

I do not think it can be mere chance that Prospero's lengthiest description of his magical powers constitutes Shakespeare's most sustained Ovidian borrowing and identifies the arts of the mage with those of Medea. The passages in question were discussed briefly in my opening chapter, in order to demonstrate that Shakespeare knew both Ovid's original Latin and Golding's translation. The dramatic significance of the correspondence must now be addressed.

Medea concentrates especially on her power to overturn the normal processes of nature:

> Ye Charmes and Witchcrafts, and thou Earth which both with herbe
>   and weed
> Of mightie working furnishest the Wizardes at their neede:
> Ye Ayres and windes: ye Elves of Hilles, of Brookes, of Woods alone,
> Of standing Lakes, and of the Night approche ye everychone.
> Through helpe of whom (the crooked bankes much wondring at
>   the thing)
> I have compelled streames to run cleane backward to their spring.
> By charmes I make the calme Seas rough, and make the rough
>   Seas plaine
> And cover all the Skie with Cloudes, and chase them thence againe.
> By charmes I rayse and lay the windes, and burst the Vipers jaw,
> And from the bowels of the Earth both stones and trees doe drawe.
> Whole woods and Forestes I remove: I make the Mountaines shake,
> And even the Earth it selfe to grone and fearfully to quake.
> I call up dead men from their graves: and thee O lightsome Moone
> I darken oft, though beaten brasse abate thy perill soone
> Our Sorcerie dimmes the Morning faire, and darkes the Sun at Noone.
>   (Golding, vii.263–77)

When she makes this appeal to Hecate and other spirits of the night, Medea is out gathering herbs by the light of the moon. She emphasizes inversion—streams running backward to their sources, darkness at noon—because what she is preparing herself for is a reversal of the ageing process: her herbs will be placed in a cauldron in which Aeson, her father-in-law, will be rejuvenated. But, as I pointed out in my discussion of *The Merchant of Venice,* a little later Medea uses her reputation as a restorer of youth to trick the daughters of old King Pelias into killing him (she pretends he's going to be rejuvenated too, but the magic herbs are left out of the pot). In the larger context of Book Seven of the *Metamorphoses,* the association between Medea and the powers of darkness serves to highlight her wickedness and unnaturalness. And yet when she is first introduced at the beginning of Book Seven, before we hear of her magical powers, Medea is portrayed as a victim of love: Ovid gives her one of the embattled soliloquies in which his characters struggle against the passion that is overcoming them. "Aliudque cupido, / mens aliud suadet": "desire draws me one way, reason another" (vii.19–20). Hers is a divided self, as may be seen from her way of addressing herself, "Medea," in the vocative. Like his master Euripides and his pupil Shakespeare, Ovid recognizes that people who torment others are usually suffering from inner torment themselves. By the end of her soliloquy, Medea seems to have staved off desire by summoning up rectitude, filial duty, and modesty ("rectum pietasque pudorque"—vii.72). Whatever dark deeds she subsequently performs, the reader cannot forget her potential for *pietas* and *pudor;* like Shakespeare, Ovid finds some soul of goodness in things evil.

The question with regard to Prospero's magic is whether the opposite applies: is there some soul of darkness in his white magic? From a technical point of view, his speech is a typical, if extremely skilfully managed, piece of Renaissance imitation. That is to say, a number of details are selected from the original passage and improvised upon. Thus the opening invocation of spirits is full of additional colour:

> Ye elves of hills, brooks, standing lakes and groves,
> And ye that on the sands with printless foot
> Do chase the ebbing Neptune, and do fly him
> When he comes back; you demi-puppets that
> By moonshine do the green sour ringlets make
> Whereof the ewe not bites; and you whose pastime
> Is to make midnight mushrooms,[17] that rejoice
> To hear the solemn curfew; by whose aid . . .
>   (V.i.33–40)

After this seven-line improvisation, Shakespeare reverts to the source-text and freely translates a sequence of elements from it—darkening the sun and raising storms, uprooting trees and shaking the earth, waking the dead and releasing them from their graves. It is the last image that is most alarming. The earlier part of the speech seems to be a lightening of the original: the playful spirits chasing the tide as it ebbs and running from it as it comes back are like children on the beach, they are by no means sinister. But for Prospero, imagined as a virtuous ruler, to bring a pagan image of raising the dead into the Christian era, in which that power should belong uniquely to Christ and his Father, is deeply disturbing.

The capacity to raise the dead, mentioned here for the first time in the play, is the final mark of the potency of Prospero's art. It is also a sign of its roughness and a reason for its abjuration. Like Medea, Prospero has achieved renewals through his magic—the spiritual rejuvenation of Alonso substitutes for the physical rejuvenation of Aeson—but, also like Medea, he has used his magic to exercise power, to control other people. Prompted by Ariel's pity for the penitent mortals, and in particular Gonzalo, Prospero recognizes that "The rarer action is / In virtue than in vengeance" (V.i.27–8). Whereas Medea goes on using her magic to act out revenge plots, Prospero renounces his and in so doing marks a movement away from the pagan world towards Christian "kindness." Medea's powers are summoned up not so that they can be exercised, but so that they can be rejected.

This is what makes the allusion so purposeful. The logical place to have put it would have been at the very beginning of the play, before the storm; in the manner of Book Seven of the *Metamorphoses,* and indeed of *Dr Faustus,* we would then have first heard the magical incantation, then seen its effect. Instead, the audience is given its incantatory fix only when the necessity of withdrawal is apparent. Recognition of the source is absolutely crucial, for it puts the audience into the same position as Prospero: as he sees that his magic must be rejected because it may so readily be abused when driven by vengeance rather than virtue, so at exactly the same moment we see that it must be rejected because it is, for all its apparent whiteness, the selfsame black magic as that of Medea.

The speech in Ovid was viewed in the Renaissance as witchcraft's great set-piece: it was cited by Bodin in *De Magorum Demonomania,* by Cornelius Agrippa in *De Occulta Philosophia,* and by Reginald Scot in his debunking *Discoverie of Witchcraft.*[18] Jonson imitates it in the principal witch's invocation in *The Masque of Queens.*[19] Middleton, in his play *The Witch,* has Hecate quoting Ovid's lines in Latin, and then translating them for the benefit of the Latinless:

> Can you doubt me then, daughter?
> That can make mountains tremble, miles of woods walk,
> Whole earth's foundation bellow, and the spirits
> Of the entombed to burst out from their marbles,
> Nay, draw yond moon to my involved designs?[20]

Playgoers who frequented the Red Bull as well as the theatres for which Shakespeare wrote would have found it especially easy to make the connection. Thomas Heywood's *The Brazen Age* had been performed by 1611, the probable year of *The Tempest.*[21] The third act of that play contains "The Tragedy of *Jason* and *Medea*": it is in all essentials a dramatization of Book Seven of the *Metamorphoses.* On her first appearance Medea says:

> I can by Art make rivers retrograde,
> Alter their channels, run backe to their heads,
> And hide them in the springs from whence they grew.
> The curled Ocean with a word Il'e smooth,
> (Or being calme) raise waves as high as hils,
> Threatning to swallow the vast continent.
> With powerfull charmes Il'e make the Sunne stand still,

> Or call the Moone downe from her arched spheare.
> What cannot I by power of *Hecate?*
>
> *(Dramatic Works,* iii.209)

A little later she gathers enchanted herbs, and begins her nocturnal soliloquy:

> The night growes on, and now to my black Arts,
> Goddesse of witchcraft and darke ceremony,
> To whom the elves of Hils, of Brookes, of Groves,
> Of standing lakes, and cavernes vaulted deepe
> Are ministers.
>
> *(Dramatic Works,* iii.215)

Heywood, then, is imitating Ovid even more closely than Shakespeare does. His particular emphasis is on the association between Medea and Hecate, "Goddess of witchcraft." Given that *The Brazen Age* was in the London theatrical repertory in 1611, it is almost certain that some theatregoers would have recognized Heywood's and Shakespeare's shared allusion to Ovid (via Golding);[22] in the wider context of the association between the speech and witchcraft, it would have been impossible for Shakespeare to empty it of its darker tones, as some critics have supposed he did.[23]

There is internal evidence as compelling as the external. Medea has a proxy in the play in the form of Sycorax, the witch on whom Prospero harps so persistently in his rehearsals of the past; Stephen Orgel has even suggested that her strange name may be derived from one of the epithets for Medea, "Scythian raven" ("Sy-," as prefix, "korax" meaning raven, a bird with which Sycorax is associated in Caliban's first speech, quoted above).[24] Sycorax, as modern criticism has recognized,[25] is a disturbing double of Prospero himself. She is his dark Other. Each of them is banished and finds new life on the island; each makes Ariel a servant and controls the spirits of the isle; Sycorax confined Ariel in a cloven pine, Prospero threatens to peg him in an oak. When Prospero confronts Caliban at the end of the play he remembers Sycorax one more time: "His mother was a witch, and one so strong / That could control the moon, make flows and ebbs" (V.i.272–3). The tidal image links her powers with Prospero's control of the spirits of the sand who go backwards and forwards with "the ebbing Neptune." Now that he has been unburdened of his magic, Prospero, who previously set himself up as the opposite of Sycorax, recognizes that his arts were as one with hers. And so it is that he can recognize that her progeny is also his: "This thing of darkness I / Acknowledge mine" (V.i.278–9). The subject hangs at the line-ending, split from its verb as a token of the split between darkness and light, the division within Prospero himself, a division that he shares with the Medea whose own self was racked across a line-ending early in Ovid's seventh book ("aliudque cupido, / mens aliud suadet").

Why is it that the darkness of Caliban is an inescapable part of Prospero? Why does the island have to contain this creature who must be subdued and controlled, who tries to rape Miranda and lead a rebellion against Prospero, who must eventually be humiliated so that he is led to seek for grace?

In answering this, we need to return to Gonzalo's Utopian vision. Though Shakespeare imitated it from Montaigne, his audience would have been more likely to identify it with Montaigne's source. As so often in the play, the "discourse of colonialism" is summoned up only to be displaced into the discourse of myth. A signal in the text alerts the listener to the original source: "I would with such perfection govern, sir, / T' excel the Golden Age" (II.i.173–4). Montaigne's vision of peace and of the absence of law, labour, and agriculture aligns the New World with the oldest world; he says that life in the "barbarian" nations exceeds "all the pictures wherewith licentious Poesie hath proudly imbellished the golden age" (*Essayes*, p. 164). He is thinking in particular of the Golden Age as it is described in Book One of the *Metamorphoses:*

> There was no feare of punishment, there was no threatning lawe
> In brazen tables nayled up, to keepe the folke in awe.
> There was no man would crouch or creepe to Judge with cap in hand,
> They lived safe without a Judge in every Realme and lande.
> . . . .
> There was no towne enclosed yet, with walles and ditches deepe.
> No horne nor trumpet was in use, no sword nor helmet worne.
> The worlde was suche, that souldiers helpe might easly be forborne.
> The fertile earth as yet was free, untoucht of spade or plough,
> And yet it yeelded of it selfe of every things inough.
> . . . .
> The Springtime lasted all the yeare, and *Zephyr* with his milde
> And gentle blast did cherish things that grew of owne accorde.
> The ground untilde, all kinde of fruits did plenteously avorde.[26]

The Latin original of this passage would have been encountered early in a boy's grammar-school education; for many playgoers it would therefore have been Ovid, not Montaigne, who would have been evoked by Gonzalo's "no name of magistrate," "Bourn, bound of land, tilth, vineyard, none," and

> All things in common nature should produce
> Without sweat or endeavour. Treason, felony,
> Sword, pike, knife, gun, or need of any engine,
> Would I not have; but nature should bring forth
> Of its own kind all foison, all abundance,
> To feed my innocent people.

> (II.i.165–70)

But man is fallen and the Golden Age is irrecoverable. The very presence of the characters on the island is a sign of this, for Ovid had pointed out that one feature of the Golden Age was the absence of travel. People remained contentedly in their own fertile land, "The loftie Pynetree was not hewen from mountaines where it stood, / In seeking straunge and forren landes to rove upon the flood" (Golding, i.109–10). It was in the Iron Age, according to Ovid, that the first sea-voyages took place. The first sea-voyagers were Jason and his Argonauts, so the encounter with Prospero's forebear Medea was a direct consequence of the decline of Ages.[27] The Iron Age also brought craft, treason, violence, envy, pride, lust, the parcelling out of land (Gonzalo's "plantation") which was previously held in common, and family quarrels ("yea seldome time doth rest / Betweene borne brothers such accord and love as ought to bee"—Golding, i.164–5). All the dark elements in *The Tempest* are of the Iron Age. Gonzalo gets into a tangle in his speech, and can be mocked by Sebastian and Antonio, precisely because of the incompatibility between the Golden Age ideal of no law, no property, no need to till the land, and his own Iron Age mentality which thinks in terms of the right to plant, of sovereignty and rule.

Shakespeare has therefore reversed Montaigne. The Frenchman idealized the New World and its inhabitants, seeing in them the Golden Age restored (or rather a realization of what poets feigned in their licentious fictions of the Golden Age). The island in *The Tempest,* on the other hand, is shot through with Iron Age characteristics, many of them embodied in Caliban, but some of them brought by Prospero—Caliban is only provoked into a claim that he owns the land, "this island's mine, by Sycorax my mother" (I.ii.333), by Prospero's appropriation of it. The play leaves open the question as to whether Caliban's fallenness is innate, as Prospero's abuses imply ("a born devil"—IV.i.188), or in some sense created by Prospero himself, as may be admitted in his acknowledgement of the darkness as his own. Either way, Shakespeare denies the myth of the Golden Age restored in a New World peopled by noble cannibals.

What positive myth is available, then? The answer comes in Prospero's masque, though the fact that its performance is interrupted by Caliban's conspiracy shows that it offers a precarious and vulnerable stasis. When the Golden Age ended, says Ovid, the Silver Age brought the seasons—as was noted in *As You Like It,* in the Golden Age it was always spring—and agriculture: "Then first of all were furrowes drawne, and corne was cast in ground" (Golding, i.139). The loss of the Golden Age, the fall of man, means that human society cannot escape the seasonal cycle and its dependence on agriculture. It becomes necessary to hope and pray for fertile land and a good harvest. Prospero's masque fuses this hope with a prayer for fertility in the marriage of Miranda and Ferdinand.

The land described in the masque is husbanded, not in a state of nature. It is under Ceres, patroness of agriculture: her "rich leas" are sown with "wheat, rye, barley, vetches, oats, and peas," her vineyards are "pole-clipped" and her flat meads "thatched with stover" (IV.i.60 ff.). The language here is that of Ovid's Ceres: "Dame *Ceres* first to breake the Earth with plough the maner found, / She first made corne and stover soft to grow upon the ground" (Golding, V.434–5, "stover" is winter forage for cattle). Where Caliban spoke of the island yielding up its own fruits in the ready abundance of the Golden Age, Prospero's actors acknowledge the need to work the land.

Agriculture is, as I have said, a Silver Age phenomenon; it was in his *Silver Age* play that Heywood placed Ceres and the story of the rape of her daughter Proserpina. It is because she presides over the period immediately after the Golden Age that Ceres also "first made lawes" (Golding, V.436, translating Ovid's "prima dedit leges"). In the Golden Age, when there was no law and all things were held in common, there could be free love (Montaigne's cannibals share their women without jealousy); in the Silver Age, love must be bounded within the laws of marriage. So it is that the masque is part of Prospero's project to ensure that Ferdinand's motives are chaste and that he is not overhasty in seeking sexual union; for fertility to be achieved, sexual desire must be controlled. The plot of the masque allegorizes this idea: Ceres is summoned to Juno, goddess of marriage, in order to ensure that Venus and Cupid, forces of sexual desire, are banished. There is an allusion to an Ovidian innovation in the Proserpine myth, namely a twist whereby Venus and Cupid are the agents who inspire in Dis the desire that prompts him to abduct Proserpina—the ambition of Venus and Cupid in this was to extend their domain from the sky, the sea, and the earth (where they already rule over the desires of Jupiter, Neptune, and all mortals) to the underworld (*Met.* V.363–79). In the masque, Iris reassures Ceres that Venus has flown off to Paphos and Cupid's arrows are broken, so the "wanton charm" they were to cast on Miranda and Ferdinand has been avoided, and accordingly "no bedright shall be paid / Till Hymen's torch be lighted" (IV.i.91–101).

The commonplace Renaissance theme of the dangers of lust is a key motif in both *The Tempest* and the age's reading of Ovid. In the interstices of the Aenean Section of the *Metamorphoses* is the tale which Lodge retold in the first Elizabethan "minor epic," that of Scylla, the nymph who is metamorphosed so that dogs and wolves encircle her loins; Prospero, who is capable of unleashing dogs himself, would have interpreted her fate as George Sandys did, as an allegory of the dual nature of human beings:

> That the upper part of her body, is feigned to retaine a humane figure, and the lower to be bestiall, intimates how man, a divine creature, endued with wisdome and intelligence, in whose superiour parts, as in a high tower, that immortall spirit resideth, who only of all that hath life erects his lookes unto heaven, can never so degenerate into a beast, as when he giveth himselfe over to the lowe delights of those baser parts of the body, Dogs and Wolves, the blind and salvage fury of concupiscence. (Sandys, p. 475)

Scylla's metamorphosis is performed by Circe, whom Frank Kermode sees as a model for Sycorax (Arden edn., p. 26). This is a suggestive link, since Prospero's obsession with Ferdinand's possible concupiscence seems to be provoked by the attempt of Sycorax's son to rape Miranda. Prospero thus unfairly associates Ferdinand with the bestial as opposed to the heaven-looking aspect of man: "To th' most of men this is a Caliban / And they to him are angels" (I.ii.483–4).

To ideologically minded critics, the theme of the need for desire to be tamed within the formal structure of marriage is political, and in this instance dynastic; to psychologically minded ones, it is connected with Prospero's possessiveness towards his daughter, his hang-ups about the idea of her having sex with another man. These readings may well be valid, but it seems to me that the play itself makes the point in terms of the decline of the Ages. Furthermore, the Ages are not politicized, as they easily could have been. As so often, Shakespeare eschews topical reference. One may see this by contrasting *The Tempest* with "De Guiana," a poem by George Chapman, published in 1596 among the prefatory material of Lawrence Keymis's *A Relation of the Second Voyage to Guiana*. The poem is a plea to Queen Elizabeth to accept Guiana as a colony; because gold is to be found there, it can become a new golden world:

> Then most admired Soveraigne, let your breath
> Goe foorth upon the waters, and create
> A golden worlde in this our yron age.
> (lines 30–2)

The pursuit of gold also leads Chapman to Jason's quest for the golden fleece: Sir Walter Ralegh thus sails to Guiana with "his *Argolian* Fleet."[28] No such connections are made in Prospero's masque. It makes moral rather than imperial use of the Ages. Free love was all very well in the Golden Age, but with the Silver Age comes the law of marriage, and if that law is broken, one is on a slippery path to the lust that deforms the Iron Age. That sex must take place within marriage is standard Christian theology; here, in characteristically Renaissance fashion, it is smuggled into a pagan nature myth.

The masque is a manifestation of the art which Prospero renounces. Even before he puts it on, he refers to it dismissively as "Some vanity of mine art" (IV.i.41). By the time he speaks his epilogue he has ceased to use pagan myth as a vehicle, and he speaks instead the unalloyed language of Christianity (despair, prayer, mercy, faults, pardoned, indulgence). This is an implicit recognition on Shakespeare's part of the distance between Ovidian art and orthodox Christianity; to use Thomas Greene's term, cited in my first chapter, it renders his imitation of Ovid "dialectical." It could be described as his equivalent to the two stanzas of the "unperfite" eighth canto of Spenser's "Mutabilitie," which come to rest on "the pillours of Eternity" that are "contrayr to [Ovidian] Mutabilitie" (*Faerie Queene,* VII.viii.2). In this sense, Leonard Barkan is both elegant and just when he describes Prospero's burial of his book as Shakespeare's magisterial closing of the book that Lavinia so clumsily opened in *Titus Andronicus.*[29] But although the masque belongs to Prospero's rejected art, for a Jacobean theatre audience it would have been the high point of the play, in terms of both spectacle and allegorical sophistication. And in this sense Shakespeare's art remains coordinate with, dependent upon, Ovid's.

For a theatre audience the most memorable thing about the masque is not the plot—it is only in a reading that we stop to think through the business about the threat of Venus and Cupid—but the sense of fruition, the harmony and the harvest. With our eyes, we wonder at certain nymphs and certain reapers, properly habited, joining together in a graceful dance. With our ears, we absorb the language of fruitfulness, the sense that the harshness of Proserpina's winter confinement in the underworld can be overstepped as spring returns in the very moment of autumn's harvest:

> Earth's increase, foison plenty,
> Barns and garners never empty,
> Vines with clust'ring bunches growing,
> Plants with goodly burden bowing;
> Spring come to you at the farthest,
> In the very end of harvest.
> Scarcity and want shall shun you,
> Ceres' blessing so is on you.
>
> (IV.i.110–17)

As Prospero's incantation intersects with the Medea of Heywood's *Brazen Age,* so this celebration of agricultural plenty resonates with Heywood's *Silver Age.* In that play, which is contemporaneous with *The Tempest,* Mercury flames amazement like Ariel, Juno and Iris work in tandem, descending from the heavens on several occasions; there is also a *Cymbeline*-like moment in which to thunder and lightning "Jupiter descends in his majesty, his Thunderbolt burning."[30] And at the centre of the play is a "harvest home" which represents the closest analogue in all Jacobean drama to the agricultural benison of Prospero's masque of Ceres. Heywood's play remains little known, so I make no apology for quoting at length:

> *Enter* Ceres *and* Proserpine *attired like the Moone,*
> *with a company of Swaines, and country Wenches:*
>
> *They sing.*
>
> *With faire* Ceres *Queene of graine*
> *The reaped fields we rome, rome, rome,*

Each Countrey Peasant, Nimph and Swaine
Sing their harvest home, home, home:
 Whilst the Queene of plenty hallowes
 Growing fields as well as fallowes.

Eccho double all our Layes,
Make the Champains sound, sound, sound
To the Queene of harvest praise,
That sowes and reapes our ground, ground, ground.
 Ceres Queene of plenty hallowes
 Growing fields as well as fallowes.

CERES. As we are *Ceres,* Queene of all fertility,
The earthes sister, Aunt to highest *Jupiter,*
And mother to this beauteous childe the Moone,
So will we blesse your harvests, crowne your fields
With plenty and increase: your bearded eares
Shall make their golden stalkes of wheat to bend
Below their laden riches: with full sickles
You shall receive the usury of their seeds.
Your fallowes and your gleabes our selfe will till
From every furrow that your plow-shares raze
Upon the plenteous earth, our sisters breast,
You shall cast up aboundance for your gratitude
To *Ceres* and the chaste *Proserpina.*
. . . .
Now that the heavens and earth are both appeas'd
And the huge Giants that assaulted *Jove,*
Are slaughtered by the hand of *Jupiter;*
We have leasure to attend our harmelesse swaines:
Set on then to our Rurall ceremonies. *Exeunt singing.*

Tempests hence, hence winds and hailes,
Tares, cockle, rotten showers, showers, showers,
Our song shall keep time with our flailes,
When Ceres *sings, none lowers, lowers, lowers.*
 She it is whose God-hood hallowes
 Growing fields as well as fallowes.
        (*Dramatic Works,* iii.133–4)

"Tempests hence"; "plenty and increase" come hither. The fruits of labour in the fields bend with "their laden riches": the tonality and the rhythm are

Shakespeare's. I am not proposing a "source" here, since it is impossible to establish which play was written first.[31] The point of my collocation is that the two plays were in the repertory at the same time. Indeed, they were performed at court within a few weeks of each other in the winter of 1611–12; *The Silver Age* was played by the King's Men and Queen's Men together, so Shakespeare's company had direct contact with Heywood's song to Ceres. Both the court audience and any playgoers who kept up with the repertory of the two leading companies would have been presented with a striking parallel between Prospero's masque and the *Silver Age,* just as they would have been presented with a striking parallel between Prospero and the Medea of *The Brazen Age.* While one parallel darkens the character of Prospero, the other lightens him and warms the audience. When watching the masque at the Globe or Blackfriars, as when watching *The Silver Age* at the Red Bull, the city-dwellers in their leisure engage with an image of country-dwellers singing or dancing in their moment of leisure once the harvest is safely gathered in.

According to Sir Philip Sidney in his *Apology for Poetry,* the poet ranges freely within the zodiac of his own wit, bringing forth the wonderful forms of myth: the heroes, demigods, and Cyclops. Thus it is that where nature's world is brazen, "the Poets only deliver a golden."[32] Heywood and Shakespeare were not so idealistic: in *The Silver Age,* shortly after the passage quoted above, Proserpina is abducted by Pluto, "his Chariot drawne in by Divels"; in *The Tempest,* the nymphs and reapers "heavily vanish" as "a strange, hollow, and confused noise" heralds the entrance of Caliban and his fellow-conspirators, the intrusion of the Iron Age of treason, violence, and envy. Shakespeare was too much of a sceptic to suppose that he could deliver up the Golden World, but for a moment, through Prospero's theatrical arts, which are of course also his own, he provides some consolation by conjuring the Silver Age back to life. The drama itself becomes a harvest home.

Notes

1. The strongest, but by no means conclusive, arguments that he did are those of Emrys Jones in *The Origins of Shakespeare* [Oxford, 1977].

2. This is not the place to rehearse the relationship between *Titus,* the 1594 ballad on the subject, and the prose chapbook *History of Titus Andronicus:* as I intimated in Ch. 3, I agree with G. K. Hunter's argument that the order is play–ballad–chapbook, not chapbook–ballad–play, as most scholars have believed. *Titus* would then be Shakespeare's only 'sourceless' tragedy. My reasons for agreeing with Hunter, together with additional supporting evidence, [are] laid out in the introduction to my . . . Arden edn. of the play [London, 1995].

3. Hamilton, *Virgil and "The Tempest": The Politics of Imitation* (Columbus, Ohio, 1990), 4.

4. Greenblatt, "Learning to Curse: Aspects of Linguistic Colonialism in the Sixteenth Century," in *First Images of America: The Impact of the New World on the Old,* ed. Fredi Chiappelli, 2 vols. (Berkeley and Los Angeles, 1976), ii.561–80, repr. as the title-essay of Greenblatt's *Learning to Curse* (London, 1990).

5.   Note to Trinculo's speech at II.ii.27–32, in Arden edn. (London, 1954).

6.   "Of the Caniballes," *The Essayes of Montaigne,* bk. I, ch. 30, Florio trans., quoted from 1933 edn., p. 164.

7.   This argument seems to have been first articulated by Colin Still in his mystically minded *The Timeless Theme* (London, 1936); more recent treatments include two essays by Jan Kott reprinted in his *The Bottom Translation* (Chicago, 1987), Robert Miola, "Vergil in Shakespeare: From Allusion to Imitation," in *Vergil at 2000: Commemorative Essays on the Poet and his Influence,* ed. J. D. Bernard (New York, 1986), 241–58, John Pitcher, "A Theatre of the Future: *The Aeneid* and *The Tempest,*" *Essays in Criticism,* xxxiv (1984), 193–215, Robert Wiltenburg, "The *Aeneid* in *The Tempest,*" *ShS* xxxix (1987), 159–68, and the book by Donna B. Hamilton cited above. Among the countless misrepresentations in Ted Hughes, *Shakespeare and the Goddess of Complete Being* (London, 1992), is the claim that "The smouldering presence of that previous life, in which Miranda was Dido, seems to become more and more the secret, poignant, smothered tragedy of this play" (p. 423).

8.   See Anthony DiMattio, " 'The Figure of this Harpy': Shakespeare and the Moralized Ovid," *N&Q* NS xxxviii (1991), 70–2.

9.   Wiltenburg, "The *Aeneid* in *The Tempest,*" 168.

10.   Ariosto provides a parallel "romance" reworking: as Daniel Javitch shows, Astolfo's adventures in hell and ascent to the moon in canto 34 of *Orlando Furioso* are a parodic rewriting of Dante's *Commedia,* inspired by Ovid's version of *The Aeneid* in bks. 13 and 14 of the *Metamorphoses*—"The *Orlando Furioso* and Ovid's Revision of the *Aeneid,*" *MLN* xcix (1984), 1023–36.

11.   Brower, "The Mirror of Analogy: *The Tempest,*" in his *The Fields of Light: An Experiment in Critical Reading* (London, 1951), 95–122.

12.   *Titus Andronicus,* II.iii.12–29, 92–108.

13.   *Met.* xiii.789–97 and 798–807 represent a formally paired set of apostrophes, the first *in bono,* the second *in male:* they could well be the model for Tamora's pair of speeches in *Titus.*

14.   Sandys, *Ovid's Metamorphosis Englished* (1632), 477–8.

15.   Ibid. 476. For Coleridge on Thersites as "the Caliban of demagogic life," see *The Romantics on Shakespeare* [London, 1992], 548.

16.   The examples from Bacon and Ralegh are both cited by Stephen Orgel in the fine introduction to his edn. of *The Tempest* (Oxford, 1987), 20.

17.   The mushrooms may be picked from Medea's subsequent flight to Corinth, where men "Did breede of deawie Mushroomes" (Golding, vii.500).

18.   See William Carroll, *The Metamorphoses of Shakespearean Comedy* (Princeton, NJ, 1985), 237–8, 284.

19.   This masque was performed at court in 1609. In a marginal note to the invocation, which includes the familiar catalogue of raising storms and darkening the noonday sun (ll. 218–47), Jonson indicates that he is combining the Medeas of Ovid and Seneca with the Erichtho of Lucan's *Pharsalia* (vi.695 ff.): "These Invocations are solemne with them; whereof we may see the formes in *Ovid. Meta. lib. vii. in Sen. Trag. Med. in Luc. lib. vi.* which of all is the boldest, and most horrid" (*Ben Jonson,* vii.295).

20.   Middleton, *The Witch,* v.ii.25–9, in *Three Jacobean Witchcraft Plays,* ed. Peter Corbin and Douglas Sedge (Manchester, 1986).

21.   *The Brazen Age* was not printed until 1613, but, as noted earlier, the address to the reader prefixed to *The Golden Age,* printed in Oct. 1611, refers to that play as "the eldest brother of three Ages, that hath adventured the Stage" (Heywood, *Dramatic Works* [London, 1874], iii.3).

22.   The presence in both plays of Golding's phrases "elves of hills" and "standing lakes" must mean that both Heywood and Shakespeare used the English translation as a crib (there are other marks of Golding's vocabulary elsewhere in each play). It is intriguing, though it may

be coincidental, that for Golding's "woods" both Heywood and Shakespeare have "groves": might there then be a direct influence between the two plays? If so, whichever way round it is (the chronology cannot be known for certain), the link between Prospero and Medea is reinforced.

23. Most influentially, Frank Kermode: "Only those elements . . . consistent with 'white' magic are taken over for Prospero" (Arden edn., p. 149).

24. Orgel's edn., p. 19 and n.

25. See e.g. Carroll, *Metamorphoses,* 238 ff., Orgel's edn., p. 20.

26. Golding, i.105–24. The phrase "to keepe the folke in awe" is an insertion by Golding which suggests a distinctively 16th cent., quasi-machiavellian, view of the law; the image of creeping to the judge, cap in hand, is also a sharpening of Ovid's original text. Shakespeare has a similarly charged sense of the relationship between the Golden Age and justice, of the absence of justice in the Iron Age of the present, when he quotes the line "terras Astraea reliquit" in the context of Titus Andronicus' discovery that there is no justice at Saturninus' court— the same idea is dramatized in the figure of the Clown in *Titus* who goes cap in hand for justice and is rewarded with hanging.

27. For Jason as the first ship-builder, see e.g. *Met.* viii.302 ("primaeque ratis molitor Iason") and *Amores,* II.xi.1–6. I would like to thank A.D. Nuttall for reminding me of this connection when I presented a version of this reading of *The Tempest* to the Oxford Renaissance Seminar.

28. Line 159, quoted from Chapman's *Poems,* ed. Phyllis Brooks Bartlett (New York, 1941). The association between the Iron Age, shipping, trade, and the pursuit of gold is also apparent from the language of Barabas in Marlowe's *Jew of Malta* (see e.g. his image of "Ripping the bowels of the earth," I.i.107, which comes from Ovid's "sed itum est in viscera terrae," i.138, in the description of the Iron Age).

29. [Leonard] Barkan, *The Gods Made Flesh[: Metamorphosis and the Pursuit of Paganism* (New Haven, Conn., 1986], 288.

30. Heywood, *Dramatic Works,* iii.154.

31. Though the scene in Heywood must come first if, as has sometimes been supposed, the masque was an interpolation in *The Tempest* for the performance at court as part of the royal betrothal celebrations during the winter of 1612–13.

32. Sidney, *Apology,* in *Elizabethan Critical Essays* [Oxford, 1904], i.156.

Discourse and the Individual:
The Case of Colonialism in *The Tempest*

Meredith Anne Skura

For many years idealist readings of *The Tempest* presented Prospero as an exemplar of timeless human values. They emphasized the way in which his hard-earned "magical" powers enable him to re-educate the shipwrecked Italians, to heal their civil war—and, even more important, to triumph over his own vengefulness by forgiving his enemies; they emphasized the way he achieves, if not a wholly "brave," at least a harmoniously reconciled new world. Within the last few years, however, numbers of critics have offered remarkably similar critiques of this reading. There is an essay on *The Tempest* in each of three recent anthologies of alternative, political, and reproduced Shakespeare criticism, and another in the volume on estranging Renaissance criticism; *The Tempest* was a focus for the 1988 SAA session on "Shakespeare and Colonialism" and was one of the masthead plays in the Folger Institute's 1988 seminar on new directions in Shakespeare studies.[1] Together, the revisionists call for a move to counteract some "deeply ahistorical readings" of *The Tempest*,[2] a play that is now seen to be not simply an allegory about "timeless"[3] or universal experience but rather a cultural phenomenon that has its origin in and effect on "historical" events, specifically in English colonialism. "New historicist" criticism in general, of which much recent work on *The Tempest* is a part, has itself begun to come under scrutiny, but the numerous historical reinterpretations of *The Tempest* deserve closer attention in their own right,[4] and they will be the subject of the rest of this essay.

In assessing the "new" historicist version of the play, it is important to realize that here, even more than in other new historical criticism, an historical emphasis in itself is not new. Since the early nineteenth century *The Tempest* has been seen in the historical context of the New World, and Frank Kermode, citing the early scholars, argued in the fifties that reports of a particular episode in British efforts to colonize North America had precipitated the play's major themes.[5] In 1609 nine ships had left England to settle the colony in Jamestown, Virginia, and the *Sea Venture*, carrying all of the

Meredith Anne Skura, "Discourse and the Individual: The Case of Colonialism in *The Tempest*," *Shakespeare Quarterly* 40 (spring 1989): 42–69. Reprinted by permission of *Shakespeare Quarterly*.

colonial officers, had disappeared. But its passengers reappeared in Virginia one year later, miraculously saved; they had wrecked off the Bermudas, until then believed demonically dangerous but now found to be providentially mild and fruitful. These events, much in the news in the year just preceding *The Tempest,* have long been seen as a relevant context for the play by all but a very few critics.[6] These earlier historical interpretations generally placed the play and its immediate source in the context of voyaging discourse in general, which stressed the romance and exoticism of discoveries in the Old as well as the New World. Even the "factual" reports in this discourse, as Charles Frey notes, were themselves colored by the romance of the situation, for better and for worse; and the traditional view was that *The Tempest*'s stylized allegory abstracts the romance core of all voyagers' experience.[7]

Nor had traditional criticism entirely ignored either Prospero's flaws[8] or their relation to the dark side of Europe's confrontation with the Other. Kermode had identified Caliban as the "core" or "ground" of the play, insofar as confrontation with this strange representative of "uncivilized" man prompts the play's reexamination of "civilized" human nature. Harry Levin, Leslie Fiedler, Leo Marx, and others had suggested that in trying to understand the New World representatives of "uncivilized" human nature, Prospero, like other Europeans, had imposed Old (and New) World stereotypes of innocence and monstrosity on the Native Americans, distorting perception with hope and fear.[9] Fiedler's landmark book had indeed placed *The Tempest* suggestively in the context of a series of plays about the Other (or, as he called it in 1972, the "Stranger") in Shakespeare, showing Caliban's resemblance to the demonized women, Moors, and Jews in the canon. O. Mannoni had added that, in this process, Prospero displayed the psychology of colonials who projected their disowned traits onto New World natives.[10]

Why, then, so many recent articles? In part they are simply shifting the emphasis. Revisionists claim that the New World material is not just present but is right at the center of the play, and that it demands far more attention than critics have been willing to grant it. They argue that the civil war in Milan that had ousted Prospero should be recognized as merely an episode in a minor dispute between Italian dynasties, of little import compared to the transatlantic action;[11] they show how the love story can be seen as a political maneuver by Prospero to ensure his return to power in Milan,[12] and how even Caliban's attempted rape of Miranda can be seen as an expression not merely of sexual but also of territorial lust, understandable in its context.[13]

These recent critics are not simply repeating the older ones, however; they are making important distinctions. First and most explicitly, they are not calling attention to history in general but rather to one aspect of history: to power relations and to the ideology in which power relations are encoded.[14] The revisionists look not at the New World material in the play but to the play's effect on power relations in the New World. What matters is not just the particular Bermuda pamphlets actually echoed in the play but rather the whole "ensemble of fictional and lived practices" known as "English colonial-ism," which, it is now being claimed, provides the "dominant discursive con-texts"[15] for the play. (Though the term "colonialism" may allude to the entire spectrum of New World activity, in these articles it most often refers specifi-cally to the use of power, to the Europeans' exploitative and self-justifying treatment of the New World and its inhabitants—and I shall use it in that sense.) If Caliban is the center of the play, it is not because of his role in the play's self-contained structure, and not even because of what he reveals about man's timeless tendency to demonize "strangers," but because Europeans were at that time exploiting the real Calibans of the world, and *The Tempest* was part of the process. It is no longer enough to suggest that Europeans were trying to make sense of the Indian; rather, the emphasis is now on the way Europeans subdued the Indian to "make sense/order/money—not of him, so much as out of him."[16] Revisionists argue that when the English talked about these New World inhabitants, they did not just innocently apply stereotypes or project their own fears: they did so to a particular effect, whether wittingly or unwittingly. The various distortions were discursive strategies that served the political purpose of making the New World fit into a schema justifying colonialism.[17] Revisionists therefore emphasize the dis-cursive strategies that the play shares with all colonial discourse, and the ways in which *The Tempest* itself not only displays prejudice but fosters and even "enacts" colonialism by mystifying or justifying Prospero's power over Cal-iban.[18] The new point is that *The Tempest* is a political act.

Second, this shift in our attitude toward the object of interpretation entails a less explicit but extremely important move away from the psycho-logical interpretation that had previously seemed appropriate for the play (even to its detractors) largely because of its central figure who, so like Shake-speare, runs the show. Where earlier criticism of Prospero talked about his "prejudice," the more recent revisionists talk about "power" and "euphemisa-tion." Thus, a critic writing in 1980 argued that *The Tempest*'s "allegorical and Neoplatonic overlay masks some of the most damaging prejudices of Western civilization";[19] but by 1987 the formulation had changed: "*The Tempest* is . . . fully implicated in the process of 'euphemisation,' the effacement of power," in "operations [that] encode struggle and contradiction even as they, or *because* they, strive to insist on the legitimacy of colonialist narrative."[20]

Psychological criticism of the play is seen as distracting at best; one recent critic, for example, opens his argument by claiming that we need to conceive *The Tempest* in an historical context that is not "hamstrung by spe-cious speculations concerning 'Shakespeare's mind.' "[21] Even in less polemical examples the "political unconscious" often replaces, rather than supplements, any other unconscious; attention to culture and politics is associated with an implicit questioning of individuality and of subjective experience. Such a stance extends beyond an objection to wholesale projections of twentieth-century assumptions onto sixteenth-century subjects, or to psychological interpretations that totally ignore the cultural context in which psyches exist. As Frederick Jameson argued in a work that lies behind many of these specific studies, it derives from the desire to transcend personal psychology altogether, because Freud's psychology remains "locked into the category of the individual subject."[22] The emphasis now is on psychology as a product of culture, itself a political structure; the very concept of a psyche is seen to be a product of the cultural nexus evolved during the Renaissance, and indeed, psychoanalysis itself, rather than being a way of understanding the Renaissance psyche, is a marginal and belated creation of this same nexus.[23] Thus the revisionists, with Jameson, may look for a "political unconscious" and make use of Freud's insights into the "logic of dreams"[24]—the concepts of displacement, condensation, the management of desire[25]—but they do not accept Freud's assumptions about the mind—or the subject—creating that logic.[26] The agent who displaces or manages is not the individual but the "collective or associative" mind; at times it seems to be the text itself, seen as a "libidinal apparatus" or "desiring machine"[27] independent of any individual creator.

The revisionist impulse has been one of the most salutary in recent years in correcting New Critical "blindness" to history and ideology. In particular it has revealed the ways in which the play has been "reproduced" and drafted into the service of colonialist politics from the nineteenth century through G. Wilson Knight's twentieth-century celebration of Prospero as representative of England's "colonizing, especially her will to raise savage peoples from superstition and blood-sacrifice, taboos and witchcraft and the attendant fears and slaveries, to a more enlightened existence."[28] But here, as critics have been suggesting about new historicism in general, it is now in danger of fostering blindness of its own. Granted that something was wrong with a commentary that focused on *The Tempest* as a self-contained project of a self-contained individual and that ignored the political situation in 1611. But something seems wrong now also, something more than the rhetorical excesses characteristic of any innovative critical movement. The recent criticism not only flattens the text into the mold of colonialist discourse and eliminates what is characteristically "Shakespearean" in order to foreground what is "colonialist," but it is also—paradoxically—in danger of taking the play further from the particular historical situation in England in 1611 even as it brings it closer to what we mean by "colonialism" today.

It is difficult to extrapolate back from G. Wilson Knight's colonialist discourse to seventeenth-century colonialist discourse without knowing more about the particulars of that earlier discourse. What is missing from the recent articles is the connection between the new insights about cultural phenomena like "power" and "fields of discourse" and the traditional insights about the text, its immediate sources, its individual author—and his individual psychology. There is little sense of how discourse is related to the individual who was creating, even as he was participating in, that discourse. The following discussion will suggest how such a relation might be conceived.

Sections I and II briefly elaborate on *The Tempest*'s versions of problems raised by new historicist treatment of the text and its relation to the historical context; sections III and IV go on to suggest that the recognition of the individuality of the play, and of Shakespeare, does not counter but rather enriches the understanding of that context. Perhaps by testing individual cases, we can avoid the circularity of a definition that assumes that "colonialism" was present in a given group of texts, and so "discovers" it there.

I

How do we know that *The Tempest* "enacts" colonialism rather than merely alluding to the New World? How do we know that Caliban is part of the "discourse of colonialism"? To ask such a question may seem perversely naive, but the play is notoriously slippery. There have been, for example, any number of interpretations of Caliban,[29] including not only contemporary postcolonial versions in which Caliban is a Virginian Indian but also others in which Caliban is played as a black slave or as "missing link" (in a costume "half monkey, half coco-nut"[30]), with the interpretation drawing on the issues that were being debated at the time—on the discursive contexts that were culturally operative—and articulated according to "changing Anglo-American attitudes toward primitive man."[31] Most recently one teacher has suggested that *The Tempest* is a good play to teach in junior colleges because students can identify with Caliban.

Interpretation is made even more problematic here because, despite the claims about the play's intervention in English colonialism,[32] we have no *external* evidence that seventeenth-century audiences thought the play referred to the New World. In an age when real voyages were read allegorically, the status of allegorical voyages like Prospero's can be doubly ambiguous, especially in a play like *The Tempest,* which provides an encyclopedic context for Prospero's experience, presenting it in terms of an extraordinary range of classical, biblical, and romantic exiles, discoveries, and confrontations.[33] Evidence for the play's original reception is of course extraordinarily difficult to find, but in the two nearly contemporary responses to Caliban that we do know about, the evidence for a colonialist response is at best ambiguous. In *Bartholomew Fair* (1614) Jonson refers scornfully to a "servant-monster," and the Folio identifies Caliban as a "salvage and deformed slave"[34] in the cast list. Both "monster" and "salvage" are firmly rooted in the discourse of Old World wild men, though the latter was of course also applied to the New World natives. In other words, these two seventeenth-century responses tend to invoke the universal and not the particular implications of Caliban's condition. A recent study of the play's history suggests that "if Shakespeare, however obliquely, meant Caliban to personify America's natives, his intention apparently miscarried almost completely."[35]

Despite this lack of contemporary testimony, the obvious reason for our feeling that the play "is" colonialist—more so than *The Winter's Tale* or *Henry VIII,* for example, which were written at roughly the same time—is, of course, the literal resemblance between its plot and certain events and attitudes in English colonial history: Europeans arrive in the New World and assume they can appropriate what properly belongs to the New World Other, who is then "erased." The similarities are clear and compelling—more so than in many cases of new historical readings; the problem, however, is that while there are also many literal differences between *The Tempest* and colonialist fictions and practice, the similarities are taken to be so compelling that the differences are ignored. Thus Caliban is taken to "be" a Native American despite the fact that a multitude of details differentiate Caliban from the Indian as he appeared in the travelers' reports from the New World.[36] Yet it does seem significant that, despite his closeness to nature, his naiveté, his devil worship, his susceptibility to European liquor, and, above all, his "treachery"—characteristics associated in writings of the time with the Indians—he nonetheless lacks almost all of the defining external traits in the many reports from the New World—no superhuman physique, no nakedness or animal skin (indeed, an English "gaberdine" instead), no decorative feathers,[37] no arrows, no pipe, no tobacco, no body paint, and—as Shakespeare takes pains to emphasize— no love of trinkets and trash. No one could mistake him for the stereotyped "Indian with a great tool," mentioned in passing in *Henry VIII*. Caliban in fact is more like the devils Strachey expected to find on the Bermuda island (but didn't) than like the Indians whom adventurers did find in Virginia, though he is not wholly a monster from the explorers' wild tales either.[38]

In other ways, too, it is assumed that the similarities matter but the differences do not: thus Prospero's magic occupies "the space *really inhabited in colonial history* by gunpowder"[39] (emphasis mine); or, when Prospero has Caliban pinched by the spirits, he shows a "similar sadism" to that of the Haitian masters who "roasted slaves or buried them alive";[40] or, when Prospero and Ariel hunt Caliban with spirit dogs, they are equated to the Spaniards who hunted Native Americans with dogs.[41] So long as there is a core of resemblance, the differences are irrelevant. The differences, in fact, are themselves taken to be evidence of the colonialist ideology at work, rationalizing and euphemizing power—or else inadvertent slips. Thus the case for colonialism becomes stronger insofar as Prospero *is* good and insofar as Caliban *is* in some ways bad—he did try to rape Miranda—or is *himself* now caught trying to falsify the past by occluding the rape and presenting himself as an innocent victim of Prospero's tyranny. Prospero's goodness and Caliban's badness are called rationalizations, justifications for Prospero's tyranny. Nor does it matter that the play seems *anti*-colonialist to the degree that it qualifies Prospero's scorn by showing Caliban's virtues, or that Prospero seems to achieve some kind of transcendence over his own colonialism when at the end of the play he says, "This thing of darkness I acknowledge mine."[42] Prospero's acknowledgement of Caliban is considered a mistake, a moment of inadvertent sympathy or truth, too brief to counter Prospero's underlying colonialism: in spite of the deceptively resonant poetry of his acknowledgement, Prospero actually does nothing to live up to the meaning which that poetry suggests;[43] it has even been argued that Prospero, in calling Caliban "mine," is simply claiming possession of him: "It is as though, after a public disturbance, a slaveowner said, 'Those two men are yours; this darkie's mine.' "[44]

Nonetheless, in addition to these differences that have been seen as rationalizations, there are many other differences as well that collectively raise questions about what counts as "colonialist discourse" and about what, if anything, might count as a relevant "difference." Thus, for example, any attempt to cast Prospero and Caliban as actors in the typical colonial narrative (in which a European exploits a previously free—indeed a reigning—native of an unspoiled world) is complicated by two other characters, Sycorax and Ariel. Sycorax, Caliban's mother, through whom he claims possession of the island, was not only a witch and a criminal, but she came from the Old World herself, or at least from eastern-hemisphere Argier.[45] She is a reminder that Caliban is only half-native, that his claim to the island is less like the claim of the Native American than the claim of the second generation Spaniard in the New World.[46] Moreover, Caliban was not alone when Prospero arrived. Ariel either came to the island with Sycorax or was already living on the island—its true reigning lord[47]—when Sycorax arrived and promptly enslaved him, thus herself becoming the first colonialist, the one who established the habits of dominance and erasure before Prospero ever set foot on the island. Nearly all revisionists note some of these differences before disregarding them, though they are not agreed on their significance—on whether they are "symptoms" of ideological conflict in the discourse, for example, or whether Shakespeare's "insights exceeded his sympathies."[48] But however they are explained, the differences *are* discarded. For the critic interested only in counteracting earlier blindness to potentially racist and ideological elements in the play, such ignoring of differences is understandable; for his or her purposes, it *is* enough to point out that *The Tempest* has a "political unconscious" and is connected in *some* way to colonialist discourse without specifying further.

But if the object is, rather, to understand colonialism, instead of simply identifying it or condemning it, it is important to specify, to notice how the colonial elements are rationalized or integrated into the play's vision of the world. Otherwise, extracting the play's political unconscious leads to the same problems Freud faced at the beginning of his career when he treated the personal unconscious as an independent entity that should be almost surgically extracted from conscious discourse by hypnotizing away the "defenses." But, as is well known, Freud found that the conscious "defenses" were as essential—and problematic—as the supposedly prior unconscious "wish," and that they served purposes other than containment.[49] Indeed, in most psychoanalytic practice since Freud, the unconscious—or, rather, unconscious mentation—is assumed to exist in texts rather than existing as a reified "id," and interpretation must always return to the text.

As in the case of the personal unconscious, the political unconscious exists only in texts, whose "defenses" or rationalizations must be taken into account. Otherwise interpretation not only destroys the text—here *The Tempest*—as a unique work of art and flattens it into one more example of the master plot—or master ploy—in colonialist discourse; it also destroys the evidence of the play as a unique cultural artifact, a unique voice in that discourse. Colonialist discourse was varied enough to escape any simple formulation, even in a group of texts with apparent thematic links. It ranged from the lived Spanish colonialist practice of hunting New World natives with dogs to Bartholomew Las Casas's "factual" account lamenting and exposing the viciousness of that hunt,[50] to Shakespeare's possible allusion to it in *The Tempest,* when Prospero and Ariel set spirit dogs on Caliban, to a still earlier Shakespearean allusion—or possible allusion—in the otherwise non-colonialist *A Midsummer Night's Dream,* when Puck (who has come from India himself) chases Greek rude mechanicals with illusory animals in a scene evoking an entirely English conflict. The same "colonialist" hunt informs radically different fictions and practices, some of which enact colonialism, some of which subvert it, and some of which require other categories entirely to characterize its effect.

It is not easy to categorize the several links between *The Tempest* and colonialist discourse. Take the deceptively simple example of Caliban's name. Revisionists rightly emphasize the implications of the cannibal stereotype as automatic mark of Other in Western ethnocentric colonialist discourse,[51] and, since Shakespeare's name for "Caliban" is widely accepted as an anagram of "cannibal," many read the play as if he *were* a cannibal, with all that the term implies. But an anagram is not a cannibal, and Shakespeare's use of the stereotype is hardly automatic.[52] Caliban is no cannibal—he barely touches meat, confining himself more delicately to roots, berries, and an occasional fish; indeed, his symbiotic harmony with the island's natural food resources is one of his most attractive traits. His name seems more like a mockery of stereotypes than a mark of monstrosity, and in our haste to confirm the link between "cannibal" and "Indian" outside the text, we lose track of the way in which Caliban severs the link *within* the text.[53] While no one would deny *some* relation between Caliban and the New World natives to whom such terms as "cannibal" were applied, what that relation is remains unclear.

To enumerate differences between *The Tempest* and "colonialist discourse" is not to reduce discussion of the play to a counting contest, pitting similarities against differences. Rather, it is to suggest that inherent in any analysis of the play as colonialist discourse is a particular assumption about the relation between text and discourse—between one man's fiction and a collective fiction—or, perhaps, between one man's fiction and what we take for "reality." This relation matters not only to New Critics trying to isolate texts from contexts but to new historicists (or just plain historicists) trying to put them back together. The relation is also vital to lived practices like censorship and inquisitions—and there are differences of opinion about what counts in these cases. Such differences need to be acknowledged and examined, and the method for reading them needs to be made more explicit before the implications of *The Tempest* as colonialist discourse can be fully understood.

II

Similar problems beset the definition of the "discourse" itself, the means of identifying the fictional—and the "lived"—practices constituting "English colonialism" in 1611. Given the impact of English colonialism over the last 350 years, it may again seem perversely naive to ask what colonialist discourse was like in 1611, as opposed to colonialism in 1911 or even in 1625, the year when Samuel Purchas asked, alluding to the "treachery" of the Virginian Indians, "Can a Leopard change his spots? Can a Savage remayning a Savage be civill?" Purchas added this comment when he published the 1610 document that Shakespeare had used as his source for *The Tempest,* and Purchas has been cited as an example of "colonialist discourse."[54] Purchas does indeed display the particular combination of exploitative motives and self-justifying rhetoric—the "effacement of power"[55]—that revisionists identify as colonialist and which they find in *The Tempest.* But, one might reasonably ask, was the discursive context in 1611, when Shakespeare was writing, the same as it would be fourteen years later, when Purchas added his marginal comment?[56]

There seems, rather, to have been in 1611 a variety of what we might call "New World discourses" with multiple points of view, motives, and effects, among which such comments as Purchas's are not as common as the revisionist emphasis implies. These are "colonialist" only in the most general sense in which all ethnocentric cultures are always "colonialist": narcissistically pursuing their own ends, oblivious to the desires, needs, and even the existence of the Other. That is, if this New World discourse is colonialist, it is so primarily in that it *ignores* Indians, betraying its Eurocentric assumptions about the irrelevance of any people other than white, male, upper-class Europeans, preferably from England. It thus expresses not an historically specific but a *timeless* and universal attitude toward the "stranger," which Fiedler described in so many of Shakespeare's plays. We might see this discourse as a precondition[57] for colonialism proper, which was to follow with the literal rather than the figurative colonizing of New World natives. But to assume that colonialism was already encoded in the anomalous situation in 1611 is to undermine the revisionist effort to understand the historical specificity of the moment when Shakespeare wrote *The Tempest.*

It is not easy to characterize the situation in 1611. On the one hand, Spain had long been engaged in the sort of "colonialist discourse" that revisionists find in *The Tempest;* and even in England at the time there were examples of colonialist discourse (in the rhetoric, if not yet often in the lived practices) produced by those directly involved in the colonialist project and expecting to profit from it. The official advertisements in the first rush of enthusiasm about Virginia, as well as the stream of defenses when the Virginia project began to fail, often have a euphemistic ring and often do suggest a fundamental greed and implicit racism beneath claims to be securing the earthly and spiritual well-being of the Virginia natives.[58] ("[We] doe buy of them the pearles of earth, and sell to them the pearles of heauen."[59]) These documents efface not only power but most practical problems as well, and they were supplemented by sermons romanticizing hardships as divine tribulation.[60] Scattered throughout this discourse are righteous defenses of taking land from the Indians, much in the spirit—and tone—of Rabbi Zeal-of-the-Land Busy defending his need to eat pig. (This was also the tone familiar from the anti-theatrical critics—and, indeed, occasional colonialist sermons included snipes at the "Plaiers," along with the Devil and the papists, as particular enemies of the Virginia venture.[61])

On the other hand, even in these documents not only is the emphasis elsewhere but often there are important contradictory movements. For example, "A True Declaration," the official record of the Bermuda wreck, refers once to the Indians as "humane beasts" and devotes one paragraph of its twenty-four pages to the "greedy Vulture" Powhattan and his ambush. It notes elsewhere, however, that some of the English settlers themselves had "created the *Indians* our implacable enemies by some violence they had offered," and it actually spends far more time attacking the lazy "scum of men" among the settlers, who had undermined the colony from within, than demonizing the less relevant Indians.[62]

And on the whole, the exploitative and self-justifying rhetoric is only one element in a complex New World discourse. For much of the time, in fact, the main conflict in the New World was not between whites and Native Americans but between Spain and England. Voyages like Drake's (1577–80) were motivated by this international conflict, as well as by the romance of discovery and the lure of treasure—but not by colonizing.[63] Even when Raleigh received the first patent to settle and trade with the New World (1584), necessitating more extended contact with Native Americans, the temporary settlements he started in the 1580s were largely tokens in his play for fame and wealth rather than attempts to take over sizable portions of land from the natives.[64]

Only when the war with Spain was over (1604) and ships were free again did colonization really begin; and then "America and Virginia were on everyone's lips."[65] But this New World discourse still reflects little interest in its inhabitants. Other issues are much more widely discussed. For example, what would the New World government be like? Would James try to extend his authoritarianism to America? *Could* he? This was the issue, for example, most energizing Henry Wriothesley, Shakespeare's Southampton, who led the "Patriot" faction on the London Virginia Council, pushing for more American independence.[66] (As for James's own "colonial discourse," it seems to have been devoted to worries about how it would all affect his relations with Spain,[67] and to requests for flying squirrels and other New World "toyes."[68]) Of more immediate interest, perhaps, to the mass of real or armchair adventurers were the reports of New World wealth that at first made Virginia known as a haven for bankrupts and spendthrifts, as well as for wild dreamers—followed by the accounts of starvation, rebellion, and hardship brought back by those who had escaped from the reality of colonial existence. Now the issue became "Is it worth it?" The official propaganda, optimistic about future profits, was soon countered by a backlash from less optimistic scoffers challenging the value of the entire project, one which sent money, men, and ships to frequent destruction and brought back almost no profit.[69]

Even the settlers actually living with the natives in the New World itself were—for entirely non-altruistic reasons—not yet fully engaged in "colonialist" discourse as defined by revisionists. In 1611 they had not managed to establish enough power to euphemize; they had little to be defensive about. They were too busy fighting mutiny, disease, and the stupidities of the London Council to have much energy left over for Indians. It is true that no writer ever treated Native Americans as equals—any more than he treated Moors, Jews, Catholics, peasants, women, Irishmen, or even Frenchmen as equals; travellers complacently recorded kidnapping natives to exhibit in England, as if the natives had no rights at all.[70] And it is true that some of their descriptions are distorted by Old World stereotypes of wild men or cannibals—though these descriptions are often confined to earlier *pre*colonial explorers' reports.[71] Or, far more insidiously, the descriptions were distorted by stereotypes of unfallen innocent noble savages—stereotypes that inevitably led to disillusionment when the settlers had to realize that the Indians, like the land itself, were not going to fulfill their dreams of a golden world made expressly to nurture Englishmen. The "noble savage" stereotype thus fueled the recurring accusation of Indian treachery, a response to betrayal of settlers' fantasies as well as to any real Indian betrayal,[72] and one to which I will return in discussing *The Tempest*.

But, given the universality of racial prejudice towards New World natives along with all "Others," in this early period the movement was to loosen, not to consolidate, the prejudices brought from the Old World. The descriptions of these extended face-to-face encounters with Native Americans were perhaps even more varied than contemporary responses to Moors and Jews, who were usually encountered on the white man's own territory, where exposure could be limited and controlled. The very terms imported from the Old World to name the natives—"savages" or "naturals"—began to lose their original connotations as the differing descriptions multiplied and even contra-dicted themselves. The reports range from Harriot's widely republished attempt at scientific, objective reporting (1588), which viewed natives with great respect, to Smith's less reliable adventure stories (1608–31), disputed even in his own time by Purchas. And although these do not by any means live up to our standards for non-colonialist discourse, their typical attitude is a wary, often patronizing, but live-and-let-live curiosity, rather than the exploitative erasure which would later become the mark of colonialist dis-course. So long as the conflicts remained minimal, Native Americans were seen as beings like the writers;[73] further, tribes were distinguished from one another, and recognition was granted to their different forms of government, class structure, dress codes, religion, and language.[74] And when conflict did trigger the recurring accusation of "treachery," the writers never presented the Indians as laughable Calibans, but rather as capable, indeed formidable, enemies whose skill and intelligence challenged that of the settlers.

Horrors had already been perpetrated by the Spanish in the name of colonialism; not learning from these—or perhaps learning all too well—the English would soon begin perpetrating their own. But that lay in the future. When *The Tempest* was written, what the New World seems to have meant for the majority of Englishmen was a sense of possibility and a set of conflicting fantasies about the wonders to be found there; these were perhaps the pre-conditions for colonialism—as for much else—but not yet the thing itself.

To place colonialist discourse as precisely as possible within a given moment (like stressing the differences between *The Tempest* and colonialist dis-course) is not to reduce the discussion to a numbers game. What is at stake here is not a quibble about chronology but an assumption about what we mean by the "relevant discursive context," about how we agree to determine it, and about how we decide to limit it. Here too there are differences of opin-ion about what counts, and these differences need to be acknowledged, exam-ined, and accounted for.

III

My point in specifying Shakespeare's precise literal and temporal relation to colonialist discourse—in specifying the unique mind through which the dis-course is mediated—is not to deny that the play has *any* relation to its context but to suggest that the relation is problematic. In the effort to identify Cal-iban as one more colonialist representation of the Other, we fail to notice how remarkable it is that such a Caliban should exist. In 1611 there were in England no literary portrayals of New World inhabitants and certainly no fic-tional examples of colonialist discourse.[75] Insofar as *The Tempest* does in some way allude to an encounter with a New World native (and I will for the remainder of this essay accept this premise), it is the very first work of literature to do so. There may be Indians, more or less demonized, in the nonliterary discourse. Outside of Shakespeare, however, there would be none in literature until two years after *The Tempest,* when they began to appear—feathers and all—in masques.[76] And Shakespeare went out of his way to invent Caliban: Strachey's account of the wreck on the uninhabited Bermuda islands—Shakespeare's main New World source—contains, of course, no island natives.[77] For these Shakespeare had to turn elsewhere in Strachey and in others who described the mainland colony in Virginia. Shakespeare was the first to show one of *us* mistreating a native, the first to represent a native from the inside, the first to allow a native to complain onstage, and the first to make that New World encounter problematic enough to generate the current attention to the play.

To argue for Shakespeare's uniqueness is not to argue that as fiction *The Tempest* is above politics, or that as a writer of fiction Shakespeare transcended ideology. It does imply, however, that if the play is "colonialist," it must be seen as "prophetic" rather than descriptive.[78] As such, the play's status immediately raises important questions. Why was Shakespeare—a man who had no direct stake in colonization—the first writer of fiction to portray New World inhabitants? Why then? Shakespeare had shown no signs of interest in the New World until *The Tempest,* despite the fact that there had been some colonial activity and some colonialist rhetoric for several years among those who did have a stake in it. How did the colonialist phenomenon spread?

To hasten over Shakespeare's relation to colonialism as if it were not a question but a conclusion is to lose one of the most important bits of data we may ever have about how such things as colonialism—and discourse—work. Problematic as it may be to speculate about an individual mind, it is even more problematic to speculate about the discourse of an entire nation or an entire period. One way to give substance to such large generalizations is to trace, in as much detail as may be available, the particulars on which they are based. Here the particulars include the individuals who produced, as well as reproduced, the larger cultural discourse—especially individuals like Shakespeare, who, more than almost any other, both absorbed and shaped the various conflicting discourses of the period.

To do this, as I have been arguing, it is necessary to consider the entire play, without deciding prematurely what is "only a distortion" or "only an irrelevance." In addition, however, we must also look to a context for *The Tempest* that is as relevant as colonialist discourse and perhaps even more essential to the presence of colonialism in *The Tempest* in the first place—that is, to the context of Shakespeare's own earlier "discourse." Only then can we see how the two fields of discourse intersect. In making use of the New World vocabulary and imagery, Shakespeare was in part describing something much closer to home—as was Jonson when he called the London brothel district "the Bermudas,"[79] or as would Donne when he found his America, his "new founde land," in the arms of his mistress. Or as was Dudley Carleton in a gossipy letter from London about Lord Salisbury enduring a "tempest" of reproof from a lady; or Sir Ralph Winwood in trying to "begin a new world by setting himself and his wife here at home."[80]

Long before writing *The Tempest,* Shakespeare had written another play about a ruler who preferred his books to government. Navarre's academy in *Love's Labor's Lost* was no island, but, like an island, it was supposed to be isolated from territorial negotiations. And Navarre, oblivious to colonial issues, though certainly not exempt from timeless aristocratic prejudice, brought his own version of Ariel and Caliban by inviting Armado and Costard to join him. Like Prospero, he asked his "Ariel" to make a pageant for him, and he imprisoned his "Caliban" for trying to "do" a wench. His relation to the two is not a matter of colonization but rather of condescension and ironic recognition, as Navarre is forced to see something of himself in the conflict between fiery Armado's over-active imagination and earthy Costard's lust.[81] Only much later did this pattern come to be "colonial."

The Tempest is linked in many other ways not only to *Love's Labor's Lost* but also to the rest of the canon, as continued efforts of critics have shown,[82] and it is revealing to see how, in each case, the non-colonial structures become associated with colonialist discourse. Indeed, the very details of *The Tempest* that revisionists see as marking the "nodal point of the play's imbrication into this discourse of colonialism"[83] are reworkings of similar moments in earlier and seemingly precolonial plays. The moment I will focus on for the rest of this paper is the one that many revisionists take as the strongest evidence in the play for the falseness of Prospero's position—the moment when the hidden colonialist project emerges openly,[84] when the "political unconscious" is exposed.[85] It occurs when Caliban's plot interrupts the pageant Prospero is staging for Ferdinand and Miranda, and Prospero is so enraged that Miranda says she has never seen him so angry. The explanation, it has been suggested, is that if psychology matters at all, Prospero's anger here, like his anger earlier when Caliban tried to rape Miranda, derives from the politics of colonialism. It reveals Prospero's political "disquiet at the irruption into consciousness of an unconscious anxiety concerning the grounding of his legitimacy" on the island.[86]

But the dramatic context counters the assumption that politics is primary in this episode. Like Caliban, Prospero differs in significant ways from the stereotyped "real life" characters in colonial political drama. Unlike the single-minded colonial invader, Prospero is both an exile and a father; and the action of the play is initiated when both these roles are newly activated by the arrival of Prospero's old enemies, those who had exiled him as well as his daughter's husband-to-be. At the moment of Prospero's eruption into anger, he has just bestowed Miranda on his enemy's son Ferdinand[87] and is in the midst of presenting his pageant as a wedding gift, wrapped in a three-fold warning about chastity.[88] If Prospero is to pass on his heritage to the next generation, he must at this moment repress his desire for power and for revenge at home, as well as any sexual desire he feels toward Miranda.[89] Both desires are easily projected onto the fishily phallic Caliban, a walking version of Prospero's own "thing" of darkness. Not only has Caliban already tried to rape Miranda; he is now out to kill Prospero so that he can turn Miranda over to Stephano ("she will give thee brave brood"); and Caliban does not even feel guilty. Caliban's function as a walking screen for projection may help explain why Caliban's sin does not consist in cannibalism, to which, one assumes, Prospero was never tempted, but rather in Prospero's own repressed fantasies of omnipotence and lust.[90] Of course Prospero is also angry that Caliban is now threatening both his authority on the island and his justification of that authority; but the extraordinary intensity of Prospero's rage suggests a conjunction of psychological as well as political passion.

This conjunction of the psychological and the political not only appears here in *The Tempest* but also characterizes a surprising number of Prospero-like characters in Shakespeare's earlier plays who provide a suggestive context for *The Tempest*. All through the canon one finds characters who escape from active lives to some kind of pastoral retreat, who step aside from power and aggression—and usually from sexuality as well—and from all the forbidden fantasies in which these are enacted. But while each adopts a disinterested stance, as if having retired behind the scenes, each sees life as a play and manipulates others still on stage in a way that suggests a fascination with what he has rejected and assigned to the "Others." And each of these has his "Caliban" and his moment of sudden, irrational anger when his "Caliban" threatens to overstep the limits defining him as "other" and separating him from "Prospero." At this moment of confrontation, boundaries threaten to disappear and hierarchies are menaced. And in each of the earlier plays, this moment is indicative of inner conflict, as the earlier "Prospero" figure confronts someone who often has neither property nor power to colonize, and whose threat is largely symbolic. In all these plays Shakespeare is dealing not just with power relations but also with the psychology of domination, with the complicated ways in which personal psychology interacts with political power.

As early as the mid-1590s, two figures show some resemblance to Prospero. Antonio, the merchant of Venice, sees the world as "A stage where every man must play a part, / And mine a sad one" (1.1.78–79). Almost eagerly accepting his passive lot, he claims to renounce both profit and love. But, as Marianne Novy suggests, a repressed self-assertion is hinted at in the passive/aggressive claims he makes on Bassanio and comes out clearly when he lashes out at the greedy and self-assertive Shylock with a viciousness like Prospero's towards Caliban, a viciousness he shows nowhere else.[91] He admits calling the Jew a dog and says,

> I am as like to call thee so again,
> To spet on thee again. . . .
>   (1.3.130–31)[92]

A related and similarly problematic exchange occurs in the *Henry IV* plays, written a year or so later, where role-playing Prince Hal, during his temporary retreat from power, had found a version of pastoral in Falstaff's tavern. After reclaiming his throne, when he finds that Falstaff has also come from the tavern to claim a role in the new kingdom, Hal suddenly repudiates Falstaff with a cruelty as cold as Prospero's anger at Caliban—and equally excessive: "I know thee not, old man." In both these cases, though the resemblance to Prospero is clear, the relation to an historically specific colonialism is hard to establish.

Then in *As You Like It* (1599) and *Measure for Measure* (1604) come the two exiled or self-exiled Dukes who leave home—one to "usurp" the deer in the forest (2.1.21–28), the other to "usurp" the beggary in the Vienna streets (3.2.93)—and who most resemble Prospero. Duke Senior in *As You Like It* is banished to the pastoral forest of Arden, where he professes himself utterly content to live a life notable for the absence of both power and women (a "woeful pageant," he calls it cheerfully [2.7.138]). He is saved from having to fight for power when his evil brother (unlike the one in Shakespeare's source) conveniently repents and hands back the dukedom; but an ambivalence about sexuality is at least suggested when this mildest of men lashes out at Jaques, precisely when Jaques returns from melancholy withdrawal and claims the fool's license to satirize society's ills—to "cleanse the foul body of the infected world."[93] "Fie on thee!" says the Duke,

> . . . thou thyself hast been a libertine,
> As sensual as the brutish sting itself,
> And all th' embossed sores, and headed evils,
> That thou with license of free foot hast caught,
> Wouldst thou disgorge into the general world.
> (2.7.65–69)

Jaques seems to have touched a nerve. Elsewhere Jaques makes a claim on behalf of the deer in the forest rather like the claim Caliban makes for himself on the island, complaining that Duke Senior has "usurped" these "velvet friends"; he even makes it "most invectively," having, like Caliban, learned how to curse. Just as in the case of Caliban, we cannot laugh away the claim the way the Duke does. But Jaques's complaint seems intended more as an insight into the Duke than a comment on the deer—whom Jaques later kills anyway.

The touchiest of these precursors, Vincentio in *Measure for Measure* (1604), is the one who most closely resembles Prospero. He too prefers study to government, and he turns over his power to Angelo, claiming "[I] do not like to stage me to their eyes" (1.1.68)—but then he steps behind the scenes to manipulate the action. Like Prospero, Vincentio sees his manipulation as an altruistic means of educating his wayward subjects into chastity, repentance, and merciful mildness; but it seems to serve more private needs of self-definition as well. For it first allows him, as "ghostly father," to deny any aggressive or sexual motives of his own, and then allows him to return at the end to claim both power and sexual rewards as he resumes his dukedom and claims Isabel.[94] Vincentio's "Caliban" is the libidinous and loose-tongued Lucio, who not only indulges his own appetites but openly accuses the Duke of indulging his, so that it is unusually clear in this case that the "Caliban" figure is a representation of the Duke's own disowned passions. Lucio's slanders include the claim that the Duke has "usurp[ed] the beggary he was never born to," but, like Jaques speaking for the deer, he is more concerned with revealing the Duke's contradictory desires here than with defending beggars' rights. Goaded by Lucio's insubordination, the Duke lashes out at him as he does at no one else and threatens a punishment much worse than the one he assigned to the would-be rapist and murderer Angelo or to the actual murderer Barnardine.

In the case of all of these "Prosperos," it is hard to see the attack on "Caliban" as part of a specifically colonialist strategy, as a way of exploiting the Other or of rationalizing illegitimate power over him rather than over what he represents in "Prospero" himself. To a logical observer, the Prospero-attack seems at best gratuitous—and the more frightening for being so. It has no political rationale. The "political" attack always takes place outside the play's old world, after the characters' withdrawal to a second world that is not so much a new world as one that projects, exaggerates, turns upside down, or polarizes the conflicts that made the old world uninhabitable. In the case of each earlier "Prospero," the conflicts seem internal as well as external, so that when he moves out to meet his "Caliban," he is always meeting himself. Political exile is also presented as self-estrangement, a crisis of selfhood expressed in social and geographical divisions. And in each case, Shakespeare exposes the fragility of such arrangements, whether they take the form of the pastoralization of the forest of Arden, or of the scapegoating of Shylock in Venice, or of Falstaff's carnival misrule in the tavern, or of the theatricalizing of the prison in Vincentio's Vienna, or of Prospero's "colonizing" of a utopian island.

Whatever varying political role each earlier "Caliban" plays as inhabitant of his second—or second-class—world, each seems to embody a similar psychological quality. In each case he displays the overt self-assertion that the retired or retiring "Prospero" cannot—or wishes not to—muster for himself, and that for Shakespeare seems to be the mark of the Other. Each is an epitome of what Shakespeare (perhaps in his own punning ambivalence about acknowledging it as his own) elsewhere calls "will."[95] This "will" includes a range of forbidden desires and appetites often attributed to the Other and always associated with the "foul body," as Jaques calls it; or with the fat appetitive body, as in Hal's picture of Falstaff; or with the body as mere pounds of flesh and blood; perhaps with what we might call, after Bakhtin, the "grotesque" body. And it is defined in opposition to the ethereal, or ariel, virtues such as "mercy," "honor," and "chastity" characterizing the various "Prosperos."

The "will" of these "Calibans" can carry suggestions of primitive oral greed, as in Shylock's desire to "feed fat" his revenge with a pound of human flesh, in Falstaff's voracious appetite, or in Caliban's name. Or it emerges in a rampant sexual greed, as in Falstaff, in Jaques's past, in Lucio, perhaps even in Shylock's reproductive miracles with sheep, and of course in Caliban himself. But the most alien aspect of self-assertion or "will" in these plays emerges in a primitive vengefulness. This vengefulness is associated with an infantile need to control and dominate and with the scatological imagery of filth—with a disgust at the whole messy, physical world that always threatens to get out of control. Thus Shylock's drive for revenge is linked to his Jonsonian "anal" virtues ("fast bind, fast find"), to his fecal gold, and to his tightly locked orifices ("stop my house's ears, I mean my casements" [2.5.34]). Thus, too, Duke Senior's description of Jaques "disgorging" his "embossed sores" suggests that he is projecting onto Jaques his disgust at the idea of "the foul body of the infected world"—and his fear that Jaques will "disgorge" and overflow his boundaries rather than cleanse; Jaques's very name associates him with this scatological vision. Caliban, very much concerned with revenge, also takes on a taint of anality through the words of Trinculo and Stephano. The latter sees Caliban hiding under his gabardine with Trinculo and takes Caliban for a monster whose first act is to "vent" a Trinculo—a Gargantuan act of defecation; Trinculo elsewhere complains that Caliban led them to a "foul lake" that o'erstunk their feet till they smelled "all horse-piss."[96]

Thus, although Caliban is like the New World natives in his "otherness," he is linked at least as closely to Shakespeare's earlier "Calibans." What is interesting in any attempt to understand *The Tempest*'s uniqueness in other aspects is that in Caliban for the first time Shakespeare shows "will," or narcissistic self-assertion, in its purest and simplest form as the original "grandiosity" or "megalomania" of a child;[97] for the first time he makes the representative of bodily existence a seeming child whose ego is a "body ego," as Freud said, a "subject" whose "self" is defined by the body. There is a childishly amoral—and almost asexual—glee in Caliban's sexuality ("O ho, O ho, would't had been done!" he says of the attempted rape [1.2.349]) and a childish exaggeration in his dreams of revenge ("brain him / . . . or with a log / Batter his skull, or paunch him with a stake, / Or cut his wezand with thy knife" [3.2.88–91]).[98] Like a child he thinks often about his mother,[99] and now that she is gone, he dreams of riches dropping from heaven and cries to dream again; like a child he was taught language and shown the man in the moon.[100] And like an imperious child he is enraged when his pie in the sky does not appear. If he rebukes Prospero for first stroking and then disciplining him, if he objects to being made a subject when he was "mine own king" (1.2.342), this is the rebuke made by every child, who begins life as "His

Majesty the Baby," tended by his mother, and who is then subjected to the demands of the community,[101] represented by the father. Childhood is the period in which anyone—even the most powerful Elizabethan aristocrat—can experience the slave's side of the master/slave relation, its indignities, and the dreams of reversal and revenge it can imbue. Appropriate and acceptable in a baby, all these traits (like Caliban himself) "with age [grow] uglier" (4.1.191)—and far more dangerous.

Caliban's childishness has been dismissed as a defense, another rationalization of Prospero's illegitimate power.[102] But if it is a defense, it is one which itself is revealing. Caliban's childishness is a dimension of the Other in which Shakespeare seems extremely interested.[103] It is a major (not peripheral) source both of Caliban's defining characteristics and of what makes his relation to Prospero so highly charged. Caliban's childish innocence seems to have been what first attracted Prospero, and now it is Caliban's childish lawlessness that enrages him. To a man like Prospero, whose life has been spent learning a self-discipline in which he is not yet totally adept, Caliban can seem like a child who must be controlled, and who, like a child, is murderously enraged at being controlled. Prospero treats Caliban as he would treat the willful child in himself.

The importance of childishness in defining Caliban is suggested by the final *Tempest* precedent to be cited here, one that lies behind Prospero's acknowledgement of Caliban as his own thing of darkness—and in which the Caliban figure is literally a child. This figure is found in *Titus Andronicus,* where a bastard child, called "devil" and "slave," is cast out by his mother but rescued by his father, who promises—in language foreshadowing Caliban's imagery in *The Tempest*—to raise him in a cave and feed him on berries and roots.[104] Here the father is black Aaron the Moor, and the childish thing of darkness, whom Aaron is at some pains to acknowledge his, is his own literally black son. What is remarkable about this portrait of a barbarian father and son is that Aaron's is the only uncomplicated parental love in a play-world where civilized white men like Titus kill their own children on principle. It is a world, by the way, which contains the only literal (if unwitting) cannibal in Shakespeare's plays, the child's white mother. Unlike Titus, Aaron can love his child because he can identify with him; as an "uncivilized" black man, he can accept the greedy, sensual, lawless child in himself: "This is my self, the vigor and the picture of my youth," he says (4.2.108). This love, which comes easily to Aaron in acknowledging his own flesh and blood, is transformed in *The Tempest* to Prospero's strained and difficult recognition of a tribal Other whose blackness nonetheless figures his own.

The echoes of Aaron not only suggest the family resemblance between Prospero and Caliban. They also suggest that here Shakespeare is changing his earlier vision of authority. In the earlier play it is white Titus who—like Prospero—gives away his power and is betrayed; but it is black Aaron who is stigmatized as the vengeful villain. And Titus maintains this black-and-white distinction even while savagely carrying out his own revenge. But distinctions in *The Tempest* have become less rigid. By merging his fantasy about a "white" (but exiled and neurotically puritanical) duke with his fantasy about a villainous (but loving) "black" father, Shakespeare for the first time shows, in Prospero, a paternal leader who comes back to power by admitting rather than denying the "blackness" in himself. Prospero may not, as several revisionists point out, physically *do* much for Caliban at the end; however, what he *says* matters a great deal indeed, for his original transgression, when he first defined Caliban as the Other, was intellectual as well as physical. When Prospero finally acknowledges Caliban, although he is a long way from recognizing the equality of racial "others," he comes closer than any of Shakespeare's other "Prosperos" to acknowledging the otherness within, which helps generate all racism—and he comes closer than anyone else in colonialist discourse. Prospero acknowledges the child-like Caliban as his own, and although he does not thus undo hierarchy, he moves for the first time towards accepting the child in himself rather than trying to dominate and erase that child (along with random vulnerable human beings outside himself) in order to establish his adult authority.

Thus, although Shakespeare may, as the revisionists claim, to some degree reproduce Prospero's colonialist vision of the island, the play's emphasis lies not so much in justifying as in analyzing that vision, just as Shakespeare had analyzed the origins of dominance in the earlier plays. The play insists that we see Prospero's current relation to Caliban in terms of Prospero's own past; it contains the "colonial" encounter firmly within the framing story of his own family history. And though that history does not extend backward to Prospero's own childhood, it does begin with family ties and Miranda's memory of "the dark backward and abysm of time" (1.2.50), before either she or Prospero had known the Other. Prospero was then, he thought, in total harmony with his world and himself, happy in his regressive retreat to his library-Eden; he was buffered from reality, he thought, by a "lov'd" brother so linked to himself and his own desires that Prospero had in him a trust with no "limit, / A confidence sans bound" (1.2.96–97), like the trust that Miranda must have had in the women who "tended" her then. Only when Antonio's betrayal shattered that trust and Prospero was ousted from Eden—newly aware of both the brother as Other and of himself as a willful self in opposition—did he "discover" the island and Caliban. In a sense, then, Caliban emerged from the rift between Prospero and Antonio,[105] just as Ariel emerged from Sycorax's riven pine. Once the brother has shown that he is not identical to the self, reflecting back its own narcissistic desire, then he becomes the Other—and simultaneously rouses the vengeful Other in the self. In *The Tempest* the distance that a "colonialist" Prospero imposes between self and Other originated in a recoil from the closest relation of all; it was a recoil that in fact *defined* both the "distant" and the "close," the public and the private—the political and the personal—as separate realms. When

Prospero acknowledges Caliban, he thus partly defuses an entire dynamic that began long before he had ever seen the island.

IV

When Shakespeare created a childish "Caliban," he was himself rounding out a dynamic process that had begun as long ago as the writing of *Titus Andronicus*. We will never "know" why Shakespeare gave to this final version of his exile story a local habitation incorporating aspects of colonialist discourse. But the answer lies not only in that discourse but also in him and in what was on his mind. Some of the most "specious" speculations about Shakespeare's mind have been stimulated by his presumed resemblance to Prospero at the end of the play: past his zenith, on the way to retirement, every third thought turned to his grave. Without trying speciously to read minds, however, it seems safe to say that to some degree Shakespeare had been for several years concerned with the aging, loss, mortality, and death that recur in so much of what we know he was writing and reading at the time. To this degree, both the play and its context deal with the end of the individual self, the subject and the body in which it is located. It is the end of everything associated with the discovery of self in childhood, the end of everything Caliban represents— and thus the greatest threat to infantile narcissism since His Majesty the Baby was first de-throned. John Bender has noted that the occasion of the play's presumed court debut in 1611 was Hallowmas, the feast of winter and the time of seasonal celebrations figuring the more final endings and death associated with winter.[106] As part of the celebrations, Bender suggests, the play might have served to structure a communal response to the recurring "seasonal mentality" brought on by the reminder of mortality. Whether or not this is true, that which "recurs" in seasons and communities comes only once to individuals; and as the final stage in Shakespeare's own "seasonal" movement from *A Midsummer Night's Dream* to *The Winter's Tale*, the play can be seen as staging a final "crisis of selfhood" and of betrayal like those in the earlier exile plays—but this time a far more extreme one.[107] For those who rage against the dying of the light, it is a crisis that awakens the old infantile narcissistic demand for endless fulfillment and the narcissistic rage and vengefulness against a world that denies such satisfactions.[108]

To one on the threshold of retirement from the Old World, the New World is an appropriate stage on which to enact this last resurgence of the infantile self. We take for granted the historical conditions generating utopian visions in the voyagers' reports outside the play. What the example of Caliban's childish presence in the play suggests is that for Shakespeare the desire for such utopias—the golden worlds and fountains of youth—has roots in personal history as well as in "history." The desire has been shaped by the most local as well as by the largest, collective, material constraints: by being born small and weak in a world run by large, strong people with problems of their own; by being born in "a sexed and mortal body"[109] that must somehow become part of a social and linguistic community. Caliban's utopia of sweet voices and clouds dropping riches (3.2.137–43) draws most directly on the infantile substratum that colored Columbus's report when he returned from his third voyage convinced "that the newly discovered hemisphere was shaped like a woman's breast, and that the Earthly Paradise was located at a high point corresponding to the nipple."[110] But the play's other "utopias" draw on it too. Gonzalo's utopia is more socialized ("nature should bring forth, / . . . all abundance, / To feed my innocent people" [2.1.163–65]); Prospero's pageant utopia is more mythic (a world without winter, blessed by nurturing Ceres); but, like Caliban's, their utopias recreate a union with a bounteous Mother Nature. And, like every child's utopia, each is a fragile creation, easily destroyed by the rage and violence that constitute its defining alternative—a dystopia of murderous vengeance; the interruption of Prospero's pageant is only the last in a series of such interruptions.[111] Each is the creation of a childish mind that operates in binary divisions: good mother/bad mother, love/rage, brother/Other.

That Shakespeare was drawn to the utopian aspects of the New World is suggested by the particular fragment of New World discourse that most directly precipitated (Kermode's suggestive term) the play—the Bermuda pamphlets, which record what was "perhaps the most romantic incident associated with America's beginnings."[112] What attracted Shakespeare, that is, was the story in which a "merciful God," a loving and fatherly protector, rescued a whole shipload of people from certain death; it was a story that countered thoughts of winter with reports of magical bounty in the aptly named "Summer Islands."

The concerns that made Shakespeare's approach to colonialist discourse possible may have been operative later in other cases as well. In analyzing the colonialist discourse growing out of political motives, it is important not to lose touch with the utopian discourse growing out of a different set of motives. Without reducing colonialism to "the merely subjective and to the status of psychological projection,"[113] one can still take account of fantasies and motives that, though now regarded as secondary, or as irrelevant to politics, may interact with political motives in ways we have not yet begun to understand—and cannot understand so long as we are diverted by trying to reduce psychology to politics or politics to psychology. The binary dynamics of infantile utopian fantasies can, for example, help explain why frustrated settlers succumbed *so easily* to the twin stereotypes of the Native Americans as innocent primitives who would welcome and nurture the settlers, and as hopelessly treacherous Others. They can serve as a reminder that the desire for friendship and brotherhood can be as destructive as a desire to exploit. Reference to irrational, outdated infantile needs can help explain why the settlers, once they actually did begin colonizing, set out with such gratuitous thoroughness to "reduce" the savage to civility. As James Axtell describes the process, "In European eyes, no native characteristic was too small to reform, no habit too harmless to reduce."[114] Such behavior seems to go beyond any immediate political or material motive and seems rather to serve more general psychological needs stirred up by conflict with the natives. The recent emphasis on the colonists' obvious material greed and rational self-interest— or class-interest—has unnecessarily obscured the role of these less obvious irrational motives and fantasies that are potentially even more insidious.

Shakespeare's assimilation of elements from historical colonialist discourse was neither entirely isolated from other uses or innocent of their effects. Nonetheless, the "colonialism" in his play is linked not only to Shakespeare's indirect participation in an ideology of political exploitation and erasure but also to his direct participation in the psychological aftereffects of having experienced the exploitation and erasure inevitable in being a child in an adult's world. He was not merely reproducing a preexistent discourse; he was also crossing it with other discourses, changing, enlarging, skewing, and questioning it. Our sense of *The Tempest*'s participation in "colonialist discourse" should be flexible enough to take account of such crossings; indeed our notion of that in which such discourse consisted should be flexible enough to include the whole of the text that constitutes the first English example of fictional colonialist discourse.[115]

Notes

1. Two of the earliest of these critiques were actually written, although not published, by 1960: George Lamming, "A monster, a child, a slave" (1960) in *The Pleasures of Exile* (London: Allison and Busby, 1984); James Smith, "The Tempest" (1954) in *Shakespearian and Other Essays*, ed. E. M. Wilson (Cambridge: Cambridge Univ. Press, 1974), pp. 159–261. Two more articles, less politicized, followed in the sixties: Philip Brockbank, "*The Tempest:* Conventions of Art and Empire" in *Later Shakespeare*, eds. J. R. Brown and B. Harris (London: Edward Arnold, 1966), pp. 183–201; and D. G. James, "The New World" in *The Dream of Prospero* (Oxford: Clarendon Press, 1967), pp. 72–123.

The recent group, returning to the political perspective of the first two, includes: Stephen Greenblatt, "Learning to Curse: Aspects of Linguistic Colonialism in the Sixteenth Century" in *First Images of America*, ed. Fredi Chiappelli, 2 vols. (Los Angeles: Univ. of California Press, 1976), Vol. 2, 561–80; Bruce Erlich, "Shakespeare's Colonial Metaphor: On the Social Function of Theatre in *The Tempest,*" *Science and Society*, 41 (1977), 43–65; Lorie Leininger, "Cracking the Code of *The Tempest,*" *Bucknell Review*, 25 (1980), 121–31; Peter Hulme, "Hurricanes in the Caribbees: The Constitution of the Discourse of English Colonialism" in *1642: Literature and Power in the Seventeenth Century,* Proceedings of the Essex conference on the Sociology of Literature, eds. Francis Barker et al. (Colchester: Univ. of Essex, 1981), pp. 55–83; Paul N. Siegel, "Historical Ironies in *The Tempest,*" *Shakespeare Jahrbuch,* 119 (Weimar: 1983), 104–11; Francis Barker and Peter Hulme, "Nymphs and reapers heavily vanish: the discursive con-texts of *The Tempest*" in *Alternative Shakespeares,* ed. John Drakakis (London and New York: Methuen, 1985), pp. 191–205; Terence Hawkes, "Swisser-Swatter: making a man of English letters" in *Alternative Shakespeares,* pp. 26–46; Paul Brown, " 'This thing of darkness I acknowledge mine': *The Tempest* and the discourse of colonialism" in *Political Shakespeare: New essays in cultural materialism* (Ithaca, N.Y., and London: Cornell Univ. Press, 1985), pp. 48–71; Peter Hulme, *Colonial Encounters: Europe and the native Caribbean, 1492–1797* (London and New York: Methuen, 1986), pp. 89–134; Thomas Cartelli, "Prospero in Africa: *The Tempest* as colonialist text and pretext" in *Shakespeare Reproduced: The text in history and ideology,* eds. Jean Howard and Marion O'Conner (New York: Methuen, 1987), pp. 99–115; I would include two essays by Stephen Orgel somewhat different in their focus but nonetheless related: "Prospero's Wife" in *Rewriting the Renaissance,* eds. Margaret Ferguson et al. (Chicago: Univ. of Chicago Press, 1986), pp. 50–64, and "Shakespeare and the Cannibals" in *Cannibals, Witches, and Divorce: Estranging the Renaissance,* ed. Marjorie Garber (Baltimore and London: Johns Hopkins Univ. Press, 1987), pp. 40–66.

2. Hulme, *Colonial Encounters,* p. 94.

3. See, for example, Paul Brown, "This thing of darkness," p. 48.

4. In fact Edward Pechter, in one of the earliest of such scrutinies, cited several of the recent *Tempest* articles as especially problematic. See "The New Historicism and Its Discontents: Politicizing Renaissance Drama," *PMLA,* 102 (1987), 292–303. See also Howard Felperin, "Making it 'neo': The new historicism and Renaissance literature," *Textual Practice,* 1 (1987), 262–77; Jean Howard, "The New Historicism in Renaissance Studies," *English Literary Renaissance,* 16 (1986), 13–43; and Anthony B. Dawson, "*Measure for Measure,* New Historicism, and Theatrical Power," *Shakespeare Quarterly,* 39 (1988), 328–41.

5. *The Tempest,* The Arden Shakespeare, ed. Frank Kermode (London: Methuen, 1954), p. xxv. For an account of the work of earlier scholars exploring the connection between the play and these documents, see Kermode, pp. xxv–xxxiv, and Charles Frey, "*The Tempest* and the New World," *SQ,* 30 (1979), 29–41.

6. E. E. Stoll and Northrop Frye are the only exceptions I have seen cited.

7. Recently there has been a renewed emphasis on the romance elements. See Gary Schmidgall, "*The Tempest* and *Primaleon*: A New Source," *SQ,* 37 (1986), 423–39, esp. p. 436; and Robert Wiltenberg, "The '*Aeneid*' in '*The Tempest,*' " *Shakespeare Survey,* 39 (1987), 159–68.

8. See, for example, Harry Berger's important essay, "Miraculous Harp: A Reading of Shakespeare's *Tempest,*" *Shakespeare Studies,* 5 (1969), 253–83.

9. Harry Levin, *The Myth of the Golden Age in the Renaissance* (Bloomington: Indiana Univ. Press, 1969); Leslie A. Fiedler, *The Stranger in Shakespeare* (New York: Stein and Day, 1972); Leo Marx, "Shakespeare's American Fable," *The Machine in the Garden* (London and New York: Oxford Univ. Press, 1964), pp. 34–72.

10. O. Manoni, *Prospero and Caliban: The Psychology of Colonization,* trans. Pamela Powesland (1950; rpt. New York: Praeger, 1964).

11. Hulme, *Colonial Encounters,* p. 133.

12. Hulme, *Colonial Encounters,* p. 115; Barker and Hulme, p. 201; Orgel, "Prospero's Wife," pp. 62–63.

13. Orgel, "Shakespeare and the Cannibals," p. 55.

14. As Paul Werstine wrote in the brochure announcing the NEH Humanities Institute on "New Directions in Shakespeare Criticism" (The Folger Shakespeare Library, 1988), "To appreciate *The Tempest* . . . today . . . we must understand discourses of colonialism, power, legitimation."

15. Barker and Hulme, p. 198.

16. Hawkes, "Swisser-Swatter," p. 28.

17. Thus stereotypes, for example, served as part of a "discursive strategy . . . to locate or 'fix' a colonial other in a position of inferiority . . ." (Paul Brown, modifying Edward Said on orientalism, p. 58).

18. Actually, this point too is a matter of emphasis. R. R. Cawley ("Shakspere's Use of the Voyagers in *The Tempest,*" *PMLA,* 41 [1926], 688–726) and Kermode, among others, had

noted in passing some similarities between the play's view of Caliban and the distortions of colonialist self-serving rhetorical purposes; but revisionists take this to be the important point, not to be passed over.

19. Leininger, "Cracking the Code of *The Tempest,*" p. 122.

20. Paul Brown, pp. 64, 66. Brown also contends that *The Tempest* "exemplifies . . . a moment of *historical* crisis. This crisis is the struggle to produce a coherent discourse adequate to the complex requirements of British colonialism in its initial phase" (p. 48).

21. Hulme, *Colonial Encounters,* p. 93. Later he does grant a little ground to the psychological critics in allowing that their "totally spurious" identification of Prospero with Shakespeare yet "half grasps the crucial point that Prospero . . . is a dramatist and creator of theatrical effects" (p. 115).

22. "From the point of view of a political hermeneutic, measured against the requirements of a 'political unconscious,' we must conclude that the conception of wish-fulfillment remains locked in a problematic of the individual subject . . . which is only indirectly useful to us." The objection to wish-fulfillment is that it is "always outside of time, outside of narrative" and history; "what is more damaging, from the present perspective, is that desire . . . remains locked into the category of the individual subject, even if the form taken by the individual in it is no longer the ego or the self, but the individual body. . . . *the need to transcend individualistic categories and modes of interpretation is in many ways the fundamental issue for any doctrine of the political unconscious*" (*The Political Unconscious: Narrative as a Socially Symbolic Act* [Ithaca, N.Y.: Cornell Univ. Press, 1981], pp. 66, 68, italics added).

23. Stephen Greenblatt, "Psychoanalysis and Renaissance Culture," *Literary Theory/Renaissance Texts,* eds. Patricia Parker and David Quint (Baltimore: Johns Hopkins Univ. Press, 1986), 210–24.

24. Jameson, p. 12. So, too, Freud's "hermeneutic manual" can be of use to the political critic (p. 65).

25. "Norman Holland's suggestive term," Jameson, p. 49.

26. Jameson, p. 67. Cf. Paul Brown, "My use of Freudian terms does not mean that I endorse its ahistorical, Europocentric and sexist models of psychical development. However, a materialist criticism deprived of such concepts as displacement and condensation would be seriously impoverished . . ." (p. 71, n. 35).

27. Jameson discussing Althusser (p. 30) and Greimas (p. 48).

28. *The Crown of Life* (1947; rpt. New York: Barnes & Noble, 1966), p. 255.

29. See Trevor R. Griffiths, " 'This Island's mine': Caliban and Colonialism," *Yearbook of English Studies,* 13 (1983), 159–80.

30. Griffiths, p. 166.

31. Virginia Mason Vaughan, " 'Something Rich and Strange': Caliban's Theatrical Metamorphoses," *SQ,* 36 (1985), 390–405, esp. p. 390.

32. Erlich, "Shakespeare's Colonial Metaphor," p. 49; Paul Brown, p. 48.

33. Even St. Paul in his travels (echoed in the play) met natives who—like Caliban—thought him a god.

34. Hulme produces as evidence against Shakespeare these four words from the cast list, which Shakespeare may or may not have written ("Hurricanes in the Caribbees," p. 72).

35. Alden T. Vaughan, "Shakespeare's Indian: The Americanization of Caliban," *SQ,* 39 (1988), 137–53. He argues that the intention miscarried not only at the time but also for the three centuries following. He adds, "Rather, from the Restoration until the late 1890s, Caliban appeared on stage and in critical literature as almost everything but an Indian" (p. 138).

36. Hulme, while noting Caliban's "anomalous nature," sees the anomaly as yet another colonialist strategy: "In ideological terms [Caliban is] a compromise formation and one achieved, like all such formations, only at the expense of distortion elsewhere" ("Hurricanes in the Caribbees," pp. 71, 72). This begs the question: Caliban can only be a "distortion" if he is intended to represent someone. But that is precisely the question—*is* he meant to represent a

Native American? Sidney Lee noted that Caliban's method of building dams for fish reproduces the Indians'; though he is often cited by later writers as an authority on the resemblance, the rest of his evidence is not convincing ("The Call of the West: America and Elizabethan England," *Elizabethan and Other Essays,* ed. Frederick S. Boas [Oxford: Clarendon Press, 1929], pp. 263–301). G. Wilson Knight has an impressionistic essay about the relationship between Caliban and Indians ("Caliban as Red Man" [1977] in *Shakespeare's Styles,* eds. Philip Edwards, Inga-Stina Ewbank, and G. K. Hunter [London: Cambridge Univ. Press, 1980]). Hulme lists Caliban's resemblances to Caribs ("Hurricanes in the Caribbees"), and Kermode cites details taken from natives visited during both the Old and the New World voyages.

37. The Indians who would appear in Chapman's 1613 masque would be fully equipped with feathers. See R. R. Cawley, *The Voyagers and Elizabethan Drama* (Boston: D. C. Heath; London: Oxford Univ. Press, 1938), p. 359, and Orgel, "Shakespeare and the Cannibals," pp. 44, 47.

38. Shakespeare had apparently read up on his monsters (R. R. Cawley, "Shakspere's Use of the Voyagers," p. 723, and Frey, passim), but he picked up the stereotypes only to play with them ostentatiously (in Stephano's and Trinculo's many discredited guesses about Caliban's identity) or to leave them hanging (in Prospero's identification of Caliban as "devil").

39. Hulme, "Hurricanes in the Caribbees," p. 74.

40. Lamming (n. 1, above), pp. 98–99.

41. Lamming, p. 97; Erlich, p. 49.

42. The play also seems anti-colonialist because it includes the comic sections with Stephano and Trinculo, which show colonialism to be "nakedly avaricious, profiteering, perhaps even pointless"; but this too can be seen as a rationalization: "This low version of colonialism serves to displace possibly damaging charges . . . against properly-constituted civil authority on to the already excremental products of civility, the masterless" (Paul Brown, p. 65).

43. Greenblatt, "Learning to Curse," pp. 570–71; Leininger (n. 1, above), pp. 126–27.

44. Leininger, p. 127.

45. As Fiedler's book implies (n. 9, above), she is less like anything American than like the Frenchwoman Joan of Arc, who also tried to save herself from the law by claiming she was pregnant with a bastard; Joan simply wasn't as successful (see pp. 43–81, esp. p. 77).

46. See Brockbank, p. 193. Even these details can be discounted as rationalizations, of course. Paul Brown, for example, explains Sycorax's presence as a rationalization: by degrading her black magic, he argues, Shakespeare makes Prospero seem better than he is (pp. 60–61). Hulme notes that Sycorax may be Prospero's invention, pointing out that we never see any direct evidence that she was present (*Colonial Encounters,* p. 115). Orgel links Caliban's claims of legitimacy by birth to James I's claims ("Prospero's Wife," pp. 58–59).

47. See Fiedler, p. 205.

48. Erlich, "Shakespeare's Colonial Metaphor," p. 63.

49. The trend, moreover, is to move away from anthropomorphic terms like "repression" or "censorship," themselves inherited from the political terminology on which Freud drew for his own. Like the vocabulary of "scientific" hydraulics on which Freud also drew for his notions of libido flowing and damming up, the older terms are being replaced by contemporary terminologies more appropriate to describing a conflict among meanings or interpretations, rather than between anthropomorphized forces engaged in a simple struggle "for" and "against."

50. Spaniards, he writes, "taught their Hounds, fierce Dogs, to teare [the Indians] in peeces" (*A briefe Narration of the destruction of the Indies by the Spaniards* [1542 (?)], Samuel Purchas, *Purchas His Pilgrimes,* 20 vols. [Glasgow: Maclehose and Sons, 1905—1907], Vol. XVIII, 91). This was apparently a common topos, found also in Eden's translation of Peter Martyr's *Decades of the Newe Worlde* (1555), included in Eden's *Historie of Trauaile* (1577), which Shakespeare read for *The Tempest.* It was also used by Greene and Deloney (Cawley, *Voyagers and Elizabethan Drama,* pp. 383–84).

51.   Hulme, "Hurricanes in the Caribbees," pp. 63–66; see also Orgel on this "New World topos" in "Shakespeare and the Cannibals," pp. 41–44.

52.   Neither was Montaigne's in the essay that has been taken as a source for the play. Scholars are still debating about Montaigne's attitude toward cannibals, though all agree that his critical attitude toward *Europeans* was clear in the essay.

53.   This blend of Old and New World characteristics, earlier seen as characteristic of New World discourse, is acknowledged in many of the revisionist studies but is seen as one of the rhetorical strategies used to control Indians.

54.   William Strach[e]y, "A true reportorie. . . ," *Purchas*, Vol. XIX, p. 62. For the citation of Purchas as colonialist, see Hulme, "Hurricanes in the Caribbees," p. 78, n. 21.

55.   Paul Brown, p. 64.

56.   This is an entirely separate question from another that one might ask: How comparable were Purchas's remarks, taken from the collection of travelers' tales which he edited, censored, and used to support his colonialist ideal, on the one hand, and a play, on the other? In *Purchas*, Richard Marienstras argues, "the multiplicity of interpretations modulates and reinforces a single ideological system. The same can certainly not be said of . . . *The Tempest*" (*New perspectives on the Shakespearean world*, trans. Janet Lloyd [Cambridge: Cambridge Univ. Press, 1985], p. 169). This entire book, which devotes a chapter to *The Tempest*, is an excellent study of "certain aspects of Elizabethan ideology and . . . the way these are used in Shakespeare" (p. 1).

57.   See Pechter (n. 4, above). This kind of "condition," he argues, is really a precondition in the sense that it is assumed to be logically (if not chronologically) prior. It is assumed to have the kind of explanatory power that "the Elizabethan world view" was once accorded (p. 297).

58.   See, for example, the following contemporary tracts reprinted in *Tracts and Other Papers Relating Principally to the Origin, Settlement, and Progress of . . . North America*, ed. Peter Force, 4 vols. (1836–47; rpt. New York: Peter Smith, 1947): R. I., "*Nova Brittania:* OFFERING MOST Excellent fruites by Planting IN VIRGINIA. Exciting all such as be well affected to further the same" (1609), Vol. 1, No. 6; "Virginia richly valued" (1609), Vol. 4, No. 1; "A TRVE DECLARATION of the estate of the Colonie in Virginia, With a confutation of such scandalous reports as haue tended to the disgrace of so worthy an enterprise" (1610), Vol. 3, No. 1; Sil. Jourdan, "A PLAINE DESCRIPTION OF THE BARMVDAS, NOW CALLED SOMMER ILANDS" (1613), Vol. 3, No. 3.

In *The Genesis of the United States,* ed. Alexander Brown, 2 vols. (New York: Russell & Russell, 1964), see also: Robert Gray, "A GOOD SPEED to Virginia" (1609), Vol. 1, 293–302; "A True and Sincere declaration of the purpose and ends of the *Plantation* begun in *Virginia* of the degrees which it hath received; and meanes by *which it hath beene advanced:* and the . . . *conclusion* of His Majesties Councel of that Colony . . . untill by the mercies of GOD it shall *retribute a fruitful harvest to the Kingdome of heaven, and this Common-Wealth*" (1609), Vol. 1, 337–53; "A Publication by the Counsell of Virginea, touching the Plantation there" (1609), Vol. 1, 354–56; R. Rich, "NEWES FROM VIRGINIA. THE LOST FLOCKE TRIUMPHANT . . ." (1610), Vol. 1, 420–26.

59.   "A Trve Declaration," p. 6.

60.   Alexander Brown, in *The Genesis of the United States,* reprints extracts from the following pertinent documents: William Symonds, "VIRGINIA: A SERMON PREACHED AT WHITE-CHAPPEL . . ." (1609), Vol. 1, 282–91; Daniel Price, "SAVLES PROHIBITION STAIDE . . . And to the Inditement of all that persecute Christ with a reproofe of those that traduce the Honourable Plantation of Virginia" (1609), Vol. 1, 312–16; and, most important, William Crashaw's sermon titled "A New-yeeres Gift to Virginea," and preached, as the title page announced, before "Lord La Warre Lord Governour and Captaine Generall of Virginia, and others of [the] Counsell . . . At the said Lord Generall his . . . departure for Virginea . . . Wherein both the lawfulnesses of that action is maintained and the necessity thereof is also demonstrated, not so much out of the grounds of Policie, as of Humanity, Equity and Christianity" (1610), Vol. 1, 360–75.

61. In Alexander Brown, see William Crashaw for two of these references (in "A New-yeeres Gift to Virginea" [1610], and "Epistle Dedicatory" to Alexander Whitaker's *"Good Newes from Virginia"* [1613], Vol. 2, 611–20); and see Ralphe Hamor in *A True Discourse of the Present Estate of Virginea* (1615), Virginia State Library Publications, No. 3 (Richmond: Virginia State Library, 1957).

62. Pp. 16, 17.

63. For the general history of the period, see David Beers Quinn, *England and the Discovery of America, 1481–1620* (New York: Alfred A. Knopf, 1974); Alexander Brown's *Genesis* identifies similar shifting motives in the history of colonization. Such voyages were made famous by often-reprinted accounts, especially in collections by Richard Eden and Richard Hakluyt, both of whose anthologies Shakespeare would consult for *The Tempest*. In the introductory material in these collections, as in the voyages themselves, the self-interest is obvious but so mixed with excitement and utopian hopes, and so focused on competition with Spain, that the issue of relation to Indians was dwarfed by comparison.

64. If he didn't succeed in establishing a settlement, he would lose his patent. His interest in the patent rather than the colony was shown by his apparent negligence in searching for his lost colony (Quinn, n. 63, above, p. 300). He could hold onto his patent only so long as there was hope that the colonists were still alive; clearly the hope was worth more to Raleigh than the colony.

65. Matthew P. Andrews, *The Soul of a Nation: The Founding of Virginia and the Projection of New England* (New York: Scribner's, 1943), p. 125. An entire popular literature developed, so much so that the Archbishop of York complained that "of Virginia there be so many tractates, divine, human, historical, political, or call them as you please, as no further intelligence I dare desire" (quoted in Andrews, p. 125).

66. It is this issue rather than colonialism that stimulated an earlier period of political commentary on the New World material in *The Tempest:* Charles M. Gayley, *Shakespeare and the Founders of Liberty in America* (New York: Macmillan, 1917); A. A. Ward, "Shakespeare and the makers of Virginia," *Proceedings of the British Academy,* 9 (1919); see also E. P. Kuhl, "Shakespeare and the founders of America: *The Tempest,"* *Philological Quarterly,* 41 (1962), 123–46.

67. Contributing to the welter of contradictory discourses was the Spanish ambassador's flow of letters to Spain insisting, not irrationally, that the whole purpose of maintaining a profitless colony like Jamestown was to establish a base for pirate raids against Spanish colonies.

68. Letter from Southampton to the Earl of Salisbury, 15 December 1609, in Alexander Brown, Vol. 1, 356–57.

69. The quantity and quality of the objections, which have not on the whole survived, has been judged by the nature of the many defenses thought necessary to answer them. See notes 58, 60, 61.

70. A practice that Shakespeare did not admire if Stephano and Trinculo are any indication.

71. As are the two monsters cited as possible prototypes for Caliban by Geoffrey Bullough (*Narrative and Dramatic Sources of Shakespeare,* 8 vols. [New York: Columbia Univ. Press, 1958], Vol. 8, 240). There were exceptions, of course, as in George Percy's *Observations . . . of the Plantation of . . . Virginia* (1606), in *Purchas,* Vol. XVIII, 403–19.

72. See Karen Ordahl Kupperman, *Settling With the Indians: The Meeting of English and Indian Cultures in America, 1580–1640* (Totowa, N.J.: Rowman and Littlefield, 1980), pp. 127–29. The origins of this nearly universal belief in Indian treachery are of course multiple, ranging from the readiness of the English to project their fears onto any available victim, whether Indians or mariners (who were also regularly accused of treachery in these narratives), to the prevailing stereotypes of the Other, to specific English acts of provocation, to the general tensions inherent in the situation. Without arguing for any one of these, I merely wish to suggest that the notion of "colonialist discourse" simplifies a complex situation.

73. Even as proto-white men, their skin as tanned rather than naturally black, etc. See Kupperman, and Orgel, "Shakespeare and the Cannibals."

74. Greenblatt, in his study of the ways in which white men verbally "colonialized" Indians, emphasizes the degree to which whites assumed that the Indians had *no* language. Although he notes that there were exceptions, he makes it sound as if these exceptions were rare and were largely confined to the "rough, illiterate sea dog, bartering for gold trinkets on a faraway beach," rather than to the "captains or lieutenants whose accounts we read" ("Learning to Curse," pp. 564–65). On the contrary, even the earliest travelers had often included glossaries of Indian terms in their reports (e.g., the Glossary in the introductory material of Eden's translation of Martyr's *Decades* [1555], as well as in various later English reports reprinted in *Purchas His Pilgrimes* [1625]); and in reading through Purchas's helter-skelter collection, one is struck by the number of writers who grant automatic respect to the Indians' language. A possibly figurative rather than literal force for comments on the Indians' "want of language" is suggested by Gabriel Archer's account of a 1602 voyage. Here it is the English, not the Indians, who are deficient in this respect: they "spake divers Christian words, and seemed to understand much *more then we, for Want of Language, could comprehend*" ("Relation of Captain Gosnold's voyage," *Purchas*, Vol. XVIII, 304, italics mine).

75. See R. R. Cawley, *Voyagers and Elizabethan Drama*, passim, and *Unpathed Waters: Studies in the Influence of the Voyagers on Elizabethan Literature* (Princeton, N.J.: Princeton Univ. Press, 1940), pp. 234–41. Neither of R. R. Cawley's two books about the voyagers' influence on contemporary English literature cites any pre-1611 passage of more than a few lines. It is true that in the 1580s Marlowe's plays took off from the general sense of vastness and possibility opened up by voyages to the New as well as to the Old World. In addition Drayton wrote an "Ode to the Virginia Voyage," perhaps expressly for the settlers leaving for Jamestown in 1606; and one line in Samuel Daniel's "Musophilis" has a colonialist ring: he speaks of "vent[ing] the treasure of our tongue . . . T' inrich unknowing Nations with our stores." True, too, that in a quite different spirit Jonson, Marston, and Chapman collaborated in *Eastward Ho* (1605) to make fun of gallants flocking to Virginia with expectations as great as those bringing foolish victims to Face and Subtle's alchemical chimeras. But while Marlowe participates in the spirit of romantic adventure associated with voyaging and treasure-hunting, and *Eastward Ho* satirizes it, neither deals at all with the New World or with the New World natives.

76. The three brief exceptions are references to Spanish cruelty to Indians, all published before the truce with Spain. The Stationers' Register lists "The crueltie of ye Spaniardes toward th[e] Indians, a ballad" (1586) and "Spanishe cruelties" (1601), now lost. Robert Greene notes in passing that the Spaniards hunted Indians with dogs, while by contrast the English treated the natives with "such courtesie, as they thought the English Gods, and the Spaniardes both by rule and conscience halfe Devils" (*The Spanish Masquerado* [1589], *Life and . . . Works,* ed. Alexander B. Grosart, 15 vols. [London and Aylesbury: privately printed, 1881–86], Vol. V, 282–83). See Cawley, *Voyagers and Elizabethan Drama*, pp. 385–86.

77. When Strachey finishes with his account of the Bermuda episode and turns to a description of Virginia, he does devote one sentence to the Indians' treachery.

78. See Frey, p. 31.

79. In his edition of *The Tempest,* Kermode notes this parallel with *Bartholomew Fair* (2.6.76–77), "Looke into any Angle o' the towne, (the Streights, or the Bermuda's) . . ." (p. 24, n. 223).

80. Letter from Carleton to Chamberlain, August 1607, in Alexander Brown, Vol. 1, 111–13.

81. Many other similarities link *The Tempest* to the earlier play, including some which might have been taken to suggest *The Tempest*'s focus on the New World. Thus, for example, Stephano cries out when he first sees Caliban, "Do you put tricks upon's with salvages and men of Inde, ha?" (2.2.58–59). But Berowne, though rooted in the Old World, resorts to similarly

exotic analogies to describe the passion which Rosaline should inspire in his colleagues. Who sees her, he says,

> That, (like a rude and savage man of Inde),
> At the first op'ning of the gorgeous east,
> Bows not his vassal head . . .?
> (*Love's Labor's Lost,* 4.3.218–20)

See Kermode's note on the line in *The Tempest.*

82. Specific resemblances between subplots here and the plots of other plays have been noted (between the plot to murder Alonso and *Macbeth,* between Ferdinand's courtship of Miranda and *Romeo and Juliet,* etc.). See Alvin B. Kernan, "The great fair of the world and the ocean island: *Bartholomew Fair* and *The Tempest,*" in *The Revels History of Drama in English,* 8 vols., eds. J. Leeds Barroll, Alexander Leggatt, Richard Hosley, Alvin Kernan (London: Methuen, 1975), Vol. III, 456–74. G. Wilson Knight has described the place of *The Tempest* in Shakespeare's overarching myth of the tempest. Even more suggestive, Leslie Fiedler has traced the less obvious personal mythology that provides a context for the play. Drawing on marginal details, he shows the play's concern with themes that pervade the entire canon, such as the interracial marriage that here, not accidentally, initiates the action of the play. His work is the starting point for mine.

83. Barker and Hulme, p. 198.

84. Hulme, *Colonial Encounters,* p. 133.

85. Paul Brown, p. 69.

86. Barker and Hulme, p. 202.

87. The last time Prospero got so angry that Miranda had to apologize was when Ferdinand began to court Miranda.

88. See A. D. Nuttall's discussion of the blend of colonialist and sexual tensions in *The Tempest,* "Two Unassimilable Men," in *Shakespearian Comedy,* Stratford-upon-Avon Studies 14 (London: Edward Arnold, 1972), pp. 210–40, esp. p. 216.

89. The incestuous impulse implicit in the situation is even clearer in Shakespeare's own earlier romances; both Fiedler and Nuttall, among others, have explored these in the context of the vast literature of romance that lies behind the play. See also Mark Taylor, *Shakespeare's Darker Purpose: A Question of Incest* (New York: AMS Press, 1982).

90. Fiedler, p. 234.

91. Marianne Novy, *Love's Argument: Gender Relations in Shakespeare* (Chapel Hill and London: Univ. of North Carolina Press, 1984), pp. 63–82.

92. All Shakespeare quotations are from *The Riverside Shakespeare,* ed. G. Blakemore Evans (Boston: Houghton Mifflin, 1974). The earlier group of critics who had pointed out the racist assumptions in Antonio's behavior made many of the same points recently made on Caliban's behalf. The two cases are indeed similar, and although both can be seen as examples of "colonialism"—with the word "colonialism" used very loosely as it is today for any exploitative appropriation—the more historically specific "colonialist discourse" does not seem to be the appropriate context for Shylock.

93. Nuttall (n. 88, above) notes the strangeness of the Duke's explosion and the fact that Jaques's request for a fool's license "has shaken Duke Senior" (p. 231).

94. See Richard P. Wheeler's analysis in *Shakespeare's Development and the Problem Comedies: Turn and Counter-turn* (Berkeley and Los Angeles: Univ. of California Press, 1981).

95. Primarily of course in the sonnets, but in the plays as well. See Novy's discussion of self-assertiveness in Shylock.

96. Caliban later joins the two courtly servants in appropriately scatological double entendres.

97. Norman Holland, "Caliban's Dream," *The Design Within: Psychoanalytic Approaches to Shakespeare,* ed. M. D. Faber (New York: Science House, 1970), pp. 521–33.

98. Compare Antonio's cold calculations as he plans to kill Alonso.

99. Albeit in a "My mommy is going to get you" fashion.

100. Nuttall, p. 225.

101. So, too, any child might complain that he was taught to speak and now his "profit on 't" is to be trapped in the prison house of language.

102. See Leininger, p. 125, for the most effective presentation of this view; also Paul Brown, p. 63.

103. Here, too, Shakespeare seems unusual. Not until our child-centered, post-Freudian age do we find writers so directly representing the aliens on our galactic frontier as children—whether as innocents like Steven Spielberg's E. T. or as proto-savages like his Gremlins. Others had associated the primitive with metaphorical childhood: De Bry's 1590 edition of Harriot's *Briefe and true report* and, later, Purchas's version of Strachey associated the primitive Indians with the childhood of the English nation, and writers spoke of the Indians as "younger brethren" (Kupperman, n. 72, above, p. 170). What is unusual in Shakespeare is the emphasis and the detailed portrayal of emotional as well as cognitive childishness. Leah Marcus argues, in another context, that the English in the chaotic and disorienting intellectual context of the seventeenth century were especially susceptible to dreams of the golden age—and to sympathetic portrayals of childhood wholeness (*Childhood and Cultural Despair* [Pittsburgh, Pa.: Univ. of Pittsburgh Press, 1978]). Most of the instances of such portrayals did not appear until later in the century, however.

104. Edward A. Armstrong, *Shakespeare's Imagination* (Lincoln: Univ. of Nebraska Press, 1963), p. 52.

105. Might the brothers' definition by opposition perhaps have influenced Shakespeare's choice of names: *Pros*pero and *Ant*onio?

106 John B. Bender, "The Day of *The Tempest,*" *English Literary History,* 47 (1980), 235–58.

107. It also marks Shakespeare's return to the pattern of withdrawal from active life used in *Love's Labor's Lost*—but this time with a difference. The earlier play had shown young men hoping to conquer death by forswearing the body and all it represents. *The Tempest* shows an old man coming to terms with death by acknowledging the body and what it represents.

108. Elliot Jacques offers a related account, in Kleinian terms, of the role of infantile demands and emotions in the effort to come to terms with death in "Death and the Mid-life Crisis," *International Journal of Psychoanalysis,* 46 (1965), 502–14.

109. John Forrester, "Psychoanalysis or Literature?" *French Studies,* 35 (1981), 170–79, esp. p. 172.

110. Cited in Levin (n. 9, above), p. 183.

111. See Bender (n. 106, above) on the way dreams are always followed by violence in the play; the violence is not a cause of the problem on the island but rather an effect.

112. Andrews (n. 65, above), p. 126.

113. Jameson cites as being "very much in the spirit of [his] present work" the concern of Deleuze and Guattari "to reassert the specificity of the political content of everyday life and of individual fantasy-experience and to reclaim it from . . . reduction to the merely subjective and to the status of psychological projection" (*The Political Unconscious,* n. 22, above, p. 22).

114. *The Invasion Within: The Contest of Cultures in North America* (Oxford: Oxford Univ. Press, 1985), p. 54.

115. The original version of this essay was presented at a session on "Psychoanalysis and Renaissance History," chaired by Richard Wheeler at the 1987 MLA annual meeting. The current version has greatly benefited from careful readings by Janet Adelman, Anne and Rob Goble, Carol Neely, Marianne Novy, Martin Wiener, and several anonymous readers.

"The Duke of Milan / And His Brave Son": Dynastic Politics in *The Tempest*

DAVID SCOTT KASTAN

It is, of course, *The Comedy of Errors* that alone among Shakespeare's plays mentions "America" (which the Syracusan Dromio exuberantly locates "upon [Nell's] nose, all o'er embellished with rubies, carbuncles, sapphires, declining their rich aspect to the hot breath of Spain"),[1] but it is Shakespeare's other comedy observing the unities of time and place, *The Tempest,* that has almost inescapably become his play of Europe's engagement with the New World. Since Malone in 1808 first called attention to the play's relation to the Virginia Company pamphlets, offering the closest thing we have to something that might be thought of as a source for *The Tempest,* the experience of Thomas Gates and his men in Bermuda has been taken to give a local habitation and a name to the stereotypical narrative of shipwreck and deliverance articulating the play's romance form.[2]

Following Malone, critics have long claimed that the accounts of the miraculous escape of Gates's ship from "the most dreadful tempest," as Strachey's report terms it, which drove it from the Virginia coast provided the material that stimulated Shakespeare's dramatic imagination. The texts of the various reports from Virginia have come to seem the determining source and subtext of the play itself. In 1901 Morton Luce, editor of the first Arden edition, argued that the wreck of the *Sea-Venture* "must have suggested the leading incidents of *The Tempest*"; "indeed," he continued, "we may fairly say that fully nine-tenths of the subjects touched upon by Shakespeare in *The Tempest* are suggested by the new enterprise of colonisation."[3] And critics have continued to insist, as John Gillies has recently put it, that the play is "vitally rather than casually implicated in the discourses of America and the Virginia Company," whose directors included the Earl of Southampton, to whom Shakespeare dedicated *Venus and Adonis* and *The Rape of Lucrece,* and the earl of Pembroke, one of the dedicatees of the First Folio, making such a connection to Shakespeare plausible if not absolutely compelling.[4]

Recently, of course, criticism of *The Tempest,* while reasserting the New World context, has effectively wrested the play from the idealizations of

This essay was written specifically for this volume and is published here for the first time.

romance (as Gillies's word "implicated" no doubt signals). The experience of the Virginia colonists is no longer merely a timely reminder of the timeless structures of a romance mode in which the world of "mortal accident" is discovered to "suffer a sea-change into something rich and strange" (1.2.403–4), in which the hand of a "great creating nature" can be felt organizing the turbulence of earthly existence, reestablishing love and human continuance. No longer is *The Tempest* a play of social reconciliation and moral renewal, of benevolent artistry and providential design; it now appears as a telling document of the first phase of English imperialism, implicated in the will to power of the Jacobean court, even as an "instrument of empire" itself.[5]

Prospero is no longer an inspiring magus but an arrogant and ill-tempered magistrate (not even the "good, authoritarian Governor" that Geoffrey Bullough sees);[6] and the romance form is no longer a utopian spectacle of wonder but itself a participant in the ideological activity of imperialism—performing the necessary act of colonialist legitimation by naturalizing domination as the activity of a "Providence divine" (1.2.159). Coleridge found *The Tempest* to be one of those plays "where the ideal is predominant,"[7] but for us the "ideal" usually now seems only the name that the powerful give to their desire. In our anxious postcolonial moment, the power of Prospero's art, once confidently viewed as benevolently civilizing, has become the colonizer's technology of domination and control. Prospero's magic in the play now appears, in Stephen Greenblatt's phrase, as "the romance equivalent of martial law," or, in Peter Hulme's version, as marking out "the space really inhabited in colonial history by gunpowder."[8] And Caliban and, if somewhat less truculently, Ariel are the natives of the New World that have been unwillingly subjected to the coercive power of European knowledge.

This is, of course, the current orthodoxy of *Tempest* criticism but not, it should be said, of *Tempest* performance, which most often has chosen, for obvious reasons, to emphasize the theme and spectacle of artistry, even as it has come to recognize the contradictions and stresses of the text. Nonetheless, there have been memorable "colonial" interpretations, such as Jonathan Miller's production of the play at the Mermaid in 1970, which cast black actors as Caliban and Ariel and explicitly depended as Miller wrote, on "the whole colonial theme as knowledge which the audience brought to bear on Shakespeare's play."[9] But though undoubtedly "colonial," this was not a "new world" *Tempest*. Miller was thinking explicitly of the then current political situation in Nigeria, and he based his characterizations upon Octave Mannoni's analysis in *La psychologie de la colonisation* (1950) of the 1947 revolt in Madagascar. And, more recently, George Wolfe's 1995 *Tempest* in Central Park (and then on Broadway), starring Patrick Stewart, staged the play as a Third World fantasy and made its colonial theme explicit, if uncertainly located both temporally and geographically. But these productions are, in any case, more the exception than the rule.

If, however, on stage *The Tempest*'s relation to the New World is still optional, the critical assertion of the play's relation to the colonial enterprise in the Americas is now seemingly inescapable, even historically extendable, as in Leslie Fiedler's claim that in the play "the whole history of imperialist America has been prophetically revealed to us."[10] Fiedler at least has the good grace not to see the play as solely a document of *English* imperialism; but clearly for Fiedler, as for most of us who have read it in his wake, the play unsettlingly defines the encounter of the old world with the new, of the powerful with the powerless, Prospero's bad faith evident in not only his bitter denunciation of Antonio's usurpation of his dukedom but also his complete blindness to his own usurpation of the sovereignty of the island. "This island's mine," protests Caliban, "by Sycorax my mother, / Which thou tak'st from me . . . I am all the subjects that you have, / Which first was mine own king, and here you sty me / In this hard rock, whiles you do keep me from the rest o'th' island" (1.2.333–46). Prospero responds angrily: "thou most lying slave," not, however, angry about Caliban's claim of alienated sovereignty but at his assertion of undeserved hard treatment: "I have used thee— / Filth as thou art—with humane care, and lodged thee / In mine own cell, till thou didst seek to violate / The honor of my child" (1.2.347–50). What Prospero calls a lie is only the claim that he is an oppressor; Caliban's claim that he is a usurper is not contested, indeed not even heard, so fully does Prospero feel his own right to rule to be beyond any question.

No doubt Prospero's bad faith (a bad faith not canceled out by the fact that Caliban's sovereign claim is itself based upon his Algerian mother's parallel domination of a native, "spirit" population) is relevant to any understanding of the encounter with the New World, whose native inhabitants could have said to their putative "discoverers," no less tellingly than Prospero to Miranda, "'Tis new to thee" (5.1.184). But it is worth reminding ourselves how thin is the thread on which the play's relation to the New World hangs.

The play is obviously set in the Old World; the tempest is called up as the Italian nobles are returning from Africa to Italy, and those who have escaped the storm are said to return "sadly" to Naples "upon the Mediterranean flote" (1.2.234). Ariel does refer to Bermuda, but pointedly as the place they are not: the Italians' ship, he tells Prospero, is safe in the harbor "where once / Thou call'd'st me up at midnight to fetch dew / From the still-vex'd Bermoothes" (1.2.227–29). The only other explicit textual connections are the two references to "Setebos," whom Caliban identifies as "my dam's god" (1.2.375) and editors have identified in accounts of Magellan's voyages as a "great devil" of the Patagonian religion. Trinculo observes that the English who "will not give a doit to relieve a lame beggar . . . will lay out ten to see a dead Indian" (2.2.32–34), but Trinculo never takes the creature hiding beneath the cloak for an Indian; it is some kind of "monster" that "smells like a fish." That's it.

Some would add Gonzalo's use of the word "plantation," its only appearance in Shakespeare, though "plantation" is a word apparently coined for *Old* World domination, to describe the English colonial project in Ireland, and even when applied to the New World is used to describe an exclusively English enclave: "a plantation of the people of your owne English nation," as John Hooker wrote to Raleigh.[11] And, of course, Gonzalo's utopian fantasy is based on a passage in Montaigne's essay on the cannibals of Brazil, but Montaigne's primitivist vision has little relevance to the dreams and desires of the Italian courtiers, as is revealed by its self-contradiction, where Gonzalo's imaginings of a world with "no sovereignty" (2.1.152) originate in its opposite, in a fantasy of power: "Had I plantation of this isle, my lord . . . And were the king on't . . . " (2.1.141, 143).

In all there is very little to go on, especially to validate the now commonplace insistence that New World colonialism provides the play's "dominant discursive con-texts."[12] Though Prospero does locate Caliban in anthropological, social, moral, and even theological discourses—"beast," "slave," "demi-devil"—that sanction and support his own hierarchical superiority, we might note that Caliban is described as "freckled" and of a "blue-eyed" dam (1.2.283, 269; and though editors regularly remind us that "blue-eyed" may well refer to the dark blue of the eyelid understood as a mark of pregnancy or may even be an error for "blear-eyed," to an English audience for whom blue eyes were not at all unusual, the term must inevitably have been heard, if not necessarily intended, conventionally, as an indication of the color of the iris). Caliban is not, therefore, easily imagined either as an indigenous American or African slave. Indeed, as long ago as 1927, E. E. Stoll emphatically denied that the play had any relation to the New World at all. "There is not a word in *The Tempest*," he wrote, "about America or Virginia, colonies or colonizing, Indians or tomahawks, maize, mocking-birds, or tobacco. Nothing but the Bermudas, once barely mentioned as faraway places, like Tokio or Mandalay."[13] And more recently Geoffrey Bullough stated bluntly: "*The Tempest* is not a play about colonization."[14]

Stoll and Bullough are, of course, too absolute, but if the play has a relation to the New World colonial activity, it is not writ deep into its texture; the relation is allusive and elusive, existing primarily in the negations, like Ariel's or Trinculo's, that deny that the experience on the island is the experience of the Americas. The negations, of course, make the New World present, in a sense, but we may wonder why, if colonialism is, as Francis Barker and Peter Hulme put it, "the articulatory principle of the play,"[15] the principle is almost completely effaced and when present is established negatively rather than by a direct engagement with the material of Virginia.

Possibly this is evidence of the play's uneasy conscience about the colonial project, or possibly our hypersensitivity to it is evidence merely of our own uneasy conscience in the postcolonial world. In any case, certainly part of the desire to locate the play within the discourses of early colonialism, to return

the play to a historical moment, is evidence of the degree to which the imagination of the past now enthralls us as once we were enthralled by the imagination of the future, and this desire seems worthily motivated by the felt need
to rescue the play from the banality of the moral claims made for it in the
name of its putative timelessness and transcendence. Yet one might ask about
the specific historicizing gesture: why this moment, why these discourses that
are arguably no less eccentric in the play than in the culture of Jacobean
England? Certainly it is possible to suggest more obvious contexts and then
perhaps to wonder why these do not appear to us to be the play's "articulatory principle," if only to suggest that the Americanization of *The Tempest* may
be itself an act of cultural imperialism.

The play is much more obviously about European dynastic concerns
than European colonial activities, but this has largely slipped from view—or
at least from critical comment. The Italian courtiers have no interest in colonizing the island on which they find themselves, no desire to "plant a nation /
Where none before had stood," as Rich's *Newes From Virginia* (1610, B2r)
defines the goals of the first English settlers. The Italians' journey was not to
explore or settle a new world but was intended as a return home, a return
from the royal wedding of Alonso's daughter Claribel to the King of Tunis.
And only Trinculo and Stephano worry about sovereignty on the island: "the
King and all our company else being drowned," says Stephano, "we will
inherit *here*" (2.2.174–75); Antonio and Sebastian, on the contrary, think only
about crowns in Europe: "As thou got'st Milan, / I'll come by Naples"
(2.1.286–87), Sebastian eagerly declares, urging Antonio to draw his sword
and murder the Neapolitan king. Even Ferdinand immediately understands
and articulates his situation in the explicitly dynastic terms of the world he
has come from. When he hears Miranda speak, he responds with amazement:
"My language! heavens! / I am the best of them that speak this speech"
(1.2.431–32), instantly locating his sorrow in a set of political relations:
"myself am Naples, / Who with mine eyes, never since at ebb, beheld / The
King my father wrack'd" (1.2.437–39), just as he, with the same alacrity,
finds political measure for his love for Miranda: "I'll make you / The Queen of
Naples" (1.2.451–52). And Alonso at the end, hearing that Prospero has
"lost" *his* daughter, thinks of her and his own lost son as a royal couple to provide the terms of loss for the tragic cutting off of their children's too brief
lives: "O heavens, that they were living both in Naples, / The King and
Queen there" (5.1.149–50).

Indeed the critical emphasis upon the New World not only obscures the
play's more prominent discourses of dynastic politics but also blinds us to dis-
turbances in the text that should alert us to this aspect of the play's engagement with its own historical moment. When Alonso mourns the apparent
death of his son, he, perhaps predictably, identifies him not by name but by
his dynastic position: "O thou mine heir / Of Naples and Milan" (2.1.107–8).
No edition of the play feels the line worthy of comment, but it seemingly

poses a problem. As son of the Neapolitan king, Ferdinand is obviously heir
to the crown of Naples, but why is he heir of "Milan"? Antonio has replaced
Prospero as duke—and Antonio has a son who presumably would be his successor: reporting on his experience of the tempest, Ferdinand expresses his
dismay at seeing Antonio "and his brave son being twain" (1.2.441), a line
that editors usually gloss by predicating some earlier, abandoned conception
of the play in which this dynastic relation would have been developed. Thus
Dover Wilson writes in his note in the New Cambridge edition (now, of
course, the "old" New Cambridge) that Antonio's son "must be one of the
Alonso group in an earlier version" of the play, as if a prior, and differing, version of *The Tempest* is certain to have existed. Stephen Orgel in his Oxford edition more cautiously writes that "possibly a parallel to Ferdinand was originally contemplated by Shakespeare, and then abandoned as the drama took
shape." And Frank Kermode, in his Arden edition, somewhat despairingly
concludes that "Shakespeare began writing with a somewhat hazy understanding of the dynastic relationships he was to deal with."

But the "dynastic relations" are adequately, indeed tellingly, developed
here. Antonio's arrangement with Naples, in which, as Prospero says, in
return for "homage and I know not how much tribute" (1.2.124), Alonso has
conferred "fair Milan, / With all the honours, on my brother" (1.2.126–27),
clearly reserves Milanese sovereignty for Naples, alienating Antonio's son
from the succession. Indeed when Alonso at the end begs Prospero to "pardon" his wrongs, it is he, not Antonio, who offers: "Thy dukedom I resign"
(5.1.118), another line that has generally escaped critical comment. The
romance action is to rescue Milan from vassalage to Naples and yet still allow
the merging of national interests that James's fantasy of European peace and
coherence demanded. As the truth of the strange events of the play emerges
fully, leading those who will to "rejoice / Beyond a common joy" (5.1.206–7),
even the utopian Gonzalo recognizes that the true source of wonder is the
dynastic miracle that has been performed: "Was Milan thrust from Milan,
that his issue / Should become Kings of Naples?" (5.1.205–6). Ariel's terms
for the success of Prospero's tempest are homonymically apt; in the play's
magical rewriting of history there is "not so much perdition as an hair"
(1.2.30). Indeed the only thing that apparently is lost in the tempest is the
usurper Antonio's disinherited son, the one "hair"—or heir—that can be cut
from the restorative action of the play.

Certainly for the audience of *The Tempest* at court in 1613, when the play
was performed as 1 of 14 selected for the festivities leading up the marriage of
the King's daughter, Elizabeth, to Frederick, the Elector Palatine (this was, it
should be noted, the second recorded performance of the play; the first was
on Hallowmas night of 1611 at Whitehall before "ye kinges Maiestie"),[16] the
play's events were more likely to resonate with political issues in Europe
rather than in the Americas. Alonso's sadness at having apparently lost his
son and married his daughter to a foreign prince might well have seemed a

virtual mirror of the situation of James I, whose son Henry had died the previous year, and who now was marrying his daughter, Elizabeth, to a foreign prince (and who would, exactly as Alonso feared for himself, never see his daughter again).

The marriage of Princess Elizabeth was, like all royal weddings, politics by other means, designed primarily to serve the political interests of the nation or at least its king, rather than the emotional needs of the marrying couple. The match had long been rumored, and negotiations for it had begun as early as 1608, though there were always other prominent candidates for Elizabeth's hand, most notably the Prince of Piedmont, heir of the Duke of Savoy, and the recently widowed King of Spain, Philip III. A contemporary discussion of "suitable alliances" for Elizabeth interestingly comments: "the Prince of Piedmont an unequal match for the Princess, unless the King of Spain will give him the Duchy of Milan on his marriage, which is not likely, as that King is said to want her for himself. She could not marry him without changing her religion, and such a marriage would be dangerous to the two that are between her and the Crown. A match with Sweden or the Prince Palatine suggested for her . . ." (*Calendar of State Papers, Domestic* [1611–18], 97).

It was the match with the Prince Palatine to which James finally agreed. In many ways the "most suitable" (*Calendar of State Papers, Domestic* [1611–18], 97), the choice, of course, was designed not least to satisfy the interests of the Protestant nation and more immediately to tie James to the Union of Protestant Princes in the struggle against the Austrian Habsburgs and the states of the Catholic League. Though James's original hope had been to avoid sectarian alliance—or rather, while Henry lived, to pair sectarian alliances (Henry to the Spanish infanta; Elizabeth to the Palatine Prince) in order to play his planned role as mediator of Europe's religious conflicts, that particular balancing act was impossible after Henry's death in 1612. Although the Treaty of Antwerp in 1609, reconciling Spain to the United Provinces, seemed initially to promise peace in Europe, within a few weeks, a dispute over succession in the Rhine principality of Cleves-Jülich divided the Protestant and Catholic States and again pushed Europe toward full-scale religious war, "a generall altercacion in Christendome," as Salisbury feared.[17] James had little choice then but to side with the Protestant princes—and indeed the marriage of Elizabeth to the Palatine Prince was finally agreed to as a result of the negotiations with the Evangelical Union, which sought English support in their struggle against the Catholic League.[18]

England seemed now fully committed to the international Protestant cause. Dudley Carleton reported that "all well-affected people take great pleasure and contentment in this Match, as being a firm foundation and stablishing of religion . . . and the Roman Catholics malign it as much, as being the ruin of their hopes."[19] Though, in fact, as James's almost immediate search for a Spanish match for Prince Charles reveals, the king never abandoned his fantasy of being rex pacificus, to play the role of mediator to secure a lasting peace between the rival religious blocs. His willingness to side with the Evangelical Union was motivated less by his commitment to international Protestantism than by the desire to counterbalance the destabilizing aggressions of the Habsburg monarchy.

This all may seem to be taking us far from the island world of *The Tempest,* even farther than the New World narratives claimed as the play's source; but it may well bring us closer to the historical center of the play—and possibly to the heart of the interpretive problem it poses—than do the tracts of the Virginia Company. While southern Europe, including the kingdom of Naples and the dukedom of Milan, was largely at peace under the administration of the Spanish monarchy, the Holy Roman Empire was marked by a crisis of authority. In 1606 the Habsburg archdukes stripped administrative control from the Emperor Rudolf II, conferring it upon his brother Matthias. In 1608 Rudolf was forced to surrender to his brother the crowns of Austria, Hungary, and Moravia, keeping only the imperial crown and the crown of Bohemia. In April of 1611, Rudolf was deposed from the throne of Bohemia as his brother was proclaimed emperor.[20]

Rudolf turned to the Evangelical Union for support, and to James. Envoys were sent to England from the Diet of Protestant Princes in November asking James to back the reinstatement of the deposed Habsburg and to agree to the marriage of Elizabeth with the Elector Palatine to secure his commitment. While James's respect for the authority of princes could perhaps alone be reasonably expected to produce support for the reinstatement—and James had dedicated his own 1609 *Apology for the Oath of Allegiance* to "the Most Sacred and invincible Prince, Rudolf the II"—the English King certainly knew that the Emperor had brought about his own troubles by being irascible, indecisive, and increasingly unavailable. As early as 1591, Sir Henry Wotton had observed that Rudolf seems "now rather to bear the title of Emperor for fashion sake, than authority to command by virtue of it."[21] Gradually the Emperor withdrew from the affairs of state, shutting himself up in his palace, dedicating himself to scientific and occult study. Indeed in 1606, the archdukes justified the reassignment of authority to Matthias by commenting that "[h]is majesty is interested only in wizards, alkymists, Kabbalists, and the like, sparing no expense to find all kinds of treasure, learn secrets, and use scandalous ways of harming his enemies" and noting his "whole library of magic books."[22] The responsibilities of government of little interest to him and increasingly beyond his control, Rudolf took refuge in his books behind the walls of his palace, uncannily like another ruler "transported / And rapt in secret studies" (1.2.76–77) who would be deposed by his brother for "neglecting worldly ends" (1.2.89).

Part two of John Barclay's popular *roman a clef, Euphormionis Lusinini Satyricon,* published in Paris in 1609 (but circulating widely in England, so much so that it is named as what any "Young Gentleman of the Universitie" would be reading in the character in John Earle's *Micro-Cosmographie,* 1628), has a readily identifiable portrait of Rudolf in the Theban ruler Aquilius who "abandons all thoughts of public matters, foreign and domestic" (K2r; translation mine) for "voluntary solitude" (I2r) in his "beloved laboratory" (K5r) where he "searches into nature's secret places" (K2r). Similarly, Jonson's *Alchemist,* performed in 1610, reveals the English knowledge of Rudolf's habits in its reference to the alchemist and medium Edward Kelly, who along with John Dee, was, like Jonson's "divine instructor" Subtle, "courted" by "the Emp'ror" (4.1.90–92) in Prague with the extraordinary commitment to alchemy and magic.

Though Rudolf's interests and political fate would inevitably have been known to many, I certainly am not claiming that Rudolf II is the sole inspiration for Shakespeare's duke.[23] I am only concerned here to show the relevance of an available and urgent European courtly context for the concerns of the play, and one that accounts for more of its textual density than the colonial theme that has come to dominate our readings. James, of course, would never have approved of either Rudolf's or Prospero's interest in magic or neglect of the concerns of state. Though George Marcelline hailed James as "[t]he king of wonders, or the wonder of Kings" (*The Triumphs of King James,* 1610, H3v), what "wonders" James achieved and his own appeal as an object of admiration were far more predictably worldly than the arcane interests and attractions of Rudolf's court in Prague or, more modestly, in Prospero's island cell.

In his *Daemonologie,* James explicitly condemns "diuerse Christian Princes" who allow magicians to live in their realms and "euen sometimes delight to see them prooue some of their practicques"; these princes, he says "sinne heavilie against their office in that poynt."[24] And in *Basilikon Doron,* he instructs his son that "it is necessarie yee delight in reading and seeking the knowledge of all lawful things, but with these two restrictions. First, that yee choose idle houres for it, not interfering therewith the discharge of your office: and next, that yee studie not for knowledge nakedly, but that your principall ende be, to make you able thereby to vse your office."[25] The renunciation of magic to return to the reponsibilities of rule allows Prospero to redeem Rudolf's kingship—or rather allows him to escape the damning parallel with Rudolf and achieve a saving one with James himself. Prospero drowns his magic book, not of course the only reading matter with which Gonzalo had provided him, and returns to the teachings of the speculum principis, like James's own *Basilikon Doron,* which always knows the priority of the arts of rule over the rules of magical art.

All interpretation is in a sense allegorical, offering a meaning other than the literal. But I am not suggesting here that we merely substitute another allegory, not the biographical one of Prospero as Shakespeare, or the humanistic one of his magic as art, or in its suspicious form, as colonial domination, in order to see Prospero as the Holy Roman Emperor; though certainly I am suggesting that the world of European politics has receded too far from our view. Shakepeare may well in *The Winter's Tale* have, in following Greene's

Pandosto, mistakenly given Bohemia a seacoast, but the complex politics of Bohemia and the other Habsburg states were arguably more deeply connected to the hopes and anxieties of the Jacobean court than were the struggling settlements in the New World.

This shift in focus from the New World to the Old is not to evade or erase the history of colonialism as it has left its traces in the play but to individualize and clarify that history—perhaps indeed to motivate it. The colonial activity of seventeenth-century Europe must itself be understood in relation to the politics of the great European powers; to recognize at once England's deep involvements in Europe (a historical dimension that has worryingly dropped out of our recent attentions to the politics of early modern England) and the differing forms of colonial activity produced by its differing impulses and circumstances in England, Spain, and the Netherlands. If our attention to early modern colonialism is to have more than sentimental force, it must see its practices for what they were, as various and admittedly overdetermined activities within the conflicts of seventeenth-century European absolutism rather than as examples of a unified and transhistorical imperial desire and administration.

Certainly European expansionism is evident in the play, but more, it must be insisted, in the marriage of Claribel to the King of Tunis or Alonso's support of Antonio in exchange for Milan's vassalage than in Prospero's domination of the island. Or rather, the Old World examples reveal the old technologies of expansion; the action on the island is symbolic of the New. And the two were always understood to support one another. Even as Europe looked west, it was mainly as it sought to thrive at home. Thinking about the incredible riches available in the New World, Hakluyt, that quintessential voice of English imperialism, observes enthusiastically (and in terms that uncannily explain something of the geopolitics of *The Tempest*): "with this great treasure, did not the emperor Charles get from the french king the kingdom of Naples, the dukedom of Milan, and all other his dominions in Italy, Lombardy, Piedmont, and Savoy?"[26]

But though I would say (indeed have said) that the play clearly engages the social and political concerns of seventeenth-century Europe, concerns that the insistent focus on the New World has largely obscured, I am not now claiming that European court politics must replace New World colonialism as the "dominant discursive con-text" that reveals the meaning of *The Tempest*. Contexts by definition can be neither singular nor inevitable; logically they are virtually infinite, valuable as they—and only as they—serve the needs of the interpreter. *The Tempest* can be profitably viewed in relation to various historical and nonhistorical (e.g., ethical, psychological, theological, and even, may I say it, literary) contexts, and no one is inevitable and determining.

If, however, one's desire is to reinsert the play into its own historical moment, into the space of its own diegetic setting as well as the performative space of its own earliest productions (and this is a thoroughly reasonable and productive desire, though hardly the only useful interpretive desire we might have), it seems to me that we should look more closely at the Old World than the New, at the wedding of Elizabeth and Frederick rather than of Pocahontas and John Rolfe, at James's own writings rather than the writings from Jamestown. The shift in focus from Bermuda to Bohemia, from Harriot to Habsburg is not to evade or dull the political edges of the play; indeed arguably it is to sharpen them, but it is also to find them less in the conquest of the New World than in the killing religious conflicts and territorial ambitions of the Old, where tragically they can be found still.[27]

The Tempest effectively stages and manages these anxieties about European politics and England's role within them, harmonizing and securing absolutist desire through the marriage of Miranda and Ferdinand. The play drives purposefully to fulfill Gonzalo's prayer: "look down, you gods, / And on this couple drop a bless'd crown" (5.1.201–2). But this utopian solution to the problem of political conflict—a solution that by temperament, ideology, and financial limitation appealed to James and led him to conduct his foreign policy through marriage negotiation—is vulnerable, if only to irony. If the crown is "blessèd," we should remember that the impending marriage will accomplish precisely what the "inveterate" (1.2.122) hatred of Alonso for Prospero attempted: the dissolution of Milanese sovereignty. However, in the reparative fantasy of the *The Tempest,* nothing—except the brave son of Antonio, who has no place in its ambitious political relations—is finally lost.[28]

Notes

1. *The Comedy of Errors*, 3.2.133–35. All quotations to Shakespeare are taken from the Arden editions of the plays. It is worth noting that "America," perhaps inevitably for a play written in the early 1590s, is here associated with a Spanish colonial interest rather than an English one.

2. Edmond Malone, *An account of the incidents, from which the title and part of the story of Shakspeare's Tempest were derived; and its true date ascertained.* (London: C. and R. Baldwin, 1808).

3. Morton Luce, ed. *The Tempest* (London: Methuen, 1901), xii, xlii.

4. John Gillies, *Shakespeare and the Geography of Difference* (Cambridge: Cambridge University Press, 1994), 149. On Shakespeare's relations with the Virginia Company, see Charles Mills Gayley, *Shakespeare and the Founders of Liberty in America* (New York: Macmillan, 1917).

5. The phrase, now a staple of *Tempest* criticism, derives from Antonio de Nebrija's justification to Queen Isabella for his Spanish grammar: "language is the perfect instrument of empire" (quoted in Louis Hanke, *Aristotle and the American Indians* [Bloomington: Indiana University Press, 1959], 8). Nebrija (or, more properly, Lebrija) was, however, a bit less explicit about the instrumental relation of language and empire; "siempre la lengua fue compañera del imperio" (a2r) is what he wrote in his *Grammatica Castellana* (1492). For the play's "implication" in the English colonial project, see, for example, Paul Brown, "'This thing of darkness I acknowledge mine': *The Tempest* and the discourse of colonialism," *Political Shakespeare: New Essays in Cultural Materialism,* ed. Jonathan Dollimore and Alan Sinfield (Ithaca: Cornell University Press, 1985), esp. 56, 64.

6. Geoffrey Bullough, *Narrative and Dramatic Sources of Shakespeare,* vol. 8 (London: Routledge and Kegan Paul, 1975), 245.

7. *Coleridge on Shakespeare: The Text of the Lectures of 1811–1812,* ed. R. A. Foakes (Charlottesville: University Press of Virginia, 1971), 106.

8. Stephen Greenblatt, *Shakespearean Negotiations* (Berkeley and Los Angeles: University of California Press, 1988), 156; and Peter Hulme, "Hurricanes in the Caribbees: the constitution of the discourse of English colonialism," in *1642: Literature and Power in the Seventeenth Century,* ed. Francis Barker et al. (Colchester: University of Essex, 1981), 74.

9. Jonathan Miller, quoted in Ralph Berry, *On Directing Shakespeare: Interviews with Contemporary Directors* (London: Croom Helm, 1977), 34.

10. Leslie A. Fiedler, *The Stranger in Shakespeare* (New York: Stein and Day, 1972), 238.

11. John Hooker, in the Epistle Dedicatory to *The Second Volume of Chronicles* in *The First and Second Volumes of Chronicles,* ed. Raphael Holinshed et al. (London, 1586), A3v.

12. Francis Barker and Peter Hulme, "Nymphs and reapers heavily vanish: the discursive con-texts of *The Tempest,*" in *Alternative Shakespeares,* ed. John Drakakis (London: Routledge, 1985), 198. Richard Halpern similarly says that "colonialism has established itself as a dominant, if not the dominant code for interpreting *The Tempest,*" in his " 'The Picture of Nobody': White Cannibalism in *The Tempest,*" in *The Production of English Renaissance Culture,* ed. David Lee Miller, Sharon O'Dair, and Harold Weber (Ithaca: Cornell University Press, 1994), 265.

13. E. E. Stoll, "Certain Fallacies and Irrelevancies in the Literary Scholarship of the Day," *Studies in Philology* 24 (1927): 484.

14. Bullough, *Narrative and Dramatic Sources of Shakespeare,* 8:241.

15. Barker and Hulme, "Nymphs and reapers," 204.

16. See E. K. Chambers, *William Shakespeare: A Study of Facts and Problems* (Oxford: Clarendon Press, 1930), 2:342.

17. S. R. Gardiner, ed., *Parliamentary Debates in 1610* (London: Camden Society, 1861), 53.

18. See Roger Lockyer, *The Early Stuarts: A Political History of England* (London and New York: Longman, 1989), esp. 15. It is perhaps of interest here that Pembroke and Southampton, to both of whom Shakespeare had connections, were proponents of an aggressive pro-Protestant foreign policy. See Thomas Cogswell, *The Blessed Revolution: English Politics and the Coming of War, 1621–1624* (Cambridge: Cambridge University Press, 1989), esp. 12–50.

19. John Nichols, *Progresses of King James the First* (1828; rpt. New York: AMS Press, n.d.), 2:601–2.

20. Henry Wotton wrote in May 1611 of how Rudolf was forced "to make Matthias King of the Romans." Commenting on the treatment of Rudolf by the supporters of Matthias, Wotton notes, "[H]aving first spoiled him of obedience and reverence, next of his estates and titles, they have now reduced him to so low a case, that he is no longer patron of his voice." See *Life and Letters of Sir Henry Wotton,* ed. Logan Pearsall Smith (Oxford: Clarendon Press, 1907), 1:507.

21. *Life and Letters of Sir Henry Wotton,* 1:268.

22. Quoted in R. J. W. Evans, *Rudolph II and His World* (Oxford: Clarendon Press, 1973), 196. See also Hugh Trevor-Roper, *Princes and Artists: Patronage and Ideology at Four Habsburg Courts 1517–1633* (London: Thames and Hudson, 1976), esp. 122–23.

23. Michael Srigley's *Images of Regeneration: A Study of Shakespeare's "The Tempest" and Its Cultural Background* (Uppsala: Academiae Upsaliensis, 1985) does make an argument for such topical allegory, though, of course, we should remember that as early as *Love's Labor's Lost* Shakespeare had begun thinking about rulers who preferred the study to the affairs of state.

24. *Daemonologie (1597) and Newes From Scotland,* ed. G. B. Harrison (London: Bodley Head, 1924), 24–25.

25. *The Political Works of James I,* ed. Charles Howard McIlwain (Cambridge: Harvard University Press, 1918), 38.

26. *The Original Writings and Correspondence of the Two Richard Hakluyts,* ed. Eva G. R. Taylor (London: Hakluyt Society, 1935), 243. See Jeffrey Knapp's fine *An Empire Nowhere: England, America, and Literature from "Utopia" to the "The Tempest"* (Berkeley: University of California Press, 1992), esp. 231–34.

27. Howard Felperin has recently argued similarly that "the colonialism of the New World" has been overemphasized. Its traces in the play, he argues, have been "overread," mistaking "the part for the whole." Felperin, however, wants finally to see the "whole" not as a larger historical picture but "as a projection of nothing less than a historical totality" itself, or, as he says, "a vision of history as a cycle of repetition." This, however, seems to me to return the play to the very idealism that historical criticism has tried to counter. See his "Political Criticism at the Crossroads: The Utopian Historicism of *The Tempest,*" in *The Tempest,* ed. Nigel Wood (Buckingham and Philadelphia: Open University Press, 1995), esp. 47–55. For a different relocation of *The Tempest* in relation to New World colonial activity, see Meredith Anne Skura's "Discourse and the Individual: The Case of Colonialism in *The Tempest,*" *Shakespeare Quarterly* 40 (1989): 42–69, and reprinted in this volume.

28. For thoughtful comments and needed encouragement, I would like to thank David Armitage, Jean Howard, Jim Shapiro, Steve Pincus, and William Sherman, this last to whom I owe additional thanks for inviting me to join the panel at the Shakespeare Association of America meeting in 1995, which he organized and at which a version of this essay was presented.

PERFORMANCE AND
PERFORMANCE HISTORY

◆

"A Quaint Device":
The Tempest at the Blackfriars

KEITH STURGESS

In Act II, scene iii of *The Tempest,* Ariel, costumed as a harpy, bursts on to stage and causes a banquet set out before the court party of Alonso and the others to disappear. The stage direction tells us that this is done "with a quaint device," where "quaint" means ingenious and thereby pleasing. It is a word Prospero uses elsewhere of Ariel himself, to praise the spirit's appearance as a water nymph (I, ii, 319).[1] The disappearing banquet is a sleight of hand. It is a conjuror's trick, real magic to the courtiers and a stage illusion to the audience. An experiment in metatheatre, the whole play explores the baffling territory marked out by "magic," "illusion" and "trick." The staging of the play is both device and meaning. Design, not narrative, is *The Tempest*'s major impulse and its structure is architectural, not dynamic. So far as we can tell it was a success on stage. Strange as it is (and "strange" is a word much used in the play), Hemmings and Condell placed it first in the First Folio. Paradoxical and enigmatic, it occupies a special place too in theatre history and dramatic criticism. It is both a summation of Shakespeare's writing career and a radically experimental, new departure. Especially, it seems a "quaintly" fashioned play appropriate to the Blackfriars.

The writing and first production of *The Tempest* can be dated reasonably accurately. Shakespeare derived a number of features of the story from the various accounts of Sir George Somers's ill-fated voyage to Virginia in 1609–10.[2] The accounts circulated in England in the last months of 1610 and the play itself was performed at Whitehall on 1 November 1611. Meanwhile, Simon Forman, an astrologer, likely to be interested in the play and perhaps himself a part model for Prospero, mentions having seen *Cymbeline* and *The Winter's Tale* at the Globe in the early summer of 1611 but not *The Tempest.* Either *The Tempest* was first played at the Blackfriars in the winter of 1610/11 but not acted at the Globe in the following summer, or, more likely, the play was premiered at the Blackfriars season of autumn 1611 and was still quite new when it was

Keith Sturgess, " 'A Quaint Device': *The Tempest* at the Blackfriars," in *Jacobean Private Theatre* (London: Routledge and Kegan Paul, 1987), 73–96, 216. Reprinted with permission.

played at court. We know of another court performance: as part of the festivities organised around the betrothal of Princess Elizabeth and the Elector Palatine in May 1613. But in 1670, Dryden wrote in the published edition of his adaptation of Shakespeare's play that the original "had formerly been acted with success in the Blackfriars." Dryden's collaborator was Davenant who should have known. On internal grounds, one would readily identify *The Tempest* as a "private theatre" play for the Blackfriars and court. And it is the Blackfriars production that is the theme of this account.

In 1611, *The Tempest* had considerable topical interest for a Blackfriars audience. Members of the Virginia Company who had organised Somers's expedition and others who were investors in it were a part of that audience. Shakespeare himself was personally acquainted with prominent figures in the Council, and he had access to a letter about the wreck and the providential escape by those on board which had been written by William Strachey in Virginia on 15 July 1610 and was not available in print until 1625. Strachey soon followed his letter home and was himself living in Blackfriars by December 1611.

No single narrative source fits the whole play, but the Bermuda shipwreck and associated ideas concerning "plantation" and New World natives provide a plausible starting-point for Shakespeare's composition. This then brought to mind, we may imagine, Montaigne's handling of similar topics in the essay "Of the Cannibals," where Gonzalo's Utopia speech of II, i, 139–64 finds its origin. Montaigne unironically paints an ideal version of the natural life free of the debilitating effects of sophisticated society. And this in turn suggests to Shakespeare Caliban (probably anagrammatised from "Cannibal") who provides an antithetical comment on Montaigne's naturalism.

The plot is more or less completed by the magician motif, which itself was of topical, even Blackfriars, interest. Jonson's *The Alchemist* had been performed by Shakespeare's company in 1610. Its Dr Subtle, Aubrey thought, was based on the astrologer, mathematician and, it was reputed, necromancer, Dr John Dee. Dee, who died in 1608, had had connections with Western travel, coined the expression "the British Empire," and advised navigators on technical matters. Forman, too, we have suggested, connects with Prospero. In September 1611 (two months before the play was certainly in production) he had predicted his own death while in good health and expired suddenly five days later. He, too, was interested in "Plantation" and was a well-known figure in theatre circles (he rated a mention in *Epicoene* and would be referred to again after his death in *Bartholomew Fair*). He had also treated Shakespeare's landlady, both medically and astrologically. For the playwright and his audience, the mage was a noted contemporary—part scientist, part neo-platonist. Shakespeare's own plays provided models for Prospero's other features: as usurped monarch (*Much Ado about Nothing*), magical operator (*A Midsummer Night's Dream*) and abdicated ruler conducting a controlled experiment on his subjects (*Measure for Measure*).

The play's dramatic power is not developed through the conventional means of character conflict. Only Prospero, a "god of power," can take significant action. The plot in effect is his, and the other *personae,* caught out of contingent time and confined by his experiment, can only react. Even the love story is developed within the master plan conceived and executed by Prospero.

The role was almost certainly written for Burbage. In 1611 he was at the height of his powers, the greatest actor of his generation, aged 37 or 38, who had played most of Shakespeare's tragic leads. Something of the character of Lear, whom he had first acted about five years earlier—banished king with faithful daughter—could be drawn on to endue the role with an epic quality which Shakespeare only sketches lightly in the later play—righteous anger dependent on a personally authentic sense of sovereignty. For Prospero is enigmatic where Lear is painfully transparent. His inner life remains largely hidden from the audience and he is aloof and magisterial in his relationship with the other characters. Indeed, his purpose in shipwrecking the court party is never clarified until the beginning of the final sequence (V, i, 28–30). Until then we know there is a design; the play is his handiwork; he organises it with clock-watching precision and constantly dispatches Ariel to fashion its individual parts. But several times (I, ii, 320, 498) the command is whispered so that the audience might not hear (not only the others on stage, note, for elsewhere in the play the convention of inaudibility is employed). Twice he refers to his "project" (V, i, I and Epilogue, I,12) and Ariel does so once (II, i, 294). But for four acts he maintains an elusiveness of intent (as opposed to a complexity of motivation) uncharacteristic of Shakespeare's leading characters. Vincentio in *Measure for Measure,* for example, explains his purpose even if underlying, unconscious motivations are only half-expressed. But Prospero is as detached from us as from the other characters. He evidently feels deeply, but we are not expected to feel with him. The modern actor, who, playing Prospero, tries to explain the enigma takes a different line from that of Burbage.

Burbage, however, brought something else. For it was he, in all probability, who had played Jonson's Dr Subtle a year earlier. *The Alchemist,* remaining in the repertory (like *The Tempest* it was played at court in 1613) would inevitably colour not only Burbage's playing but also an audience's reception of Shakespeare's play about a conjuror. Subtle is the other side of the coin—magician as charlatan. He is an illusionist whose art is cheating not charming and he is exiled from his little empire at the end of the play, not welcomed home in triumph. Prospero is a "projector" too and his solemn intensity was in part permitted by the shadow figure of the comic magician of the earlier play remaining in Burbage's portrayal. A Blackfriars audience at *The Tempest* would not only see a Burbage-Lear-Prospero stage figure but also a Burbage-Subtle-Prospero stage figure.[3]

Prospero's is the dominant role in *The Tempest* in all important respects. He has over 600 lines of a short play (the second shortest in the canon), and the next biggest part, Ariel's, tops 200 lines only if we add in (as we probably may) Ceres' lines as well. (At IV, i, 167 Ariel explains that he played Ceres in the masque.) In fact, ten of the seventeen speaking (and singing) roles only have between 100 and 200 lines, so that character development outside Prospero is flattened out in an unusual manner. Only Pericles, elsewhere in Shakespeare, and possibly Hamlet, so out-talk their fellow characters.

The casting of the play by the King's Men would have caused little difficulty (and granted, perhaps, small satisfaction). There are thirteen parts for adult actors and four for boys if we assume, as we should, that Ariel was played by a boy. There was no doubling, because all the adult male characters are on stage together at the end of the play and all four characters for boys appear together. (The King's Men normally had four boy actors and so the doubling of Ariel and Ceres, or something like it, becomes inevitable; Shakespeare makes a virtue of necessity by referring to it in the play.) The Master's is a strange role—three lines in scene i when he abdicates responsibility (and the stage) to the Boatswain, and no word on his other appearance at the end when, by rank, he might be expected to relate the events on board ship. (It is tempting to see this as a Hitchcockian cameo for Shakespeare himself in his last play.) All other parts, including the three very minor ones of Adrian, Francisco and the Boatswain, have something clear and theatrically emphatic to do at some point of the play, even though it is rightly maintained by critics and experienced by actors that, apart from Ariel and Caliban, they are handled in a perfunctory and flat manner. They lack an individual language and sharp personality and are subordinated to the overall design.

Beside the speaking roles, the play calls for a squad of supernumaries who people the spirit world. The company would normally provide extras from the backstage staff to play walk-ons like the mariners of I, i. But something more organised is needed for the Shapes (III, iii), the dance team of Nymphs and Reapers (IV, i) and the hunting dogs (also IV, i). Especially in the masque scene the normal company personnel would be overstretched, though actors of other roles might here have doubled the roles of Reapers. For none of these episodes does Shakespeare specify an exact number of spirits, though only three dogs are named in the hunting. But in that characteristic self-reflexivity of the play, Prospero demands that to the masque Ariel "bring a corollary, Rather than want a spirit," and the outer play would benefit from the same generous treatment. Evidently, the King's Men could draw on a number of trained extras to fill the ranks. For *The Winter's Tale* of the previous year, a scene required on stage six principals, shepherds and shepherdesses to make up a dance, and then a troupe of twelve satyrs. Perhaps the Chapel Royal, now without a regular playing operation of their own, might have supplied these choreographed (and in I, ii singing) extras. They would need to be well trained.

Who filled the other roles is mere (though interesting) speculation. Ariel, we have assumed, was played by a boy. Prospero, whether affectionate or vexed, treats him like a child, certainly as someone small of stature: he calls him "delicate," "dainty" and "chick." The spirit adopts for much of the play the costume of a sea-nymph and he evidently plays the part of Ceres in the masque. William Poel, whose instincts in these matters were often right, evidently thought he was played by an adult. But an Elizabethan boy actor would not bring to his playing of Ariel the kind of naive charm that a child actor of today would, and his training would provide the physical and musical skills necessary for the part. Richard Robinson was the principal company juvenile at the time, but, an experienced female impersonator, he may well have played Miranda rather than Ariel.

Lowin customarily played the second leads. In this play devoid of major supporting roles, that of Caliban might well have gone to him, although Shakespeare developed the part oddly. For, as Caliban begins as a strong protagonist set in opposition to Prospero, he features increasingly as a comic foil for Trinculo and Stephano. Nevertheless, a figure of physical menace and no longer youthful, Caliban would need to be played by a mature actor capable of both the passion and the poetry of the part. Lowin may well have been cast here, his large frame made suitably grotesque by the tiremen.

Trinculo would presumably be played by the King's Men's regular comedian, Robert Armin. Armin had played Shakespeare's other professional fools, Touchstone, Feste and probably the Fool in *King Lear.* But this fool is kept away from the ranking characters in the play and is forced to expend his wit on a man-monster and a drunken butler. Rather than providing a stalking-horse for the playwright's satire, he becomes the comic butt of the true wit of the play, Ariel. Outside the characters of Prospero and to a limited extent Ariel and Caliban, there is little challenge here for the King's Men's actors. It is not, in fact, an actor's play.

In a specialised sense, *The Tempest* is a designer's play. Short of conflict and rounded characterisation, it has always been staged in a spectacularly visual way. At the Restoration, rewritten by Dryden and Shadwell, it was rapidly converted into a baroque melodrama, complete with elaborate, moveable scenery and complex flying effects. When restored to Shakespeare's script in the nineteenth century, *The Tempest* was still the excuse for a lavish display of pantomime stage effects. A reviewer of Beerbohm Tree's production at His Majesty's in 1904 observed that Tree had "stage-managed Shakespeare out of sight."[4] Meanwhile, William Poel's non-scenic, "Elizabethan" production of the play in 1897 encouraged Bernard Shaw to see the special gains of simple staging:

> It requires the nicest judgment to know exactly how much help the imagination wants. There is no general rule, not even for any particular author. You can do best without scenery in *The Tempest* and *A Midsummer Night's Dream,* because the best scenery you can get will only destroy the illusion created by the poetry.[5]

Much earlier, Coleridge, talking of *The Tempest,* had argued against "the complicated machinery and decorations of modern times" which in Shakesperian productions distracted "the moved and sympathetic imagination" of the audience from the true focus, "the spiritual vision" of the play.[6] It is all about delusion versus illusion, the "glistering apparel" set before Caliban and his crew versus "the most majestic vision" presented to Ferdinand and Miranda. The play at large is constantly concerned with the matter and so must have been the Blackfriars production and its audience.

The Blackfriars playhouse where, according to Dryden, *The Tempest* was a popular success, was non-scenic. The stage was a platform for the actors, not a locale realistically presented through flats, borders and curtains. The "scene" is the architectural, upstage wall providing entrances, discovery-space and gallery over; and stage left and right the action is closed in by the stage-sitters. "Design" for the play will concern actors, properly costumed and carefully blocked, together with a few, simple properties. And it will create a series of shows, which is largely the substance of the play.

It is worth referring here to the persuasive argument that in its court performance in the Banqueting Hall, Hallowmas night, 1611, the play might have been decked out with stock scenic elements built for, and left over from, previous masques. A whole topography for the play, it is argued, can be assembled out of the timber and canvas realisation of masques such as *Oberon* (ten months earlier) and others: a seashore, rocks, clouds, a cave and a wood.[7] But it is difficult to imagine that a play intended for the Blackfriars repertory should receive a radically different staging at court; and though "canvas for the booths and other necessaries" were provided for *Bartholomew Fair* at court in 1614 and Inigo Jones built scenery for *The Faithful Shepherdess* for its court revival in 1634, on economic grounds alone it is unlikely that plays were regularly produced in this way at Whitehall. The King's Men themselves gave twenty-two plays at court between 31 October 1611 and 26 April 1612.

Nevertheless, it is clear that in *The Tempest* Shakespeare was experimenting with graphic kinds of stage imagery. A special poetry is developed in place of the verbal richness of the earlier plays.[8] The audience is given a series of stage pictures which, like the visions in a dream, have a sharp-edged clarity and a sense of careful composition. They seem, again as in a dream, to be both emblematic and not readily accessible to simple interpretation. For the play moves in a masque-like way, proceeding by way of a series of counter-pointed events that act like revelations or epiphanies. Again, the relation to dream is insistent, and the characters themselves suspect they are inhabiting a dream. But the shows are not dream-work but a species of art-work, created by artist Prospero.

In a special way, it is imperative that the magic island should not be scenically realised. To the different characters it becomes a different place; they each impose on it a construction that comes from their personality and their moral bias. Though fictively "real" (it exists prior to Prospero's discovery of it), it is a symbolic landscape: for Gonzalo, a Utopia; for Ferdinand, a new Garden of Eden where Adam re-meets Eve; for Antonio and Sebastian, a desert place; for Caliban, an empire and possession; for Ariel, a prison; for Prospero, a "poor isle" where he refinds his dukedom and loses his daughter. The realistic topography is amply created by the one most concerned to live in and by it, Caliban. His densely specific poetry realises a world of plants, animals and fish, rocks and springs, and the attendant diseases and discomforts of nature in the raw. But the island is essentially a pastoral, unreal world incapable of being imaged concretely. What the actors had was the "magic" space of the Blackfriars stage, unlocalised, where they might "enact [Shakespeare's] present fancies."

Legitimate visual display derives partly from the action, partly from the characterisation. For the latter, to an unremarkable extent it concerns the conventional Elizabethan emphasis on costume denoting the man and his function. For much of the play, Prospero wears his "magic garment" over normal clothes (we might assume a robe covered in cabalistic signs, the badge of the magician) and he carries a staff. But at the climax of the play he changes costume onstage to mark his resumption of his true role as duke: "I will discase me, and myself present As I was sometime Milan" (V, i, 85–6). And so his rapier and hat are brought out, his robe taken away. We should expect Trinculo to wear the Fool's outfit of suit of motley and coxcomb. Perhaps he carried a bauble. Stephano would have been costumed as Butler to the King to make his assumption of regal power the more ridiculous. His and Trinculo's final appearance in their "stolen apparel" is an apt comment. The court party's clothes too would describe their wearers in social terms, and it is interesting that Shakespeare insists, twice over, that they are unspoiled by the sea-drenching they have received. Indeed they are "rather new-dyed than stained with salt water" (II, i, 61–2). For the courtiers are not firstly shipwrecked survivors; they are aristocrats and rulers of men exiled from their preferred surroundings into a pastoral world.

So far, then, there is nothing unduly taxing for the keeper of the King's Men's wardrobe, all stock commodities. But in Ariel and Caliban, the company confronted a significant design challenge, perhaps the most crucial in the whole of Shakespeare. In a play which moves easily within a nexus of ideas we recognise as neo-platonic, by their very appearance these two non-realistic figures necessarily impose a large element of the play's meaning. We shall return to them.

Visual display which derives from the play's action is present at every turn in a composition almost excessively full of variety and invention. Five episodes in particular, each a spectacular *coup de théâtre,* show Shakespeare's confidence in the staging ability of the Blackfriars company, though each works through simple theatrical means contrived from actors, their costume and careful blocking. These are the shipwreck of I, i, Ferdinand's meeting with Miranda in I, ii, the banquet of III, iii, the masque of IV, i and the chess game of V, i. (It is worth mentioning here that the first printing of the text, in the First Folio, contains unusually detailed and impressionistic stage directions. They might be Shakespeare's or those of an eye-witness. Either way, they enable the "reconstruction" of several of these episodes with more confidence than we might normally allow.)

In Act I, scene i, Shakespeare writes the first of two prologues for the play, the "dramatic" one[9] which will make possible the leisurely, recapping, story-so-far that occupies a good deal of scene ii. The location is shipboard, the action is tempest at sea and, at the moment, the audience is not aware of Prospero's control through his agent, Ariel. Later productions have sometimes shown Prospero's hand too early. It is important that to the audience, as to those aboard, it is a "real" storm. For a Jacobean audience and for us, the initial "meaning" is human frailty confronted by the elemental powers in nature.

The first effect is aural. No dimming of the houselights, of course, but in the enclosed (roofed) space at the Blackfriars, an emphatic opening: "*A tempestuous noise of thunder and lightning is heard.*" The comic illogicality (the noise of lightning?) happily catches the notion of cosmic chaos and the play will exploit at other moments a richly combined assault upon the senses of the audience. Squibs from the upper level of the Blackfriars facade or a resin box provided the lighting and the thunder was mimicked by drums in the tiring-house or music room or by cannonballs rolled in a thunder run, perhaps a combination of the two. And offstage sound effects from a sea machine (small pebbles revolved in a drum) and a wind machine (a loose length of canvas turned on a wheel) would complete a compelling storm sequence, probably enhanced by an echo from the high roof-space over the auditorium. Jonson deplored this kind of thing. He preferred his own kind of naturalistic theatre where

> [No] nimble squib is seen to make afear'd
> The gentlewomen; nor roll'd thunder heard
> To say, it thunders; nor tempestuous drum
> Rumbles, to tell you when the storm doth come.[10]

Shakespeare and Prospero were not so purist. They both had greater faith in the power of theatrical illusion.

The ship itself is largely presented through dialogue and action. The first, carefully placed word is "Boatswain" (is this the major function of the Master?) and the next eight lines, nautically technical but explicit to the layman, deftly present ship, storm, nearness of land and imminence of shipwreck. Shipboard scenes are frequent in Elizabethan drama and more ambitious stage action is required in other plays than here. With confidence, the playwright expects the actors to create and sustain the illusion. "*Enter mariners wet*" (after l. 50) is a graphic piece of theatre shorthand, and the offstage voices—"*A cry within*" (l. 35) and "*A confused noise within*" (l. 58)—combine with onstage shouting and a good deal of frantic rushing about to present a little world of fear and disaster at sea. A. C. Sprague, describing the New Mermaid production of 1951, bears testimony to the effectiveness with which this scene will work when staged in a simple, "Elizabethan" manner:

> The scene began with a clap of thunder and howling wind. In each of the two windows [above the stage, on the "gallery"] a ship's lantern swung back and forth. Ropes and a ladder were lowered from somewhere above the gallery. A trapdoor opened and became a hatchway; the upper stage, the upper deck. Sailors, shouting orders, clung for support to the pillars, or swarmed up the tackling. It was as if the ship were there before our eyes! Yet, as crew and passengers departed and the ropes dropped out of sight through the trap, it was gone again in an instant.[11]

And so it must, for the play structurally makes much of abrupt transitions and the opening of scene ii "explains" and completes scene i. We hear straightway of Prospero's Art (insistently capitalised throughout the First Folio) and it is that art that controls nature, evoking a harmless "tempest" first "believed in" by the audience. Miranda knows that the tempest is Prospero's but she does not know how it was done (nor, indeed, that it is harmless). But Ariel's entrance, in a little while, clarifies the matter finely, for he "perform'd to point the tempest" (l. 194) as his master had bade him; or, in other words, the tempest was a theatrical illusion, a device or trick. Scene i is a brief masterpiece, possible to stage at the Globe, but deriving from the enclosed and smaller Blackfriars greater affective power, and offering a literate audience an iconographic statement, bound up in conventional emblem book imagery, of human constancy in an inconstant world (Gonzalo's ironies about the Boatswain alerted the spectators to this).

The scenery of the first scene is in fact largely acoustical, and before an analysis of the other "shows," it is appropriate to discuss the importance of sound effects generally in the play. The thunder will recur throughout. It opens II, ii—"*A noise of thunder heard*"—and is present again at Ariel's entrance as the Harpy in III, iii ("*Thunder and lightning*") and his exit ("*He vanishes in Thunder*"). Alonso hears the thunder, conscience-stricken as he is, pronounce Prospero's name (III, i, 97–8), and it is one of the devices in the list of magical powers that Prospero resolves to abandon (V, i, 44–5). But noises of all kinds, as Caliban famously describes at III, ii, 133–41, fill the island, and Shakespeare scored these with a frequency that suggests an artist's pleasure in a new resource, new in its controllability.

The principal sound is music and *The Tempest* is Shakespeare's most musical play, a genuine melodrama. Music expresses both the functioning and the effect of Prospero's magic, the world of spirit, hallucination and dream, and it relates the group of ideas concerned with the harmony of the spheres and astral influences. But disharmonious sound is also prominent, sound effects which tell of chaos, pain and punishment. There is the thunder which surrounds the wicked with the promise of retribution, and the fear of the sailors in I, i, "*a confused noise within.*" "Confused" is used again of the interrupted masque in IV, i when the masquers vanish "*to a strange, hollow and confused noise.*" Hollow, too (an effect of the roofed auditorium), would be the baying of the dogs as a prelude to the routing of Caliban and the others at the end of the same scene—"*a noise of hunters*" is heard, and then the pain of the hunted: "Hark, they roar." The characters' senses are heightened in the animistic world of the magic island and other sounds tug at the mind. Antonio claims to hear the roaring of bulls or lions in II, i, but Gonzalo, wakened by Ariel's song, remembers confusedly "a humming, And that a stange one too." Trinculo, taken up with simpler problems, hears the storm "sing i' th' wind." And Alonso, made mad by the Harpy's peroration, is accused by voices in the elements:

> Methought the billows spoke, and told me of it;
> The winds did sing it to me; and the thunder,
> That deep and dreadful organ-pipe, pronounced
> The name of Prosper.
>
> (III, iii, 96–9)

As for the actual theatre music, Alonso's "dreadful organ-pipe" may have been actually employed at the Blackfriars. In the play, song and instrumental pieces alternate in a rich score that exists now largely in the suggestive descriptions of the stage directions. There are nine songs in the play (three of them, all in II, ii, probably unaccompanied), six pieces of orchestral music and, most probably, four *entr'acte* sequences that Shakespeare's pedantic observation of a five-act structure gives opportunity for, or is deliberately accommodated by. Settings survive for "Full Fathom Five" (I, ii) and "Where the Bee Sucks" (V, i). They were written by the King's musician, lutenist Robert Johnson, and it is suggested they were composed for a court revival. But Johnson wrote music for several King's Men's plays (including the madmen's song in *The Duchess of Malfi*) and he may well have played in the Blackfriars orchestra. Perhaps he composed the whole score for the original production; certainly something more is required than a rehashing of popular melodies.

The orchestra might well have been a broken consort of strings and woodwind. But this was probably augmented by an organ to produce the sonorous and unearthly music the play requires. For though music in *The Tempest* evidently provides a continuum of localising references and a prompting of sensuous impressions that makes it the play's true scenery, in particular, and at the various climaxes except the last, music enacts Prospero's magic power—

drawing Ferdinand to his meeting with Miranda, charming the court party asleep and rousing them again, accompanying the dance of the Shapes around the banquet and finally leading the court party, "spell-stopped," into the magic circle where their brains are unscrambled by "A solemn air, and the best comforter to an unsettled fancy." Only a full sympathy towards the Renaissance belief in the ethical, religious and therapeutic effects of music will release all the significance of what Shakespeare is doing in this music-theatre. But his (or his editor's) grace notes (in stage direction) help: "solemn," "solemn and strange," "soft," "soft," and "solemn." And to these we may add the character's responses: "Sure, it waits upon some god o' th' island"; "what harmony is this? . . . Marvellous, sweet music"; "harmonious charmingly"; "some heavenly music." "Charm" is the key word—meaning magical incantation, song (Latin *carmen*), and the mixed warbling of birds. The island is literally charming. And most musical of all is Prospero's own bird, Ariel, whose name and Folio description, "an airy spirit," contain the pun on air (= ether and melody).

Ariel's whole being is expressed through the power of song. He plays pipe and tabor and probably also accompanied himself at the Blackfriars on the lute. And he tells Prospero, with pride, that he so lured Caliban and the others with his playing that

> they prick'd their ears,
> Advanc'd their eyelids, lifted up their noses,
> As they smelt music: so I charm'd their ears.
> (IV, i, 176–8)

The final sound of the play, rhythmic and life-enhancing like the music, and able, too, to effect a magical release, is also scored by Shakespeare. Prospero, in abrogating his magic powers, also gives up his music. So the play does not end with a festive dance to celebrate the forthcoming marriage. Instead, "his charms o'erthrown," Prospero requests in the Epilogue that the audience will work its own magic to release him from the confinement of the stage: by applause.

Much of Act I, scene ii is occupied by the careful introductions of first Ariel and then Caliban. Shakespeare, in almost mannered fashion, contrives that we think of them in opposition to each other. When Prospero demands Caliban's entrance and his grumble has been heard offstage (ll. 315–17), suddenly Ariel reappears ("*like a water-nymph*") and is promptly despatched before Caliban's actual (and smouldering) first appearance. The sequence demands exact timing (the entrances are upstage left and right) and the stage business is complicated by the fact that Miranda, reluctantly awaiting Caliban, does not see Ariel (who is "invisible") or catch her father's aside. The whole episode runs thus:

PROS   What, ho! slave! Caliban!
             Thou earth, thou! speak.
CAL *within*   There's wood enough within.
PROS   Come forth, I say! there's other business for thee;
            Come, thou tortoise! when?
               [Re-] enter ARIEL *like a water-nymph*
            Fine apparition! My quaint Ariel,
            Hark in thine ear.
ARI   My lord, it shall be done. *Exit*
PROS   Thou poisonous slave, got by the devil himself
            Upon thy wicked dam, come forth!
               Enter CALIBAN

So, much of the play proceeds by pairing opposites and the stagecraft here emphasises that.

The stage appearances of Ariel and Caliban are vital and a Jacobean record would be invaluable. In many ways they are a precise pairing—servants to Prospero, but opposite in their temperaments and physiques. They have complementary, elemental allegiances, to air and fire the one, to earth and water the other. Ariel is a thing of spirit and without human sentience; Caliban a thing of matter, bestial and sensual. In an allegorical reading of the play, they act as linked cyphers. An audience aware of the conventions of the court masque, as a Blackfriars audience would be, would see them as hieroglyphs.

Ariel, who probably owes his origins to Shakespeare's reading in Agrippa and other hermetic writings, is a type of Mercury, the winged god associated by Renaissance emblem writers with the notion, so germane to the play, that "Art is a help to nature." (In this role, Mercury is pictured mending a lute.) Ariel is the arch shape-changer in a play of metamorphosis. He shifts costumes readily to act out roles assigned by Prospero, a kind of Face to Prospero's Subtle, and in his own person he is seen only by his master. It was suggested earlier that he was played by a boy and we should expect a boy to express the character's sexlessness well (Caliban is all male libido). One idea for his appearance comes from Jonson's Jophiel, in the masque *The Fortunate Isles* (1625). Jonson may be making, in fact, a deliberate allusion to Shakespeare's character. Jophiel is part of a sustained Rosicrucian satire but is also "the intelligencer of Jupiter's sphere." (Dee's presiding spirit, Uriel, a variant of Ariel, was also connected with Jupiter.) In fact, Jonson's description of Jophiel in the text does not square with Inigo Jones's design. But Ernest Law neatly conflates description and design to give Ariel

a close-fitting tunic of silk in rainbow colours, wings tinctured in harmony with it, a scarf over his shoulders, buskins or blue stockings, and on his head a chaplet of flowers.[12]

If the whole effect strikes us as too pretty for Shakespeare's moody sprite, we should remember again that a boy actor would not bring to the part the naive charm (in its modern sense) characteristically expressed by child performers of today.

There is no certain indication in the text that Ariel was flown, though that became his customary form of locomotion at the Restoration. The Folio text marks his entrance and exits in conventional manner except for "*Vanishes*" at the end of the Harpy episode. In any case, for much of the play he is habited like a sea-nymph and flying would be indecorous. Jophiel "entereth in running" and we can assume that for the actor of Ariel, a shimmering costume, light and speedy stage movements and the verbal imagery of rapid motion which he employs would do the trick.

His first costume change into sea-nymph requires attention. It is often taken to be a whimsy on Shakespeare's part or a mere excuse to get him off stage. But Prospero's purpose is clear enough: the sea-nymph appearance will guarantee invisibility in the presence of all mortals in the play bar Prospero himself. The relevant lines run:

> Go make thyself like a nymph o' th' sea:
> Be subject to no sight but mine; invisible
> To every eyeball else. Go take this shape,
> And hither come in 't. Go; hence.
> ARI   With diligence. *Exit*
> (I, ii, 301–6)[13]

When Ariel returns, he earns the praise quoted at the start of this chapter: "Fine apparition! My quaint Ariel." He is then promptly despatched so that he might invisibly (but audibly) draw Ferdinand to the meeting with Miranda.

The sea-nymph costume that confers invisibility (and Ariel is "invisible" in stage directions twice—a little later in this same scene, after l. 375, and in III, ii, after l. 39) is evidently not the conventional costume in the inventory of the Admiral's Men ("robe for to go invisible") often quoted in connection with this. Ariel's costume confers invisibility by making him look like a sea-nymph, as though the costume merged with the surroundings—the marine ambience of the play-in-performance. How so is not clear, unless (mere speculation, this) the tiring-house facade, or part of it, were hung with curtains representing a seascape. Tapestries or painted cloths were used on stage facades[,] and at least once in the public playhouses we hear of the stage being draped with black for a tragedy (see the Induction to *A Warning for Fair Women*, 1599). Perhaps Ariel, at will, by standing against such a cloth, "disappears"—exactly the kind of theatre illusion that evokes and parallels the magic of a spirit world. And of course, almost uniquely here, the playhouse architecture of doors and the like is irrelevant narratively to the play. Ariel's other costumes will be discussed with the staging of those episodes in which they appear.

For Caliban, the text tells us much, even too much about his appearance; it is difficult to create a coherent stage image out of seemingly inconsistent references. For the literary critic, ambiguity is exciting, something that is part of Shakespeare's purpose.[14] But for the King's Men, Caliban needed a precise shape and texture and these had to be created by Lowin (probably) with the careful aid of costume and make-up.

The way of playing Caliban has undergone radical transformations over the centuries (as Hamlet's psyche has yielded to the prevailing ethos, so has Caliban's appearance). There are no contemporary references to his Jacobean shape save those in the text. Resuming stage life at the Restoration in the Davenant and Shadwell adaptations, he is remembered as a type of drunkard and an apt comparison for the bucolic Sir Wilful Witwoud in *The Way of the World:* "When [Sir Wilful] is drunk, he's as loving as the monster in *The Tempest,* and much after the same manner." Pepys, going backstage, found Caliban's costume "very droll." Rymer stressed his humanity: "'Tis not necessary for a man to have a nose on his face, nor to have two legs: he may be a true man though awkward and unsightly, as the Monster in *The Tempest.*" But the Restoration Caliban is Trinculo and Stephano's. Only they call him monster.

The First Folio *dramatis personae* gives us three separate ideas in "a salvage and deformed slave." "Slave" refers both to a political status and a moral character, for Caliban became slave only after the attempted rape of Miranda. (It was current doctrine that those incapable of being good Christians should be made slaves.) "Deformed" has both a physical and an ethical colouring, in a play suffused with neo-platonic ideas. "Salvage," as spelt here, retains an archaic form that refers us back to the word's etymological connection with Latin *silva,* a wood. In part, Caliban is that medieval, mythic creature, the wild man of the forests, hairy and primitive, capable of rudimentary social habits but one "on whose nature Nurture can never stick." And his name is probably an anagram of "cannibal" which itself derives from Carib (a native of the southern West Indies).

Of physical details in the text, fish references begin early (II, ii, 24–39) and return late (V, i, 265–6). But elsewhere Caliban has hands with fingers and nails (IV, i, 245; IV, i, 220; II, ii, 168), bare feet (II, i, 11), is not ape-like with low forehead (IV, i, 246–8) and can be pinched from toe to crown (IV, i, 233). Prospero calls him a tortoise (though probably because of his inertia) and to Trinculo he is "puppy-headed" (which may only mean stupid). Prospero implies he has a human shape (I, ii, 281–4) and Miranda first regards him as a man (I, ii, 447–8), then later appears not to do so (III, i, 50–2). Prospero calls him "slave" (five times), "hag-seed," "beast" and "demi-devil." To Trinculo and Stephano he is "moon-calf" (four times), "monster" (thirty-three times) and various "monster" combinations—"man-monster," "half fish half monster," "servant-monster" and "bully-monster." He might be dark coloured ("this thing of darkness") though born freckled. And he wears a gaberdine in II, ii, a cloak large enough for Trinculo to crawl under and play the monster with four legs. There is a description of a sea monster encountered in a voyage of 1597 and not published till 1625 which picks up many of the physical details referred to here. Perhaps Shakespeare read something like this in manuscript. In any case, it seems we can arrive no nearer to how the King's Men's actor got himself up to play the role:

> He was ash-coloured on the back, and white on the belly, hairy like an oxe but rougher. . . . He was ten spans long, thicker than a man; his tail thick, a span long, ears of a dog, arms like a man without hair, and at the elbows great fins like a fish . . . [the natives] thought him (they said) the son of the Devil.[15]

What Shakespeare created was not some version of the noble savage (although Caliban frequently and fashionably appears like that on today's stage) but a genuine grotesque, half man half beast, something outside nature. Jonson scorned Caliban's unrealism in the prologue to *Bartholomew Fair:* "If there be never a servant monster in the fair, who can help it?" His own mooncalf, Ursula's tapster, is a "natural" in the Jacobean sense of congenital idiot. When Trinculo calls Caliban a "natural" (III, ii, 31) he alerts us to Shakespeare's confidence in what he is about as a creative artist (it is of the playwright's invention of this character that Dryden first used "create" in the literary sense). As a show and taken to Europe, as Trinculo would have him, Caliban, a thing of nature, is the opposite of "a quaint device." As Shakespeare's invention, he is exactly that. Finally, it is worth stressing that in the comic, underplot scenes Caliban shares with Trinculo and Stephano (II, ii, III, ii and IV, i), he is consistently presented as a comic butt and the excuse for a series of *lazzi*. He is the Indian drunk on fire-water who crassly judges Stephano to be god-like and would exchange him as master for Prospero. He leaves the stage at the end of the play chastened and seeking grace. Though his significance as victim of "plantation" was far from lost on Shakespeare, inevitably, on the modern stage we create a sentimentalised version far from the original. Prospero and Shakespeare knew Caliban was "A devil, a born devil on whose nature Nurture can never stick." We no longer have the confidence of a Blackfriars audience in the value of nurture, but Shakespeare's play, in its "quaintness," is about that very issue.

Caliban's grumbling exit in I, ii is followed immediately by the second of the five major shows that Prospero contrives as part of his moral experiment: the meeting of Ferdinand and Miranda. As Caliban exits through one stage door, Ariel leads in Ferdinand by the other. Prospero and Miranda are downstage, and Miranda remains unaware of the entrance, and of the music which accompanies it, for several minutes. Probably Prospero indicates to the audience that he shields her from it. Ariel, invisible through the sea-nymph costume and accompanying himself perhaps on the lute, sings "Come unto these yellow sands," which re-enacts the stilling of the sea-tempest, and then "Full fathom five." He has a chorus of offstage spirits and the music from above appears to be handled quadraphonically, so that Ferdinand cannot place its origin. Here, especially in rehearsal and conducting, Robert Johnson's skills were essential. The second song acts as a dirge for the dead father. It expresses lyrically the idea of nature renewed by art into beauty, and in the music that remains of Johnson it is surprisingly cheerful, almost gay. The intention is clear. Music that mourns Alonso's assumed death is also therapy that permits Ferdinand to go on living; he grows through the experience from funeral to marriage without appearing heartless. The knell of "Ding dong bell" is thus also the signal for the magic meeting, and Ferdinand becomes a piece of theatre presented by Prospero to Miranda:

> PROS   The fringed curtains of thine eye advance,
>   And say what thou seest yond.
> MIR   What is 't? a spirit?
>
> (I, ii, 411–12)

Now the climax of the episode is reached as the couple "change eyes." Prospero's commentary and assumed brusqueness have a deflationary force and the whole love-match will proceed only with his hidden connivance. So Ferdinand is humiliated and overpowered. A gesture of the magic staff defeats his attempt at self-assertion: "*He draws, and is charmed from moving.*"

The scene then ends twice over. In the outer play mounted by Prospero, Ferdinand the traitor is harshly imprisoned, but succoured by the affectionate concern of Miranda. In the inner play, Ferdinand's courage and constancy are tested in a rite of passage. And meanwhile, Ariel is organised to oversee the next part of the project.

In III, iii, Prospero's testing of the court party has a profoundly different flavour. The episode is elaborate and full of high design and the stage business is described in three detailed stage directions nominated here (a), (b) and (c).

Alonso and the others enter exhausted and demoralised. There are six named characters onstage and others in attendance (the entry ends with "*&c.*"). Several sit down while Sebastian and Antonio move to one side to reaffirm their decision to kill the king at "the next advantage." Then

(a)   Solemn and strange music; and PROSPER *on the top (invisible). Enter several strange Shapes, bringing in a banquet; and dance about it with gentle actions of salutations; and inviting the King, & c., to eat, they depart.* (after l. 17)

After some discussion, the courtiers approach the banquet to eat.

(b) Thunder and lightning. Enter ARIEL *like a Harpy, claps his wings upon the table, and with a quaint device, the banquet vanishes.* (after l. 52)

Ariel as Harpy charms the courtiers, reproves Alonso, Antonio and Sebastian as "three men of sin," and demands "heart sorrow And a clear life ensuing."

(c) *He vanishes in thunder; then, to soft music, enter the Shapes again, and dance, with mocks and mows, and carrying out the table.* (after l. 82)

Sound effects, mime, props and costume all combine here to create a piece of theatre that is (characteristically in this play) both emblematic and dream-like. The Shapes carry in the table from behind the curtain across the discovery-space opening and position it well upstage. There are at least four of them but possibly more and they are both stage-hands and grotesques in Prospero's "happening." We can only guess at their appearance (they are called *"fantastics"* in the Restoration adaptation), but the courtiers are struck by the contrast between their uncouth appearance and the civilised gentleness of their gestures. Caliban at his most primitive had no (verbal) language with which to express his ideas, even to think (I, ii, 357–60); but Alonso sees in the Shapes' actions a species of communication through art that transcends normal discourse:

> I cannot too much muse
> Such shapes, such gestures, and such sound, expressing—
> Although they want the use of tongue—a kind
> Of excellent dumb discourse.
>
> (III, iii, 36–9)

In effect, a kind of non-verbal theatre, which this play at its most profound moments consistently is.

At the centre of the episode is another grotesque, a classical hybrid, the Harpy, half woman and half bird, but played here, it is important for the audience to register, by Ariel in a costume. He is winged and perhaps wears a bird mask and claws and his meaning (another hieroglyph) is instantly clear as he arrives as a Jovian judgment in thunder and lightning. But like the courtiers, the audience is unprepared for this thrilling moment (typically there is no forewarning except of a most general kind) and the effect should startle.

However, within their visual frame throughout the episode, the audience has Prospero *"on the top, invisible"* (a). "Invisible" may mean only unseen, but perhaps he (like Ariel elsewhere) is costumed to make him "invisible" to the other characters. *"On the top"* is an unusual expression. To oversee the action, the actor need only to have been "above"—on the gallery, 10 feet or so above the Blackfriars stage. The actual expression appears once elsewhere in Shakespeare, in *I Henry VI*, III, ii: *"Enter Pucell, on the top. . . ."* This was a play written for the Theatre, and in the scene Pucell, having tricked her way into Rouen, signals to her forces with a torch from a tower (called so in the dialogue and also "turret"). Later in the same scene she appears "on the walls" while her enemies appear below. Clearly, a position higher than the gallery was necessary for the first appearance. In Fletcher's play for Blackfriars, *The Double Marriage,* there is a *"boy atop"* referring to the main-top of a ship. Action is played below the boy but on the gallery. In the masque *Hymenaei,* on a scenic stage, a statue of Jupiter overviewing the action is described as *"in the top, figuring the heaven."* Prospero, *"on the top,"* is evidently in a position above the gallery, perhaps twenty feet above the stage. He occupies a god-like position, observing the action like God in the mystery play. Why he is not merely on the gallery we must answer shortly.

Sixty years later, in the Dryden adaptation on the Restoration stage, the banquet episode had become two separate but parallel events, at III, iii and IV, ii. In the first, a table was carried on stage by two spirits: *"after the Dance, a Table furnish'd with Meats and Fruits is brought in by two Spirits."* Alonso and the others prepare to eat but *"Two spirits descend, and fly away with the Table."* In the second event, as Caliban and his crew get drunk,

> *A Table rises, and four Spirits with Wine and Meat enter, placing it, as they dance, on the Table. The Dance ended, the Bottles vanish and the table sinks again.*

At the Blackfriars, the table was evidently neither flown nor raised on a trap: it was carried in by the Shapes (see (a)) and carried out again (see (c)). The banquet (meat and drink and *alfresco* refreshment) *"vanishes"* when Ariel/Harpy claps his/her wings over it. What seems to happen is that the actor thus provides a temporary masking so that the top of the table (a trick table) may be flipped over by a stage assistant hiding behind (that is upstage) of it. But the best vantage point for the boy actor playing Ariel would be on top of the table itself. There, he not only acts like a Harpy, spoiling the food by touching it, but he is in a strong position to read over the moral disablement to the wicked threesome beneath him.

Now we can assemble the whole sequence. After Antonio and Sebastian's *sotto voce* plotting, *"solemn and strange music"* is played in the music house and Prospero appears above the gallery. The Shapes enter from the discovery space and bring on the trick table carrying an apparent banquet. They dance a dance of welcome to the court party and exit. The table has been placed upstage, close to the tiring-house facade. As the court party approaches it there is thunder and lightning, appearing almost to have been hurled from above by Prospero, and in the distraction so caused Ariel is flown from the gallery on to the table. In the clapping of his wings over the table a stage-hand from the discovery-space spins the table or rather that part (the inner section) carrying the banquet. Ariel/Harpy then speaks to the court party downstage of him, mocks at them as they draw their swords and are charmed, and, as thunder again echoes round the auditorium, is flown out *via* the gallery. (He *"vanishes"* according to (c), so a simple door exit is unlikely. He could slip out through the tiring-house curtains, but flying would best complete an exciting but morally eloquent episode.)

During this, Prospero surveys the whole action and comments on it from a position where he sees all and never masks it: very much the puppet master pulling strings, though not quite, because Ariel as performer is able to fail and so is praised in succeeding:

> Of my instruction hast thou nothing bated
> In what thou hadst to say.
>
> (III, iii, 85–6)

Not the puppeteer—but the magician that joins hands with the playwright and the director and is proud of his own work, a work of "quaint" illusion. And an episode like this insistently cries out for exact direction.

Pride marks Prospero's next show, the masque of IV, i—but a pride overtaken by anguish at the inevitable ephemerality of the theatrical moment, "this insubstantial pageant," which brings in turn a painful awareness of the fragility of life itself and of human values. The masque is a donation in the form of an art-work. It enacts a divine visitation which confers blessings and guarantees fertility. Unlike the pantomime of the banquet, the audience inside the play, Ferdinand and Miranda, know that it is a show. The reality for them lies not in the "majestic vision" *per se* but in its demonstration of Prospero's high art and its promise. For him it is "such another trick" (IV, i, 37) as the banquet.[16]

What he gives them is a pastoral. The entertainment enacts through its ornate style the sense of civilised values within which, Prospero twice insists, the Ferdinand-Miranda relationship should be conducted. Venus (physical love) and Cupid (erotic anarchy) are banished, so that "ceremony" (a key Renaissance value) may have pride of place. Ariel, as we later hear, is to play Ceres and so he is despatched to get into yet another costume. Practically speaking, the actor has only a few minutes offstage, during which there is a short discussion of chastity, *"soft music,"* Iris's entrance and then her first fourteen lines of verse. Just as Prospero directs Miranda first to see Ferdinand, now with a fine sense of theatre, he directs the couple to see this "vanity" of his art: "No tongue! all eyes! be silent!" And they sit stage left and right, Ferdinand and Miranda one side and Prospero the other in front of the stage-sitters, to enjoy the spectacle of the wedding masque.

Iris and Ceres' verse dialogue is spoken, perhaps in a kind of recitative, against the soft music. The language has a leisurely, pageant-like quality and the couplets, quite properly, sound like nothing else in the play. During the exchange *"Juno descends."* We might expect here a throne descent, winched down from above with the Juno actor on board. The stage direction comes early (opposite 1. 72) to allow time for the operation and for a decorous leaving of the throne. Thirty lines later, Juno is ready to step forward and join the downstage Iris and Ceres: "Great Juno comes; I know her by her gait" (1. 102).

After the song of blessing sung by Juno and Ceres (three verses, perhaps the first by Juno, the second by Ceres, and the third by the two in unison), comes the revels of the Naiads and Reapers. This is pastoral choreography in its most civilised accoutrements. Iris, Ceres and Juno have retreated upstage where Juno sits in the throne, the other two either side of her and the four or six pairs of dancers weave elegant patterns over the stage: the nymphs are "temperate" (1. 132), the Reapers are *"properly habited"* (stage direction) and the dance itself, *"graceful"* (stage direction). There is a strict formality in the stage picture and the effect is quite different from that of the dance at the equivalent moment in *The Winter's Tale*. There, in a different kind of pastoral, "a gallimaufrey of gambols" is performed by "Twelve rustics habited like satyrs," and the celebration, properly in its context, is a folk festival. Here, we have an aristocratic revel in a play in which the satyr figure is the rapist, Caliban.

However, the revel of course is not played out to an aesthetically satisfying conclusion. Prospero's "present fancies" are abruptly dismissed precisely because the satyr intrudes into Prospero's mind:

> PROSPERO *starts suddenly, and speaks; after*
> *which, to a strange, hollow and confused noise,*
> *they heavily vanish.*
>
> PROS   I had forgot that foul conspiracy
>   Of the beast Caliban and his confederates
>   Against my life; the minute of their plot
>   Is almost come.—Well done! avoid; no more!
>   (IV, i, 139–42)

We can imagine him rising from his stage-side place and speaking, moving stage-centre on his last line. *"Vanish"* in the stage direction, the third time in the play, again cannot signify a conventional, tiring-house door exit for the six or eight dancers and three masque characters. Its modifier, "heavily," must mean "dejectedly" (for "sluggishly" clearly will not do). As the spirits, their roles snatched from them by Prospero's command, leave the stage informally, perhaps through the discovery-space curtain, what vanishes, in effect, is the formal construct of the masque itself. So the music breaks off in disharmony, the throne, empty, is winched back up, and *"a strange, hollow and confused noise"* enacts the return to the real world of violence, power and, especially, death. And Prospero, marvellously distempered, fills the uneasy moments while the Ariel actor returns to his sea-nymph costume with the profoundly mannerist imagery of the play's best known lines, "Our revels now are ended . . ." (ll. 418–58).

A court masque of 1604, Daniel's *The Vision of Twelve Goddesses* helps us imagine the main characters of Prospero's show. There, Iris, as here, presents the goddesses and they descend from a mountain:

> First here imperial Juno in her chair
> With sceptre of command for kingdoms large,
> Descends all clad in colours of the air,
> Crown'd with bright stars.

Penultimate comes Ceres:

> Next plenteous Ceres in her harvest weed
> Crown'd with th' increase of what she gave to keep
> To gratitude and faith.

Jacobean companies were always prepared to spend lavishly on costumes. And Shakespeare could not lose here, for if the effect were somewhat poverty-stricken compared with the no-expense-spared practice of the court masque, that in effect is what Prospero alludes to in the disillusioned tenor of his distempered speech. But probably the costumes were splendid.

Prospero's last show, perforce, is contrived of homelier materials, for by then he has joined the workaday world and abjured his "rough magic." Nevertheless, with characteristic confidence, he promises to those assembled at the end of the play "a wonder, to content ye as much as me my dukedom." Probably he draws the curtains of the discovery-space to reveal the inside of his cell: "*Here* PROSPERO *discovers* FERDINAND *and* MIRANDA *playing at chess*" (V, i, after l. 171). The moment has an almost sacramental quality for the onlookers onstage. To Alonso it suggests "a vision of the island" and to Sebastian "a most high miracle" (ll. 175, 6). As with the incident of Hermione's statue which comes to life and gives back to Leontes a dead wife, so Ferdinand is restored to a grieving father as restitution beyond his deserving. Never are Prospero's god-like powers more palpable than at this moment when he has given them up. Indeed, he has no music to set off the event, for the "rough magic" is past. Instead, a pair of lovers sit opposite each other across a small table and engage in love-talk about a homely game of chess. It is as affecting as it is simple. And perhaps it is not all that simple, either. For the chess game, which is the excuse for holding the effect for a couple of minutes until those inside the discovery-space see those outside and join them, carries overtones of the power game of Antonio, Alonso and Prospero which starts up the story, but rendered in the lovers' affectionate teasing into the commerce of love and a kind of communication: love's kingdom is already lost and won; its battles are bloodless.

Alonso sees a miracle and identifies Miranda as the goddess responsible, and Ferdinand must assure him that she is mortal (l. 188). The remainder of the play will be suitably downbeat. There is no wedding celebration, which would normally end a play of this kind. Prospero's response (it may be an aside) to Miranda's excitement in the "brave new world" she now meets is devastating—"*'Tis new to thee.*" There is his anticipation that in retirement to Milan "Every third thought shall be my grave," and intimations of mortality will not be dismissed. In a heart-rending moment, Ariel's promised freedom is granted; and then as Prospero-Burbage is left alone on stage, an isolated figure down-centre, the indulgence of the audience is begged in the most poignant Epilogue in all the drama. For that, from the Blackfriars audience, will alone release the theatre-artist which Prospero-Shakespeare has consistently been in the play:

> As you from crimes would pardon'd be,
> Let your indulgence set me free.

For 150 years it has been fashionable to identify Prospero and Shakespeare to the extent of seeing in the magician's abjuration of his Art the playwright's retirement from the stage. In fact, Shakespeare was still to write *Henry VIII* and collaborate (probably) on *The Two Noble Kinsmen* (both 1613). But it is difficult not to read into *The Tempest* a sustained analogy between Prospero and the theatre-artist, capable always of creating "far other worlds and other seas" but drawn back always to the reality of the human condition in an imperfect world.

The Tempest is insistently an art-object. It does not imitate in vigorous action the hurly-burly dynamic of human experience but reduces the story to the unified and elegant shape of Keats's urn. It does this by turning narrative into anecdote, creating out of the world of Italianate revenge drama a dream-play complete with the abrupt transitions, the lack of compelling logic and the procession of profoundly engaging symbols that we associate with the world of dream. And as with dream, the play has a remote and inaccessible air. Its delicate strategies and carefully mounted shows would have been blown away in the open air at the Globe. A precise control of pace, of aural effects and of the staging of individual episodes is more necessary than perhaps anywhere else in Shakespeare's plays. It is difficult to imagine this produced without careful direction (though the director is unindentifiable on the Jacobean stage). If we cannot play the play well now it is because it is a "quaint device" that defeats our clumsy handling. We would turn it into our own—as "cruel" theatre, or psychological theatre, or political theatre. Shakespeare tells us what it is—"an insubstantial pageant," given significance by an indulgent audience. If that is a disappointingly reductive valuation, it is also bracingly true.

Notes

1. Quotations are taken from the Arden edition, ed. F. Kermode, 1962.

2. For narrative sources and the topicality of the play, see G. Bullough, *Narrative and Dramatic Sources of Shakespeare*, VIII, London, 1975, pp. 237–74.

3. See Harry Levin, "Two Magian Comedies: 'The Tempest,' and 'The Alchemist,' " *S.S. {Shakespeare Survey}*, XXII, 1969, pp. 47–58.

4. *The Star*, 15 September 1904.

5. Quoted in David William's *"The Tempest* on the Stage," *Jacobean Theatre*, ed. J. R. Brown and B. Harris, London, repr., 1965, p. 149.

6. *Shakespearean Criticism*, ed. T. M. Raysor, I, London, 1960, p. 118.

7. The argument is developed in E. Law's *Shakespeare's "Tempest" As Originally Produced at Court*, Shakespeare Association Pamphlet, London, n.d. (?1920).

8. The verbal plainness of the play is often remarked—especially a thinness of metaphor and a lack of "fine" speeches.

9. Jan Kott, *Shakespeare our Contemporary*, trans. B. Taborski, London, 1964, p. 180.

10. Prologue to the revised version of *Everyman in his Humour*, 1616. Jonson may well refer directly to *The Tempest* here.

11. Sprague, *Shakespearian Players and Performances*, London, 1954, p. 157.

12. Law, *op. cit.*, p. 20.

13. I have adopted, in part, the proposed emendation of these lines in Kermode, p. 161, except I have given to Ariel "With diligence." The argument is unaffected.

14. See, for example, N. Frye, *A Natural Perspective: The Development of Shakespearean Comedy and Romance*, New York, 1965, p. 177; and W. Farnham, *The Shakespearean Grotesque*, Oxford, 1971, p. 165.

15. Quoted in J. E. Hawkins's, *Backgrounds of Shakespeare's Thought*, Hassocks, 1978, p. 174.

16. Kermode, p. 95n., quotes E. Welsford on "trick" as a technical expression derived from French *truc:* "an elaborate device or ingenious mechanism used for pageantry, etc."

"This Island's Mine": Caliban and Colonialism

TREVOR R. GRIFFITHS

The political and colonial themes of *The Tempest* excited a considerable degree of theatrical interest in Britain, both in the later part of the nineteenth century, at a time when Social Darwinian ideas and Imperialistic doctrines were making a major impact on the British public, and in the 1970s, when the retreat from Empire permitted a very different view of the relationship between Prospero and Caliban. In this paper I propose to trace such politico-colonial interpretations of *The Tempest,* and critics' responses to them from their beginnings in the nineteenth century to the present day. In so doing, I do not wish to suggest that a theatrical or critical interpretation of *The Tempest* which gives prominence to the play's specifically colonial elements has more or less intrinsic worth than one that does not. Nor will I confine myself rigidly to what might be seen as the purely colonial aspects of the Prospero–Caliban relationship since, as we shall see, these aspects are often both treated as part of a continuum of ideas involving domestic as well as colonial attitudes and also discussed in language which has been applied virtually interchangeably to matters of class and race. Rather, I am concerned with a cluster of ideas, associated with Caliban in particular, which have been applied to or directly influenced a considerable number of interpretations of *The Tempest* over the past 150 years.

Prior to the nineteenth century, critical responses to Caliban were dominated by the interest in "preternatural beings" which exercised most notably Dryden, Rowe, Warton, Johnson, and Mrs Montagu. In the theatre the supremacy of Dryden–Davenant based alterations of *The Tempest* over Shakespeare's original meant that Caliban was characterized as a comic woodwose, albeit one whose strong rebellious streak was a medium for the adapters' anti-democratic sentiments. With critical and theatrical interest directed elsewhere, little attention was paid in the eighteenth century to the colonial elements in Shakespeare's *Tempest.*

The play, however, written at the time of England's first major overseas expansion and under the very direct influence of accounts of the wreck of the

Trevor R. Griffiths, " 'This Island's Mine': Caliban and Colonialism" *Yearbook of English Studies* 13 (1983): 159–180. © Modern Humanities Research Association. All rights reserved. Reprinted by permission of the editor and the Modern Humanities Research Association.

Sea Adventure, is thoroughly imbued with elements which have encouraged actors and reviewers in the nineteenth and twentieth centuries to approach it through its responses to colonial topics.[1] The main focus of such attention has been, naturally enough, the relationship between Prospero and Caliban, the colonizer and the colonized, the ruler and the ruled, the white and the black, the aristocrat and the democrat. In the nineteenth-century theatre, interpretations of Caliban gradually came to reflect broadly colonial and republican themes with Caliban appearing as, variously, an "underdeveloped native," a "red Republican," a Darwinian missing link, and latterly, to some sensitive critics, an oppressed minority.

Although 1838, the year of Macready's successful restoration of Shakespeare's text as the basis for *Tempest* productions, was also, coincidentally, the year of the final abolition of slavery in the British Empire, the anti-slavery campaigners appear not to have used Caliban as a vehicle for propaganda. Perhaps the misshapen creature was too double-edged a weapon to be readily adopted in such a cause, even if George Bennett's subtle and sympathetic interpretation of the role for Macready encouraged at least one member of the audience to develop an analysis of Caliban along colonial lines. Although P. MacDonnell was exceptional in developing his response in this way, and at pamphlet length, he was not alone in recognizing the importance of Bennett's interpretation. This recognition was manifested in two main ways: through engagements to repeat the part for Phelps in 1847 and 1849 and at the Surrey in 1853, and through universal praise, well encapsulated in the *Era*'s response to the Surrey revival: "Even Caliban, with all his grossness and hideous deformity, is a poetical character, and Mr George Bennett . . . gave to it great breadth and vigour, without a particle of vulgarity" (9 October). Part of Bennett's success presumably stemmed from his close attention to the text, which is exemplified in his adopting long nails and high foreheads in response to Caliban's offer to dig for pignuts with his long nails and his fear of being turned into a low-browed ape. None of the productions Bennett appeared in aimed at making specifically colonial points, indeed only the single "Indian Landscape" in the Surrey playbill's scenery synopsis could be construed as having direct colonial connotations.

Nevertheless, Bennett's attention to detail and presentation of much of Caliban's complexity was enough to move MacDonnell to declare that his performance was an example, like Macklin's Shylock, of how "some of the characters drawn by Shakespeare, were never altogether understood, till the excellence of the histrionic art developed them" and to express a truly Romantic "degree of pity for the poor, abject, and degraded slave." He believed that Prospero was partly to blame for Caliban's behaviour, since he imprudently placed "this wild and untutored creature" in a position which made his rape attempt more feasible. Furthermore he argued that Caliban "amidst the rudeness of his nature and possessing an exterior ugly and misshapen . . . stimulated to revenge, by the severity he suffers . . . has withal, qualities of a

redeeming nature." From this perception it was but a small step for MacDonnell to make a link with a moral obligation to civilize the natives: Bennett
delineated "the rude and uncultivated savage in a style, which arouses our
sympathies in behalf of those, whose destiny, it has never been, to enjoy the
advantages of civilisation."[2] Here, then, we have, in MacDonnell's response to
Bennett's subtlety, the germ of an idea which was to grow in importance
under the stimulus of the popularity of Darwinian and Imperialist theories.

Although the readoption of Shakespeare's text and Bennett's sensitivity
to Caliban's complexity led the way for a gradual displacement of the traditional comic wild man associated with the Dryden–Davenant versions, progress was by no means regular, and there were many simplistic interpretations
after Bennett's breakthrough. His immediate successor James Bland, for
example, who played the part for Charles Kemble in 1842, was "wholly
appetite," "grossly corporeal," and, appearing like the "grotesque ready to
change into the clown of a pantomime," succeeded only in "giving a very
broad burlesque of the part."[3]

Burlesque as a form was, in fact, responsible for the next development in
approaches to Caliban since William and Robert Broughs' *The Enchanted Isle*
offered the first overtly republican Caliban.[4] The play, written and first performed in 1848, is full of satirical allusions to the social upheavals of that
year, many of them made through Caliban, who is described in the cast list as
"an hereditary bondsman who, in his determination to be free takes the most
fearful liberties" (p. 164). Although contemporary illustrations give no indication that the Broughs' Caliban "blacked up," he is certainly identified textually with anti-slavery campaigns. When Miranda calls him a slave he
replies "Slave! Come, drop that sort of bother; / Just let me ax, 'Ain't I a man
and a brother?,' " and he also appeals to the "Sons of freedom" (the audience)
to "Pity and protect the slave" (pp. 179, 180). The anti-slavery slogan was
later to prove its versatility by being applied to an ape in a *Punch* cartoon about
evolution, thus illustrating the close popular interlinking of ideas about evolution and slavery which was to include Caliban's assumption of increasingly
ape-like characteristics. The Broughs' Caliban, as well as appropriating anti-
slavery slogans, turned revolutionary, entering to the Marseillaise, *"with a Cap
of Liberty on his head"* and *"a red flag in one hand"* (p. 186). When the revolution fails he capitulates to Prospero with considerable insouciance:

> Governor, we surrender at discretion,
> And to your government send in adhesion;
> We own that this a just and fair defeat is,
> So take these chains off, and let's sign some treaties.
>
> (p. 197)

The Broughs appear to have been aware of the implicit contradictions
between their use of language which elicited sympathy for the slave and their

deploring the revolutionary, since they give the final plea for applause to Caliban in these terms:

> [*Pushing forward and interrupting.*]
> Excuse me, pray, my lawless acts completing,
> With stirring language I'll inflame this meeting.
> [*To audience.*]
> Be noisy—and excuse this observation—
> Get up a *devil* of a *demon*stration;
> But not with *arms*—no, only with the *hand*. [*Indicating clapping.*]
> That's all we want and please to understand,
> Tho' noise 'mongst you we're wishing to increase—
> Here on the stage we wish to *keep the piece!*
>
> (p. 200)

The plea for applause must not be mistaken for an incitement to riot, the audience's enthusiasm must be contained within the theatre, their appreciation of Caliban must be confined to the purely aesthetic dimension. With the success of *The Enchanted Isle,* however, the idea of Caliban as a republican and as a "native" was established as a strand in nineteenth-century interpretations of the Shakespearian character.[5]

The period between the first performances of *The Enchanted Isle* and the publication of *The Origin of Species* in 1859 offered little development in colonial interpretations of *The Tempest.* At the Marylebone Theatre in 1852, for example, there was a programme redolent with imperial overtones in which a routine *Tempest* production shared the bill with a ballet divertissement called "Britannia the Gem of the Ocean," in which "Europe, Asia, Africa and America dance *pas seuls,* while *Britannia* looks on, until the end, when she achieves her triumph and all pay her homage" (*Illustrated London News,* 17 April, p. 310). In Charles Kean's 1857 revival, the major *Tempest* production of the period, archaeology and spectacle so eclipsed the play that there was, as one disenchanted critic remarked, comparatively little room for the acting. Despite this, the production did move Henry Crabb Robinson to the thought "that Caliban was innocent after all and ill treated but this was a theological impression."[6] Unlike MacDonnell, Crabb Robinson did not develop his impression into a colonial reading, though one can see how easily such a perception of innocence could lead in that direction.

The promulgation of Darwin's evolutionary theories in *The Origin of Species* and *The Descent of Man* (1871) served to enhance Caliban's status as a representative figure. Although Caliban had been referred to as ape as early as 1770,[7] the widespread impact of Darwin's ideas in the 1860s caused him to be seen as Shakespeare's imaginative precreation of Darwin's "missing link" as well as an under-developed native and a member of a rebellious proletariat. These categories were by no means discrete and the virtual interchangeability of typifications of class and race in much later nineteenth-century thought makes it particularly difficult to differentiate between Caliban as native, as proletarian, and as missing link.

The anti-slavery slogan, "Am I not a man and a brother," provides a good example of the way in which concepts like natural selection, slavery, and the proletariat could be associated linguistically. We have already seen that the Broughs' republican Caliban utilized the slogan, thus linking republican and anti-slavery sentiments. On 18 May 1861, *Punch* linked natural selection with the Wedgwood cameo which showed a black with the famous slogan, by printing a cartoon of an ape carrying a placard inscribed "Am I a man and a brother?." This was accompanied by a poem in the name of "Gorilla":

> Am I satyr or man?
> Pray tell me who can,
> And settle my place in the scale.
> A man in ape's shape,
> An anthropoid ape,
> Or monkey deprived of his tail?

Although Caliban is not referred to in the poem, one can see that his combination of bestial and human qualities makes him a potential analogue to "the missing link," and future theatrical treatments of the character would develop along the lines of "an anthropoid ape." They would also take account of the slavery element in Caliban which allowed *Punch* to appropriate him in an anti-American Civil War cartoon on 24 January 1863. In the cartoon a black talks to a Union soldier whilst a Confederate glowers in the background; the caption reads "CALIBAN (SAMBO). '*YOU* BEAT HIM 'NOUGH, MASSA! BERRY LITTLE TIME, I'LL *BEAT HIM TOO*'—SHAKESPEARE. (*Nigger Translation*)." Caliban was thus now intellectually available as a (black) slave and as a republican and, although he had, as yet, been presented only incidentally as an ape, *Punch*'s and the Broughs' use of the anti-slavery slogan together illustrate his potential for development as gorilla and missing link. The connexions between Caliban, blacks, evolution, and apes were not, of course, logical but rather a matter of association of ideas and by no means unrelated to what Greta Jones has described as the liberal belief in the 1860s that "the question of arbitrary government and political and racial equality was indivisible."[8]

The evolution controversies established Caliban the missing link along-side Caliban the slave and Caliban the republican. In *The Descent of Man* Darwin presented the theory that the races were separated along a graduated evolutionary chain of development. The "primitive" races were assumed to represent earlier stages in evolution than civilized European man, and psychological faculties such as intelligence and moral sense were also seen as part of a graduated evolution. Thus races "lower" in the evolutionary scale also had "inferior" mental development. Caliban as a creature who could learn language but had no developed moral sense could be slotted very neatly into such a scheme, which could also be appropriated to justify European tutelage of "underdeveloped" (that is, black) natives in colonial territories.

In the light of these developments and the intellectual ferment generated by the evolution controversy, it is not surprising that John Ryder's 1871 production of *The Tempest* boasted in George Rignold the first Caliban since Bennett's to give a complex reading of the character and also a significant innovation in staging which was to bear full pro-Imperial fruit in Herbert Beerbohm Tree's production. The final scenes of nineteenth-century *Tempest* productions had concentrated on Ariel and Prospero, often with spectacular scenes of Ariel's flight and Prospero's departure on the restored ship. In such versions no specific provision was made either for leaving Caliban on the island or taking him away. Ryder, whose production was otherwise very heavily influenced by Kean's, offered the usual departure of Prospero in his ship and release of Ariel, "who is seen suspended in the air over a glittering expanse of ocean" but added to this "the abandonment of the island to the sole charge of *Caliban,* who as the curtain descends lies stretched upon the shore basking in the rays of the setting sun."[9] Clearly this was a Caliban glad to be left behind in charge of his island and, if we are to judge from Richard Dickins's comments on George Rignold's characterization, there was a distinctly "aboriginal" tinge to Rignold's interpretation:

> He was, I believe, exactly what Shakespeare intended, fierce, strong, hideous, almost all animal, but with glimmerings of human intellect, the undeveloped soul feeling up for the light through the mass of brute instinct in which it is encased. Shakespeare's scheme was admirably conveyed of animal strength and passion (typified in Caliban), and irresponsible, amiable mischief (exemplified by Ariel), controlled by educated developed human intellect.[10]

Dickins's response to Rignold's performance is similar to MacDonnell's reaction to Bennett's. Rignold's sensitivity to Caliban's emotional and intellectual range encourages Dickins to a colonial analysis with Caliban as the "undeveloped" native who may be controlled by Prospero's "educated developed" intellect. Rignold re-established Caliban as a character with intellectual as well as brutish aspects, which fitted readily into the climate established by the evolution debates.

The process of claiming Caliban as imaginative evidence for evolution received its greatest boost with the publication of Daniel Wilson's *Caliban: The Missing Link.* In this book, written from Toronto where the author was Professor of History and English Literature, Wilson argued explicitly the case advanced implicitly by MacDonnell, the Broughs, and Dickins. In Caliban, Shakespeare had anticipated the missing link in the Darwinian evolutionary chain: "The not wholly irrational brute, the animal approximating in form and attributes as nearly to man as the lower animal may be supposed to do while still remaining a brute, has actually been conceived for us . . . in one of the most original creations of the Shakespearean drama." Wilson was, however, something of a degenerationist, arguing that Caliban was a creature not only in whom "the moral instincts of man have no part; but also in whom the degradation of savage humanity is equally wanting. He is a novel anthropoid of a high type—such as on the hypothesis of evolution must have existed intermediately between the ape and man—in whom some spark of rational intelligence has been enkindled, under the tutorship of one who has already mastered the secrets of nature." The argument is splendidly double-edged: Caliban is in need of tutoring and development, an argument similarly advanced by Imperialist theorists in defence of the European "civilising mission," but he is also more advanced than the actual "underdeveloped" peoples: "the half-human link between the brute and man" who "realises, as no degraded Bushman or Australian savage can do, a conceivable intermediate stage of the anthropomorphous existence, as far above the most highly organized ape as it falls short of rational humanity." Even Caliban's fear of being turned into an ape with a low forehead is grist to the Wilsonian mill since, as he notes, "Darwin claims for the bonnet-monkey 'the forehead which gives to man his noble and intellectual appearance.' "[11] In the same discussion Wilson also suggests that Caliban's jaws would have been prognathous. Thus Caliban's incidental expression of fear becomes further proof of Shakespeare's prophetic anticipation of Darwin's scientific analysis, and his presumed ability to crack pignuts an indication of his negritude and, by extension in later scientific theorizing, proof of his lack of culture since "the decrease of the action of jaw muscles is concomitant with rise in culture, that is to increased mental activity."[12] There is, of course, a certain circularity in such arguments, but we are discussing not rigorous scientific proofs but much looser processes of association in which prejudice and simplification distort popular perceptions of complex scientific analysis.

Whereas Wilson pursued a broadly Darwinian and degenerationist line in his discussion of Caliban, Andrew Lang argued that Caliban and the "primitive" peoples were exploited innocents whose potential was abused by the colonizers. In an article for *Harper's New Monthly Magazine,* 84 (April 1892), Lang put what was to become a standard defence of Caliban:

> He was introduced to the benefits of civilization. He was instructed. The resources of his island were developed. He was like the red men in America, the blacks in Australia, the tribes of Hispaniola. Then he committed an offence, an unpardonable offence, but one that Caliban was fated to commit. Then he was punished. Do we not "punish the natives" all over the world, all we civilized powers? . . . All this appears to be as inevitable as it is odious, and all this occurred in Caliban's island. My own sympathies have always been with "the natives," with Caliban. He is innocent and simple; he only asks Stefano [*sic*] not to torment him. He is modest, and addicted to a mistaken but generous hero-worship. . . . Poor Caliban, like all these lower peoples, is easily misled by

the juice of the grape. . . . If Caliban wants to kill Prospero, as he does, can one blame him? Prospero had taken his land, had enslaved him, had punished him cruelly. (p. 660)

Lang's interpretation of Caliban was more liberal than Wilson's but both were to bear some fruit in theatrical productions at the turn of the century.

At the end of the nineteenth century, two major actors played the part of Caliban in ways which made explicit many of the various strands of interpretation we have examined thus far. F. R. Benson and Beerbohm Tree each wielded tremendous influence but in very different contexts: Benson, by reason of his tireless touring for fifty years, left his impression on generations of actors and audiences throughout Britain, whereas Tree captured the fashionable and influential London audience. Benson first played Caliban in the 1890s and, although he was not (as he believed) the first actor "to bring out his responsive devotion to music, songs and sweet airs that give delight and hurt not," he was the first consciously to play the part "as a sort of missing link." Constance Benson, who was not altogether impressed by the performance, records that Benson took his missing-link conception seriously enough to spend "many hours watching monkeys and baboons in the zoo, in order to get the movements in keeping with his 'make-up.'" Attired in a "curious costume," which his wife all too accurately described as "half monkey, half coco-nut," the future knight would swarm up trees, hang head down from branches and gibber at Trinculo. His devotion to animal realism extended to carrying a real fish in his mouth, an almost Stanislavskian ploy which caused considerable distress to both Benson and his casts when the property master forgot to change it often enough.[13]

Benson was to admit later that he probably carried his athleticism as Caliban to extremes, and it certainly tended to overshadow the other elements in his performance when he first essayed the part at Stratford in 1891. The *Illustrated Sporting and Dramatic News* (2 May) was moved to contrast Shakespeare's Caliban with Benson's:

Shakespeare's Caliban is a monster, but human. The product of superstition and ignorance, he is surly, brutal, cunning, servile, lustful and vindictively cruel. The best use to which he can put the language he has been taught is the uttering of horrible curses against his teacher, whom he at once fears and hates. His chief pleasure is eating, and he is ready to sell his soul for drink to Stephano and be his slave for ever if he will kill Prospero and give him Miranda. Mr Benson's Caliban is a comic and amusing one; it provoked peal after peal of merry laughter. He was a kind of man-monkey performing various acrobatic feats, and passing through a series of grotesque antics, grimacing and gesticulating, grinning and chattering and making a series of discordant, inarticulate noises expressive of delight, or, when the master showed his whip, of mingling rage and terror, slavishly licking the dust from the footsteps of the drunken butler as he implores him to be his god.

However much one may take issue with this picture of Shakespeare's Caliban, it is clear that, despite Benson's own later claim to have done justice to the responsive side of Caliban, the initial critical response to his portrayal was shaped by his athletic antics. A "Lady Visitor," writing in the Stratford *Herald* (1 May) found Benson's Caliban inferior to Cathcart's in Charles Calvert's Manchester revival. She felt that Benson saw him as "not even on a level with the beasts" and despite "the evidence of much careful study and thought" she was moved to ask

> what purpose is served by such an impersonation? Is it artistic? Is it not straining the text to its utmost limits of coarseness, to say the least of it? And, if we might venture to point out, there *are* better things even in the vile and hateful slave Caliban, as Shakespeare gives him to us, than Mr Benson ever hinted at. It is possible from time to time to feel pity mix with our loathing for the ill-used, down-trodden wretch, who, having had his peaceful island wrested from him, is wantonly tortured and tormented for not obeying the despot, who has despoiled him of all his possessions with alacrity and cheerfulness. . . . In Mr Cathcart's Caliban we had this subtle discrimination. There was no need of apish jabberings, nor display of athletic powers; certainly no attempt to set before the audience, from a Darwinian point of view, a hideous and degraded, and after all, only hypothetical phase of evolution.

In the same journal a correspondent under the name of "Druid" also objected to Benson's conception of the character: "His idea seemed that of a man monkey or monkey man; mine was that of a monster of vice and ignorance of the human kind, distorted and deformed not in body only, but in mind and heart." In all these judgements, and in the Bensons' own comments, there is no sense of an ideological framework underlying the interpretation. The idea of Caliban as man-monkey or missing link is handled perfectly neutrally, although the "Lady Visitor" in her charitable feelings for Caliban's sufferings at the hands of the despotic Prospero shows some inkling of an understanding of the ramifications of the play.

When Benson offered his *Tempest* production at the Lyceum in London in 1900, the first professional performance in the capital for twenty-five years, his performance once again elicited baffled admiration for its athleticism. Gordon Crosse, for example, commented in his diary only on the more technical aspects of Benson's performance in 1900:

> *Caliban* is on the whole one of *Mr Benson's* good parts. It gives him a chance of displaying his athletic propensities in monkey like feats of climbing etc, without marring the effect; and he plays it with sincerity as well as with realism. His get-up was good, but his face should have been coloured to match: a pink and white countenance looking out from all that hairiness was inappropriate. In the comic scenes he played artistically, and was amusing without clowning.

In his published collections, however, Crosse's judgement extended to Benson's conception of the part: "It added to the realism of his missing-link Caliban that he could clamber nimbly up a tree and hang head downwards from a branch, chattering with rage at Prospero." This judgement is an amalgamation of his reactions to the 1900 performance and to one he saw at the King's, Hammersmith, in 1924, when he wrote in his diary: "His own Caliban was as monkey-like as ever; a missing link between the ape and the lowest savage."[14]

As far as I have been able to discover, Crosse was typical in not developing his description of Benson's Caliban beyond this categorization. Often critics made references to Benson's Caliban in terms which might have led to further comment on the wider implications of his interpretation, but the point is never fully developed. The *Era* (7 April 1900), for example, used terms like "simian," "submission," and "rebellious" and another journal discussed Benson's make-up as "a link in the chain between 'a wild man of the woods' and an orang-outang," but that is as far as it goes. Similarly the critics were content to describe rather than analyse J. H. Leigh's 1903 Caliban, although the terms they used emphasized familiar aspects of the character. The *Daily Telegraph* (27 October), for example, described it as "that strange character, Caliban, in which the poet seems to have anticipated Darwin's missing link" and the *Era* (31 October) noted that Leigh emphasized the "moral, rather than the physical, ugliness of the creature" and presented him as "more of a man and less of a four-footed animal than usual" (p. 14). Ultimately, as with Darwinism itself, audiences found in Benson's and Leigh's Calibans reflections of their own prejudices. Two points, however, are inescapable: Benson's Caliban was deliberately based on monkeys, making Caliban, the dispossessed native, an ape as well as a sympathetic character; and it was seen by vast numbers over a very lengthy period all over the British Isles, thus fixing an interpretation of Caliban for several generations of actors and audiences.

It is one of the ironies of Benson's work that, however widely influential it may have been elsewhere, it was seldom seen in London and so received much less press coverage than was accorded to a fashionable metropolitan manager like Beerbohm Tree. Tree was an adept publicist and his attention to the press ensured that there would be lengthy and detailed accounts of his productions in the newspapers. These accounts and the souvenir text of Tree's version show that his production represented a very full flowering of many nineteenth-century approaches to Caliban. Indeed, discussion of the role began before the production even opened. In a letter to the *Referee* (4 September 1904), Walter Parke asked the question: "What was Caliban like?" His answer more than encompassed the whole gallery of nineteenth-century analogues: downtrodden peasants, savages, monkeys, and Saxon serfs:

> Shakespeare describes him merely as "a savage and deformed slave," which does not imply that he was any more unearthly or uncouth than some of the

actual "natives" whose portraits appear in "The Living Races of Mankind." Prospero calls him "abhorrèd slave" and, "a freckled whelp, hag-born," and this seems to indicate that Caliban did not belong to any of the darker races, whose complexions are proof against freckles. A white savage is a prodigy in keeping with the wonders of Prospero's "Enchanted Isle."

But Caliban on the stage is frequently an outrageously grotesque being with brick dust complexion, rampant elf-locks, distorted features, teeth like tusks, and a habit of gibbering, howling and grovelling, with ape-like attitudes and gestures. In some illustrations there is a suggestion of scaly limbs and webbed feet, as if he were an amphibious monster of the deep.

Surely this is not a correct portrait, for Caliban, however debased, is still something above the brutes. He has human feelings, and words to express them, and there are moments when he can even win our sympathy. His expressions of sullen malignity and revengeful discontent might have been used by an oppressed Saxon serf in the time of the Normans, or could, perhaps, be heard even in the present day in countries where the peasants are downtrodden, ignorant and superstitious.

Parke's letter exemplifies the ease with which discussions of Caliban could move freely from racial to class ideas, and serves as a further reminder of the character's long association with both racial and class typifications.

Tree's *Tempest* was, in fact, organized round his own performance of Caliban and culminated in a pro-Imperial final tableau. Two weeks before the production even opened, the *Era* (27 August) was informing its readers that Tree "realises that the 'savage and deformed slave' is not a comic character and will enact it accordingly" (p. 14). In practice this meant that Tree's customary massive reorderings and massagings of Shakespeare established Caliban as the star of the show, eating fish, cracking oysters, catching flies, and regarding Ferdinand as a rival in his continued aspirations to Miranda.

The Imperial overtones were most marked in the last act. The *Era* (17 September) described the poetic effect of "the uncanny figure of Caliban seated on a rock and silhouetted against an azure sky watching the departing vessel sailing away from the enchanted shores sped by auspicious gales" (p. 17); but Tree's own published acting arrangement was much more specific, and clearly indicates that Caliban regrets being deprived of the human companions who have "gladdened and saddened his island home, and taught him to 'seek for grace.' " He turns "sadly" in the direction of the ship, stretches out his arms to it "in mute despair" and, as night falls, he is left "on the lonely rock" as "a king once more."[15] The implications of all this are quite clear: Caliban is lost without the civilizing influence exerted upon him by Prospero and his companions; the islander needs the Europeans, the slave needs the master as much as the master needed the slave. Although Benson's "missing-link" Caliban was political in the sense that analogies had been drawn between "underdeveloped natives" and the missing link in nontheatrical contexts, Tree expanded the political dimensions of his Caliban, who was clearly

the ignorant native to whom the colonist Prospero had brought an enlighten-
ment which he had spurned before learning its true value.

The analogy was not lost on the contemporary audience, but it was
somewhat controversial. Indeed, W. T. Stead, visiting his first play at the age
of fifty-five, was struck by so many analogies that it is impossible to do them
all justice.[16] Nevertheless, several of them are particularly relevant to the current discussions. Under the heading, "What About Rhodesia?" Stead raised
some central questions of Imperialism:

> When the man-monster, brutalised by long continued torture, begins, "This
> island's mine, by Sycorax my mother, which thou takest from me," we have the
> whole case of the aboriginal against aggressive civilisation dramatised before
> us. I confess I felt a sting of conscience—vicariously suffered for my Rhodesian
> friends, notably Dr Jameson—when Caliban proceeded to unfold a similar case
> to that of the Matebele. It might have been the double of old King Lobengula
> rehearsing the blandishments which led to his doom: "When thou camest first
> / Thou strok'dst me, and mad'st much of me; would'st give me"—all that was
> promised by the Chartered Company to secure the charter. Who could help
> sympathising with his outburst after recollecting how he had helped the new-
> comer? (pp. 364–65)

Under the heading "The Instinct of Paternity" Stead remarks that Caliban's
desire to people the isle with Calibans implies "more of a craving for paternity
than the satisfaction of a brute instinct" and has some sternly eugenic reflections: "Poor Caliban! Ferdinand and Miranda nowadays would have one
child, or perhaps two, leaving the task of perpetuating the race almost
entirely to Caliban. It is he who fills the isle with progeny. The cultured, the
wealthy and refined shrink from the duty of replenishing the earth." On the
same tack, Caliban's profiting from language only to curse is "a result that
not unseldom follows our educating of the common people even in the twentieth century" (p. 365). Ignoring the Calibanization of the theatre, latter-day
parables of the fall, and Stead's worries about the raising of the age of consent
after his successful campaign, we come to "Contemporary History in Parable," "Trinculo-Rosebery," "Stephano-Chamberlain," "Mafeking Night," and
"The Khaki Election of 1900." Out of Tree's interpretation, Stead wrests one
which seems to run counter to the emotional appeal of the final tableau. To
Stead, Caliban is "the representative of the democracy, robbed of its rightful
inheritance, punished without end for an attempted crime, endowed with just
enough education to curse its master, and abandoned by him to a condition of
brutish ignorance and hopeless slavery" (p. 365). Rosebery (Trinculo) shelters
from the storm under Caliban's gaberdine and "there for a time they lie. Trinculo-Rosebery with Caliban-Democracy, head to feet—even as it was."
Stephano is "the incarnate representative of Jingo Toryism" carrying "the
bark-made flagon—I looked to see if it was labelled the *Daily Mail* or *Daily
Telegraph*—full of the heady wine of Jingoism!" (p. 366).

Allegory is now in full spate and Caliban, Lobengula only a page before, is now the British electorate deluded by the politicians into attacking the Boers. Stead appears to be unaware of the inherent contradictions of the two analyses:

> Then we see the pitiful tragedy of the Jingo fever and the South African War. Both political parties combine to pass the bottle to the poor monster, but even while assisting at the process Trinculo, after Lord Rosebery's fashion, cannot resist a sneer at the shallow wits of the half-witted monster who swallows with trusting simplicity the absurd stories and the heady liquor of his "brave god." Nevertheless, despite the Roseberian gibes and sneers, the poor, scurvy monster kisses the foot of the Jingo Party, and finally the scene ends with a deliriously drunken dance, in which Caliban-Democracy, supported by Trinculo-Rosebery and Stephano-Chamberlain, howl in maudlin chorus: "'Ban, 'Ban, Ca-Caliban / Has a new master—Get a new man." As the curtain fell amid the roars of laughter, I remembered I had seen it all before on a much larger scale. It was Mafeking night over again.

From this it is but a short step to the Khaki Election of 1900:

> After Mafeking we have a still further development of the close parallel. Caliban-Demos being now well drunk with Jingo wine takes the lead. Just as Mr Chamberlain himself shrank with reluctance from the policy of farm burning and concentration camps, which was nevertheless pressed on ruthlessly by a populace maddened by its daily drench of Jingo journalism, so Caliban incites his drunken god Stephano to murderous exploits. "Monster," says the sailor sententiously, "I will kill this man; his daughter and I will be king and queen"—and in that saying I seemed to hear the decision proclaimed to annex the Boer Republics!
>
> In the next scene, in which the worthy trio appear, we have the true and faithful presentment of the Khaki Election of 1900, in which the drunken Caliban, despite the scoffing of Trinculo, in humbly abject fashion licks the shoe of Stephano. (p. 366)

Stead's was the most fully allegorical reading of Tree's production and he certainly turned some aspects of it on its head, but he was responding to a quite obvious invitation from the production's treatment of Caliban. All Stead's allegorizing was too much for the Era (22 October 1904), which took the resolutely pragmatic line one might expect from the theatrical trade-paper, only to prove equally susceptible to the allegorical tendency which characterizes so much Tempest criticism of all kinds:

> It would have been just as easy to see an equivalent of Caliban in the Boer nation, and take Prospero as fore-shadowing Lord MILNER, and Ariel as a composite of Lord ROBERTS, Lord KITCHENER, and the British Army. Caliban was undoubtedly in possession of the island when Prospero, the "medicine man," arrived as an emigrant; so were the Boers. To put it mildly, he was some-

what rude and primitive in his ideas; so, admittedly were the Boers. Prospero tried giving him personal independence, but he behaved so badly that his republican arrangements had to be extinguished; thus it was with the Boers. And Mr STEAD—who, of course, believes that eventually we shall be out-numbered by his friends in the Transvaal, and ejected from South Africa—may complacently complete the parallel by pointing to Prospero's exit from the isle after burning his books and breaking his rod. How explicit a prophet SHAKE-SPEARE was may be proved by Caliban's straightforwardly expressed inten-tion to "people the isle with Calibans"—evidently a *clairvoyant* allusion to the extinction of the British from South Africa by the sheer force of multiplication of the Dutch. (p. 21)

In all of the *Era*'s comments there is, of course, no mention of any other inhabitants of South Africa but, having disposed to its own satisfaction of Stead's case, the *Era* was moved, without preliminaries, to declare that "analysed, Caliban is much nearer to a modern decadent Frenchman than he is to the chimpanzee or the Wild Man of the Woods." One allegorical reading disposed of and another enemy of the Empire sniped at, the *Era* is safe to demolish any associations of Caliban with "the common herd." Such direct political controversy is unusual, but after Benson's and Tree's performances Caliban was established as a barometer of attitudes to imperialism and democracy, if not, *pace* Stead, of attitudes to eugenics or the raising of the age of consent.

During and after the First World War, Caliban continued to be treated along the lines established at the turn of the century. Thus we find Ben Greet's Old Vic programme for 19 November 1917 describing Caliban as "a solitary savage—a member of an almost prehistoric race with witches as ancestors," neatly encapsulating the Darwinian idea that contemporary "sav-age" races exemplified the prehistory of modern civilized man. At the same time there was a swing towards a costuming which, unlike Tree's or Benson's, stressed the fishy side of Caliban. For example, Murray Carrington, a former member of Benson's company, played the role at Stratford in 1919 as "half-seal, half-man" (*Stage,* 14 August) and George Foss, who directed the play at the Old Vic in 1918, believed that Caliban should be "slow moving and walrus-like." Although Foss's production was virtually ruined by war-time difficulties, he was able to develop his analysis of Caliban at some length in his book, *What the Author Meant* (London, 1932). Curiously, his "walrus-like" description of Caliban's appearance was matched with an analysis of his char-acter which was more generally associated with a missing-link or ape-like appearance:

The part typifies Demos—just one degree above the beasts, of immense strength but with brutalised, degrading passions that had not been eradicated or refined by education, and with no human sympathies. . . . On several occa-sions throughout the ages Caliban has got free for a little time and indulged in a senseless orgy of blood and destruction. He has "made a hell of earth" until some strong hand has forced him into subjection again. (p. 40)

With these views it is not surprising that Foss suggests that "Prospero typifies paternal wise government" (p. 41), and once again we can see how closely linked are ideas of democracy, family, and colonial government. As Greta Jones has remarked, the Victorians in describing subordination "took much of their imagery from an area where subordination was legitimised—that of the family." They "talked in terms of dependence, of development, of benevolent and paternal supervision and of the 'child' or the childlike qualities of the 'primitive' peoples" (p. 144). Similarly, Foss's Prospero was both the head of a family and a governor doing his best to keep an unruly population in check.

Generally we find that the missing-link/native interpretation was the norm against which the Calibans of the twenties were judged. Sometimes the judgement was overt, as in the case of one journal's reaction to Russell Thorndike's 1919 Old Vic Caliban which, "though hideous enough to have been studied from the new gorilla at the Zoo, managed to combine the grossness with flashes of almost profound intelligence, just in the way that one feels Shakespeare meant his inspired aboriginal to do." This production clearly encouraged such a reaction with its concluding tableau of the cast departing, "leaving Caliban to resume his erstwhile savage existence, a lonely and solitary figure" (*Era,* 15 October 1919, p. 6). Sometimes the norm was used to castigate an aberrant actor like Louis Calvert, whose 1921 Caliban in Viola Tree's Aldwych production ("a simple figure like a Neapolitan lazzarone in skins") the *Athenaeum* (11 February) compared unfavourably with Beerbohm Tree's "plaintive, savage child with the ear for music." Sometimes it was so deeply engrained as to be almost invisible, as when the *Era* (9 February), reviewing the Aldwych production, described Caliban as a "tragic blend of brutishness and intelligence" which often "evoked our pity" (p. 8).

The continued association of the ideas of Caliban as a missing link, as a "native," and as a gorilla is well exemplified in the *Daily Herald's* reaction to Robert Atkins's 1921 Old Vic Caliban: "Less of a beast and more of a savage than is customary, labouring for his words, pawing the air in brutish impotence, he is a Caliban to be remembered next century. No one who has seen it will ever forget the unpent, tempestuous lust for liberty" revealed in his farewell to Prospero and singing of his song (21 February). Similarly, Gordon Crosse thought that Atkins was superlative in showing "the malevolent brute nature with the dim half-formed human intellect just breaking through."[17] By the 1924 Old Vic production, however, Atkins's conception was more familiar, and the *Observer* (10 February) objected that "Caliban began to impinge upon my imagination less as a strange sea-fish than as an only too engrossingly natural gorilla. His was a truly marvellous make-up, a poignantly realistic study of the ape turned human, too close a shot at the missing link."

Although this critical reaction against missing-link make-ups continued, it did not extend to a rejection of the connotations of such make-ups. Thus in 1926, when there were two *Tempest* productions in London and one at Stratford, we find three quite different approaches to the part of Caliban. Henry Baynton's Caliban for Robert Courtneidge's company was fishy and monstrous, Randle Ayrton's was beastlike and repulsive at Stratford, and Baliol Holloway's was missing link with fishy and democratic overtones at the Old Vic. Baynton followed Murray Carrington's lines, offering a fishy rather than a gorilla-like monster. St. John Ervine praised his effort "to interpret his author's intentions" by giving Caliban "a fish-like body, with green scales and a most dejected green face," but objected to the lack of "mind." The *Era* (13 January) shared this view; even if the fish costume was rather too clean, it was "nearer the mark than the shaggy bear costume in which the moon-calf sometimes appears," but the real problem was that, although Baynton "roared with great spirit" and "tried to get the monstrous character by breaking up all the lines into pieces," "he was never able to suggest that his Caliban had ever come under the spell of the island, that he had any realisation of anything greater than the drunken Stephano" (p. 1). At Stratford, Randle Ayrton also tried to convey the beastlike nature of the character by mangling his blank verse with "staccato and broken utterance" and the result was "amply repulsive and beast-like in this strange half-man, half-animal creation" (Stratford *Herald,* 20 August). In both these interpretations the monster predominated to the detriment of the overall complexity of the character.

At the Old Vic, however, the contrast between Baliol Holloway's make-up and his acting permitted a more subtle reading. He adopted a particularly gruesome make-up, with an ape's face, "but more hideous, with hidden, deadly eyes, a monstrous flat nose, long, thick protruding lips, and two prongs of teeth projecting," long "steel" nails on each finger and toe, and a "sickly yellowish green" skin covered with long hair to provide the terrifying side of Caliban. In contrast to all this, he used restraint in his acting and thereby "conveyed more of the symbolical meaning of Caliban." Holloway apparently saw this "symbolical meaning" in terms of Caliban's status as an oppressed minority, assuring one interviewer that "Caliban comes in for a good deal of sympathy from the modern audience" and that "Caliban was justified in his grudge" against Prospero. The problem with playing against costuming in this way is that the contrast may not be perceived as useful and creative. St John Ervine, for example, felt that Holloway's costume, "a mixture of hog and gorilla," denied the sensitivity of his playing the part as "a creature aspiring to be a man," "one who looks up from his slime and sees the stars." Ervine also favoured the view that Caliban represented "the embodied crowd," an opinion which is not unsurprising in the year of the General Strike.[18] When Holloway repeated the role, at Stratford in 1934, his monstrous appearance continued to dominate critical responses, although *The Times* (17 April) thought that he "kept the offending animal in Caliban vigorously alive while interfusing with its grossness the tragic yearning for humanity without which the monster is maligned."

In general, however, despite the relative frequency of comments about Prospero's mistreatment of Caliban, there was no developed approach to the colonial subtext in performance or in criticism during the inter-war period. The final large-scale pre-war *Tempest* exemplifies this situation very well. Tyrone Guthrie's 1934 Old Vic *Tempest* was given major press coverage because of the presence in the cast of Charles Laughton as Prospero and Elsa Lanchester as Ariel, but Caliban did not bulk large in the critics' responses to the production, and the more extended discussions of Caliban's "meaning" are to be found in weekly or monthly journals rather than in daily newspapers.

Roger Livesey's scaly and hairy Caliban, perhaps over-liberally covered in black grease-paint, was generally regarded as bringing out both Caliban's pathos and his monstrosity. Peter Fleming extended this to argue that Livesey's "distinctly aboriginal make-up underlined the parable of Civilization and the Savage which Shakespeare has here prophetically presented" (*Spectator,* 12 January 1934). Similarly Ivor Brown pursued a line that was to become familiar in his reviews of subsequent productions: "Caliban should be the oppressed aboriginal as well as the lecherous monster, a case for the radical politician's sympathy as well as for Prospero's punishment" (*Observer,* 14 January). Prince Nicolas Galitzine also developed a political insight from the play, objecting to Livesey's Caliban helping with the comedy instead of interpreting "the message of humanity's suffering, blindness and progress that is so clearly at the disposal of its sub-human prototype" (*Saturday Review,* 20 January). Livesey appears to have been the first Caliban to have actually blacked up, but this excited virtually no critical comment, except for complaints that the black came off on Trinculo and Stephano. George Warrington's remark that one way of staging the *Tempest* was in "a pantomime-set for 'Robinson Crusoe' complete with Caliban's footprints" (*Country Life,* 20 January) may have been inspired by Livesey's costuming and indicates the possibility, at that time, of an equation of Caliban with a black character from another colonial fiction.[19]

Throughout the thirties and forties the broad pattern of incidental references to simian and missing-link Calibans, occasionally expanded to a couple of lines, remained much the same: James Dale "touchingly suggested the monstrous reaching up to the human" at Stratford in 1938; Jack Hawkins was "an unregenerate Darwinian orang-outang" at the Old Vic in 1940; and Baliol Holloway, "getting uglier" was "still a child-like savage" at Stratford in 1941 and 1942.[20] Among the critics, Ivor Brown was the most consistent propagator of the colonial Caliban, moving on from his analysis of Livesey's performance to see Holloway as a "dispossessed aboriginal" at Stratford in 1934, Bernard Miles minimizing "the appeal to sympathy for an oppressed aboriginal" at the Mermaid in 1951, and Michael Hordern as "a most human and even poignant representative of the Backward and Underprivileged Peoples" at Stratford in 1952.[21]

There were few productions of *The Tempest* in the fifties and sixties. At Stratford, after productions in 1946–47 and 1951–52, there was a gap until 1957 and further longer gaps between the subsequent productions in 1963, 1970, 1974, and 1978. At the Old Vic, the first post-war production was in 1954, the second in 1962, and the third, by the National Theatre, not until 1974. The majority of such productions as there were yielded little in the way of colonial insight until Jonathan Miller's 1970 Mermaid revival, which offered a full-scale colonial analysis. The status quo before Miller's production is well exemplified by the reaction to Oliver Neville's generally undistinguished 1962 Old Vic revival. Only Roger Gellert commented on Caliban in imperial terms: "Mr Selway looked genuinely and quite solemnly aboriginal, with the wild dignity that this implies. One was all the more inclined to join him in cursing the White Settler" (*New Statesman,* 8 June). This solitary comment is, perhaps, surprising in that the programme made the point that "the island does not in fact belong to Prospero, but to the man monster Caliban, both by inheritance and by right, for it is Caliban who 'knows the best springs,' 'how to snare the nimble marmoset,' and 'where to dig for pignuts.' " It appears that the production failed to convey the point with enough vigour to elicit a critical response. In the case of the 1963 production at Stratford the colonial references were again submerged, in this instance beneath the directors' attempts to stress what they saw as the play's deliberate irresolution. This innovatory conception was highly controversial and dominated critical response to the production, so that a programme note which stressed that "the Elizabethans, like ourselves, had a prickly conscience about the ethics of their colonial enterprise" elicited only the usual incidental use of words like simian or aborigine to describe Roy Dotrice's Caliban, "black and almost naked, with a forehead as low as that of the Java man" (*The Times,* 3 April 1963).

So, during the great period of British withdrawal from Empire there were few productions of *The Tempest,* and the play's colonial themes were largely uncanvassed. In the early sixties, however, three sociological studies were published in which the Prospero–Caliban relationship was taken as a paradigm of Imperialism. In George Lamming's *The Pleasures of Exile* (1960), Prospero was the colonist and Caliban the West Indian who has an alien language and culture imposed on him. Philip Mason actually took the magician into the title of his analysis, *Prospero's Magic: Some Thoughts on Class and Race* (1962), in which both Ariel and Caliban are seen as black nationalists, with Caliban the more extreme. Mason's book, which is also concerned with the interchangeability of the vocabulary of class and race, was a response to O. Mannoni's *Prospero and Caliban: The Psychology of Colonization* which, however, was not published in English translation until 1964. Mannoni, like Mason and Lamming, used an analogy between Caliban and the natives, and Prospero and the colonists, in his study of the French in Madagascar.

It was partly under the influence of Mannoni's study that Jonathan Miller chose to give serious consideration to the colonial dimension in his 1970 revival of *The Tempest*. Perhaps the new willingness to present the colonial dimension arose from a sense that it was now feasible to approach the colonial elements more dispassionately than had been possible during the retreat from Empire. Miller's production was certainly the most overtly colonial since Tree's, although the analysis of colonialism was far removed from its predecessor's. Apart from Mannoni, Miller's decision to treat the play in terms of colonialism was influenced by his own reading of accounts of the Elizabethan voyages of exploration and a production of Lowell's *The Old Glory*, with its long account of Puritan sailors making Indians drunk. In the programme, which included a lengthy extract from Mannoni, Caliban was without his traditional description as "a savage and deformed slave" but Ariel was still "an airy spirit." In the production, Ariel and Caliban, played for the first time by black actors (Norman Beaton and Rudolph Walker), became examples of two opposing ways in which native black populations responded to the Europeans. Ariel was the accomplished servant who learnt European ways and literally picked up Prospero's broken wand at the end, dressing in European breeches but carrying a Kenyatta flywhisk, whilst Caliban was a detribalized field hand, with faint memories of matrilineal gods, who got drunk with Trinculo and Stephano (whom Miller likened to sergeants getting off the boat at Port Said). The frippery became trade goods and the goddesses were black sopranos.[22]

In general, the critical reaction was extremely favourable to Miller's conception, although the *Financial Times*, 16 June, dismissed the theory on the grounds that "colonialism, the dominion of one race (as opposed to one nation) over another, is something that Shakespeare had never heard of" and that "it isn't possible to set any party unequivocally in the position of colonialist or of subject." Other critics, however, found no difficulty in relating Miller's production specifically to the Bermuda wreck and generally to the subsequent history of colonialism:

> Alonso and his courtiers . . . are half-bewildered, half-enraptured by an island which seems to them, as the Bermudas seemed to Shakespeare's contemporaries, "a most prodigious and enchanted place"; and they are almost immediately discontented. They scarcely listen to the old courtier, Gonzalo's, proposals for founding an ideal commonwealth; no sooner have they grasped the possibilities of this magical new world, than they fall—much as the "Sea Venture's" company did—to plotting murder.
>
> It will be hard after Mr Miller's production, ever again to see *The Tempest* as the fairytale to which we are accustomed—or indeed to see it in any other terms than as Shakespeare's account, prosaic and prophetic, of the impact of the Old World on the New: a confrontation which, beginning in amazed delight, moves so swiftly to drawn swords and "bloody thoughts" that the opening storm seems only a prelude in a minor key to the "tempest of dissension" that sweeps Prospero's island. (Hilary Spurling, *Spectator,* 27 June)

As this response (which was much more typical than the *Financial Times*'s) suggests, it is not necessary for an investigation of the colonizing impulse to set up unequivocal colonists and colonized, each acting in accordance with one fixed approach, and, moreover, it is surely desirable that within a complex dramatic structure different characters should manifest different aspects of a central theme. Indeed one of the strengths of Miller's colonial interpretation lay in the way that it embraced all the characters. Thus the often criticized scenes between Caliban, Stephano, and Trinculo were "transformed from irrelevant low comedy into another expression of the main theme" (*Plays and Players*, 17 August 1970, p. 29). Miranda fitted into the theme by showing "a mind awakening to many things new and strange" (*Stage*, 18 June) and the *Observer* discovered "a terrible new irony" in Miranda's "welcome to the master race." Perhaps most significantly, the relationship between Caliban and Ariel gained new associations in Miller's interpretation and, as with the other great colonial interpretation, we find that the last vision is of the island's original inhabitants: "Ariel you'd say is the Uncle Tom, Caliban the black rebel. In fact as the play reminds you, it's Ariel who insists on his liberty, and gains it, Caliban who demands a master to worship and serve. As the Europeans depart, Caliban picks up Prospero's wand and points it icily at his fellow: *uhuru* has begun" (*Observer*, 21 June). In fact it was Ariel who picked up Prospero's wand, but the difference between Tree's tableau and this picture is truly indicative of the aesthetic and political distance between the two productions.

The success of Miller's *Tempest* ensured that the colonial themes would be accorded a greater significance than they had had in the fifties and sixties. Even in productions which operated on different intellectual premises to Miller's, the colonial elements were inescapable. In John Barton's 1970 Stratford production, for example, Ben Kingsley's Ariel was "a slow moving, secretive native servant, naked except for a G string and a Sioux hairpiece, suggesting the victims depicted in those ancient prints of the Conquest of the Americas" (*Guardian*, 16 October). Similarly, although the main thrust of Peter Hall's "emblematic" production for the National Theatre at the Old Vic in 1974 was directed elsewhere, he succeeded in presenting Caliban as a savage, a democrat, and a missing link through an ingenious costume design. Dennis Quilley did full justice to the "paradoxical dignity" and "impressive seriousness" of Caliban's "blunt rhetoric" in a bisected make-up, "one half the ugly scrofulous monster whom Prospero sees, on the other an image of the noble savage . . . striving to break from the first stage into the second. His delivery of the word 'freedom' even in the catch . . . echoes with more passion and meaning than anything else in the evening."[23] Quilley's costuming represented a considerable breakthrough in terms of doing full justice to the complexity of Caliban, and would seem to be an entirely appropriate visual representation of the paradoxical elements which make up the character.

Miller's black Ariel and Caliban had been a successful and integral part of the whole conception of his production, but, when Keith Hack used the black actor Jeffrey Kissoon as Caliban at The Other Place in Stratford in 1974, the result was not so happy. Several critics complained that the actor was far too handsome for Caliban, and the *Coventry Evening Telegraph* (23 October) argued that "in attempting to illustrate the white man's mental and physical cruelty to the black races" Hack had succeeded "only in being offensive to them." In this case it would seem that casting a black actor as Caliban misfired, but there is no doubt that the casting was intended to emphasize the play's colonial elements.

Indeed, some emphasis on colonialism is now expected, and Michael Billington castigated the most recent Stratford *Tempest,* directed by Clifford Williams in 1978, for not going far enough "in mining the play's political-colonial sub-text," despite the blacked-up David Suchet's "stunning performance with both the anger and the pathos of the unreasonably exploited" as Caliban (*Guardian,* 4 May). Bernard Levin also praised Suchet's performance in terms of its colonial elements: "no deformed monster but a Man Friday conscious of his usurped rights, and clutching a voodoo figure to help him curse his enemy" (*Sunday Times,* 7 May). Here, with Caliban once more linked with that other great colonial fiction, the story ends for the moment, but there seems to be little likelihood that the "political-colonial sub-text" of *The Tempest* will not remain an important part of theatrical productions in the future.

In discussing *The Tempest* in terms of theatrical responses to its colonial themes I have, of course, done scant justice to its multi-faceted brilliance, both on the page and in the theatre. I have been more concerned with tracing the often fragmentary process in which approaches to the play have reflected attitudes to colonialism, imperialism, evolution, and democracy. Any analysis of these elements in one play can provide only a partial picture of responses to colonialism or any of the issues of evolution, race, class, and politics which were frequently associated with it. Nevertheless, the various interpretations we have examined, particularly Tree's and Miller's, do show that *The Tempest* has acted as a barometer of the changing fortunes and particular relevances and resonances, critical, social, political, and theatrical, of these themes.

Notes

1.   For a discussion of the Bermuda pamphlets and the influence of the New World on *The Tempest,* see *The Tempest,* edited by F. Kermode (London, 1954), pp. xxv–xxxiv. My quotations from reviews, where page-references are not given, are from clippings in collections held variously at the Shakespeare Centre Library, Stratford-upon-Avon; the Harvard Theatre Collection, Cambridge, Massachusetts; Birmingham Public Libraries; the Library of the Vic-Wells Association; and the Enthoven Collection at the Victoria and Albert Museum.

2.   P. MacDonnell, *An Essay on the Play of The Tempest* (London, 1840), pp. 18–19.

3.   *John Bull,* 12 November 1842, and *Sunday Times,* partially unidentified clipping in the Enthoven Collection, Victoria and Albert Museum.

4.   Page references are to the text reprinted in *English Plays of the Nineteenth Century,* edited by Michael R. Booth, 5 vols (Oxford and London, 1969–76), v, *Pantomimes, Extravaganzas and Burlesques* (1976), 163–201.

5.   "Ariel," F. C. Burnand's *Tempest* burlesque, also illustrates this. In it Caliban sang, "You *landed* on dryland on this *Is*land which is *my*land / And by night [*sic?*] belongs to me; / O I was so riled and vexed to see it 'annexed'/ By a foreign authoritee," *Selections from the Songs and Words of the Concerted Pieces in "Ariel"* (London, 1883), p. 10.

6.   *The London Theatre, 1811–1866,* edited by Eluned Brown (London, 1966), p. 204.

7.   In Thompson's *Trinculo's Trip to the Jubilee,* second edition (London, 1770), Trinculo's song includes the lines "There was Caliban too, a most monstrous ape, / No beast had before such a whimsical shape" (p. 33).

8.   *Social Darwinism and English Thought* (Brighton, 1980), p. 140. My discussions of Darwinism and of typifications of race and class are greatly indebted to this work.

9.   Dutton Cook, *Nights at the Play* (London, 1883), pp. 123–24.

10.   *Forty Years of Shakespeare on the English Stage* (London, [1908]), pp. 13–14.

11.   *Caliban: The Missing Link* (London, 1873), pp. 9, 79, 89–90, 78.

12.   A. C. Haddon, *The Study of Man* (London, 1898), p. 63, quoted in Jones, p. 106.

13.   F. R. Benson, *My Memoirs* (London, 1930), p. 298; Constance Benson, *Mainly Players* (London, 1926), p. 179. For the fish, see J. C. Trewin, *Benson and the Bensonians* (London, 1960), p. 150.

14.   Gordon Crosse's 21-volume MS diary, now in the Birmingham Reference Library, formed the basis of his *Fifty Years of Shakespearean Playgoing* (London, 1940) and *Shakespearean Playgoing* (London, 1953). The diary entries record performances he saw in April 1900 (MS diary 2, pp. 138, 140) and February 1924 (MS diary 8, p. 135). The published version is on page 31 of *Fifty Years* and page 29 of *Shakespearean Playgoing.*

15.   *The Tempest, as Arranged for the Stage by H. B. Tree* (London, 1904), p. 63.

16.   "First Impressions of the Theatre," *Review of Reviews,* 30 (October, 1994), 360–67.

17.   *Shakespearean Playgoing,* p. 58.

18.   Unidentified clippings in the library of the Vic-Wells Association.

19.   Malcolm Keen's Caliban in the 1933 Old Vic revival reminded the *Daily Mail* (19 April) of another colonial hero, since his make-up suggested "a compromise between Tarzan and the Old Man of the Sea."

20.   *Birmingham Mail,* 3 May 1938; *Catholic Herald,* 7 June 1940; Stratford *Herald,* 24 April 1942.

21.   *Observer,* 29 April 1934; 23 September 1951; 30 March 1952.

22.   Based on notes of a telephone conversation with Dr Jonathan Miller, 22 September 1977.

23.   *New Statesman,* 15 March, and *The Times,* 6 March.

Rough Magic and Heavenly Music: *The Tempest*

ROGER WARREN

The first of *The Tempest*'s many problems begins with the opening stage direction in the First Folio text: "*A tempestuous noise of thunder and lightning heard.*" This has usually been taken as a cue for a great deal of noise from the very start, which may give a general impression of a storm at sea but which tends to obliterate the dialogue. For that reason the Folio direction is unlikely to be correct. The text has all the hallmarks of the scrivener Ralph Crane, who probably prepared it for publication in the First Folio, and other evidence demonstrates that Crane had a habit of expanding, varying, and possibly distorting the stage directions in his copy to provide a more literary account for the reader. It has been suggested that Crane's expansions may be recalling actual performances; but if so, he is less likely to be providing an exact description than a generalized impression to help his reader. The experience of the National Theatre's rehearsals suggested that these directions need to be treated with caution, especially this first one.

The point is important because that direction misleadingly appears to launch a scene dominated by noisy chaos. Yet the opening lines suggest not panic but professional men acting quickly and efficiently to prevent disaster before it strikes, taking in the topsail (1.1.6) to make the ship lighter and to prevent it steering towards the rocks of the island, and when that proves insufficient and the situation becomes more serious, lowering the topmast (1.1.33) and eventually the mainsail too ("try wi'th' main-course," 1.1.34). The Boatswain's "Blow till thou burst thy wind, if room enough" (1.1.7) may be a response to a loud sound effect; but otherwise the tension in the first part of the scene comes from the angry exchange between the professional Boatswain and the members of the court who keep getting in his way. A major function of this scene is to reveal, fleetingly, what Antonio, Sebastian, and Gonzalo are like, and

Roger Warren, "Rough Magic and Heavenly Music: *The Tempest*," in *Staging Shakespeare's Late Plays* (Oxford: Clarendon Press, 1990), 159–207. © Roger Warren 1990. Reprinted by permission of Oxford University Press. *Editors' Note:* During 1987–1988, Roger Warren attended the rehearsals for Peter Hall's *Tempest* at the National Theatre. This essay is based on conversations that took place during that experience. Quotations from Shakespeare's *Tempest* are from the Oxford Shakespeare: *William Shakespeare: The Complete Works,* ed. Stanley Wells, Gary Taylor, John Jowett, and William Montgomery (Oxford, 1986).

this will not be achieved if the dialogue is drowned in noisy confusion. That quickly became apparent the hard way in the early rehearsals of Peter Hall's version. The company tried assiduously to follow the hints provided by the references to practical nautical manoeuvres, but this was not sufficient to open up the scene, as Hall gloomily concluded after several dispiriting rehearsals: "The scene is becoming what it always is, just a lot of desperate noise."

He therefore suggested a more formalized approach. The first image facing the audience would be the bare boards and overhanging heavens of Alison Chitty's basic set. The ship would simply be suggested by dropping in rope ladders and a sail from above. The Shipmaster stood at the front of the stage, the Boatswain behind him, their gentle swaying suggesting the movement of the ship, as they stared out front at the island and its rocks, towards which they seemed to be inexorably drawn. The scene began not noisily but in a kind of deadly quiet that seemed much more dangerous. The first noise was an eerie howl to provoke the Boatswain's "Blow till thou burst thy wind"; the court emerged from the two traps at the front of the stage, and it was their altercation with the Boatswain that raised the volume, rather than external noise. They subsequently mimed the lurching of the ship when the storm intensified. As the scene became more stylized, it also became much clearer. It is after all a strange kind of realistic storm which stops for Gonzalo to make his extended jests about the Boatswain's destiny on the gallows (1.1.27–32 and 44–6) and which ends, not with the cracking of the ship, but with Gonzalo's quiet coda. In keeping with this, the sounds punctuating the scene were more surrealistic—and much more disturbing—than the usual violent storm which drowns everything. The scene, in fact, is much less realistic than is often claimed: the moment when the ship cracks is marked by *a confused noise*, according to the stage direction, yet the phrases which make up that confused noise, and which Crane sets out as prose, actually fall into the regular rhythms of blank verse, as the Oxford Shakespeare prints them:

> Mercy on us!
> We split, we split! Farewell, my wife and children!
> Farewell, brother! We split, we split, we split!
> (1.1.57–9)

Accordingly Hall had this spoken rhythmically, hypnotically, rather than as a confused babble; the mainsail fell as the ship apparently split, but the formality of the ending was emphasized by having Gonzalo wrap the sail around himself as he spoke the quiet coda; as he turned upstage into the darkness, Miranda was standing there in his place, gazing appalled at Prospero, who had entered through the audience and now knelt at the front of the stage facing her, exhausted by the terrible ordeal of raising the tempest.

Hall concluded that "although it is often described as a naturalistic scene, it isn't wholly naturalistically written," and he summarized it in terms of the paradoxes and contradictions which increasingly came to seem essential to the technique of these late plays: "It is a quiet scene about an external storm, followed by a noisy scene about an internal storm." Prospero's "internal storm" seemed much greater than the external one. This usefully emphasized the extent to which this play centres on Prospero's spiritual crisis. The two most important questions facing the play's interpreters concern the precise nature of that spiritual journey and particularly of his "rough magic" and how best to present these in theatrical terms: as Hall put it at the introductory session: "We have to create a world where we can believe in Prospero's magic."

PROSPERO'S FIRST SCENE

Both issues are sharply focused in the long scene between Prospero and Miranda that follows the shipwreck. There was a marked and instructive contrast between the laborious progress, spread over many rehearsals, on the first scene and the sheer speed with which the second opened up. In his published diaries, Hall recalls a rehearsal of this scene in his previous production of the play at the National Theatre in 1974, "one of those afternoons when the scene comes into one's head without any beating of the brains."[1] That was exactly the impression at the first rehearsal of the scene in this version too, as Hall and his Prospero, Michael Bryant, worked closely together, mapping out the whole scene swiftly and easily. Although Bryant naturally deepened and varied the details during the following months of rehearsal and performance, the basic shape and content of the scene were discovered at this first rehearsal, giving Bryant a firm foundation for subsequent development.

The first thing to be established was the close connection between the "rough magic" which created the storm and what Hall called the "psychotic storm" within Prospero himself. As with Innogen, Posthumus, and Leontes, it became clear at a very early stage that Prospero is undergoing a purgatorial experience. In her opening speech, the sheer violence of the language with which Miranda expresses her concern for the shipwreck victims alerts us to the potential dangers of Prospero's magic, and although Prospero urges her to be collected and seems in control himself, there is a connection, running through the scene and surfacing frequently in the tortuous syntax of his speeches, between the violence in her speech and his inner turmoil as he recalls the past. For when he takes Miranda back through "the dark backward and abyss of time" (1.2.50), he is of course going back there himself, vividly reliving experiences that have clearly not become distanced or tranquillized by the passing of twelve years. In *The Winter's Tale,* Paulina keeps Leontes' memories alive, and his wounds open, for sixteen years. In *The Tempest,* Prospero does this for himself.

It is with the emphatic repetition of "twelve year since" (1.2.53) that Prospero starts to move back into the past. At Stratford-upon-Avon in 1970, Ian Richardson delivered the first "twelve year since" factually, but dwelt on the second in a way that implied "Can it really be twelve years?" For him, the memories had not faded. Nor for Michael Bryant. Prospero's fury against his brother emerges in the parentheses which break up the flow of his speeches. It is sometimes absurdly suggested that his narration is so tedious that Miranda's attention keeps wandering. Bryant demonstrated that the peremptory snapping at Miranda is designed to bring home to her the iniquity of Antonio, as in "I pray thee mark me, that a brother should / Be so perfidious!" (1.2.67–8) or in "Thy false uncle— / Dost thou attend me?" (1.2.77–8). But the extremity of this Prospero's disturbance was made the more agitated by his bitter realization that he was himself partly responsible for his misfortunes. When he recalled that as ruler of Milan he was "the prime duke," Bryant invested the phrase with a grandeur that left no doubt about the issues of power that were at stake. But in the next phrases, Prospero reveals that he neglected his dukedom:

> And Prospero the prime duke—being so reputed
> In dignity, and for the liberal arts
> Without a parallel—those being all my study,
> The government I cast upon my brother.
>
> (1.2.72–5)

His phrasing admits the drawbacks of his action, or inaction:

> I, thus *neglecting* worldly ends, all dedicated
> To closeness and the bettering of my mind
> With that which but by *being so retired*
> O'er-priced all popular rate, in my false brother
> Awaked an evil nature.
>
> (1.2.89–93)

This is clearly an acceptance of at least partial responsibility for what happened, and balances "the bettering of my mind" against the cost. Hall expanded the point. In terms of the power politics which this interpretation of the late plays emphasized, "Prospero has done the *wrong* thing. He was born to rule. Instead he indulged himself in introspection, and so was worthily deposed. It is not necessarily better to study white magic." Prospero admits:

> [I] to my state grew stranger, being transported
> And rapt in secret studies.
>
> (1.2.76–7)

The phrase "secret studies" is an evasive one, and Bryant marked it with a sidelong glance at Miranda; if she expected clarification, she did not get it.

This phrase is typical of Shakespeare's curious reticence about the magic. Its frightening power is evident from the start of the play, but its dangers are not fully spelled out, nor its source implied, until the moment when Prospero renounces it (5.1.33–50).

Prospero tells Miranda that without "the present business" the story he has told her "were most impertinent" (1.2.136–8). The climax of his narrative brings together his past experiences, his present situation, and his magic powers, into a single moment:

> by my prescience
> I find my zenith doth depend upon
> A most auspicious star, whose influence
> If now I court not, but omit, my fortunes
> Will ever after droop.
>
> (1.2.181–5)

I have already cited Hall's view that these late plays are concerned with seizing the moment when people are ready—Pisanio with Innogen in 3.4 of *Cymbeline*, Paulina restoring Hermione to a spiritually ready Leontes in the statue scene of *The Winter's Tale*—and this is perhaps the supreme instance. Everything is in the right place. Prospero must act *now*. But this is a dangerous business for him, and his inner turmoil is reflected, Michael Bryant pointed out, in the short, staccato phrasing—"If now I *court not,* but *omit,* my fortunes / Will *ever after droop*"—and in the "pounding rhythm" of the whole "auspicious star" speech. The entire scene builds to it, suggesting that time is catching up with him. During the first rehearsal, it became clear precisely why Shakespeare observes the unity of time in this play: not out of some neoclassical belief that it is more skilful to tell a story ranging over a long period of time by means of a report rather than through a narrative sequence as in *Pericles* and *The Winter's Tale,* but in order to throw all the focus upon the fusion of past and present, and upon the tremendous pressure that this places upon Prospero himself.

We feel this pressure throughout the play—in his arguments with Ariel, Caliban, and Ferdinand, as well as in his attitude to his enemies and to the Caliban/Stefano/Trinculo plot; and that pressure contributes to the climax and crisis of the play, his tense forgiveness of his enemies, his renunciation of his magic, and the strange depression—"despair" is the word he uses—in the sombre final moments of the play (Epilogue, 15). As with Pericles and Leontes, there is a dangerous psychological jolt as the years seem to speed up and he seems to re-experience the past in the present. What differentiates his crisis from theirs is that he appears to feel no exaltation, no great sea of joys rushing upon him, as they do. Part of him, Hall suggested to Bryant, would let that ship run on and avoid it all; but he must act now or never. And this concentration upon a precise moment of time also brings out another important reason why this is such a dangerous crisis for Prospero: his relation to his magic. His reference to his "prescience" reminds us of those "secret studies" which have given him his power; but the crucial point is that his "zenith" *depends* upon an "auspicious star." His power, in short, is a relative one, a collaboration with the spirits "by whose aid," as he later tells us (5.1.40), he can work the magic—which is one explanation of the tensions underlying the scene with Ariel that follows.

Michael Bryant's interpretation of the scene grew with every rehearsal; it was noticeable how different it seemed in detail each time, within the same framework. He gave the impression of re-experiencing the past every time he did it, so that the scene seemed constantly new-minted. It also seemed a terrifying experience for Prospero: the balanced sage of traditional interpretation, represented for instance by the introduction to the Arden edition—"As a mage he controls nature; as a prince he conquers . . . passions . . .; as a man he learns to temper his passions"[2]—seemed as remote from this Prospero as from the language of the play. Bryant lent particular emphasis to the shifty sense of guilt about being "*transported* / And *rapt* in *secret* studies" (1.2.76–7). At the beginning of rehearsals Hall was speaking of "white magic"; but by the third rehearsal he was interpreting the phrase "secret studies" as something more than a neutral description, carrying implications of the occult and of "dabbling in the black arts." Shakespeare is never specific about that, but the evasiveness can certainly be taken to support such a view, and the speech in which Prospero renounces the magic at the end of the play strongly reinforces it. For the present, however, this hint increased Prospero's tension and turbulence. But Bryant also took every opportunity to counterbalance these dark implications with what Hall called "little colours of tenderness and amusement" for instance in his dulcet, smiling memory of the "noble Neapolitan, Gonzalo":

> of his gentleness,
> Knowing I loved my books, he furnished me
> From mine own library with volumes that
> I prize above my dukedom.
>
> (1.2.166–9)

Bryant modulated subtly between one line and the next from tenderness towards his preserver to sombre uneasiness at the thought of the sinister secrets those books contained, and in doing so caught contrasting aspects of Prospero's personality. He did this still more in his scene with Ariel.

As this huge scene opens out from the painfully remembered past to the equally difficult present, Prospero's exchanges with Ariel, Caliban, and Ferdinand dramatize, often in tense form, Prospero's attitudes to his art, to power, and to sexuality. Like other Prosperos, Bryant suggested that it took a great effort to summon his spirit-servant, just as it had cost him a great deal to conjure up the tempest in the first place, a tempest in which Ariel played an important part, as he now tells the audience in detail. The first question that Hall raised about Ariel was whether he needs to fly at his first appearance. It depends partly on what the scene is thought to be about. In Hall's previous production, which was based upon Renaissance emblematic images, Ariel flew in on a bone-like stirrup above a Prospero who never looked at him, suggesting that Ariel symbolized Prospero's imaginative powers, and more specifically his magic powers. Ariel is visible to other people only when he assumes theatrical roles (the harpy, the goddess Ceres) and sometimes not even then: when Prospero instructs him to appear "like to a nymph o'th' sea'," he is to be visible "to no sight but thine and mine" (1.2.303–4). The relationship between Prospero and Ariel, therefore, which is sometimes tense and effortful and at other times relaxed and delighted, is an externalization in theatrical terms of Prospero's relation to his magic art, and helps to emphasize the conditional nature of his power. Prospero is at once master of Ariel and dependent on him just as he is dependent on the influence of that "auspicious star" in bringing about the shipwreck. As that speech also insists, everything depends upon acting at this present moment, and an uncooperative Ariel could wreck what Prospero frequently calls his "project," which partially explains the tension between them.

Hall concentrated on bringing out their relationship. As in his previous version, Ariel flew down on a stirrup, a slim, androgynous sprite in bleached make-up and body-stocking; but, far from ignoring him, Michael Bryant moved eagerly upstage to greet him, and Steven Mackintosh's Ariel left the stirrup to join him on the ground, energetically entering into the conversation with his account of his contribution to the tempest, "flaming amazement" in the form of St. Elmo's fire. Part of Prospero's "project" is to subject his enemies to a purgatorial ordeal similar to the one he has been enduring and reliving himself, driving them mad and purging them, as far as possible, of their sins. That is the force of his question:

> Who was so firm, so constant, that this coil
> Would not infect his reason?

Ariel has certainly achieved this:

> Not a soul
> But felt a fever of the mad, and played
> Some tricks of desperation.
> (1.2.208–11)

Hall detected a "malicious glee" in Ariel's description of his exploits, adding that he is to some extent "a spirit of anarchy" unbounded by issues of morality. He urged Steven Mackintosh to communicate Ariel's non-human quality less by a high, fluting register than by sheer energy, using the verbs in his first speech—"be't to fly, / To swim, to dive . . ., to ride" (1.2.191–2)—to emphasize Ariel's volatility and unpredictability: "Prospero has great trouble in organizing this creature"—especially as the scene develops into an argument between them when Ariel rebels and demands his freedom.

Steven Mackintosh began this section of the scene by hardening his tone on "Is there *more toil?*" Michael Bryant responded with a testy, edged "How now? Moody?" (1.2.243–5): the intonation on "Moody?" verged on the comic; but irony gave way to violence as Prospero sought to cow him by compelling him to relive the torments that Sycorax imposed. After a few rehearsals the quarrel reached a pitch of intensity on both sides in which Prospero's accusing description of Ariel as a "malignant thing" (1.2.258) seemed at least partly justified. But once Ariel had moved from extreme rebellion to extreme servility, Bryant allowed himself to relax from sternness to geniality as he laughingly instructed Ariel:

> Go make thyself like to a nymph o'th' sea. Be subject
> To no sight but thine and mine, invisible
> To every eyeball else.
>
> (1.2.303–5)

In his edition for the Oxford Shakespeare, Stephen Orgel suspects corruption in these lines; in his note on the passage he says: "The disguise is, of course, logically pointless if Ariel is invisible to everyone except Prospero. But he is visible to the audience, and the costume is the appropriate one to adopt in singing to Ferdinand on the shore."[3] Bryant and Mackintosh offered a convincing justification for "Be subject / To no sight but thine and mine." Bryant was enjoying the prospect of collaborating with Ariel on another imaginative transformation: he wanted Ariel to himself, a shared experience between the two of them for no one else's benefit—hence "invisible / To every eyeball else." And when Ariel appeared as a water nymph, Prospero turned in evident relief from the necessity of dealing with Caliban with a pleased "Fine apparition! My quaint Ariel, / Hark in thine ear" (1.2.319–20). But this Ariel did not need to be told Prospero's wishes; he divined them, with a smiling "My lord, it shall be done," and vanished. Bryant capped the moment with a delighted laugh in recognition of Ariel's skilful ingenuity, and of their collusion. These two actors captured both sides of this relationship, its tense acrimony and its affectionate co-operation.

Bryant used this delighted, and delightful, moment to suggest that Prospero would rather deal with the world of Ariel's airy imagination than with Caliban's earthiness. Just before he is pleasantly distracted by Ariel's entry as the nymph, Prospero says to Caliban "there's other business for thee," but since he never specifies what that is, it presumably reflects some kind of psychological necessity in Prospero himself: Caliban represents something he has to confront. Hall resisted the idea of Caliban as a noble savage, arguing that he is an embodiment of dark animal desire, which is why he so disturbs Prospero. That disturbance is indicated even before Caliban appears, in the repellent language with which Prospero describes Caliban's mother, "the foul witch Sycorax." "This blue-eyed hag" evokes his disgust at her pregnancy; "the son that she did *litter* here" describes the birth in the language of the farmyard (1.2.259–83). Such language reveals what Hall called a "psychopathic loathing" of what Prospero sees as certain extreme forms of animal sexuality. But, as with his hatred of Antonio, he may be reacting as much against the dark side of himself, as Stephen Orgel suggests in his Oxford Shakespeare edition. Orgel's introduction, which Hall greatly admired, sometimes provided clues for the rehearsal; sometimes the discoveries of rehearsals provided independent corroboration for Orgel's analyses.

On Prospero's attitude to Sycorax, and so ultimately to Caliban, Orgel is especially illuminating:

> On the surface, Prospero and Sycorax are antitheses . . . but as the play progresses, the similarities between the two sorcerers grow increasingly marked. . . . The rage, the demand for unwilling servitude, the continual threats of constriction and painful imprisonment are characteristic of both. And late in the play, the identification of the two in Shakespeare's mind becomes strikingly manifest.

For Prospero's renunciation of his magic is based on a speech of the sorceress Medea in Ovid's *Metamorphoses,* who is also a model for Sycorax. Orgel makes explicit the implications of this identification:

> If Prospero in his moment of triumph speaks as Medea, then we have no grounds for making easy distinctions between white and black magic, angelic science and diabolical sorcery. The battle between Prospero and Sycorax is Prospero's battle with himself, and by the play's end he has accepted the witch's monstrous offspring as his own: "this thing of darkness I / Acknowledge mine." (pp. 20–3)

To some extent, the way in which Caliban was presented visually reflected Prospero's attitudes to him, and treatment of him. Two small horns protruded from his forehead: these could be taken as an illustration of Prospero's abusive "Thou poisonous slave, got by the devil himself / Upon thy wicked dam" (1.2.321–2), but not insistently so: they could equally suggest the faun or Pan-like side of Caliban which responds to the beauties of the island. Tony Haygarth, who played the part, said that Caliban should "look bestial and sound lyrical." He certainly achieved this. At his own request, he was equipped with vampire-like fangs; he was completely naked, apart from a huge wooden block imprisoning his genitals, unmistakably Prospero's response to his attempt to rape Miranda and more generally to his upsetting sexuality. His body was covered not only with mud and filth, but also with blood, where he had been scratching his sores against the walls of the "hard rock" in which Prospero "sty[s]" him (1.2.344–5). This "sty" was represented by one of the two traps at the front of the stage, from which he first emerged. If the tensions between Prospero and Caliban are about sexuality they are also about usurpation. Caliban and Prospero circled one another warily, sizing each other up. Tony Haygarth quickly subdued an initial tendency to roar, realizing that such accusations as "This island's mine, by Sycorax my mother" (1.2.333) would disturb Prospero much more if they were less of a threat and more of a challenge. In fact they disturbed him so much that he actually threatened to strike Caliban with his magic staff. At this moment, the distinction between the civilized man and the brute wore very thin.

Both the sexual and the political aspects of the confrontation are carried through into the next development of the scene with the arrival of Ferdinand, who has been through the purgatory, induced by Prospero's magic, of apparently seeing his father drown. Ariel's first song momentarily calms his grief, as therapeutic music does elsewhere in the late plays, only to intensify it in the second song:

> Full fathom five thy father lies.
> Of his bones are coral made;
> Those are pearls that were his eyes.
> (1.2.399–401)

Hall stressed that "the body is returning to the world of nature," an image also powerfully evoked in Arviragus' picture of the robin covering Innogen's body with "furred moss" in winter (*Cymbeline,* 4.2.219–29), and in Pericles' imagining Thaisa's body becoming part of the sea-bed, "lying with simple shells" (*Pericles,* Scene 11, 63). In all three cases, despite the serene beauty of the language, the image expresses the piercing grief of the bereaved. Prospero, through Ariel, takes Ferdinand on a journey that keeps the wounds open even in the act of apparently soothing them. Earlier in the scene, Ariel describes Ferdinand sitting with "his arms in this sad knot" (1.2.225), usually taken as a sign of sorrow. Hall and Peter Woodward, who played Ferdinand, interpreted it as something stronger than that: his arms were crossed in front of his face in "a frantic gesture" such as Alonso uses at 5.1.57, after he too has been put through a purgatorial experience, driven almost out of his mind by Prospero's magic.

Why does Prospero subject Ferdinand to such an ordeal, prolonging it in the subsequent imprisonment and wood-carrying? He explains just before the masque that these were "but my trials of thy love" (4.1.6) but the explanation always seems inadequate. A more plausible answer concerns Prospero's ambiguous attitude to Ferdinand. The marriage of Ferdinand and Miranda, and the consequent alliance of Naples and Milan, is part of Prospero's "project." On one level, therefore, he wants it; but on another, he does not. The sight of Ferdinand, the son of his enemy, brings him face to face with political realities once again; but more than that, he is about to lose his daughter to a predatory male, and in this respect Ferdinand seems to Prospero "adolescent and libidinous," in Stephen Orgel's succinct phrase in his edition (p. 18). By imprisoning Ferdinand in a trap at the front of the stage symmetrically opposite Caliban's, Hall emphasized that Prospero's harsh treatment of the one mirrors his treatment of the other, and reflects his view of the libidinous potential of both. Like Giorgio Strehler's staging for the Piccolo Teatro company in Milan, Hall brought out the deliberate patterning of 2.2 and 3.1, in which Caliban and Ferdinand enter carrying logs, by having both characters enter from the same place and convey a sweating servitude which had much to say about Prospero as a taskmaster and potential father-in-law.

During this scene, Prospero several times expresses satisfaction that his plan is working: "At the first sight / They have changed eyes," "It works," and so on (1.2.443–4,496). Michael Bryant delivered such phrases with an ironic lightness of touch that implied "It works; I knew it would." It is the way of the world. But he also coloured some other phrases more mordantly, as in "No, wench, it eats and sleeps, and hath such senses / As we have—such" (1.2.415–16), where he invested the last word with the same worldly wisdom, even disillusion, that was apparent in his response to Miranda's delight at the "brave new world" in the final scene: "'Tis new to thee" (5.1.186–7). The hint of darker implications hovered around such phrases in Bryant's delivery. This did not mean that the relationship between Ferdinand and Miranda was soured. Indeed, especially in the earlier rehearsals, it had a freshness and immediacy that few performances of these parts ever achieve—to the frequent disappointment of reviewers.

It is possible, though, that mutual innocence is not really the point of this relationship. As rehearsals proceeded, it became noticeable that this is an unequal match. Ferdinand is sophisticated in the ways of the world, Miranda innocent of them. One of his first questions to her, which she does not fully understand, is "how I may bear me here" (1.2.428). It is the enquiry of a man who has been around, who, as he frankly if euphemistically tells Miranda, has "liked several women" in the past (3.1.43), and who—to put it provocatively— may be putting on a mask of purity, which would of course provide further justification for Prospero's "trials of [his] love." This would help to account for the odd phrasing, chilly and formal, stilted even, of his reply to Prospero's obsessive insistence on their pre-marital chastity in the masque scene:

> The white cold virgin snow upon my heart
> Abates the ardour of my liver.
>
> (4.1.55–6)

Ferdinand may be deliberately adopting an extreme version of a chaste lover's hyperboles to suit what he thinks Prospero wants to hear; if so, Prospero's decidedly non-committal "Well," nicely turned by Bryant, may be a recognition of what Ferdinand is up to (4.1.55–6). And if Miranda lags behind him in sophistication at the start of the play, she catches up by the end. In their chess game in the final scene, as Hall insisted, Miranda accuses him of cheating, but adds that she doesn't mind:

> Yes, for a score of kingdoms you should wrangle,
> And I would call it fair play.
>
> (5.1.177–8)

Stephen Orgel's tart summary of this moment is: "Italian *Realpolitik* is already established in the next generation" (p. 30). The experienced impression was reinforced in performance by Peter Woodward's appearance as a Caroline dandy with a pointed Charles I beard, almost foppish in his initial elaborate courtesy to Miranda, but not without humour: "My language! Heavens!" (1.2.431) was lightly thrown off and always drew laughter. This made for a big contrast with his log-carrying scene, where he was half-naked and barefoot. Something of the contrast between the earlier and later stages of Woodward's Posthumus in *Cymbeline* were present here, though of course in less extreme form, appropriate to the lesser ordeal that Ferdinand undergoes.

THE COURT

The huge scene for Prospero, Miranda, Ariel, Caliban, and Ferdinand, comprising almost the entire first act, is followed by another, for the shipwrecked court, almost as long. They could hardly be more different; and the contrast was reflected in the National Theatre rehearsals by the simple fact that, whereas the Prospero scene opened up swiftly and excitingly, it took several laborious rehearsals for the court scene to yield up its secrets. But if the progress was slow, it was also sure. By the time the production opened, this scene had gained a firm foundation, and was emerging as one of the most important in the play. It is also one of the most difficult for actors to perform and for audiences to concentrate upon; but that is part of the point of it, and when reviewers complain—as they usually do, though not as it happens about this cast—that the court scenes are slow or dull or that their jokes are stale, they blame actors for providing what is plainly required by the text, at least in the early part of the scene.

The contrast between this scene and the previous one was reflected in Hall's approach to each. Whereas he had plunged into the Prospero scene with great energy, simply working line by line with Michael Bryant on the text, and scarcely hesitating as they interpreted it together, he approached the court scene warily, squaring up to what he knew was a difficult challenge; the first session was a low-key, careful probing of the tone and rhythm of the scene. The first point to emerge was the court's sense of displacement on the island: Hall's image of "an overdressed court in the middle of a beach" was subsequently precisely caught in Alison Chitty's costumes for these grandees in full Caroline fig, with their silks and broad-brimmed, plumed hats lending special point to Gonzalo's remark that their garments, though "drenched in the sea, hold notwithstanding their freshness and glosses" (2.1.67–8), set against the circle of sand which constituted the central acting area. "Why," asked Hall, "after such concentrated scenes as the shipwreck and Prospero's first scene, despite its length, does this court scene take so long to get going?" Unlike the Prospero scene, the rhythm is hard to catch, and that is partly because it is deliberately laborious. Sebastian's caustic remark that Gonzalo is "winding up the watch of his wit" (2.1.13) seems the key to it. The witticisms of Gonzalo and Adrian, and the counterbalancing ones of Antonio and Sebastian at their expense, especially the notorious running gag about "widow Dido" (2.1.81–106), express their situation: these are the remarks of sophisticated but very frightened men who are under great pressure as a result of their ordeal. Gonzalo and Adrian find relief from their tension in their witticisms; Antonio and Sebastian derive similar relief from sniping ill-naturedly at those witticisms. Ken Stott's and Basil Henson's handling of Antonio's and Sebastian's sneering was a brilliant demonstration of Coleridge's point that "Shakespeare never puts habitual scorn into the mouths of other than bad men."[4]

When it came to staging these exchanges, Hall again emphasized the court's sense of displacement. When Alonso collapsed in the middle of the circle of sand, the court did not know how to behave: there could be no congregating around the throne in this situation. Antonio paced relentlessly around the periphery of the circle, suggesting a man waiting to operate; his sniping jokes with Sebastian were initially played as asides, as their lines are sometimes marked by editors. But they did not work when played as asides in these rehearsals; the energy of the scene flagged, and Hall concluded that *none* of the lines should be asides. So Antonio and Sebastian then delivered their mockery of Adrian and Gonzalo provocatively, flinging their remarks back and forth from either side of the stage, across Adrian and Gonzalo who were trying to console Alonso stage-centre, and whose jokes became in part a conscious response to this irritating jibing. Now the scene began to crackle into life as an acrimonious exchange between people whose nerve-ends were very raw. That is surely what the stale witticisms are for. Setting two groups of the court at odds in this way also helped to focus the exchange about the appearance of the island:

GONZALO   How lush and lusty the grass looks! How green!
ANTONIO   The ground indeed is tawny.

                                          (2.1.57–9)

These lines sparked off a long discussion between Hall and Alison Chitty about the design, and especially about the sandy floor. If it looked too "tawny," this would suggest that Antonio is right and Gonzalo wrong, the one cruelly realistic, the other self-deludingly idealistic. This interpretation is of course possible. But Hall, arguing that the point of the exchange is that the island is multi-faceted, and that how it appears depends upon who is looking at it, suggested that "the design of *The Tempest* should be like a prism," and proposed lighting the white sand in such a way that it would change colour, thus avoiding supporting any single viewpoint.

Hall's emphasis upon the openness of this exchange was carried further in the interpretation of Gonzalo, and especially in his description of an ideal commonwealth. Again, there is a clash of opinion: Gonzalo's idealism and its illogicalities are mercilessly pilloried by Antonio and Sebastian. But how seriously are *we* to take it? And what are we to make of Gonzalo himself? Hall raised various possibilities at different times. On one occasion he suggested it was moving that an old politician should still harbour such a dream of an ideal world, on another that it was curious how a loyal instrument of absolute power should now *in extremis* dream of a republic. These possibilities came together fruitfully when Tony Church joined the company during the rehearsal period to play the part. As in his performance of Cymbeline, Church skilfully modified his sonorously eloquent verse-speaking from time to time with a querulous tone that had the effect of undermining, but not destroying, Gonzalo's positive qualities. When Sebastian heartlessly criticized Alonso for marrying his daughter to the King of Tunis, without any regard for Alonso's feelings, Tony Church invested Gonzalo's protest "My lord Sebastian!" (2.1.141) with all his considerable vocal power. Basil Henson froze him with a withering stare; instantly Church backed down, modifying his tone and rubbing his hands in an instinctive gesture of time-serving: there was, clearly, a limit to courageous protest. The demonstration of strength and weakness coexisting in Gonzalo drew from Hall a conclusion about the part: "an old politician with dirty hands." Prospero's view of him, quoted by Ariel, as "the good old lord Gonzalo" (5.1.15), reflects only one aspect of the character: it ignores the fact that Gonzalo was the agent of Prospero's expulsion from Milan (1.2.164), revealing only how he appears to Prospero. As in the varying accounts of the island vegetation, things in this play are described according to people's perceptions of them. Tony Church kept the options open even in performance, refraining from pushing the part too far in any one direction. He was, at different times, "the good old lord" *and* the impractical idealist of the commonwealth speech *and* the political time-server who had dirtied his hands. This satisfyingly complex performance grew out of the options discovered in rehearsal, and its openness usefully focused not just this one character but what Stephen Orgel in his edition aptly calls "the characteristic openness of the text" and its variety of implication (p. 12).

A further example of this variety was the novel context for the common-wealth speech provided by John Hirsch in his thoughtful production of the play at Stratford, Ontario, in 1982. In this, Adrian was a young boy (perhaps Antonio's "brave son" so mysteriously referred to at 1.2.441?), and so Gon-zalo was able to aim his idealism at one character, at least, who had not yet become tarnished by Italian *realpolitik*. Adrian's exchange with Gonzalo about Tunis, Carthage, and widow Dido came across less as pedantic hair-splitting than as recently acquired classical knowledge that Adrian was keen to display. His relationship with Gonzalo was like that between a bright pupil and his tutor, anticipating the contrast between Miranda's "O brave new world" and Prospero's knowing "'Tis new to thee" at the end of the play (5.1.186–7). The general effect was to make the witticisms seem less jaded and Gonzalo's idealism less impractical, almost vulnerable; and this lighten-ing of the mood made for a greater contrast between the wit-cracking in the first part of the scene and the sinister political realities of the conspiracy in the second half.

When Ariel enters playing music that immediately puts Gonzalo, Adrian, and Francisco to sleep, Hall pointed out that Antonio's line "They dropped as by a thunderstroke" (2.1.209) is a clue as to how the actors should play it: all three fell abruptly, under Ariel's influence—a strong indication that Prospero is, through Ariel, creating the conditions for Antonio's conspir-acy. As Stephen Orgel puts it in his edition, "the murderous conspiracy is cer-tainly part of his project. . . . Prospero is restaging his usurpation, and main-taining his control over it this time" (p. 54). Through it, he is also testing his brother, and discovering that time has not softened his nature. E. M. W. Till-yard puts his finger on the crux of this scene when he says that "Antonio's transformation from the cynical and lazy badgerer of Gonzalo's loquacity to the brilliantly swift and unscrupulous man of action is a thrilling affair."[5] One reason why the earlier part of the scene has to be so long and so slow, flaccid even, and why the rhythm is so tricky to capture exactly, is to edge this trans-formation.

No sooner has Antonio observed that the others fell as by a thunder-stroke than he begins—in the same verse line—his temptation of Sebast-ian, with some of the elliptical phrasing that occurs frequently in the late plays:

> What might,
> Worthy Sebastian, O, what might—? No more!—
> (2.1.209–10)

There is something almost Pinteresque in the perfectly timed pauses and hes-itations in this dialogue; and Hall, a seasoned interpreter of the implications of Pinter's ambiguities, mapped out precisely the shape of these clipped exchanges, together with the two actors, Ken Stott and Basil Henson:

```
ANTONIO              Will you grant with me
   That Ferdinand is drowned?
SEBASTIAN                    He's gone.
ANTONIO                            Then tell me
   Who's the next heir of Naples?
SEBASTIAN                 Claribel.
```
(2.1.248–50)

Basil Henson delivered the name "Claribel" with an acerbic, challenging finality, as if to say "where can you go from here?" He was testing Antonio as much as Antonio him, and Antonio's "She that is Queen of Tunis; she that dwells / Ten leagues beyond man's life" (2.1.251–2) was an ironical response to that challenge. When, later in that speech, Antonio says that they were preserved

```
              by that destiny, to perform an act
       Whereof what's past is prologue, what to come
       In yours and my discharge
```
(2.1.257–9)

this Sebastian cut through what he plainly considered verbiage by briefly summarizing the facts and thus revealing that he had understood Antonio's drift perfectly:

```
              What stuff is this? How say you?
       'Tis true my brother's daughter's Queen of Tunis;
       So is she heir to Naples; 'twixt which regions
       There is some space.
```
(2.1.259–62)

Basil Henson offered a fresh view of the scene in suggesting that Sebastian was thinking as quickly as Antonio, and probably ahead of him, as their next exchange made clear:

```
ANTONIO             Do you understand me?
SEBASTIAN
   Methinks I do.
ANTONIO            And how does your content
   Tender your own good fortune?
SEBASTIAN                    I remember
   You did supplant your brother Prospero.
```
(2.1.273–6)

The tone of that last speech, Hall said, is "pure Machiavelli"; and with it, this Sebastian sharply indicated that he had realized all along where Antonio's drift was leading, in part because he knew precisely the kind of man he was dealing with. Ken Stott's smiling but equally sharp delivery of the monosyllable "True" which completes Sebastian's line, clinched the point. In Basil Henson's rethinking, Sebastian emerged as a dangerous Machiavellian politician whose "hereditary sloth" (2.1.228) was merely a mask for a lethal intelligence, every inch Antonio's equal. It came as no surprise at the end of the play that these two should remain outside the general reconciliation, nor that Sebastian's "A most high miracle," on realizing that Ferdinand was alive and all hopes of the crown of Naples therefore lost (5.1.180), should become an ironical snarl.

The next court scene (3.3), in which the banquet served by the spirits is broken up by Ariel's apparition as a harpy, marks the next stage of the purgatorial process through which Prospero puts the "three men of sin" [3.3.53]. As in the storm scene, he conjures up a magical (and therefore theatrical) spectacle that will drive them mad. The spirits who bring on the banquet are deceptive in a complicated way: Gonzalo says that although they are of "monstrous shape," yet their "manners are more gentle-kind" than most human beings (3.3.31–2); but this is itself a deception, since they are only being courteous in order to lull the court into a false sense of security, so that Ariel's attack on them as the harpy may have extra impact. The harpy itself is a further deceptive image, a bird of prey with a beautiful woman's face. Its significance is spelled out in *Pericles:*

> Thou art like the harpy,
> Which, to betray, dost, with thine angel face,
> Seize in thine eagle talons.
>
> (Scene 17, 47–9)

Ariel's apparition needs to be terrifying, in order to communicate the ferocity of Prospero's arraignment of the men of sin, and in the process to drive them into madness. It does not take Ariel long to achieve this:

> I have made you mad,
> And even with suchlike valour men hang and drown
> Their proper selves.
>
> (3.3.58–60)

This is, as Hall pointed out, the climax of Alonso's spiritual journey, and he suggested that Alonso's "O, it is monstrous, monstrous!" (3.3.95) should be "a great cry of sheer madness," and that he should exit with the same "frantic gesture" with which the Folio directions to 5.1 specify that he enters in the later scene. Ariel's threat that the madness he inflicts on them will drive them to drown themselves works with Alonso; but the madness drives Sebastian and Antonio, not to repent, but desperately to take on the spirits:

> SEBASTIAN   But one fiend at a time,
>   I'll fight their legions over.
> ANTONIO   I'll be thy second.
>   (3.3.102–3)

The effect of Ariel's "madness" is to make the men of sin a more extreme version of what they were before.

Working on this scene convinced Hall that the spirits and the harpy provide a valuable key to interpreting the play as a whole: "Everything is the opposite of what it seems." It is as if Shakespeare, like Gonzalo in his ideal commonwealth, "would by contraries / Execute all things" (2.1.153–4). The storm and shipwreck turn out to be theatrical illusions: the victims are not drowned, the ship is not split. The shapes in the banquet scene look like predators but are (for a while, at least) civilized; Antonio and Sebastian look civilized but are treacherous killers. Gonzalo, who has beautiful instincts, has soiled his hands as the agent of Prospero's expulsion. Miranda is the obedient daughter who nevertheless quickly disobeys her father in her passion for Ferdinand (3.1.36–7). Caliban looks hideous, but has some of the most beautiful lyrical language. Prospero himself seems contained, but is undergoing a purgatorial crisis. As rehearsals proceeded, Hall was fond of quoting a phrase of Groucho Marx: "the contrary is also true." The play goes wrong, he suggested, when actors pick out only one thing from each scene and go for that. He urged everyone to be continually aware of the opposite of what they were doing. He admitted that this was far from easy, and the difficulties proved to be particularly acute in the so-called clowns' scenes.

THE "CLOWNS"

Much of these scenes consists of sheer comedy of situation, as Hall's first image for Trinculo emphasized: "a court jester stranded incongruously in the middle of a beach." This image of displacement firmly related these scenes to the experience of the court. Stefano, too, is a low comedy echo of the world of political intrigue; with his bullying urge to dominate both Trinculo and Caliban and to "inherit here" (2.2.174), he is a small-scale version of the struggle for inheritance elsewhere. And when Caliban declares his freedom from Prospero by worshipping Stefano, he has obviously exchanged one master for another. But Hall suggested that these scenes represent a different kind of reality from the court. Taking Stefano's claim that he arrived on the island "upon a butt of sack which the sailors heaved o'erboard" (2.2.119–20) and Trinculo's that he "swum ashore . . . like a duck" (2.2.127) at face value, and not as more of Ariel's illusionist tricks, he concluded that their arrival on the island was not part of Prospero's "project." This would make their conspiracy with Caliban more of a threat to Prospero than it might seem, if only because it has an element of the unexpected about it. This is perhaps supported by Ariel's comment on their plot, "This will I tell my master" (3.2.117), as if it were a surprise, whereas Ariel himself creates the conditions for the Antonio/Sebastian conspiracy and intervenes to "keep them [the others] living" on Prospero's instructions, "for else his project dies" (2.1.190–203, 302–4). To draw a distinction between their experience and the court's, their clothes were wet and bedraggled, as the court's were not, and of course they became more so towards the end of the play when Ariel leads them through the mire: they undergo a physical ordeal, whereas the court undergoes a spiritual one.

Their resemblance to, and contrast with, the court has to be made through the broadest of comic routines, and this is where the real difficulty of these scenes lies. Hall agreed with Tim Pigott-Smith, playing Trinculo, that Shakespeare "takes the clown figures and makes them creatures of avarice and greed." Pigott-Smith argued that they had to "create a reality" for the scenes. This is normally a valuable approach to similar scenes elsewhere—to Bottom and the mechanicals, to the villagers in *Love's Labour's Lost*, to Sir Toby and Sir Andrew, and, in the late plays, to the fishermen and brothel-keepers in *Pericles* and to Autolycus. But Trinculo and Stefano seem not to work in quite the same way. To begin with, our sense of reality in those other characters is due in large measure to the way they talk: the characters emerge through the rhythms of their speech. This is even true in *Pericles,* where we are dealing with a reported text, but where the speech rhythms are so strong that they survive the process of being transmitted at one remove: good examples are the rueful tone of the professional man emerging from the Pander's "Neither is our profession any mystery, it's *no calling*" (Scene 16, 36–7) or the Bawd's "What have we to do with Diana?" (Scene 16, 145). But Stefano's and Trinculo's humour depends much less on what they say than on what they do.

These two express themselves primarily through comic, almost pantomimic, routines as old and hoary as their jokes. Hall suggested that it is impossible to get through to what the scenes had to offer until "the mechanics are right": "You're all looking for something more," he said at an early rehearsal, "and there isn't more, at least not at this stage." As in other plays, Shakespeare makes points by means of humour; the difference in this case is that the humour is so much broader here than elsewhere. The breakthrough in their first scene with Caliban, for instance, came with something very simple. All kinds of elaborate routines had been tried out for Caliban and Trinculo in order to create a monster with four legs as they sheltered under the gaberdine, none of them very satisfactory. Then Tony Haygarth, playing Caliban, suddenly hit on a simple solution. As Caliban rose in fear that Stefano was one of Prospero's spirits, and Trinculo rose with him, they created a pantomime horse with the gaberdine, their legs protruding from under it. This extremely basic vaudeville routine provided a perfect focus for all the jokes about four legs in 2.2.56–105. And it worked because it *was* so simple, so basic. That is how these scenes are written.

The kind of humour upon which these scenes depend was aptly caught by an anonymous but astute review of Peter Brook's 1957 production at Stratford-upon-Avon. While enjoying the contrast between Patrick Wymark's rotund, bowler-hatted butler and Clive Revill's lanky jester, this reviewer admitted that he had longed to see Trinculo and Stefano played by Laurel and Hardy: "For years I have hoped that some producer of genius would enable me to hear Mr Hardy, glaring sternly down over his chins, say to Mr Laurel, 'Prithee, do not turn me about. My stomach is *not constant*' or . . . to see Mr Laurel's sad face pucker into tears at the sight of Caliban" (*Leamington Spa Courier,* 16 August 1957). Such broad effects underlie the games Ariel plays with them in their second scene (3.2). For the "Thou liest" routine, in which the invisible Ariel imitates Trinculo's voice and so draws Stefano's wrath upon Trinculo, Hall proposed an elaborate manoeuvre that involved Trinculo himself delivering the various repetitions of "Thou liest" as a ventriloquist, while Ariel glided about in different positions on a flying track above his head. It did not work because it was too sophisticated. Here again is a basic, broad gag. Once Trinculo abandoned the ventriloquism and restored the repeats of "Thou liest" to Ariel, and once Ariel abandoned the flying and simply moved nimbly around the stage behind Trinculo, the gag made its effect on its own basic terms. Once such manoeuvres were in place, other aspects of the scene could be explored.

The first of these is the way in which their drunkenness makes them more like themselves, much as Antonio and Sebastian become more like themselves in the state of madness which Ariel inflicts upon them. Trinculo is nastier but also more craven, Stefano more anarchic and megalomaniac, Caliban more brutally violent. But Caliban is also of course more complicated than the other two. Amidst their prose, his verse lines stand out:

> I'll yield him thee asleep
> Where thou mayst knock a nail into his head.
> (3.2.61–2)

That second line, as Hall pointed out, is a perfect blank verse line which expresses great brutality, and Tony Haygarth caught it exactly. The combination of brutish impulse and noble expression (especially by contrast with the other two) is a good example of the contrasts or contradictions inherent in the play, here caught in a single line. This tendency is developed in Caliban's celebrated speech about the "sounds, and sweet airs" of the island (3.2.138–46).

Hall was not slow to point out that it is typical of the play—"the contrary is also true"—that having been lulled to sleep by the sounds and sweet airs, and then woken up, he "cried to dream again" in part because of the other kind of reality he faced when awake, in the form of torments from Prospero's spirits. So the lyrical speech leads back to Caliban's murderous plan: Stefano will have his music for nothing only "when Prospero is destroyed."

The dramatic context in which Shakespeare places famous set-pieces like this must always be carefully considered, since it often radically affects how the audience takes them. The context of Caliban's speech raises various issues. The reaction to the music that Ariel provides is crucial. At first, Stefano and Trinculo are terrified by it, and Hall suggested to Tony Haygarth that he might turn Caliban's question "Art thou afeard?" to imply that if Stefano wants to be king of the island, he shouldn't start by being afraid of it. Like John Hirsch's treatment at Stratford, Ontario, in 1982, this focused upon the contrast between Stefano's pretensions and his cowardice. Hirsch took this further than Hall in having Nicholas Pennell's strikingly vivid, homicidal bully of a Stefano collapse in gibbering terror, so that Caliban had to comfort him with "Be not afeard. The isle is full of noises," thus absolutely integrating the set-piece into the scene. On the other hand, Hall's version made a telling point about their changing response to the music. After listening to Caliban's explanation about the sounds and sweet airs, they became entranced by the music, so that Ariel could lead them away from the cell—into the mire. Once again, contraries prevail: the music is at first frightening, then soothing, then deceptive.

In their reaction to the music, this version touched upon something more fully explored in Giorgio Strehler's Piccolo Teatro version. Perhaps because the humour of these scenes is not primarily verbal, this version in Italian translation made some particularly telling points. The routines (and the costumes) were based on those of the *commedia dell'arte,* or at least what a modern Italian director took that to have been like. They were much less inhibited than any other Stefano and Trinculo I have seen; they roared, they crashed noisily around the stage, they strutted and bellowed, and they certainly set their Italian audiences on a roar. This had its drawbacks—it seemed to go on for ever—but its advantages too. It served to emphasize how these scenes are constructed around traditional theatrical routines; but it also provided one superb moment of contrast. Ariel, played by an actress in a white skull cap, white face make-up, and billowing, shapeless white costume, was a still more androgynous figure than the Ariel of Hall's production with his figure-hugging body-stocking. And since she was in part a *commedia dell'arte* figure herself, she was able to enter the routines of these *commedia* clowns with unusual abandon. But when she delicately played the tune of their catch on her tabor, Caliban stretched out luxuriously at full length on the floor to enjoy the music, and the clowns sat slumped in a maudlin alcoholic stupor: a strange harmony took over the stage, from which these lumbering *commedia* drunks were not excluded.

Strehler, then, brought out a harmony underlying the crude routines, Hirsch the political menace beneath them. Hall's version touched on both, but did not take the scenes so fully in either direction, perhaps because of his concern not to seize upon any one aspect of a scene to the exclusion of others, but to keep the contrasts as visible as possible. If his staging of 3.2 was less decisive than either Hirsch's or Strehler's, it succeeded in catching the contradictions of a trio of characters who are at once an "act" and a threat to Prospero. Perhaps the most memorable moment of these scenes occurred as Trinculo was about to shelter under Caliban's gaberdine. Tim Pigott-Smith made it clear exactly what kind of humour we were dealing with as he shot an indignant glance at the audience and excused his conduct in the affronted tones of a Frankie Howerd: "there is no other shelter hereabout!" Then, as he snuggled down beside Caliban, he again looked the audience straight in the eye to observe: "Misery acquaints a man with strange bedfellows" (2.2.38–9). In the context of this season, it was impossible not to think of Innogen waking beside Cloten's corpse and recoiling with "soft, no bedfellow!" (*Cymbeline*, 4.2.297). These plays exploit the varied potential of extreme situations within each play and within the group.

THE SPIRITS AND THE MASQUE

Prospero tells Ferdinand that the masque represents his "present fancies," enacted by spirits (4.1.120–2). Ariel and his "meaner ministers" (3.3.87) are at once the executants of his magic and the externalization of what he imagines. As Hall put it, "when he imagines Juno, or a rainbow, these appear as he imagines them," embodied by the spirits. And apart from Ariel, these spirits have no independent theatrical life in the text except when they are playing monstrous shapes, or goddesses, or dogs pursuing Caliban, Stefano, and Trinculo. But since they are the embodiment of Prospero's "rough magic," a way has to be found to present them in convincing theatrical terms, as Hall pointed out at the introductory session. He did not, however, discover how to do this until well into the rehearsal period.

What seemed to me one of the two major breakthroughs of this interpretation of *The Tempest* occurred while Hall was considering how to present the masque. As in all the major developments of this rehearsal period, it happened suddenly and was then rapidly developed at that and subsequent rehearsals. Seven years earlier, Hall had directed Britten's operatic version of *A Midsummer Night's Dream* at Glyndebourne. In Britten's opera, even more than in Shakespeare's play, the wood is a living presence: where Shakespeare achieves this effect in the vividly evocative language, Britten has composed an introduction and interludes in which orchestral sighs and breaths suggest that the wood is alive. Hall had paralleled this in movement: a group of actors with branches, leaves, and bark attached to their black body-stockings animated the bushes, trees, and logs of the wood, so that it moved mysteriously in the moonlight to the sighing phrases, and reformed to provide a different framework for each scene. Apart from these "tree people," there was no other woodland setting: the actors created the wood. And it was this fact which made Hall realize that not only the spirits, but the island itself, could be animated like the wood in *A Midsummer Night's Dream*. He therefore arranged that a group of actors playing the spirits should appear at the first entry of Ariel, linked to him visually in their sand-coloured body-stockings, so that as they stood, sat, or sprawled around the edge of the sandy circle, they would appear to be of its element, to grow as it were out of the island. Unlike Ariel, however, they wore fencing masks so as to appear faceless: amorphous natural forces, only taking specific shape when they became theatrical embodiments of Prospero's art, playing goddesses, nymphs, reapers, or hounds.

Their first appearance quickly established their double function: at the same time, they reflected the natural forces of the island and Prospero's varying moods. When he turned on the rebellious Ariel and reminded him of his servitude under Sycorax, they shrank away, recoiling still further at the mention of the "cloven pine" in which she had imprisoned him. On the other hand, when Ariel submitted and asked "Say what, what shall I do?" (1.2.302), they all gathered round Prospero, ready for the next job. That was to lead Ferdinand to Miranda, a task they entered into with zest, providing a choral background to Ariel's songs, and miming the watchdogs and strutting cockerels of the first song. Their contributions continually edged the sense of the lines: there was something disturbing about their barking and crowing in that song which prepared for the ambiguous way in which the second song, "Full fathom five," at once consoles Ferdinand and keeps his wounds open. And when Ferdinand drew his sword on Prospero, they simply weighted down his arm like lead with a gesture, palpable instruments of Prospero's control.

Hall proposed that after their initial appearance, they should be introduced into every scene and then, by trial and error, be "weeded out" of those episodes in which they were unnecessary or intrusive. Their presence or absence, for instance, helped to point the extent of Prospero's control over the two conspiracies. As representatives of the island, they watched over the arrival of the court in 2.1, their shifting presence usefully underlining the ambiguities of the lords' dispute about the appearance of the island (2.1.57–60). They helped Ariel put the court to sleep; and the fact that they left Antonio and Sebastian awake established beyond doubt that this conspiracy was part of Prospero's "project." By contrast, since Hall believed that the arrival of Stefano and Trinculo on the island is something outside Prospero's plan, and that their conspiracy with Caliban releases a dangerously anarchic threat to Prospero which spirits representing his power would keep under control, the spirits did not appear in those scenes; the island itself is in any case vividly evoked there by the speeches of Caliban.

Hall's method of showing a group of faceless shapes gradually assuming the specific form of goddesses, nymphs, or dogs reinforced Shakespeare's dramatization of Prospero's magic power as a series of theatrical shows. Prospero's comment on the performance of Ariel and the spirits in presenting the deceptive banquet and the harpy is:

> Of my instruction hast thou nothing bated
> In what thou hadst to say. So with good life
> And observation strange my meaner ministers
> Their several kinds have done.
>
> (3.3.85–8)

A key phrase here is that what Ariel "had to say" was of Prospero's "instruction," which may imply that Prospero actually wrote Ariel's speech as the harpy. It certainly sounds like Prospero. His role as author/director is emphasized by the Folio's stage direction that places him *on the top,* overlooking the action, *invisible* to the other people on stage but visible to the audience. Hall placed Michael Bryant at the highest point of this stage, on the roof of the cell, not only here but in the masque as well; for a key to its interpretation is that, like the harpy's speech, it is almost certainly of Prospero's composition and unmistakably represents his own views, his "present fancies." Bryant edged the point by mouthing important phrases with the performing spirits.

This fact helps to explain one of the most puzzling features of the play, the curious language of the masque. For a celebration of a wedding, there is a surprising amount of emphasis in its first speech upon coldness, chastity, disappointed love, and even sterility. Iris summons Ceres not just from "thy rich leas" but also from:

> Thy banks with peonied and twillèd brims
> Which *spongy* April at thy hest betrims
> To make *cold* nymphs *chaste* crowns; and thy broom-groves,
> Whose shadow the *dismissèd* bachelor loves,
> Being *lass-lorn;* thy pole-clipped vineyard,
> And thy sea-marge, *sterile* and rocky-hard.
>
> (4.1.64–9)

Moreover the celebrations break off in the middle for a curious episode about Venus and Cupid plotting "some wanton charm" against the betrothed couple. It seems certain that these features of the masque reflect Prospero's obsessions, his ambiguous attitude to the marriage itself and to the bridegroom, and his reiterated concern for Miranda's chastity. The contradictions within him emerge powerfully in one astonishing speech to Ferdinand before the masque, a blessing which is almost a curse—he does and does not want to lose his daughter to the son of his enemy:

> Then, as my gift and thine own acquisition
> Worthily purchased, take my daughter. But—

The line ending there serves to emphasize Prospero's reservation even in the act of giving away his daughter, and the language becomes darker and more intense:

> If thou dost break her virgin-knot before
> All sanctimonious ceremonies may
> With full and holy rite be ministered,
> No sweet aspersion shall the heavens let fall
> To make this contract grow; but *barren hate,*
> *Sour-eyed disdain,* and *discord,* shall bestrew
> The union of your bed with weeds so *loathly*
> That you shall hate it both.
>
> (4.1.13–22)

It is scarcely an auspicious blessing; and it draws corresponding language from Ferdinand:

> the murkiest den,
> The most opportune place, the strong'st suggestion
> Our worser genius can, shall never melt
> Mine honour into lust . . .
>
> (4.1.25–8)

Perhaps, in echoing Prospero's tone so exactly, Ferdinand is indignantly refuting his suggestions; or perhaps, courtier-like, he is using Prospero's own language to tell him what he wants to hear. The wedding masque which Prospero imagines inevitably contains an extended allusion to the destructive sexuality upon which he so harps, in the episode of Venus and Cupid.

To grasp why the masque is written as it is does not, however, make it any easier to stage. It would be much less of a problem if its language were simpler and more uniform, if it were a simple celebration. The difficulty is to make the words, and Prospero's sentiments which they express, clear. Many approaches have been tried: sometimes the masque has been largely spoken, sometimes wholly sung, sometimes delivered in a kind of quasi-recitative. Hall asked for it to be sung with much emphasis on the rhythm, "on the pulse," and speeded up "with the speed of dreams" in the same rapid way that the apparitions' speeches in *Cymbeline* had been delivered. As in that scene, the delivery was often too rapid to allow the actors to come to grips with the peculiarities of the language, or the audience to hear the words clearly. The rhythm slowed down, with sinister accompaniment, as Ceres introduced the topic of Venus and Cupid (4.1.86), and this was one of the places where Michael Bryant mouthed the words with the spirit-actors, in order to mark this passage as of particular importance to him. But none of these devices made the sense, and therefore the significance, much clearer.

The difficulty is compounded by a staging problem during the Venus/ Cupid section. At 4.1.72, the Folio text has the direction *"Juno descends,"* and Iris' phrase "Her peacocks fly amain" two lines later may—but need not— imply that she is visible at this point. In his text for the Oxford *Complete Works,* John Jowett alters the Folio direction to *"Juno appears in the air."* He believes that the original direction indicates a floating appearance, but not yet a descent, Juno hovering over the action: as goddess of marriage, she waits for assurance that her rival Venus, goddess of love, is not in the vicinity before completing her descent, at 4.1.101, when Ceres says "Highest queen of state, / Great Juno, comes." This is possible, and if handled with extreme care, it might help to clar- ify the sense and function of the Venus/Cupid episode. But to have Juno sway- ing about up there for nearly thirty lines is more likely to distract completely from the speeches, thus sacrificing any hope that the audience will get the point of the episode. I must admit, however, that I have never seen any production that communicated the sense of the Venus/Cupid passage, and I have some sympathy with those directors who simply omit it, as John Hirsch did at Strat- ford, Ontario, in 1982, the staging which in other respects was the only one in my experience to make dramatic sense of the masque, as described in my open- ing chapter. Hall assumed that the Folio's direction for Juno's descent is in the wrong place, and flew her down just before "Great Juno comes"; a trumpet fan- fare accompanied her as she descended and alighted from her car in time for Ceres to say "I know her by her gait" (4.1.102). She subsequently flew back up, remaining in mid-air to supervise the dance of nymphs and reapers.

Hall used this dance to differentiate between Ferdinand's experience and Miranda's inexperience: he, knowing what a court masque was, led her into the circle of sand to dance with the spirits; she had to pick up the dance and the style from his example, using her own instinctive grace to do so. As the movements of all the dancers became hotter and more sexually charged, Pros- pero became increasingly agitated; and when he finally broke up the dance, Shakespeare's—or Ralph Crane's—direction *"To a strange, hollow, and confused noise, they heavily vanish"* was interpreted as a cry of great disappointment from the spirits that they could not carry their theatrical performance to its logical conclusion. This interruption is of course a complex moment. It reflects Pros- pero's fury at remembering the "foul conspiracy / Of the beast Caliban" (4.1.139–40), and there was a strong suggestion that, once more, Prospero is linking the "libidinousness" of Caliban with—is perhaps reminded of it by— that of Ferdinand. Another factor considered at rehearsal was that Prospero, absorbed in the delights of his masque, suddenly becomes aware of a replay of the past: once again, he almost falls victim to a conspiracy by becoming "rapt in secret studies," or at least in the artistic consequences of those studies.

The tension between his magic power and his realization that it cannot enable him to change the natures of those who conspire against him leads directly into the celebrated speech beginning "Our revels now are ended" (4.1.148–63). As he had done with Caliban's "The isle is full of noises," Hall stressed the context of the set-piece. It is not simply a generalized lament for the passing of things, as it can seem to be when quoted out of context. Its mood is sharply focused by the lines which end it:

> Sir, I am vexed.
> Bear with my weakness. My old brain is troubled.
> Be not disturbed with my infirmity.
> . . . .
> A turn or two I'll walk
> To still my beating mind.
>
> (4.1.158–63)

The whole passage is dominated by his turbulent response to Caliban, and in this speech his thoughts about the passing of things are clearly coloured by his disillusion with a magic which enables him to conjure up theatrical spectacles but not to alter, or even radically affect, the impulses and desires of the human heart. Michael Bryant caught this disillusioned tone, and so prepared the way for Prospero's rejection of his "rough magic" in his next scene. He established a definite connection between the two speeches.

Between the two comes the episode in which Prospero and Ariel hunt Caliban, Stefano, and Trinculo "even to roaring" (4.1.193). The disturbance underlying the "revels" speech intensifies in this episode. Why is Prospero so enraged with Caliban? Partly because whatever the power of his magic, it cannot change him: he remains, for Prospero,

> A devil, a born devil, on whose nature
> Nurture can never stick; on whom my pains,
> Humanely taken, all, all lost, quite lost
>
> (4.1.188–90)

but partly because he sees in Caliban the dark, potentially violent and uncontrolled side of himself, as he admits near the end of the play, where "This thing of darkness I / Acknowledge mine" (5.1.278–9) seems more than a simple identification of Caliban and himself as servant and master. Hall thought it essential to build up the level of intensity during this sequence. The temperature is certainly maintained by the turbulent language with which Ariel describes the three conspirators—

> I told you, sir, they were red-hot with drinking;
> So full of valour that they smote the air
> For breathing in their faces, beat the ground
> For kissing of their feet—

and by the vividness with which he suggests their animal natures:

> Then I beat my tabor,
> At which like unbacked colts they pricked their ears,
> Advanced their eyelids, lifted up their noses
> As they smelt music.
>
> (4.1.171–8)

And when Ariel says that they were "always bending / Towards their project" (4.1.174–5), his use of "project," the word Prospero himself has used and will use again in the first line of the next scene to describe his own activities, is surely deliberately provocative: Ariel is spurring him on to vengeance against Caliban, providing him with a genuine temptation to take a violent revenge and so to risk reducing himself to Caliban's level. And Prospero does not resist the temptation: his hunting of these conspirators with hounds is a physical equivalent of his driving those other three conspirators, the "men of sin," to madness. Hall used the spirits to emphasize this: they played the dogs, of course, wearing huge masks, especially sinister in the tense pause as they stood straining at their leashes, before Prospero and Ariel released them to pursue the hapless conspirators through the audience. The moment had been still more effective in rehearsal, when the actors playing the spirits gave an uncanny impersonation of hounds scenting their prey, backs erect, nostrils flared. The violent image of Prospero *hunting* the three conspirators is crucial at this point in the play, and is emphasized by the violence of the language:

> Go, charge my goblins that they grind their joints
> With dry convulsions, shorten up their sinews
> With agèd cramps, and more pinch-spotted make them
> Than pard or cat o'mountain.
> . . . .
> Let them be hunted soundly. At this hour
> Lies at my mercy all mine enemies.
>
> (4.1.256–61)

The transition in those last two lines from these to his other enemies underlines the point of the episode: the more intensely Prospero is seen to pursue a savage vengeance on Caliban, and the more excited he seems by it, the more revenge on his other enemies remains a real possibility as the play moves into the final scene and the climax and crisis of Prospero's career.

FROM ROUGH MAGIC TO HEAVENLY MUSIC

The final scene begins with a crucial exchange for Prospero and Ariel (5.1.1–32) which balances, in important respects, the exchange between the two of them in the previous scene (4.1.164–87). Ariel, especially, has two balanced speeches describing Prospero's two sets of victims, and the language of the second one, though less turbulent, is equally vivid. Having wound Prospero up to revenge in the previous speech, Ariel now shifts to a new tactic, bringing him to face fully what he has done to his enemies in driving them to madness, and hinting at the possibility of forgiving them. He does this by describing Gonzalo's grief in an image from the natural world as vivid as that of the colts in his earlier speech:

> His tears run down his beard like winter's drops
> From eaves of reeds.

The image leads straight into the crucial point Ariel has to make:

> Your charm so strongly works 'em
> That if you now beheld them your affections
> Would become tender.
> PROSPERO   Dost thou think, so, spirit?
> ARIEL
> Mine would, sir, were I human.
>
> (5.1.16–20)

This is, of course, one of the great moments of the play, as the non-human spirit confronts the human being who is faced with the temptation of being inhuman, and Ariels usually make the most of it. The moment was especially affecting in Giorgio Strehler's Milan version, coming from one who was quite remote from human experience, dangling puppet-like, half androgyne, half pierrot, on a flying wire.

As Steven Mackintosh in Hall's version spoke of "the good old lord Gonzalo," Michael Bryant was recalled to humanity by Gonzalo's own humanity to himself in the past: he beautifully suggested how near he had been to revenge, and to forgetting his debt to Gonzalo, by the simple device of passing his hand, dazed, across his eyes. The ensuing choice of virtue over vengeance was, however, no easy matter, the more so because the vengeful hunting of Caliban had been so uncompromisingly presented. "You needed that hunt," Hall said to Bryant, who proceeded to think his way through the speech to his decision. There was no skimping the still-lingering resentment of "Though with their high wrongs I am struck to th'quick," but the next lines were simple, measured, and above all devoid of any hint of the smug or the sentimental:

> Yet with my nobler reason 'gainst my fury
> Do I take part. The rarer action is
> In virtue than in vengeance.
>
> (5.1.25–8)

Yet there is irony in his next phrase. "They being penitent" is a large assumption, and his decision to forgive them is triggered by Ariel's description of Gonzalo, where penitence is not an issue. Prospero's final line expresses more truth than he is himself aware of: "they shall be themselves." Antonio and Sebastian prove, indeed, to be more "themselves" after the madness Prospero has put them through. Perhaps, too, Prospero will be as much himself as they themselves: forgiving, yes, but finding it a terrible struggle. He is certainly not transformed overnight by Ariel's prompting, any more than Posthumus and Leontes are. Repentance and reconciliation are difficult processes that take time; they are as hard-won here as in the other two plays; and "affliction" has as great a part to play here as there. Prospero refers in this speech to the "afflictions" of his victims (5.1.22); but the process they are undergoing parallels his own—and that in turn connects with Posthumus, "happier much by his affliction made" in *Cymbeline* (5.5.202), and Leontes, who feels that the "affliction" of beholding Hermione's statue "has a taste as sweet / As any cordial comfort" (*The Winter's Tale*, 5.3.76–7). Prospero now takes the decisive step of identifying and renouncing one of the causes of his affliction.

The first danger in delivering Prospero's renunciation of his magic (5.1.33–57) is generalization. It easily becomes a set-piece, a sequence of familiar, resonant phrases, from which the audience receives only a general impression of grandeur, rather than responding to the sense of the very specific details which build up to the renunciation, and explain it. But Hall's production, having created a group of spirits who embodied Prospero's magic power, could now use them to focus the detail of this passage in which he renounces it. As Prospero began his speech, they all gathered around the perimeter of the circle, and Michael Bryant addressed "Ye elves of hills" directly to them. By this means, the speech grew directly out of the scene, and more generally out of the action of the play. It was spoken to specific things. One of the points that this served to reinforce was the collaboration between Prospero and the spirits, "by whose aid, / Weak masters though ye be," Prospero has worked the magic: they are weak in themselves, but powerful when harnessed to his art (5.1.40–1).

They are also spirits of darkness, rejoicing to hear the curfew that heralds it, and creating the "sour" circles of grass that animals avoid and mushrooms that spring up overnight (5.1.36–40). Gradually the speech intensifies from these touches of the unpleasant and the mildly sinister to revelations of wholesale violence and destruction. The collaboration between Prospero and the spirits has eclipsed the sun, raised a tempest, split oaks with lightning, made the coastline tremble, uprooted trees. While the hypnotic rhythms express the awesomeness of all this, phrases drawn from rebellion and war emphasize the violence of these events:

> I have bedimmed
> The noontide sun, called forth the *mutinous* winds,

> And 'twixt the green sea and the azured vault
> Set *roaring war*—to the *dread rattling* thunder
> Have I given fire, and *rifted* Jove's stout oak
> With his own bolt; the strong-based promontory
> Have I made shake, and by the spurs *plucked up*
> The pine and cedar . . .
>
> (5.1.41–8)

What is most striking about this list is that there is not a single positive achievement mentioned; when Prospero characterizes this power as "*rough magic*" (5.1.50), the description is in one way a literal one.

But "rough" implies more than that. The climax to which this series of acts leads is a terrifying revelation:

> graves at my command
> Have waked their sleepers, oped, and let 'em forth
> By my so potent art.
>
> (5.1.48–50)

In resurrecting the dead, Hall emphasized, Prospero has been "playing God." Marlowe's *Dr. Faustus* seems to have provided Shakespeare with a model for some aspects of Prospero, and was an insistent presence during these rehearsals, especially in this scene. Faustus sets out to gain "a deity" through black magic; he rejects the study of medicine in his first speech because it does not enable him to "raise [men] to life again"; but his magic does not enable him to do that either: the Alexander the Great and Helen of Troy that he conjures up are not the real Alexander or Helen, but illusions acted out by devils. Faustus challenges God through his necromancy but does not succeed in usurping God's prerogative of resurrecting the dead. But insofar as Prospero has succeeded in doing this, he has been "playing God" in a much more far-reaching and dangerous sense. All this seems to underlie the phrase "rough magic."

But there is more. If Faustus provided one model for Prospero, the sorceress Medea in Ovid's *Metamorphoses* provided another, for many of the details of Prospero's renunciation speech are derived from her invocation in Ovid's Book 7, 179–219, including the detail of bringing back the dead. Shakespeare drew on sources with sinister associations for this moment when Prospero comes nearest to specifying the sources of his magic power, and the kind of magic it is. But it is characteristic of the reticence of this play in yielding its secrets that Shakespeare should imply but not explicitly state that Prospero's art is black magic. The source in Ovid merely confirms what the language suggests, that the magic has a terrifying power; in raising the dead Prospero has encroached upon God's territory, as he has also done in attempting to change the natures of Caliban, Alonso, and Antonio, by hunting them or driving them into madness. That is why it is important not to underplay the savagery of these processes, or Prospero's turbulent agitation about them. The temptation to be inhuman is not simply to take revenge upon his enemies, but to go further along the road of trying to change them. It is not surprising that he should call such activity a "rough magic"; and if, as seems the inevitable conclusion, he has challenged God's authority in raising the dead, then God has much to forgive him for.

That is the force of the contrast between the "rough magic" which he renounces and the "heavenly music" which he asks for (5.1.50–2). It was in interpreting this climactic moment that, for me, the other main breakthrough of Hall's *Tempest* rehearsals occurred. I had always carelessly assumed that "heavenly" here was a figurative rather than a literal expression, implying harmony and healing to contrast with the "rough" images of destruction, and that it was something which Prospero himself could create through his magic art. But at the second rehearsal of this scene, Hall suddenly suggested that when Prospero says he needs "heavenly" music, he is being very specific: "he prays, asks forgiveness of God" for his indulging in "rough magic"; he promises to break his staff and drown his book, then "waits for the music which will signal God's forgiveness, and eventually receives it" in the following stage direction, "*solemn music.*" The suggestion that the music is literally from heaven transforms the scene. It is also, I think, quite original. I cannot recall seeing it suggested either in criticism or in a previous performance.

Having hit on the point, Hall then worked on the scene with Michael Bryant in order to explore its implications to the full, with regard both to the gravity of the "rough magic" and to the contrasting connotations of the "heavenly music." At first, Bryant simply delivered "graves at my command" sombrely; but as he realized the full implications of this revelation, he paused in mid-line before "graves" and turned away, his hand across his mouth, unable to pronounce the word, shutting out the awful spectacle. The phrase began to express a major crisis for Prospero: he thus acknowledged his extreme act of *hubris* in "playing God" in this way, and asked for forgiveness. To match the gravity of the fault, the forgiveness was slow in coming. After "I'll drown my book" (5.1.57), he knelt in prayer, a penitent. In the long silence that followed, Bryant assumed that his fault was not to be pardoned (a very Faustian moment), and bowed his head in despair. Then, very quietly, music sounded. Bryant slowly raised his head, hardly daring to believe it, relief flooding his face; and, keeping his contract with God to renounce his magic, he snapped his staff in two and threw the two pieces into the sand. As the music grew in intensity and the court appeared, two of the spirits slipped across the sand, retrieved the broken pieces, and vanished away with them. All the other spirits finally disappeared at this point too, a concrete image of the departing of Prospero's magic power.

This interpretation of the "heavenly music" fits the text astonishingly well, and has some far-reaching consequences. The first is that if *The Tempest* is about forgiveness, then Prospero needs to receive it as much as to give it; and having been forgiven himself, he is the readier to forgive others. It seemed to provide a "warming" of the play such as I have not encountered in other versions. The only textual objection is that if Prospero so decisively renounces his magic and breaks his staff at this moment, then technically his ability to control Ariel ceases. It means, therefore, that Ariel must carry out his remaining duties voluntarily, and that Prospero's final liberating of him (5.1.322) is a formality. This proved to present no difficulties, and indeed had several advantages. Their relationship throughout the play is a mixture of tension and affection; now, with his freedom in sight, it is the affection that is uppermost in Ariel's behaviour, marked here by the enthusiasm and gaiety with which Steven Mackintosh infused

> I drink the air before me, and return
> Or ere your pulse twice beat
> (5.1.104–5)

which suggested that Ariel was enjoying his last co-operation with Prospero. Everything fitted the interpretation easily, especially the lines which describe the court emerging from the madness imposed by Prospero's magic:

> The charm dissolves apace,
> And as the morning steals upon the night,
> Melting the darkness, so their rising senses
> Begin to chase the ignorant fumes that mantle
> Their clearer reason.
> (5.1.64–8)

These lines make even better sense as a description of people gradually emerging from the influence of a magic power which has been completely destroyed than they do if taken as Prospero's replacement of one magic spell with another, which is what is involved if the "heavenly music" is taken to be a description of something that his spirits can provide.

As the court entered, they were frozen in typical poses which revealed, in distorted form, their essential characters, no longer concealed partially or wholly behind masks. Alonso was still arrested in the "frantic gesture" he had adopted as he left the stage after Ariel's accusations as the harpy in 3.3; the faces of Antonio and Sebastian were twisted into grimaces of rage and frustration, as when they resolved to attack the fiends, also at the end of 3.3; even Gonzalo's tears and Adrian's and Francisco's gestures of solicitation were frozen, caught *in extremis*. The effect of the magic was not to change them but to make them all more like themselves; and as the charm wore off, they gradually returned to "normal" versions of themselves. Although Alonso was repentant, it was really Prospero himself who had changed most, through the influence of the heavenly music. Bryant was like a man emerging from a purgatorial process of his own creation, from whose shoulders the great weight of the magic had been lifted. He was noticeably lighter, quicker, more genial in his exchanges with the court than he had been at any point in the play.

Even so, as elsewhere in the late plays, the change is not achieved all at once; a sense of the magic and of its dark characteristics, communicated by Prospero's speech of renunciation, still hangs over the final scene, and something of the old antagonism colours Prospero's forgiveness, as the lines themselves suggest. If Antonio and Sebastian remain unrepentant, his attitude towards them hardly encourages them to behave otherwise:

> But you, my brace of lords, were I so minded,
> I here could pluck his highness' frown upon you
> And justify you traitors. At this time
> I will tell no tales.
>
> (5.1.128–31)

Sebastian's reply "The devil speaks in him" is an exaggeration, but in view of what Prospero has told us about his magic, it is not entirely wide of the mark; and Prospero responds only with a clipped "No": it is safest not to go into further detail. His speech of forgiveness to Antonio—

> For you, most wicked sir, whom to call brother
> Would even *infect* my mouth, I do forgive
> Thy *rankest* fault, all of them—
>
> (5.1.132–4)

suggests a man scarcely able to overcome a great weight of resentment even in the act of forgiveness. Michael Bryant had no difficulty with this speech. Having gone from an extreme of violent rage in the dogs scene, through an admission of the activities of his magic art, to repentance and the experience of forgiveness, all within a short space of time, it seemed only natural that forgiving Antonio should cost him a great deal. The whiff of rough magic haunts Alonso's suspicious questions during the scene:

> This is as strange a maze as e'er men trod,
> And there is in this business more than nature
> Was ever conduct of.
>
> (5.1.245–7)

Prospero's reply is evasive; he does not intend to explain himself, nor to allow others to travel down the dangerous road from which he himself has drawn back:

> At picked leisure,
> Which shall be shortly, single I'll resolve you,

> Which to you shall seem probable, of every
> These happened accidents.
>
> (5.1.250–3)

The phrase "which to you shall seem probable" suggests that he will invent a plausible fiction to satisfy their curiosity.

It has often been pointed out that the language turns Prospero's epilogue into far more than a conventional plea for applause, especially in the phrasing of

> my ending is despair
> Unless I be relieved by prayer.
> (Epilogue, 15–16)

"Despair" is a strong word, and in this interpretation it was illuminated by the way the heavenly music had been taken earlier. During the long wait for the music to sound, this Prospero was brought to the verge of despair. In the epilogue, the word once again raises the associations of *Faustus*. Despair is the gravest of the sins because it denies the possibility of God's forgiveness; Faustus refuses to repent because he thinks, with typical *hubris*, that his sins are so great that he has placed himself beyond God's forgiveness. But in Prospero's epilogue, the danger of despair is to be avoided, not by applause, but by prayer; so the last moments of the play keep the tension between "rough magic" and "heavenly music" before us: Prospero has been granted forgiveness, but the dark shadow of the magic, and the cost of exercising it, cannot be easily shrugged off and forgotten. In putting Prospero through a purgatory that brings him close to despair, *The Tempest* mirrors the purgatorial journeys of the other late plays, Innogen's despair beside Cloten's body and Posthumus' nihilistic searching for death in *Cymbeline*, Paulina urging Leontes to "nothing but despair" in *The Winter's Tale* [3.2.209], Pericles' state of demoralization from which Marina rescues him with such difficulty. But all these characters rise from the depths of their despair with more confidence and hope than Prospero seems able to achieve.

AFTERWORD: PERFORMANCE

Of the two major discoveries in this staging of *The Tempest*, the sounding of the heavenly music was the more striking in performance. The pause as Prospero waited for it to sound was prolonged to an almost unbearable length; Prospero's potential despair seemed fully justified, and Michael Bryant had plenty of time in which to express it. But then the emblematic heavens tilted, a blinding light shone through them, and Monteverdian trumpets brilliantly announced God's forgiveness of Prospero. Most reviewers took the point, and Michael Billington usefully related the moment to Bryant's performance as a whole: this Prospero

> is almost a Mediterranean Faust. The concept is not wholly original . . . but Bryant pushes the idea much further than anyone I have seen. From the first scene with Miranda it is clear that this Prospero has spent twelve years simmering with rage at his usurpation. . . . But Bryant's wry chuckle at the mention of the noble Neapolitan, Gonzalo, hints that his humanity is not quite dead. . . . When Bryant comes to the celebrated abjuration of his powers he stops dead in his tracks on "graves at my command / Have waked their sleepers, oped, and let 'em forth" as if confronting the fact that he has been practising the blackest of magic. The conjuration of heavenly music . . . thus becomes an urgent plea from a man who has been dabbling in Satanism. (*Guardian*, 21 May 1988)

And the brilliant embodiment of the heavenly music was of course the kind of effect that gained rather than lost impact in the transfer to the larger Olivier stage.

The other major discovery of the rehearsals, the physical representation of the magic and the island by the spirits, was less decisively executed, so that it seemed less significant in performance than it had done in rehearsal. When the spirits were simply dressed in their sand-coloured body-stockings and could use their considerable skills as mimes to suggest dogs or strutting Chanticleer, the impression of the magic was strong. But when Ariel was laden down with wigs, masks, dresses, and even plastic breasts as the sea-nymph, the harpy, or the goddess Ceres, or when Iris, Juno, and the nymphs and reapers were buried beneath classical costumes and impassively staring full masks, the impression of potent magic evaporated, and the production began to seem decorative in the manner of those traditional stagings which Hall had specifically sought to avoid. As in the apparitions scene in *Cymbeline,* the expressionless masks and classical disguises were not only a barrier to clarity and communication, they also clashed with the fastidiously Caroline costumes and sets. These supernatural figures might well have been modelled instead upon the seventeenth-century-style deities who flew in and out of Peter Hall's magnificent stagings of Monteverdi and Cavalli operas at Glyndebourne. However that may be, *The Tempest,* like the other two productions, was interestingly weakest and had least illumination to offer at those very places which have led commentators to argue that these are specifically Blackfriars plays.

By contrast, the clash of personal and political interests in the first court scene, which had been slowly but surely unearthed during the rehearsals, grew and blossomed in performance. The stale witticisms actually seemed funny when bounced off contrasting personalities. A remarkable effect in the later performances, when the personalities were really sharpened, and the

timing and rhythm firmly settled, was the extraordinary amount of spontaneous audience reaction to Gonzalo's garrulity: remarks like Sebastian's "He
will be talking" (2.1.29) drew gales of laughter such as I have never known in
other performances of these scenes. The explanation, I think, is that the
laughter comes when the characterization is sharply focused, as it certainly
was in the case of Tony Church's and Basil Henson's exceptionally vivid
accounts of Gonzalo and Sebastian. The first court scene in particular continued to grow in the large spaces of the Olivier theatre; and it emphasized that
the chief illumination provided by this late Shakespeare season was of the personal and political issues of the plays.

In my introductory chapter, I said that the earlier production of *The Tempest* which kept coming to mind during the National Theatre rehearsals was
Clifford Williams's at Stratford-upon-Avon in 1963. It did so even more insistently in the Olivier performances. Its central feature was a sour, censorious
Prospero from Tom Fleming. This made an even more decisive break with the
serene enchanter of stage tradition than John Gielgud's in the 1957 Stratford
production by Peter Brook, who collaborated with Clifford Williams on the
1963 version, and it was the performance which most anticipated Michael
Bryant's in 1988. Both Fleming and Bryant adopted a lynx-eyed approach to
the language, avoiding generalization and attempting to present it as specifically as possible. Most reviewers admitted that Fleming's performance came
as a shock, but several found it a salutary one. Philip Hope-Wallace, for
instance, wrote that Fleming made "the character unusually interesting up to
and including the point where he must choose virtue and not vengeance; but
at that point the last expansion of spirit which would mark the interpretation
of a really great Prospero seemed to escape his grasp, and at once the [final]
scene seemed unimportant as a sequel" (*Guardian,* 3 April 1963).

The assumption here is that the text provides an "expansion of spirit" to
which the actor failed to rise. But, as Michael Bryant pointed out in rehearsal,
"Ye elves of hills" is less an expansive statement than a confession of guilt. If
there is an "expansion of spirit," it comes in Prospero's recognition of his need
for forgiveness, symbolized by the "heavenly music." But what I found especially interesting was that even in Hall's innovative interpretation the final
scene *still* seemed, in Hope-Wallace's terms, "unimportant as a sequel"; or, if it
was not exactly unimportant, there was no inevitable relation between the
"expansion of spirit" and what follows. Hall's interpretation did not attempt to
simplify an ending which, in Stephen Orgel's admirable phrase, "does not
exhaust the energies of the drama" (p. 55). This *Tempest* in performance finally
reinforced a point Hall made at the beginning of the rehearsal period: "the
moment you think you've got it, the play contradicts itself." In this way it
remains what Robert Speaight called it when writing about Clifford Williams's
version in his book *Shakespeare on the Stage:* "this almost inaccessible play."[6]

Notes

1. *Peter Hall's Diaries,* ed. John Goodwin (London, 1983), p. 77.
2. *The Tempest,* ed. Frank Kermode, the Arden Shakespeare (London, 1954). p. xlviii.
3. *The Tempest,* ed. Stephen Orgel, the Oxford Shakespeare (Oxford, 1987). p. 117.
4. S. T. Coleridge, *Shakespearian Criticism,* ed. T. M. Raysor, I (London, 1960), p. 121.
5. E. M. W. Tillyard, *Shakespeare's Last Plays* (London, 1938), p. 51.
6. Robert Speaight, *Shakespeare on the Stage* (Boston, 1973), p. 286.

CRITICISM

♦

Prospero, Agrippa, and Hocus Pocus

Barbara A. Mowat

> If by your Art (my deerest father) you have
> Put the wild waters in this Rore; alay them.
> —*The Tempest, I.ii.1–2*

After years of discounting Prospero's magic Art as simply a metaphor for creative imagination, critics of *The Tempest* since the 1930s have been making serious efforts to come to terms with Prospero as a Renaissance magician, a mortal with spirits at his command and with power over the natural and supernatural worlds.[1] In the 1960s, new interest in Renaissance attitudes toward the occult led to an outpouring of attempts to place Prospero as a magician and to discover the shape and parameters of his magic.[2]

Today, the issue is not that Prospero's Art is likely to be discounted, but that it is likely to be taken far too seriously and treated in far too ponderous a manner. In recent journals, one actually senses a battle shaping between those who follow Curry, Sisson, Kermode, and Yates in seeing Prospero as the quintessential Renaissance philosopher-magus or theurgist, who "exercises the supernatural powers of the holy adept" (Kermode, p. xlvii) and those who say, instead, that since all magic is evil, Prospero is actually "a type of the potentially damned sorcerer" who shows "in his actions something infinitely more malevolent" than the positive magic claimed for the magus.[3] The problem here is twofold. In the first place, Prospero's magic is far more complex than such an easy dichotomy would suggest. Robert West has long since demonstrated that Prospero cannot be safely ensconced in either of these magic traditions, black or white, and his essay linking *The Tempest* to Shakespeare's world of "outer mystery" is a fine corrective to those who would attempt to so limit Prospero's Art.[4] In the second place, those who argue about Prospero as magus or Prospero as witch tend to ignore the fact that these are only two of the many images of magicians current in Renaissance England, and thus tend to overlook aspects of Prospero's Art which radically affect audience response to him and to his creations of illusion and transformation.[5] Prospero is, I would argue, more various and more fascinating than the insubstantial, all-too-solemn magus or the

Barbara A. Mowat, "Prospero, Agrippa, and Hocus Pocus," *English Literary Renaissance,* 11:2 (1981): 281–303. Reprinted by permission of the editors from *English Literary Renaissance.*

vengeful, finally repentant witch now being proffered by critics for our contemplation. By examining the language, and, to a lesser extent, the actions which reveal Prospero's magic to us, I hope to make clear the complexity of his image and of the response which he summons from his audience. My hope is to open us up once again to the blend of seriousness and jest, of belief and skepticism, which is the climate of Shakespeare's magic island.

I

Let me begin with a portion of Prospero's long narrative to Miranda about his life in Milan. He is explaining to her the coup d'état which hurled them from their palace into a "full poor cell" on an unnamed island. The lines, although familiar, deserve our close attention:

> The Government I cast upon my brother,
> And to my State grew stranger, being transported
> And rapt in secret studies. . . .
>
> I thus neglecting worldly ends, all dedicated
> To closeness, and the bettering of my mind
> with that, which but by being so retir'd
> Ore-priz'd all popular rate: in my false brother
> Awak'd an evill nature. . . .
>
> . . . hence his Ambition growing . . .
>
> . . . he needes will be
> Absolute *Millaine,* Me (poore man) my Librarie
> Was Dukedome large enough: of temporall roalties
> He thinks me now incapable. . . .
>
> [Gonzalo,] of his gentlenesse
> Knowing I lov'd my bookes, . . . furnishd me
> From mine owne Library, with volumes, that
> I prize above my Dukedome.
>
> . . . by my prescience
> I finde my *Zenith* doth depend upon
> A most auspitious starre, whose influence
> If now I court not, but omit; my fortunes
> Will ever after droope. . . .[6]

Within this narrative, those who see Prospero as a magus could find solid evidence to support their stand. Separate from the text or replaced within the larger narrative, these lines give us a recognizable Hermetic magus, a Prospero much like Agrippa, Trithemius, and John Dee, men who linked magic to intellectual study, who said with Ficino and with Pico that magic is the greatest of the philosophies, the greatest of the sciences, taking the magus away from the pettiness of this world and drawing him close to the gods.[7]

Look carefully at Prospero's words: "transported and rapt in secret studies." This is the kind of language used by Agrippa and Trithemius in their correspondence about *The Occult Philosophy,* where they speak of "that ancient Magick, the discipline of all wise men" as "sublime and sacred"; Agrippa refers to Trithemius's knowledge as "transcending" and to Trithemius himself as a "man very industrious after secret things"; Trithemius commends Agrippa for having "penetrate[d] into such secrets as have been hidden from most learned men," and exhorts him to keep these secret things hidden from the "vulgar." Agrippa later celebrates Ceremonial Magic as the "divine science" by which, if one is "alwaies busied," contemplating it "every moment . . . by a sage and diligent inquisition," one ascends "by all the degrees of the creatures . . . even to the Archetype himself."[8] John Dee, too, uses language of rapture and transport when he writes of his "studies and studious exercises." He defends his magical endeavors from charges of sorcery, describing them as, instead, the means by which he sought the truth "by the true philosophicall method and harmony: proceeding and ascending (as it were) *gradatim,* from thinges visible to consider of thinges invisible: from thinges bodily, to conceive of thinges spirituall: from thinges transitorie, & momentanie, to meditate of things permanent. . . ."[9] For Prospero, as for the real-life magus, studies of secret things stand in contradistinction to mundane concerns, to Trithemius's "vulgar" and Dee's "transitorie & momentanie." Similarly when Prospero a moment later talks of "neglecting worldly ends," he reflects the language of these same men, to whom things "worldly" and "temporal" meant precisely things of this world, transitory rewards acquired through ambition and love of wealth and power. "Worldly ends" and "temporal roialties" are the goals of Prospero's brother, who "drie . . . for Sway," turns traitor both to Prospero and to Milan.

Prospero's dedication to "closeness" (i.e., to solitude or perhaps to secrecy) and to the "bettering of [his] mind" likewise recalls the real-life magus, as does his prizing of his books above his dukedom. For the magus—even an emperor-magus like Rudolf II—the magic books which open to the adept the secrets of the universe are properly valued above mere mortal power and station.[10] Note that in the famous lines "he furnished me / From mine own Library, with volumes, that / I prize above my Dukedome," Shakespeare has Prospero use the present tense verb *prize,* an indication that the Prospero we meet on the island is even yet, "twelve yere since," very much the Hermetic magus.[11] The reiteration of the phrase "my Library" is also of interest, echoing as it does some of the more passionate statements of John Dee about his treasured volumes.[12]

In Prospero's long narrative to Miranda, there are only two points at which the language seems potentially at odds with that used by the magus. The first is the phrase "and to my State grew stranger," with its hint of self-recrimination foreign to the language of the magus; the second is the phrase "but by being so retir'd," which again attaches guilt to magic studies, and is thus unlike the language used by maguses in their writings. One final passage deserves our close attention, inasmuch as it is usually read as Prospero's apology, his admission that his studies, his retreat into magic, were morally wrong. "I thus neglecting worldly ends," he says, "all dedicated / To closeness . . . in my false brother / Awak'd an evill nature." Were Prospero here saying that he had neglected his duty and that he was therefore blameworthy, then this passage would place him outside the world of the magus. But, as I noted earlier, Prospero does not here say that he neglected his duty; he says, rather, that he neglected "worldly ends"—a virtue for neo-Platonist and Christian alike; and though his giving over of "temporal sway" to his brother did allow Antonio's worldly ambitions to grow, the analogy that Prospero uses in his own defense suggests no sense of self-condemnation. "My trust," he says, "Like a good parent, did beget of him / A falsehood in it's contrarie, as great / As my trust was, which had indeede no limit, / A confidence sans bound." To paraphrase, using Miranda's words: "Good wombes have borne bad sonnes."

Further, within this supposed apology, Prospero gives us his most affirmative evaluation of his secret studies. He was, he said, "all dedicated / To . . . the bettering of my mind / with that which . . . / Ore-priz'd all popular rate," or, as David Horne glosses it in the Yale Shakespeare, "surpassed in value everything the world rates highly." Such a description of dark and secret studies echoes Hermetic magi from Agrippa to John Dee.[13]

In Prospero's early narrative about his magic, then, he speaks almost entirely in the vein of the Renaissance philosopher-magus. The image given of him here, drawn throughout from the magus tradition, is sharpened by the contrasting image drawn in the same scene of Sycorax, the witch who copulated with the devil, who whelped Caliban, who worshipped the god Setebos, and whose sorceries were "terrible to enter human hearing."

II

Thus far, then, those who would see Prospero as quintessential magus would seem justified in their reading of his character. Yet move with me to another set of lines, where Prospero is again speaking of his magic, of himself as magician. "I have," he says,

bedymn'd
The Noone-tide Sun, call'd forth the mutenous windes,

> And twixt the greene Sea, and the azur'd vault
> Set roaring warre: To the dread ratling Thunder
> Have I given fire, and rifted *Joves* stowt Oke
> With his owne Bolt: The strong bass'd promontorie
> Have I made shake, and by the spurs pluckt up
> The Pyne, and Cedar. Graves at my command
> Have wak'd their sleepers, op'd, and let 'em forth
> By my so potent Art.
>
> (V.i.41–50)

Such claims, such diction, lift us suddenly into a world quite antithetical to Hermetic magic, into a world of Medeas, of Thessalian witches, of such "old enchantresses" as Lyly's Dipsas or such enchanters as Owen Glendower, who kept poor Hotspur awake with many such skimble-skamble tales of earthquakes and fiery cressets, curious arts and deep experiments.

Both West and Sisson note the incongruity of having a speech derived from Ovid's Medea coming from the lips of a theurgist or magus. But they fail to note the larger significance of Shakespeare's use of these lines: namely, that this speech links Prospero to a tradition as venerable as that of the magus, a tradition which was seen in the Renaissance as the antithesis of Hermetic magic. Ovid's Medea is an enchanter, a magician who, unlike the magus, does not seek spiritual growth, but seeks instead godlike control over the natural and supernatural worlds. Apuleius's enchantress, Meroe, is another figure from this tradition; she has "power to rule the heavens, to bring down the sky, to bear up the earth, to turn the waters into hills and the hills into running waters, to lift up the terrestrial spirits into the air, and to pull the gods out of the heavens, to extinguish the planets and to lighten the deep darkness of hell." Agrippa, writing in 1510, quotes this passage as an example of the outrageous claims, the "cursed and detestable fooleries," which had brought the sacred discipline of magic as practised by himself and other Hermetic magi into disrepute.[14] Medea and Meroe are not alone in making such claims. Lyly's Dipsas can, she says, "darken the sun by my skill and remove the moon out of her course, . . . restore youth to the aged and make hills without bottoms." Glendower can summon spirits, command the devil, raise tempests. Reginald Scot scoffed at such claims: only God and Jesus had, he said, such powers. Hotspur, too, scoffed, as did Trithemius, who warned friends to beware of such braggarts as Faustus, the kind of conjuror who gave good magic a bad name.[15]

When Prospero extols his magic control over the sun, the winds, the sea; when he claims that, through his "potent Art," graves have "op'd" and let forth their sleepers, he stands before us briefly as a kind of pagan enchanter. The moment is a powerful one, with Prospero alone onstage *"in his Magicke robes,"* celebrating in potent language his enchanter's Art. Yet the moment is also a brief one. As he reaches the culmination of his "hybrisrede"[16] he immediately dismisses it, and dismisses the magic that it celebrates. "My so potent Art" becomes, within a single line, "this rough Magicke," and Prospero's language takes him into yet another world, another magic tradition:

> But this rough Magicke
> I heere abjure: and when I have requir'd
> Some heavenly Musicke (which even now I do)
> To worke mine end upon their Sences, that
> This Ayrie-charme is for, I'le breake my staffe,
> Bury it certaine fadomes in the earth,
> And deeper then did ever Plummet sound
> Ile drowne my booke.
>
> (V.i.50–57)

This speech of abjuration, with its dismissal of magic Art as "rough" and its promise to destroy both staff and book, is not the language of the great enchanters, who tend to remain proud of their powers, disappearing like Ovid's Medea in a cloud "as dark as the music chanted in her spells" (Book VII). Nor is this speech suggestive of the Hermetic magus. John Dee, called upon to recant, went to his pauper's death still composing passionate letters to the King and Parliament defending his Hermetic beliefs and practices, though his library had been destroyed by irate citizens lashing out at his necromancy, his magic glass, and his converse with spirits. Trithemius never admitted to any conflict between his Hermetic practices and his position as a Christian abbot. If Agrippa recanted, he did so only within the context of a total recantation and a cry of "all is vanity."[17]

I would suggest that Prospero's recantation, his use of the term "abjure" (with its links to the Christian church through association with the word "heresy"), and his promise to drown his book, place him in yet a third tradition. This is the tradition of the wizard—the pagan enchanter brought into the Christian world, the magician with the magus's pride in his secret knowledge, the enchanter's power over the elements, the sorcerer's control over spirits, and, finally, the Christian's concern over the fate of his soul. Those who fall into the camp of the wizard are a diverse lot; we find them in medieval legend, in commedia dell'arte scenari, in Renaissance prose "histories"—like those, for example, about "Fryer Bacon" and about "J. Faustus"— and in the elaborate wizard dramas of the 1590s.[18]

We recognize the wizard wherever we find him by his dual role. He is a magician who uses what D. P. Walker calls "transitive magic"[19] to affect other people and to effect wondrous happenings; at the same time, he is a human being with moral concerns. He delights in his magic powers; however, as a human in a Christian world, he must eventually admit the "roughness" of his magic. This moral imperative sets him apart not only from his pagan predecessors and his Hermetic contemporaries (who thought that they had reconciled magic and the Christian moral world) but also from such figures as

Shakespeare's Oberon, who, contemporary with the stage versions of Faust and Bacon, shares many of the characteristics of the wizard, but, not being mortal, need not recant and give over his power.

The line separating the wizard from the enchanter is not a rigid one. Shakespeare, for example, following Holinshed, chooses to treat Owen Glendower as an enchanter, and omits from his portrait the wizard-legends that tell of his repentance and his years of hermit life.[20] The real-life Friar Roger Bacon never admitted that his "magic" studies were evil, and is thus more like a magus or an enchanter than a wizard; but the legends, narratives, and dramas about him show him as repentant and self-condemnatory.[21] In *The Famous Historie,* for example, the Friar "cries out upon himself" for neglecting divine studies and, in a passage very reminiscent of Acts 19.19, where the "practicers of curious arts" are forced to burn their books, he decides to remove the cause of the "heavie burthen" of his knowledge of magic by publicly burning his books, and thenceforward devotes his life to pious meditation as an anchorite (G2v–G3v). Greene's Bacon also recants, of course, repenting "that Bacon ever meddled in this art." Faustus, too, although pictured by his contemporary Trithemius as a conjuror-sorcerer, develops in legend into a powerful wizard figure with the wizard's guilty conscience. Marlowe's Faustus, like his model in the *Faustbuch,* seriously attempts to repent, ending his final soliloquy with "Come not, Lucifer, / I'll burn my books. . . !" Lyly's Dipsas, described as "an old enchantress" and pictured as one throughout most of *Endymion,* suddenly moves into the Christian moral world at the end of the play, and as a reward for renouncing the filthy trade of magic, regains her lost husband.

Prospero is like his wizard predecessors in a variety of ways. First, he has the noted duality of the wizard. Like the magician-hero of such *scenari* as "Pantaloonlet,"[22] he is a father concerned for his daughter as well as a worker of beneficent magic; like Faustus and Bacon, he is both a maker of spectacles and a man with "a beating mind." Prospero, *"on the top, invisible,"* performing magic acts, is at the same time Prospero, the wronged Duke of Milan.

Second, Prospero's magic acts follow the tradition of those acts performed by wizards in earlier plays. While the acts of wizards in legends are grand and magnificent, those performed by commedia dell'arte magicians are more limited in scope, and they form a pattern which carries over into the more elaborate wizard dramas. Commedia dell'arte wizards use charms to interfere in the lives of others, they produce and destroy food magically, and they use "spirits" to cudgel and torment their enemies.[23] The wizard dramas of Greene and Marlowe include this same set of magic acts and add to it the summoning of spirits in the guise of famous persons or gods to entertain noble patrons and to give evidence of the magician's power.[24] The magic acts which we see Prospero perform—the placing of charms on Miranda and Ferdinand, the summoning of spirits to present shows, the use of magic to aid friends and punish enemies, the creation and dissolution of a magic banquet—these acts are predictable stage-wizard magic: as Prospero says of the Masque of Spirits, "they expect it from me."

But it is the renunciation of magic, the return to the conventional world, and the concern with his own mortality, that most clearly link Prospero to the wizard tradition. The suddenness of his renunciation is reminiscent of such commedia dell'arte magicians as the magician-hero of "Pantaloonlet" who, after having used his magic to bring about a happy ending for himself, his friends and his daughter, abruptly declares that "he does not wish to practice his magic art any longer but instead he will live with [the ordinary mortals]; [and] he throws away his rod and his book" (Lea, II, 642). But the language with which Prospero abjures his magic reminds us strongly of the Bacons and Faustuses of narrative and drama. The pattern established by Prospero's magic acts and the duality of Prospero's role, as both a worker of transitive magic and as a man whose fate concerns us, place him among the wizards, and lead directly to his repudiation of magic, phrased in the language of the wizard: "Ile drown my book," and "retire me to my *Millaine,* where / Every third thought shall be my grave."

III

Thus far, we have seen reflected in Prospero's language several familiar worlds of magic—the lofty, proud world of the magus, the thrasonical, hyperbolic world of the enchanter, the ambiguous world of the wizard who, at the end, turns his back on magic books and wands. In the final bit of dialogue which I will consider, we will seem, at first, to have left the recognizable traditions behind. This dialogue begins when Prospero summons Ariel: "Come away, Servant, come. . . ." Ariel approaches: "All haile, great Master, grave Sir, haile: I come / To answer thy best pleasure . . ." (I.ii.198–200). The lines which most interest me occur a bit later, but we should pause and attempt to place ourselves linguistically.

Although the magician is here summoning a spirit, we are clearly not in the world of spirit-summonings inhabited by "callers and conjurors of wicked and damned Sprites"—to use John Dee's phrase. Shakespeare had twice before shown us that world, and it is one far removed from Prospero and his summoning of Ariel. The witches' conjurations in *Macbeth* we can immediately dismiss as irrelevant; the spirits are not the witches' servants but their masters, who "will not be commanded." Bolingbroke's conjuration of a spirit in *2 Henry VI* is only slightly more reminiscent of Prospero and Ariel. Instead of Prospero's open, daylight world, Bolingbroke's conjuring is done at night: "Deepe Night, darke Night, the silent of the Night / . . . The time when Screech-owles cry, and Bandogs howle, / And Spirits walke, and Ghosts breake up their Graves; / That time best fits the worke we have in hand"

(I.iv.15–19). A witch grovels on the ground, the spirit appears under the temporary compulsion of the magic rites, speaks cryptically, and surrounded by thunder and lightning, quickly returns to his true master in the infernal realms below. Prospero has little in common with such conjury. He is Ariel's "great Master"; Ariel is Prospero's industrious "Servant," "correspondent to command."

The language of Prospero and Ariel also seems foreign to the world of the Hermetic magi and their *daemons*. Curry saw Ariel as a neo-Platonic *daemon* under Prospero's control; Kittredge and others follow Curry; and many critics explain Ariel by citing recondite sources: Plato's reference to spirits who act as messengers, Iamblichus's description of the various spirits who inhabit the air and act as guardians of man, Hermes Trismegistus's lines and Agrippa's passages discussing the higher forms of invisible life which link man to the demi-urge.[25] Yet nowhere in such writings can I find evidence that the magus may take as his servant a *daemon* who will come at his command, call him master, and present himself as a willing, obedient servant. Iamblichus and Agrippa come closest to suggesting that the magus eventually "controls" *daemons*. Yet Iamblichus gives us, at best, a rather murky picture in which divine energy flows and power is mystically exerted between the "priest" and various levels of *daemons* (IV.i–ii). Agrippa, though claiming that "the understanding of Divine things . . . compels even good Angels . . . unto our service" (*Occult Philosophy*, p. 342), states unequivocally that although the magus may "call up good spirits," these spirits "can by no bonds . . . be allayed by us"; rather, they must be beseeched "by some sacred things" (p. 447). Spirits thus beseeched through religious signs "sometimes apply themselves to humane uses" yet "not as being compelled by any kind of necessity, but of their own accord . . . being overcome by the prayers of them that called on them." It is the "good spirits" that overcome and control the more useful "evil spirits" for the magus (pp. 447–48).

The relationship of Prospero, Ariel, and the lesser spirits (the "rabble," as Shakespeare at one point calls them) could suggest a kind of translation of Agrippa's three-fold grouping of the magus, the "good spirit" whom he beseeches and the "evil spirits" whom the good spirit can control. But if we consider the tone in which Prospero addresses Ariel, remember the larger context of Agrippa's discussion of Ceremonial Magic, and consider such phrases from *The Tempest* as Prospero's command to Ariel—"Goe bring the rabble / (Ore whom I give thee powre)"—we are unlikely to see the Prospero-Ariel relationship in Agrippan terms, unless we conclude that Shakespeare was being fanciful, either tongue-in-cheek or through a rather monumental kind of dramatic license. John Dee's accounts of his summoning of spirits is much more in line with the Agrippan model, and seems far afield from Prospero's "Come away, Servant," or from Ariel's "Grave Sir, haile: I come / To answer thy best pleasure." Dee claims to have been successful in calling into his chambers a succession of spirits who grudgingly speak with him, but he must beseech them continually (as Agrippa had warned) and never are they under his command. Dee's rather pitiful attempts to get from the spirits any of their secrets or to persuade them to stay once their real master in the world beyond calls them are quite unlike Prospero's peremptory commands and Ariel's quick obedience.[26]

In the traditions of magic which we have thus far examined, there are, of course, magicians who have spirits at their command. These are the enchanters and the wizards. Glendower holds Hotspur "at least nine howres, / In reckning up the severall Devils Names, / That were his Lacqueyes." The historical Faustus, we are told, had a familiar spirit in the guise of a black dog who did his magic work for him; the legends surrounding John a Kent always included a familiar spirit who accompanied and served him; and James I wrote that the devil himself will often act as a familiar, and will, to some magicians, "be a continual attender, in forme of a Page."[27] The master-servant relationship that we hear at Prospero's meeting with Ariel would therefore be appropriate to the enchanter and wizard traditions, but only if we were willing to see Ariel as Prospero's "familiar"—i.e., a demon under Prospero's command. If we look further into the Prospero-Ariel dialogue, though, we realize that we need not be driven to that extremity, for their language leads us to yet another world of magic in which Ariel's position is far less sinister than that of a "familiar," and in which Prospero appears as neither conjuror nor enchanter:

PROSPERO:	*Ariel,* thy charge
	Exactly is perform'd; but there's more worke:
	What is the time o'th'day?
ARIEL:	Past the mid season.
PRO:	At least two Glasses: the time 'twixt six & now
	Must by us both be spent most preciously.
AR.	Is there more toyle? Since ÿ dost give me pains,
	Let me remember thee what thou hast promis'd,
	Which is not yet perform'd me.
PRO.	How now? moodie?
	What is't thou canst demand?
AR.	My Libertie.
PRO.	Before the time be out? no more;
AR.	I prethee,
	Remember I have done thee worthy service,
	Told thee no lyes, made thee no mistakings, serv'd
	Without or grudge, or grumblings; thou did promise
	To bate me a full yeere.

PRO.   Do'st thou forget
                       From what a torment I did free thee?

                       If thou more murmur'st, I will rend an Oake
                       And peg-thee in his knotty entrailes, till
                       Thou hast howl'd away twelve winters.
AR.   Pardon, Master,
                       I will be correspondent to command
                       And doe my spryting, gently.
PRO.   Doe so: and after two daies
                       I will discharge thee.
AR.   That's my noble Master:
                       What shall I doe? say what? what shall I doe?
PRO.   Goe make thy selfe like a Nymph o'th'Sea,
                       Be subject to no sight but thine, and mine: invisible
                       To every eye-ball else: goe take this shape
                       And hither come in't: goe: hence
                       With diligence.
                                                    (I.ii.237–304)

Several aspects of Prospero's relationship to Ariel become clear in this dialogue. First, there are obvious resemblances between their "contract of servitude" and that of Faustus and Mephistophilis: the charge to be invisible "to every eye-ball else," to take the whimsical form commanded by his master, is almost an echo of the Faust-Mephistophilis contract. As in the Faust story, Prospero's contract binds the spirit to "at all times appear at his command" and "doe for him whatsoever."[28] Ultimately the contracts are quite different, inasmuch as Prospero's terminates not with his own damnation but with Ariel's freedom. Nevertheless it is possible that the relationship between Faustus and his "swift-flying Spirit" may have helped shape Prospero and Ariel.

More important, though, is that aspect of the relationship which emerges in their use of words such as "discharge thee" and "before the time be out," and in the emphasis throughout the passage on Ariel's proper behavior. According to the terms of the contract as implied in the dialogue, Ariel must be diligent, must be obedient, must be truthful. In the face of Prospero's anger, Ariel insists that he has indeed been diligent, "told . . . no lyes, made . . . no mistakings, [and] serv'd / Without or grudge, or grumblings." "Remember," he says, "thou did promise / To bate me a full yeere." This kind of language occurs repeatedly between Prospero and Ariel, and it leads us to that other world of magic reflected in *The Tempest* (and, to some extent, in *A Midsummer Night's Dream* and *John a Kent and John a Cumber* as well).[29] I would suggest that Ariel's language is not that of a demon, nor of a *daemon,* but of a servant boy ready for his freedom, and further, that the language with which he and Prospero haggle over a few more hours of service belongs more to the mundane world of the streetcorner "art-Magician" or "Jugler" (these are Reginald Scot's terms for Houdini-type illusionists) than to the arcane, terrifying Hermetic or demonic spheres.

The tradition of the Jugler is, like that of the magus and the enchanter, an ancient one. Cornelius Agrippa, writing in 1527, traces "this Arte of delusions or juglinges" back into antiquity. "There are bookes extant," he notes, "of the delusions or juglinges of Hermes touchinge this skill," and he gives examples of tricks of legerdemaine done by Numa Pompilus and Pythagorus. Through illusions, he says "the Magitiens doo shewe vaine visions, and with Juglinge castes doo plaie many miracles, & cause dreams, which thinge is not so much done by Geoticall inchauntmentes . . . [as] with a readie subteltie and nimblenesse of the handes, as wee dayly see stage players and Juglers doo. . . ." "The ende of this skil," he says, is "to stretche out imaginations even unto apperaunce, of which there shall afterwarde no signe appeare." And in a statement of particular relevance to readers of *The Tempest,* he notes that "we have reade also that one Pasetes a Jugler was wonte to shew to straungers a very sumptuouse banket, & when it pleased him to cause it vanishe awaie, all they whiche sate at the table beinge disappointed both of meate & drinke."[30]

Performing magicians of the kind described by Agrippa were familiar figures in Elizabethan and Jacobean England. They played on street corners, in "Fayres and Markets," in the provinces, and in London theaters.[31] In his *Discovery of Witchcraft,* Reginald Scot names several prominent illusionists: "one Kingsfield of London" who performed the difficult "decollation of John Baptist" with his boy assistants at "a Bartholomewtide, An. 1582, in the sight of diverse that came to view this spectacle" (p. 349); one "John Cautares," in S. Martins, "who getteth not his living thereby, but . . . nevertheless hath the best hand and conveiance (I thinke) of anie man that liveth this daie" (pp. 351–52). There are, in Jacobean documents, many references to one William Vincent, licensed "to exercise and practize the Arte of legerdemaine . . . in any Convenient place within any his Ma^{ts} Dominions" (Bentley, II, 612–13). And probably most famous of all the illusionists, appearing in provincial [records] and mentioned twice by Ben Jonson in his plays, "one man more excelling in that craft than others, that went about in King *James* his time, and long since, who called himself, *The Kings Majesties most excellent Hocus Pocus.*"[32]

That these performing magicians were "conjurors" of the "I have no tricks up my sleeve" variety is clear from the description given of their devices in Scot's *Discovery of Witchcraft* (many of which are still part of the stage magician's repertoire) as well as from an interesting phrase which appears in George Abbott's attack on Giordano Bruno. Bruno, during his famous visit to Oxford in 1583, preparing to give his public lecture on Copernicus and Hermetic magic, is described by Abbott as an "Italian Didapper" who "more boldly than wisely got up into the highest place of our best and most renowned schoole, stripping up his sleeve like some Jugler. . . ."[33] And that the Juglers were proficient in the creation of illusions is also clear. S[amuel] R[id], in 1612, notes not only that "Jugling is now become common, I mean the professors who make an occupation and profession of the same" but also that "I must needs say that some deserve commendation for the nimbleness and agility of their hands, & might be thought to performe as excellent things by their Legerdemaine, as any of your wizards witches or magitians whatsoever."[34] Scot, in 1584, Rid, in 1612, and "Hocus Pocus Junior," in 1634, all wrote detailed explanations of how the Juglers' tricks worked in order to clear them of the imputation that they were witches. Thomas Cooper, writing in 1617, insisted nevertheless that Juglers worked with the devil's aid.[35] As Thomas Ady put it: "the craft of Jugling, to them that are not acquainted with it, breedeth great admiration in the beholders, and seemeth, to silly people, to be miraculous, and yet being known is but deceit and foolery" (pp. 28–29). Even in the days of Cromwell, notes Ady, people "will stand like Pharaoh and his Servants, and admire a Jugling Imposture," thinking the Jugler is working "true miracles," or "will stand affrighted, or run out of the room scared like fools, saying, The Devil is in the room, and helpeth him to do such Tricks; and some saying absolutely, He is a Witch, and ought to be hanged" (p. 29).

Since it is Prospero's master-servant talk with Ariel which first led us to the Jugler tradition, it is important to note that Juglers did indeed have young servants who aided them in the creation of illusions. The Juglers carried small animals in their pockets who they pretended were their "familiars," and they led their astounded audiences to believe that the "familiar" created supernatural events. But it was the illusionist's boy who was the confederate in the creation of the illusion: the boy who hid behind the post and blew wine "miraculously" through the wall by means of a pipe; the boy who allowed himself to be "decapitated" and "healed"; the boy who fetched, who carried, who obediently served his master.[36]

In one description of a Jugler (probably Hocus Pocus himself), we read about their "boys," and we hear how their masters spoke to them:

> then the Jugler calleth to his Boy, and biddeth him bring him a glass of Claret Wine. . . ; the silly Spectators thinking [they see] the same wine which he drank to come again out of his fore-head; then he saith, If this be not enough, I will draw good Claret Wine out of a post . . . and then is one of his boys on the other side of the wall, with a Bladder and a pipe . . . conveyeth the Wine to his Master thorow the Post . . . and being all drunk up but one small glass at the last, he calleth to his Boy, saying, Come, sirrah, you would faine have a cup, but his Boy maketh answer in a disdainful manner saying, No Master not I, if that be good Wine that is drawn out of a Post I will lose my head; yea sirrah saith his Master, then your head you shall lose; come sirrah, you shall go to pot for that word; then he layeth his Boy down upon the Table . . . commanding him to lye still. (Ady, pp. 37–38)

The language of this passage, with its "Come, sirrah," and its "No, master, not I," its emphasis on the master's control and the boy's cooperation, suggests that the Jugler's assistant is one of those servants described in Renaissance handbooks for servants, a boy bound by contract to serve his master for certain years, and bound as well to be diligent, to be obedient, and to be truthful:

> [Servants] must be obedient at a worde, at a call, and at a becke. . . : they must say and doe as the lad *Samuell* did who served under *Eli*. . . : when the voyce called him, *Samuell, Samuell,* he answered by and by, heere I am, and ranne quickly to *Eli* and sayd, *behold heere I am, for thou callest me.*[37]

In Prospero's dialogues with Ariel we hear strong echoes of the master magician and his "boy," and we see in Ariel (except for his moments of moodiness, of "malignant"[38] rebelliousness) the good servant who, like Samuel, comes at a beck, a call.

It is perhaps shocking to hear between Prospero and Ariel the language of Elizabethan master and servant. Even more disturbing is to note the relationship of Prospero to the illusionists, the master Hocus Pocuses of Stuart England. Yet I find that Louis B. Wright, in 1927, noted the resemblance of Prospero and Ariel to the magician and his assistant, and pointed out that, in *The Tempest,* "in one scene, at least, there appears to have been a trick of legerdemain by Ariel, who makes a banquet disappear."[39] There are other tricks of legerdemain in the play. The Jugler's assistant, disguised as a Harpy, himself vanishes in thunder and lightning; the entire cast of the pre-nuptial masque "to a strange, hollow, and confused noise . . . heavily vanish." Many of the illusions Prospero creates—the omnipresent music, the magically appearing banquet, the masque of spirits, the hunt with the spirit dogs—these would be known in the Jugler's trade as "acts done through confederacie" (i.e., with the help of assistants arranged in advance), just as the various disappearing acts would be called "acts done through 'deceptio visus.' "[40] Even the tempest itself, as we hear Ariel describe it in I.ii, seems as much the result of "deceptio visus" and trickery as of supernatural control over Jove's own lightning.

IV

I noted earlier that Prospero is a product of several magic traditions; interestingly and significantly, each of these traditions brings with it into the play a different set of attitudes toward man and toward marvels. In spite of their differences, it is possible to conflate the magus, the enchanter, and the wizard into one figure, the "serious magician" who believes in supernatural powers, who believes that he is in touch with those powers, and that through those powers he can bring about genuine transformations. This figure stands in stark contrast to the juggler-illusionist or "art-Magician," a figure who pretends to use spirits to bring about transformations, but who is only a trickster.

It would seem an impossible feat to combine within a single hero the dichotomous images of the serious magician and the carnival illusionist, the magician as Agrippa and the magician as Hocus Pocus. Yet I would argue that Shakespeare has done just that, that Prospero's own transformations between the poles of "serious magician" and "Jugler" can be traced through scene after scene of the play, and that those transformations and the shifts in tone and in our attitude toward the magician which accompany the transformations are at the heart of the play and of the questions the play poses about reality and illusion, about creativity and theatrical fakery, and about disturbing resemblances between the dramatist and the magician.[41]

If we can entertain the idea that Prospero is as much Hocus Pocus as he is Agrippa, then we can look at key moments in *The Tempest* with a fresh eye: at Prospero, "on the top," congratulating Ariel on his Harpy-performance and vanishing act; at Prospero explaining to Ferdinand the relationship between the masque-illusion and the illusion that we call life, the "revel" which, as a creator himself of insubstantial shows, the master jugler suspects of equal insubstantiality; at Prospero, in the epilogue, "stripping up his sleeve like some Jugler" to reveal the tricks, to let us know, finally that his magician's project, which Ariel has been at such pains to keep alive, is finally the Jugler's project: "to please."

Annie Dillard compares the illusions to which we are treated by Nature to a kind of carnival show. She watches the light change in late afternoon, watches clouds and mountains turn from pink to gray, disappear, appear again in new forms, until finally "the show pull[s] out." "Nothing is left," she says, "but an unreal blue and a few banked clouds low in the north."

> Some sort of carnival magician has been here, some fast-talking worker of wonders who has the act backwards. "Something in this hand," he says, "something in this hand, something up my sleeve, something behind my back . . ." and abracadabra, he snaps his fingers, and it's all gone. Only the bland, blank-faced magician remains, in his unruffled coat, barehanded, acknowledging a smattering of baffled applause. When you look again the whole show has pulled up stakes and moved on down the road. It never stops. New shows roll in from over the mountains and the magician reappears unannounced from a fold in the curtain you never dreamed was an opening. Scarves of clouds, rabbits in plain view, disappear into the black hat forever. Presto chango. The audience, if there is an audience at all, is dizzy from head-turning, dazed.[42]

The blending of seriousness with jest, of revelation with bewilderment, which Miss Dillard suggests is the kind of tone which *The Tempest* achieves. Nature presents spectacles which we perceive as best we can through our easily deluded senses. Presto chango, the racks vanish; the globe itself will one day vanish like a carnival show, an Inigo Jones masque, Prospero's revels or Shakespeare's play. Prospero's magic powers slide into fakery; Ceres and Iris are "really" only spirits who are in turn "really" only actors. The "reality" or fakery of the magician's power and our inability to fix this power as supernatural or as sleight-of-hand are central to the play and its vision of life, just as they point to the central ambiguities in our own vision of man in the natural and supernatural worlds.

In Prospero's role we can read the story of a man's personal growth from vengeance to mercy, and from rough magic to deep spirituality; or we can simply enjoy the magician's struggles to bring about the play's remarkable happy ending. But however we view him, the final image of Prospero which lingers in our minds is of the mortal creature of the epilogue—the magus who has learned to think of his mortality, the Faustus who successfully destroyed his book, the illusionist who stands before us revealing the tricks of his trade. The applause for which he begs we give to end his play and to free him from his island, but we give it also to celebrate the wonder of Prospero himself.[43]

Notes

1. The seminal work on Prospero's magic was Walter Clyde Curry's "Sacerdotal Science in Shakespeare's *The Tempest*," *Archiv*, 90, Bd. 168 (1935), 25–36, 185–96, rpt. in *Shakespeare's Philosophical Patterns* (Baton Rouge, 1959; orig. prtd. 1937), pp. 163–99. See also C. J. Sisson, "The Magic of Prospero," *Shakespeare Survey*, 11 (1958), 70–77; and Frank Kermode, "Introduction," *The Tempest*, Arden edition (London, 1954), pp. xlvii ff.

2. On Renaissance attitudes toward the occult, see especially D. P. Walker, *Spiritual and Demonic Magic from Ficino to Campanella* (London, 1958); Frances Yates, *Giordano Bruno and the Hermetic Tradition* (New York, 1969; orig. prt., 1964); Eugenio Garin, "Magic and Astrology in the Civilisation of the Renaissance," *Science and Civic Life in the Italian Renaissance*, trans. Peter Munz (Garden City, New York, 1969), pp. 145–65; Keith Thomas, *Religion and the Decline of Magic* (New York, 1971); and Wayne Shumaker, *The Occult Sciences in the Renaissance* (Berkeley, 1972).

Among recent studies of Prospero's magic, see, e.g., D. G. James, *The Dream of Prospero* (Oxford, 1967), pp. 45–71; Hardin Craig, "Magic in *The Tempest*," *Philological Quarterly*, 47 (1968), 8–15; Harry Levin, "Two Magian Comedies: 'The Tempest' and 'The Alchemist'," *Shakespeare Survey*, 22 (1969), 47–58; Kurt Tetzeli von Rosador, *Magie im Elisabethanischen Drama* (Braunschweig, 1970), pp. 164–86; Elizabeth Sewell, " 'As I was sometime Milan': Prospects for a Search for Giordano Bruno, through Prospero, Coleridge, and the Figure of Exile," *Mosaic*, 8 (1974), 127–37; David Woodman, *White Magic and English Renaissance Drama* (Cranbury, N.J., 1973), pp. 64 ff.; Robert Egan, "This Rough Magic: Perspectives of Art and Morality in *The Tempest*," *Shakespeare Quarterly*, 23 (1972), 171–82; Frances Yates, *Shakespeare's Last Plays: A New Approach* (London, 1975), pp. 87–106; D'Orsay Pearson, " 'Unless I Be Relieved by Prayer': *The Tempest* in Perspective," *Shakespeare Studies*, VII (1974), 253–82; and David Young, *The Heart's Forest: A Study of Shakespeare's Pastoral Plays* (New Haven and London, 1972), pp. 146–91, and "Where the Bee Sucks: A Triangular Study of *Doctor Faustus*,

The Alchemist, and *The Tempest,"* in *Shakespeare's Romances Reconsidered,* ed. Carol McGinnis Kay and Henry E. Jacobs (Lincoln and London, 1978), pp. 149–66.

Unpublished dissertations which study Prospero as a magician include Richard John Beebe's "The Genesis of Prospero" (University of Michigan, 1975); Geoffrey C. Goodale's "Black Spirits and White. Shakespeare's Use of Goetic and Theurgic Tradition in *Macbeth* and *The Tempest"* (Boston University, 1975); John Spencer Mebane's "Art and Magic in Marlowe, Jonson, and Shakespeare: The Occult Tradition in *Dr. Faustus, The Alchemist,* and *The Tempest* (Emory University, 1975); and Barbara H. Traister, "Heavenly Necromancy: The Figure of the Magician in Tudor and Stuart Drama" (Yale University, 1973).

3. D'Orsay Pearson, p. 256. Pearson accepts the idea that Prospero is a "theurgist"; his argument is that (as Augustine had made clear), theurgists were only self-deluded witches in serious danger of damnation. Augustine attacks the theurgists in *The City of God,* Book X, chapters 9–11. The word "theurgist," applied by Curry to Prospero, was used by Iamblichus to describe the priest/magician who uses ritual magic to invoke superior natural powers; the term is frequently used to distinguish the "good" or "white" magician from the "goetist" or "black" magician. See Iamblichus, *On the Mysteries of the Egyptians, Chaldeans, and Assyrians,* trans. Thomas Taylor, 2nd ed. (London, 1895). The term "theurgist" is not synonymous with "Hermetic magus" or "mage"—terms which today, following Kermode and Yates, are more usually applied to Prospero; but, since both "theurgist" and "magus" describe magicians who use ceremonial magic to achieve spiritual ascendancy, distinctions between the terms need not bother us here. On the Hermetic magus, see especially Frances Yates, *Giordano Bruno and the Hermetic Tradition.* An excellent discussion of Hermeticism is A.-J. Festugière's *Hermetisme et Mystique Païenne* (Paris, 1967).

4. Robert West, "Ceremonial Magic in *The Tempest," Shakespeare and the Outer Mystery* (Lexington, Kentucky, 1968), pp. 80–95.

5. In their dissertations, both Richard Beebe and Barbara Traister recognize that a variety of images of the magician were current in Renaissance England. I will note later the points at which my research and Professor Traister's are congruent and where we differ; Professor Beebe's approach is quite different from mine.

6. All quotations from Shakespeare's plays are taken from the *Norton Facsimile First Folio.* The line numberings, in place of the through-line numbering of the Facsimile, are those of the Riverside edition of the plays (1974). The passage here quoted is from I, ii, 75–77, 89–93, 105–11, 165–68, 180–84.

7. See especially Eugenio Garin, "Magic and Astrology in the Civilisation of the Renaissance" (note 2, above).

8. The letters between Cornelius Agrippa and Johannes Trithemius, Abbot of Saint James of Herbipolis, written in 1510, are printed in Agrippa's *Three Books of Occult Philosophy,* trans. J. F. (1651), pp. A2–A5. The later letter from Agrippa, "To the most Renowned & Illustrious Prince, Hermannus of Wyda" (written, as indicated by internal evidence, in 1531), prefaces Book III of *Occult Philosophy* ("Ceremonial Magic"), pp. 341–42.

9. "A Letter Containing a most brief discourse Apologetical . . ." (1599), p. A2v. See also Dee's "Monas Hieroglyphica" (Antwerp, 1564), trans. and introduced by C. H. Josten, *Ambix* xii, 1964, pp. 102, 197.

10. Rudolf, King of Bohemia and Holy Roman Emperor from 1576 to 1612, was described by a contemporary, Melchior Goldast (1612) as an "intelligent and sagacious Prince" who "contemned all vulgar things, loving only the rare and miraculous." He was, according to his biographer R. J. W. Evans, "a notorious patron of occult learning who trod the paths of secret knowledge with an obsession bordering on mania." *Rudolf II and His World: A Study in Intellectual History, 1576–1612* (Oxford, 1973), esp. pp. 196–242, where Evans quotes Goldast and discusses "Rudolf and the Occult Arts."

11. Robert Egan (note 2, above) also notes the significance of the fact that Prospero "still prizes his volumes above his dukedom," but for Egan this is one more piece of evidence of

Prospero's morally flawed vision, an indication that, throughout most of the play, Prospero is "disastrously short-sighted," and that he has a "serious misconception of himself as god rather than man," a character flaw which causes him to cross the thin line from theurgy to necromancy. See pp. 176–77, 179.

12.   See, e.g., John Dee, "A Letter, Nine Yeeres Since, written and first published: Containing a most brief discourse Apologeticall . . ." (1603), p. B3, where he refers to the "volumes . . . which by Gods providence, have been preserved from the spoile made of my Librarie . . . here . . . Anno 1583. In which Librarie, were about 4000 bookes: whereof, 700 were ancientlie written by hand. . . ." A partial catalogue of Dr. Dee's extensive library is appended to *The Private Diary of Dr. Dee,* ed. J. O. Halliwell (1842).

13.   See, e.g., the letters of Dee and of Agrippa and Trithemius, noted above; see also Garin (note 2, above).

14.   West, pp. 92–93; Sisson, pp. 75–76. *The Golden Ass of Lucius Apuleius,* trans. William Adlington (orig. pub. 1566), ed. F. J. Harvey Darton (London, 1924), p. 49. Agrippa, *Three Books of Occult Philosophy,* p. A3. Agrippa himself complicates this whole issue, however, by later claiming that sometimes the magus "receiveth this miraculous power" to "command the Elements, drive away Fogs, raise the winds . . . raise the dead" (*Occult Philosophy,* p. 357).

15.   John Lyly, *Endymion, The Man in the Moon,* I, iv. Although Glendower, in *1 Henry IV,* does not actually claim the ability to raise tempests, he implies that he has control over the weather, and he is credited by Holinshed with tempest-raising powers. Reginald Scot, *The Discoverie of Witchcraft* (1584), pp. 1–2. Trithemius's letters about Faustus are quoted by William Rose in his introduction to *The Historie of the Damnable Life and Deserved Death of Doctor John Faustus, 1592* (South Bend, Indiana, 1963), pp. 3–5.

16.   The term "hysbrisrede" is used by Tetzeli von Rosador to describe such bragging speeches by magicians; see his *Magie in Elisabethanischen Drama,* pp. 65–71.

17.   Cf. John Dee, "To the Kings most excellent Maiestie: the true copy of M. John Dee his petition to the Kings most excellent Maiestie, exhibited: Anno 1604, Junii 5, at Greenewich" and "To the Honorable Assemblie of the Commons in the Present Parlament, Anno 1604, Juni 8." These petitions are bound in the Folger Library copy of *Dr. Dee's Letters.*

The problem of how we are to take the tone and intention of Agrippa's "recantation" in his *De incertitudine . . .* (translated by Ja. San[ford] in 1569) remains a vexing one inasmuch as he published *De Occulta philosophia* in 1531, several years after he wrote *De incertitudine. . . .* In addition, the letter to Hernanus of Wyda in which ceremonial magic is highly praised (see note 8, above) is itself dated 1531.

18.   For a complete study of this tradition, one would want to begin with legends of wizards in *The Golden Legend,* and to examine carefully the relationship between Merlin and the various figures of the wizard which one finds in sixteenth century narrative and drama. One can find typical legends about wizards in J. Payne Collier's Introduction to *John a Kent and John a Cumber,* by Anthony Munday (London, 1851), especially pp. xxii–xxvi; in John William Ashton's "A Critical Edition of Anthony Munday's *John a Kent and John a Cumber*" (University of Chicago unpublished dissertation, 1928), pp. 61 ff.; in William Godwin's *Lives of the Necromancers, or an account of the most eminent persons in successive ages, who have claimed for themselves, or to whom has been imputed by others, the exercise of magical power* (1834); and in E. M. Butler's *The Myth of the Magus* (Cambridge, Eng., 1948).

Commedia dell'arte magicians are mentioned by K. M. Lea in her *Italian Popular Comedy: A Study in the Commedia dell'arte, 1560–1620, with special reference to the English Stage,* II (Oxford, 1934), pp. 444–45; she also includes several *scenari* which involve magicians in the same volume, pp. 555–674.

The prose "histories" to which I here refer are, specifically, *The Famous History of Fryer Bacon: Contayning the wonderfull things he did in his Life. Also the manner of his death, with the Lives and Deaths of the two Conjurors, Bungay and Vandermast* (1640[?]) and *The Historie of the damnable life, and deserved death of Doctor John Faustus. . . ,* trans. by P. F. (1592).

Recent editions of wizard dramas are Robert Greene's *Friar Bacon and Friar Bungay,* ed. Daniel Seltzer, Regents Renaissance Drama Series (Lincoln, Neb., 1963), and Christopher Marlowe's *Doctor Faustus,* in *Christopher Marlowe, The Complete Works,* II, ed. Fredson Bowers (Cambridge, Eng., 1973).

That Prospero shares characteristics with the commedia dell'arte magician has been noted by Lea (II, 443–55), by Sharon L. Smith, "The Commedie dell'Arte and Problems Related to Source in *The Tempest,*" *Emporia State Research Studies,* XIII (1964), 11–23, and by David Young, *The Heart's Forest,* pp. 149 ff. That Prospero is related to such wizard figures as Green's Bacon and Marlowe's Faustus has been noted by Jeffrey P. Hart, "Prospero and Faustus," *Boston University Studies in English,* II, no. 4 (1956–1957), 197–206, by Robert R. Reed, Jr., *The Occult on the Tudor and Stuart Stage* (Boston, 1965), by David Young, "A Triangular Study" (note 2, above), and by Barbara Traister, "Heavenly Necromancy" (note 2, above).

In this section of my paper, there are several points at which my research overlaps significantly with that of Professor Traister, whose dissertation I saw after I had completed this essay. Since Professor Traister's study does not include reference to the commedia dell'arte or to the wizards of legend or to other major magic-traditions which are important parts of my study, and since she includes plays and narrative poems in her study which I do not consider, our approaches are inevitably different, and our conclusions complementary rather than identical. Our major points of agreement concern the dual nature of the magician hero and the importance of the magician as a presenter of shows. We disagree most importantly in our interpretation of the conclusion of *Friar Bacon,* in many of our readings of *Doctor Faustus,* in our reading of Agrippa (her work being based on *De incertitudine . . .* and mine primarily on *De occulta . . .*). And our readings of *The Tempest* differ significantly.

19. Walker, *Spiritual and Demonic Magic,* p. 82 ff.

20. See Collier's Introduction to *John a Kent and John a Cumber,* pp. xxiv–xxv, for two such legends about Owen.

21. On the historical Bacon, see, e.g., S. C. Easton, *Roger Bacon and His Search for a Universal Science* (Oxford: Oxford University Press, 1952). Waldo F. McNeir, in his "Traditional Elements in the Character of Greene's Friar Bacon," *Studies in Philology,* 45 (1948), 172–79, gives some attention to the "growth of the Bacon legend." See especially fn. 2, pp. 172–73.

22. Lea, II, 636–42.

23. See, e.g., "The Magician" (Lea, II, 612 ff.); "The Enchantress" (Lea, II, 618 ff.); "The Great Magician" (Lea, II, 648 ff.); "The Magic of Pantalone" (Lea, II, 587 ff.).

24. For a similar renunciation in another commedia dell'arte play, see Lea's notes to "The Great Magician," p. 657, which refer to a fuller version of the play in which "the Magician announces that his reign is at an end now that all his spells are finished within one day," and, in the final scene, "the Magician renounces his magic art."

25. Curry, *Shakespeare's Philosophical Patterns,* pp. 186–194; George Lyman Kittredge, Introduction to *The Tempest,* in *Sixteen Plays of Shakespeare* (Boston, 1946), p. 11. On Ariel as a *daemon,* see also A. Koszul, "Ariel," *English Studies,* XIX (1937), 200–04, and W. Stacey Johnson, "The Genesis of Ariel," *Shakespeare Quarterly,* II (1951), 205–10. For Plato on *daemons,* see "The Symposium," trans. W. Hamilton (Baltimore, Md., 1951), p. 81; for Iamblichus's discussion of *daemons,* see Section IV, pp. 203–24 (note 3, above). In the Hermetic writings see *Hermetica,* ed. and trans. by Walter Scott, 4 vols. (Oxford, 1924), I, 293; Agrippa, *Three Books of Occult Philosophy,* pp. 390 ff.

26. See *A True and Faithful Relation of What passed for many yeers between Dr. John Dee (a mathematician of Great Fame in Queen Elizabeth and King James their reignes) and Some spirits . . . out of the Original Copy, Written with Dr. Dees own Hand.* Kept in the Library of Sir Tho. Cotton . . . with a Preface . . . by Meric Casaubon (1659).

27. *1 Henry IV,* III. i; the "historical personage" of Faust is discussed by William Rose, *The Damnable Life,* pp. 3–22; for legends about John a Kent, see Collier, pp. xxii–xxv; *Daemonologie, in Forme of a Dialogue* (Edinburgh, 1597), p. 20.

28.   In *The Historie of the Damnable Life* (ed. Rose, 1963), p. 73, Faustus sets as his "primary Articles" of the contract:

1.   That he might be a Spirit in shape and quality.

2.   That Mephostophiles should be his servant, and at his commandment.

3.   That Mephostophiles should bring him anything, and do for him whatsoever.

4.   That at all times he should be in his house, invisible to all men, except only to himself, and at his commandment to shew himself.

5.   Lastly, that Mephostophiles should at all times appear at his command, in what form or shape soever he would.

Marlowe follows this wording closely in *Doctor Faustus,* II.i.

29.   The relationship between Anthony Munday's *John a Kent and John a Cumber* and both *A Midsummer Night's Dream* and *The Tempest* remains to be fully explored. It is clear, however, that John a Kent's servant, Shrimp, is highly reminiscent of both Puck and Ariel; Shrimp probably prefigures both Puck and Ariel; and Shrimp's relationship to his master may well come from the same tradition to which I am now directing the reader's attention. For suggestive comments on Munday's play and its possible impact on Shakespeare, see Robert R. Reed, *The Occult on the Tudor and Stuart Stage* (note 18, above); see also I. A. Shapiro, "Shakespeare and Mundy," *Shakespeare Survey,* 14 (1961), 25–33, and I. A. Shapiro, "The Significance of a Date," *Shakespeare Survey,* 8 (1955), 100–05.

30.   *Of the Vanitie and uncertaintie of Artes and Sciences* (note 17, above), pp. 62–63.

31.   Frank Aydelotte, in his *Elizabethan Rogues and Vagabonds* (Oxford Historical and Literary Studies. Under the direction of C. H. Firth and Walter Raleigh) Vol. I (Oxford, 1913), pp. 49–52, draws our attention to the conjuring tricks of the Juglers described by Reginald Scot, and notes that in the sixteenth century, "vagabond jugglers . . . wandered up and down the land, reaping a harvest in every market, fair, and tavern; they are mentioned in every statute against vagabonds, and doubtless had a prosperous life, in spite of the constables and judges." Reginald Scot refers to the "poore men as live" by "the secrets of [the] mysterie" of jugling (*Discoverie,* p. 321), and refers by name to several professional art-magicians.

That legerdemaine artists performed in the provinces is clear in the "Notices of Dramatic Companies in the Provincial Records, 1558–1642" collected by John Tucker Murray, *English Dramatic Companies, 1558–1642,* Vol. II (London, 1910), esp. pp. 247–53, where, among the listings of anonymous "art and skill men, wonder exhibitors, etc." we find certain conjurors—William Vincent, and Hocus Pocus, for example—listed by name, along with the fees paid them for their entertainments.

Among the theaters at which legerdemain artists performed were the Hope and the Fortune. See Gerald Eades Bentley, *The Jacobean and Caroline Stage, Dramatic Companies and Players.* In Seven Volumes (Oxford: Clarendon Press, 1941–1968), II, 612–13, and VI, 209.

32.   Thomas Ady, *A Candle in the Dark: or A Treatise Concerning the Nature of Witches and Witchcraft* (1656), pp. 28–29. That Hocus Pocus was indeed a famous illusionist in Stuart England is attested to not only by records of payments to him in the provinces (Murray, II, 253), but also by a dialogue reference to him in Jonson's *The Magnetic Lady,* where, when the audience wants a miracle, a character suggests that they bring on Hocus Pocus (chorus between Acts I and II), and by a dialogue exchange in Jonson's *The Staple of Newes,* where the Vice in the old drama is compared to Iniquity coming in "like Hokus Pokos, in a Juglers jerkin, with false skirts, like the Knave of Clubs!" (Second Intermean after Act II). For a discussion of Hocus Pocus as a professional conjuror during James' and Charles' reign, see Trevor H. Hall, *Old Conjuring Books: A Bibliographical and Historical Study* (London, 1972), pp. 126–29.

33.   Quoted by Frances Yates, *Giordano Bruno and the Hermetic Tradition,* pp. 208–09.

34.   Rid, *The Art of Jugling, or Legerdemaine* (1614), p. 82.

35.   "Hocus Pocus Junior," *The Anatomie of Legerdemaine, or the Art of Jugling set forth in his proper colours* . . . (1634); Thomas Cooper, *The Mysterie of Witchcraft* (1617).

36.   See, e.g., Scot, p. 339, where "the boie" is made to dance naked, as if bewitched by the familiar; and p. 349, where two boy assistants are used in the "decollation of John Baptist" trick. See also Ady, pp. 36–40. In John Fletcher's *The Fair Maid of the Inn,* IV, ii, Forobusco the Conjuror uses his Boy to perform Scot's "naked dancing" trick in order to "con" the spectators.

37.   Thomas Fosset, *The Servants Dutie or the Calling and Condition of Servants. Serving for the instruction, not only of Servants, but of Masters and Mistresses* (1612), pp. 22–23. See also pp. 18–19, and pp. 25 ff. Equally interesting is *The Cities Advocate . . .* (1629), which discusses the contracts of bondage and of apprenticeship; J. Fit John, *A Diamonde Most Precious, worthy to be marked: Instructing All Maysters and Servauntes, how they ought to leade their lyves . . .* (1577), esp. pp. 47 ff.; and *St. Paul's Threefold Cord: wherewith are severally combined; the mutuall Oeconomicall Duties, Betwixt . . . Master-Servant* (1635), p. 273.

38.   The *OED* (1933 ed.) gives as its first definition of "malignant": "disposed to rebel against . . . constituted authority; disaffected, malcontent." When Prospero says to Ariel (I.ii.257) "Thou liest, malignant Thing," it is quite possible that "malignant" has the above meaning (in that it occurs within the context of a master-servant quarrel) rather than the sense of "having an evil influence." Whittaker and West, assuming that the word has this latter meaning, stress its importance in linking Ariel at least temporarily to pernicious demons. See West, p. 88.

39.   Wright, "Juggling Tricks and Conjury on the English Stage before 1642," *Modern Philology,* 24 (1927), 276.

40.   See Scot, pp. 307 ff., and Rid, p. B3.

41.   See, e.g., B. A. Mowat, " 'And that's true, too': Structures and Meanings in *The Tempest,*" *Renaissance Papers 1976,* pp. 37–50, for some reflections on the play's shifting modes of presentation and on its mixture of representational and presentational styles—dramaturgical patterns which parallel the transformations in the figure of Prospero.

42.   Dillard, *Pilgrim at Tinker's Creek* (New York, 1974), p. 11.

43.   Research for this essay was undertaken at the Folger Shakespeare Library, and funded in part by a grant from Auburn University.

Reading *The Tempest*

RUSS MCDONALD

My subject is *The Tempest*—how it has been read recently and how it might be read otherwise. My vehicle for approaching this subject is the poetic style, its most minute formal details. My immediate purpose is to read *The Tempest* in a way that offers an alternative to, and an implicit critique of, certain readings produced by American New Historicism and British Cultural Materialism. My larger aim is to discover uses for stylistic criticism that will reassert the value of textuality in a nontextual phase of criticism and that may contribute to the reconciliation of text and context, the aesthetic and the political.

I

It will come as no surprise to anyone who has followed developments in Renaissance studies that treatments of *The Tempest* seldom concern themselves with the verse. Recent criticism looks beyond textual details and formal properties to concentrate on cultural surroundings, addressing the play almost solely in terms of social and political contexts, particularly its relation to colonial discourse. The essay by Francis Barker and Peter Hulme in John Drakakis's *Alternative Shakespeares* is typical: "The ensemble of fictional and lived practices, which for convenience we will simply refer to here as 'English colonialism,' provides *The Tempest*'s dominant discursive 'con-texts.' We have chosen here to concentrate specifically on the figure of usurpation as the nodal point of the play's imbrication into this discourse of colonialism."[1] If American New Historicists seem slightly less virulent than British Cultural Materialists, their concerns are scarcely less political and their methods similarly contextual.[2] The Virginia pamphlets, Shakespeare's personal association with contemporary colonial projects, Montaigne on cannibals, twentieth-century racism and political oppression and their relation to Caliban—these are the contexts that have dominated recent treatments of this text.[3]

Russ McDonald, "Reading *The Tempest*," *Shakespeare Survey* 43 (1991):15–28. Reprinted with the permission of Cambridge University Press.

Many of the readings that regard *The Tempest* primarily as what Paul Brown calls an "intervention" in European colonial history are tendentious in conception and narrow in scope. In disputing them, however, I do not wish to neglect their nuances nor to suppress the differences among them: Greenblatt's 1976 essay, "Learning to Curse: Aspects of Linguistic Colonialism in the Sixteenth Century," for example, contextualizes *The Tempest* in a way that is balanced and sensitive to ambiguity,[4] but recent readers have become increasingly single-minded and reductive, often adopting a censorious and shrill tone in delineating the text's relation to the problems of cultural tyranny, political freedom, and exploitation. One of the most notable of these discussions, Paul Brown's " 'This thing of darkness I acknowledge mine': *The Tempest* and the discourse of colonialism," printed in Dollimore and Sinfield's *Political Shakespeare,* states its purpose in a way that fairly represents the revisionist reading. "This chapter seeks to demonstrate that *The Tempest* is not simply a reflection of colonialist practices but an intervention in an ambivalent and even contradictory discourse. This intervention takes the form of a powerful and pleasurable narrative which seeks at once to harmonise disjunction, to transcend irreconcilable contradictions and to mystify the political conditions which demand colonialist discourse. Yet the narrative ultimately fails to deliver that containment and instead may be seen to foreground precisely those problems which it works to efface or overcome."[5] Something like this point of view is expressed more succinctly by Walter Cohen: "*The Tempest* uncovers, perhaps despite itself, the racist and imperialist bases of English nationalism."[6] And some critics decline to treat the work at all. Richard Strier, for example, considers *The Tempest* "more conservative than the plays, from *Hamlet* on, which precede it,"[7] and the adjective is not intended as a compliment.

As these remarks show, a basic argumentative move on the part of many poststructuralist critics has been to attack the play's sophistication. This gambit follows an earlier one, a critical usurpation of the dramatic sovereignty of Prospero and a concomitant attack on the idealist reading set forth in Frank Kermode's Introduction to the Arden edition.[8] Having cast the benevolent Prospero out to sea, New Historicists and Cultural Materialists have sought to exert their hegemony over the text (and interpretation of it) by urging the claims of discourse, usually asserting that *The Tempest* cannot be aware of its own participation in the language of oppression and colonial power.[9] Such readings are not simply uninterested in the contribution of poetic texture; in fact, much criticism of *The Tempest,* like much political reading in general, is deliberately anti-aesthetic. The verbal harmonics can too easily be considered a means of textual mystification, a tool in Prospero's magic trunk contributing to the "enchantment" that has made this play especially appealing and thus especially dangerous, made it "a powerful and pleasurable narrative." Some voices have been raised against the tendentious and monochromatic quality of much interpretation of *The Tempest:* Meredith Anne Skura, for example, in a persuasive psychological essay, argues that "recent criticism not only flattens the text into the mold of colonialist discourse and eliminates what is characteristically 'Shakespearean' in order to foreground what is 'colonialist,' but it is also—paradoxically—in danger of taking the play further from the particular historical situation in England in 1611 even as it brings it closer to what we mean by 'colonialism' today."[10] Despite this and a few other protests, the colonialist reading in the past decade has demonized Prospero, sentimentalized Caliban, and tyrannized conferences and journals with a new orthodoxy as one-sided as that which it has sought to replace.

Sensitivity to the verse offers an alternative to both of these restrictive interpretations. In the first place, awareness of the poetic complexity of *The Tempest* suggests that the play is considerably more self-conscious than the recent demystifiers will allow. Repetition—of vowels and consonants, words, phrases, syntactical forms, and other verbal effects—is a fundamental stylistic turn in *The Tempest;* these aurally reiterative patterns serve to tantalize the listener, generating expectations of illumination and fixity but refusing to satisfy those desires. Such poetic echoes function in concert with the open-endedness of the romance form and with the reappearance of a host of familiar Shakespearian topoi: verbal and ideational patterns entice the audience by promising and withholding illumination, demonstrating the impossibility of significational certainty and creating an atmosphere of hermeneutic instability.

Moreover, the style and form of *The Tempest* engage the audience textually with the same issues of control and mastery—the problem of power—that are brought into sharp focus by considerations of historical context. The tendency of words and phrases to repeat themselves may be linked to the play's profound concern with reproduction, in various senses from the biological to the political. Versions of this very broad topic appear especially in those episodes that have appealed to recent critics: the story of the deceased Sycorax, the absent wife of Prospero, Antonio's usurpation, Prospero's taking the island from Caliban, the attempt of the "savage" to rape Miranda, the enslavement of Ariel, the political ambitions of Stephano and Trinculo, the arranged marriages of Claribel and Miranda, the masque's concern with fertility and succession, the problem of dynasty, the effort to reproduce the self through art. I shall argue that the stylistic implications of repetition offer a way of treating these political topics that is considerably more nuanced than most recent discussions of the play, more responsive to its balances and contradictions. The repetitions of the dramatic poetry help to expose the problems inherent in the act of cultural re-creation and to magnify their complexity, not to supply answers. Virgil Thomson described "structural elements" in music as "expressive vocabularies, . . . repertories of devices for provoking feelings without defining them."[11] In *The Tempest,* as in late Shakespeare generally, the effect of the poetry is to promote *un*certainty and to insist upon ambiguity, and attention to the verse makes one increasingly dubious about the bluntness of most political interpretation.

II

Repetition becomes a prominent figure in Shakespeare's late style generally, and *The Tempest* in particular derives much of its poetic power from phonetic, lexical, and syntactical reiteration.[12] From the confused echoes of the first scene ("We split, we split!") through Prospero's re-creation of the past ("Twelve year since, Miranda, twelve year since") to the pleasing assonantal chiming of the Epilogue, aural patterns impart a distinctive texture to this text. And yet *The Tempest* is something of a stylistic paradox, being simultaneously one of the most pleonastic and one of the briefest plays in the canon. The incantatory tone is in turn reinforced by the ellipses that represent a complementary and equally prominent feature of the late verse. But the repetition of sounds and words is only one type of larger and more frequently discussed modes of iteration, to which Jan Kott in particular has directed our notice: the replicated actions of usurpation and assassination, the structural mirroring of the aristocratic and the servant plots, the allusion to and reproduction of major motifs from *The Aeneid,* the creation of a masque within the play, and Shakespeare's representation of some of his own most familiar dramatic actions and topics.[13] Likewise, omission makes itself felt narratively as well as stylistically. By this stage of his career Shakespeare has told the story of, say, regicide so many times that he now presents it in its most abbreviated and indicative fashion. Such a mimetic approach might be called abstract: the artist is sufficiently confident of his ability to tell a story and of his audience's capacity to receive it that he is able to signal an action rather than develop it in detail.[14] We are in the realm of the comedian performing at a convention of comedians: since everybody knows the jokes, he need only refer to a gag by number, and the house breaks into laughter.

Presence being easier to demonstrate than absence, I shall concentrate on figures of repetition, but a few words are in order about Shakespeare's impulse to omit. The gestural approach to storytelling corresponds to the poet's attempt at concentration and density throughout the last plays: Shakespeare strives for power of expression not only by contracting words and skipping over non-essential syllables, but also by discarding participles, pronouns (especially relative pronouns), conjunctions, and even nouns and verbs. Asyndeton appears about as frequently as in *King Lear* and *Antony and Cleopatra,* two plays of much greater length.[15] And the play is replete with verbless constructions: "Most sure the goddess / On whom these airs attend" (1.2.425–6); "No wonder, sir, / But certainly a maid" (1.2.431–2). Participles often do the work of longer noun/verb phrases, thus accelerating the tempo: "I, not rememb'ring how I cried out then, / Will cry it o'er again" (1.2.133–4). Anne Barton, in a brilliant discussion of this stripping away of nonessentials, points out that the vocabulary of *The Tempest* is spiked with spontaneous compounds ("sea-change," "cloud-capped," "hag-seed," "man-monster"), proposing that such phrases "seem to be driving towards some ultimate reduction of language, a mode of expression more meaningful in its very bareness than anything a more elaborate and conventional rhetoric could devise." She groups Shakespeare's urge towards linguistic compression with his disjunctive approach to characterization, observation of the unities, and reluctance to supply apparently pertinent details, all strategies by which *The Tempest* "continually gives the impression of being much bigger than it is."[16]

For all its compression and abbreviation, however, it is also pleonastic and reiterative—phonetically, rhythmically, lexically, syntactically, and architectonically. Although the structural and narrative replications are more likely to be the subject of critical interest than the aural, most listeners find themselves beguiled by the musical repetition of vowels and consonants, reduplication of words, echoing of metrical forms, and incantatory effect of this musical design. Even enthusiasts of prosody, however, are apt to weary of the repetitions of my close analysis, and so I beg the reader's indulgence as I lay the groundwork for the demonstration, in the second half of this essay, of how these effects function ideologically.

One of the play's most distinctive stylistic properties is the interlocking of aural effects in a way that recalls the etymology of *text* in weaving. Instances of consonance and assonance call attention to themselves in virtually every line: in a phrase such as "There's nothing ill can dwell in such a temple," "ill" is glanced at in "dwell," then both are altered with the repetition of the *e* and *l* in "temple," and these harmonies are augmented by the reiteration of the *th* and *n* sounds. Such interweavings are audible in lines that seem merely declarative ("For thou must now know farther") as well as in the obviously musical ("Wound the loud winds, or with bemocked-at stabs / Kill the still-closing waters"). They dominate Prospero's recitation of Ariel's history:

> within which rift
> Imprisoned thou didst painfully remain
> A dozen years, within which space she died
> And left thee there, where thou didst vent thy
>   groans
> As fast as mill-wheels strike. Then was this
>   island—
> Save for the son that she did litter here,
> A freckled whelp, hag-born—not honoured
>   with
> A human shape.
>
> (1.2.279–86)

To begin with the smallest units, a series of vowel sounds spin themselves out to almost absurd lengths ("within which rift / Imprisoned thou didst painfully remain"); pairs of long vowels alternate with short ("she did litter here"); consonants can be repeated independently and then combined and split apart (in "put thyself / Upon this island as a spy," the *p, s,* and *i* sounds establish themselves separately and then coalesce in "spy"). This practice of joining and splitting phonemes creates what Stephen Booth has called "pulsating alliteration," a sensation of expansion and contraction that implies density and activity, making the text effectively "poetic" even when it may not sound conventionally so.[17]

Lexical repetition is largely responsible for the incantatory appeal of *The Tempest,* and thus for some of the most memorable passages in the play. Even in the prose of the opening shipwreck—"All lost! To prayers, to prayers! All lost!"; " 'We split, we split, we split!' "—the confused shouts of desperation take a reiterative form that functions poetically in the early speeches of Prospero and then throughout the work. Here, for instance, is a seven-line passage from the beginning of the play.

PROSPERO   . . . Tell your piteous heart
            There's no *harm done.*
MIRANDA   O woe the day!
PROSPERO   *No harm.*
            I have done nothing but in care *of thee,*
            Of thee, my dear one, *thee, my* daughter, who
            Art ignorant of what thou *art,* naught knowing
            Of whence *I am,* nor that *I am* more better
            Than Prospero, master of a full poor cell
            And thy no greater father.
                                        (1.2.14–21)[18]

In addition to the italicized repetitions, the passage echoes with phonetic duplication: "heart . . . harm," "O, woe," "my dear . . . my daughter," "naught . . . daughter," "naught knowing," "full . . . cell," and "greater father." (Our uncertainty about Elizabethan pronunciation may limit but surely does not invalidate speculation about such phonetic echoes.) The regularity of certain metrical patterns and the isocolonic arrangement of clauses intensify the effect of the repeated words, notably "thee, my dear one, thee, my daughter" and "Of whence I am, nor that I am." And then there are all the negatives: "No," "no," "nothing," "naught," "knowing," "nor," "no."

To catch the repetitive flavour of Prospero's narrative to Miranda is to learn how to hear the language of the text as a whole; the following examples are taken from the first two hundred lines of the long second scene:

            Which thou heard'st cry, which thou saw'st
                sink. Sit down,
            For thou must now know farther.

If thou rememb'rest aught ere thou cam'st here,
How thou cam'st here thou mayst.

Twelve year since, Miranda, twelve year since

What foul play had we that we came from
    thence?
Or blessed was't we did?
                    Both, both, my girl.
By foul play, as thou sayst, were we heaved
    thence,
But blessedly holp hither.

                  how to grant suits,
How to deny them, *who t'*advance and *who*
To trash for over-topping, new *created*
The *creatures* that were mine, I say—*or* changed
    'em
Or else new formed 'em; having both the key
Of *officer* and *office,* . . .

                no screen between this part
    he played
And him he played it for

Which now's upon's, without the which this
    story

To cry to th'sea that roared to us, to sigh
To th'winds, whose pity, sighing back again

Sit still, and hear the last of our sea-sorrow.
Here in this island we arrived, and here
Have I, thy schoolmaster . . .

Since stylistic criticism often founders in an elaborate summation of what its examples have already disclosed, I leave it to the reader to note the poetic and rhetorical details, the instances of assonance, alliteration, epanalepsis, isocolon, several species of paronomasia (polyptoton, syllepsis, antanaclasis), not to mention the fundamental pleasures of the repeated sounds. The various kinds of verbal play impart energy and motion to what is dramatically a notoriously static scene.

That such echoing patterns are not confined to the protasis or to the protagonist but resound throughout the work is apparent by a glance at the episode in which Antonio seeks to inveigle Sebastian into fratricide, the temptation scene (2.1.204–311). The villain begins his scheme by priming his partner with anaphoric and rhythmic restatement: "They fell together all, as

by consent; / They dropped as by a thunder-stroke" (2.1.208–9). He continues by arguing that Ferdinand's disappearance is Sebastian's good fortune,
demonstrating the transformation linguistically:

SEBASTIAN   I have *no hope*
                That he's undrowned.
ANTONIO   O, out of that *'no hope'*
                What *great hope* have you! *No hope* that way is
                Another way *so high a hope* that even
                Ambition cannot pierce a wink beyond,
                But doubt discovery there.
                            (2.1.243–8)

Apart from the obvious echoes, the passage rings with assonance and consonance; in addition to the aural repetition, we also catch the relentless negatives characteristic of Shakespeare's villains; the glance at sleep imagery
("wink") to which the dramatic atmosphere of the scene and the island has
acclimated us; and the self-conscious worrying of words that extends the
game begun earlier, when the conspirators toy with the metaphor of "standing water" (226). As is often the case in *The Tempest,* language emerges as a
subject itself, as speakers play with it, take pleasure in it, test its capacities,
and misuse it consciously and unconsciously, sometimes, as here, at the same
time.[19]

    Antonio's principal trick is structural recapitulation, the stringing
together of formally similar clauses. Consider his appositional elaboration of
Sebastian's one-word speech, "Claribel":

        She that is Queen of Tunis; she that dwells
        Ten leagues beyond man's life; she that from
          Naples
        Can have no note—unless the sun were post—
        The man i'th'moon's too slow—till newborn
          chins
        Be rough and razorable; she that from whom
        We all were sea-swallowed, though some cast
          again—
        And by that destiny, to perform an act
        Whereof what's past is prologue, what to come
        In yours and my discharge.
                     (2.1.251–9)

This string of clauses—the reader will have noticed that it is not even a sentence—is calculated to inveigle the auditor into rhythmic sympathy with

and, finally, assent to the speaker's claims. It depends for its seductive power on the reiterative disposition of phrases, specifically on the pattern known as *conduplicatio,* the repetition of words in succeeding clauses. Antonio/Shakespeare strives for a kind of hypnosis with simplicity of diction, at least in the first half, where until "razorable" no word is longer than two syllables and most are monosyllabic; with regular disruption of the normal metrical structure, each of the "she that" phrases being a trochee substituted for an iamb;[20] and with syntactical recapitulation. Even those qualifying clauses that violate the pattern of "she that" develop their own rhythmic echo: "unless the sun were post" and "The man i'th'moon's too slow" are identical in length and regularity, similar in the importance of consonance and assonance, and completed with the repeated "o" sound. In these dramatic circumstances, Antonio's periphrastic style amounts to verbal overkill, as even the dim Sebastian seems to perceive in his response to the "Claribel" speech: "What stuff is this?" But the local effect is less important than the overriding dramatic goal: Antonio and Sebastian are merely the agents of a playwright seeking to seduce his audience with words.[21]

So it goes through other scenes and with other speakers. Some of the richest passages in the text depend upon such lexical and sonic echo. One of the play's axiological cruces, for example, the complex relation between biology and culture, is set forth in an aurally pleasing and complex frame:

> A devil, a born devil, on whose nature
> Nurture can never stick; on whom my pains,
> Humanely taken, all, all lost, quite lost.
> (4.1.188–90)

"Full fathom five thy father lies," "Where the bee sucks, there suck I"—the power of the play's songs is at least partly attributable to various kinds of echo. Finally, the notorious mystery surrounding Gonzalo's "Widow Dido" has been examined in almost every conceivable context except, I think, that of aural identity, simple rhyme. Is it perhaps just another case of internal rhyme that sounds as if it ought to mean more than it does? Such density and concentration are essential to the sense of pregnancy upon which *The Tempest* depends.

III

Verbal patterns are congruent with and supported by larger networks of reiteration, most of them narrative and structural. Internal repetition of action has been a staple of Shakespearian dramatic structure since the early 1590s, the double wooing of Katherine and Bianca in *The Taming of the Shrew* being perhaps the most illustrative case. But rarely are the symmetries and parodic constructions made so obvious—or so obviously the subject of comment—as in *The Tempest*. The play is famous for the density and congruity of its mirrored actions.[22] To mention only those events associated with the celebrated example of usurpation, "the nodal point" of colonialist readings: Antonio's prompting Sebastian to regicide and fratricide seeks to repeat in Naples his own theft of power in Milan and re-enacts Prospero's seizure of the island and enslavement of Caliban, and all are burlesqued in "that foul conspiracy / Of the beast Caliban and his confederates / Against [Prospero's] life" (4.1.139–41). This reticulum of stories contributes to a dramatic design that seems both familiar and wonderful.

But the pattern of narrative and thematic recapitulation goes far beyond this text. *The Tempest* is flagrantly intertextual, and the cluster of echoes is especially audible, again, in the temptation scene. As commentators since Coleridge have noticed, both in general structure and particular details— Antonio's hectoring Sebastian about "What thou shouldst be," the image of the crown, the sleep imagery implying failure to understand or to act, the suppression of conscience, even the image of the hungry cat (although it is used differently)—the episode restages the scene between the Macbeths before the killing of Duncan.[23] Everywhere in the scene Shakespeare is repeating himself, unashamedly gazing back over his entire *oeuvre* and summoning up scenes, persons, themes, metaphors, bits of vocabulary, and other minor theatrical strategies, so much so that the personal allegorists can hardly be blamed for the vigour with which they have approached this text. The recreated actions and speeches function as all allusions do, giving pleasure by exercising the mind and flattering veteran spectators on their perspicacity; and this audacious kind of authorial self-cannibalism contributes another layer of complexity, another apparently meaningful pattern of familiar and yet rearranged material. The duplication which constitutes the original source of meaning and pleasure, and which contains all the other patterns I have mentioned, is the troping by the play of the actual world: reality is (re)presented on the stage.[24] This act of repetition is the most general instance of the process I have been describing in little, in that the relationship of play to life would seem to amount to a meaningful pattern, and yet it is immensely difficult to articulate that meaning. As Stanley Wells puts it, "The enchanted island reverberates with sounds hinting at tunes that never appear fully formed."[25]

IV

The prominence of the figure of repetition in both the verbal style and dramatic structure of *The Tempest* leads perforce to the question of its importance—what does the figure import through the text to the audience? what is its function? how does it mean? Although for the most part I would decline to assign specific stylistic functions to particular sounds, certain aural configurations do undeniably accomplish certain small tasks of characterization and tone.[26] The hieratic style suggested by Prospero's repetitions is clearly appropriate to his vatic persona and elegiac frame of mind, it is a commonplace that some of his poetically knotted reiterations attest to his agitation at narratively recreating his deposition, and Caliban's exultant "Freedom, high-day! High-day, freedom! Freedom, high-day, freedom!" ironically establishes his personal entrapment, his exchange of one master for another. But for the most part these and other such instances of functional echo constitute special cases. There is small profit in seeking "meaning" in Miranda's antanaclastic quibble on "your reason / For raising this sea-storm," in the vowels and consonants of Gonzalo's "If I should say I saw such islanders," or in most other lines.

I would argue that the operation of these acoustic and lexical echoes is musical, and that this music is only indirectly functional. The mutual effect of concentration and repetition creates a poetic counterpoint that challenges and exhilarates the auditor—Jan Kott describes *The Tempest* as a fugue[27]—and this contrapuntal effect induces aurally a sense of wonder corresponding to the aims and effects of the romantic or tragicomic mode. The operation of these verbal patterns is thus paradoxical, their greatest significance being precisely their ostensible significance combined with their refusal to signify. The effect is dream-like.[28] The verbal music is related to the oneiric and unreal atmosphere that attends and complicates the action of Shakespeare's late romantic forms; it promises much and delivers little, and I propose that it is just this dynamic that makes *The Tempest* uncommonly meaningful.

The insistent poetic reiterations interact with the elliptical verse style to mystify the audience about a function that never manifests itself. The play encourages its audience to scrutinize the linguistic and structural patterns for meaning, but it stoutly refuses to yield those meanings easily or fully. Eager to satisfy the desire for comprehension, we find ourselves both stimulated and frustrated. On the one hand, the repeated sounds or phrases in a brief and complicated text offer a kind of aural comfort: specifically, they create a richness of texture that seems to promise profundity. On the other, the text never fulfils the expectations of clarity which the discovery of such patterns engenders: in the rapid flow of the dialogue the repetitions themselves are succeeded by more repetitions which seem equally promising and equally unyielding. Such a strategy tantalizes the audience with the hope of clarification and fixity that art seems to promise, but it also demonstrates the difficulty and perhaps, finally, the impossibility of attaining them. Since order and comprehension seem always available but never thoroughly realized, the audience participates directly in the atmosphere of evanescence vital to this play.

The Tempest thus addresses itself directly to the problem of language and meaning, about which it registers extremely serious doubts. Denied or delayed communication becomes a minor but explicit motif as the action proceeds: numerous acts of communication (a speech, a song, a banquet, a masque) are broken off or delayed or redirected. Our position is something like that described by Caliban in his most memorable speech:

> Be not afeard. The isle is full of noises,
> Sounds, and sweet airs, that give delight and
>   hurt not.
> Sometimes a thousand twangling instruments
> Will hum about mine ears, and sometimes
>   voices
> That if I then had waked after long sleep
> Will make me sleep again; and then in dreaming
> The clouds methought would open and show
>   riches
> Ready to drop upon me, that when I waked
> I cried to dream again.
>   (3.2.138–46)

Often cited as evidence of natural sensitivity or of the magical atmosphere of the setting, these lines are most helpful as a statement of how the music of *The Tempest* impresses an audience. Robert Graves has shown that the confusion of tenses contributes to a feeling of arrested time;[29] lovely sounds "hum" about our ears; we seem to be about to receive the riches of meaning which remain forever elusive. The desired unity and gratification are contradicted by the brevity and compression of the text, and thus we find ourselves in what A. D. Nuttall has called an "atmosphere of ontological suspension" that pervades *The Tempest,* a region midway between promise and fulfilment.[30] And lest this seem too solemn let me add that this state of expectancy is also the source of immense pleasure. At this point one of my old teachers would have said, "You know. The Keats thing."

V

Tantalization is also one of the principal effects of the new mode of romance or tragicomedy that Shakespeare adopted in the late phase of his career, and the structure of the drama reinforces the fundamental erotic appeal of the verse by protracting but never seeming to supply the imminent resolution. Peter Brooks, commenting on an essay of Freud's, "Creative Writers and Day-Dreaming," writes about the aesthetic values of literary form, specifically what Freud calls "forepleasure."

The equation of the effects of literary form with forepleasure in this well-known passage is perhaps less trivial than it at first appears. If *Lust* and *Unlust* don't take us very far in the analysis of literary texture, *Vorlust*—forepleasure—tropes on pleasure and thus seems more promising. Forepleasure is indeed a curious concept, suggesting a whole rhetoric of advance toward and retreat from the goal or the end, a formal zone of play (I take it that forepleasure somehow implicates foreplay) that is both harnessed to the end and yet autonomous, capable of deviations and recursive movements. When we begin to unpack the components of forepleasure, we may find a whole erotics of form, which is perhaps what we most need if we are to make formalism serve an understanding of the human functions of literature. Forepleasure would include the notion of both delay and advance in the textual dynamic, the creation of that "dilatory space" which Roland Barthes, in *S/Z,* claimed to be the essence of the textual middle. We seek to advance through this space toward the discharge of the end, yet all the while we are perversely delaying, returning backward in order to put off the promised end and perhaps to assure its greater significance.[31]

This suggestive paragraph is relevant to the way that Shakespeare's late style functions in, and in concert with, the voguish new dramatic mode. A more or less contemporary description of the process of narrative teasing is found in William Cartwright's prefatory verses in the 1647 Beaumont and Fletcher Folio:

> None can prevent the fancy, and see through
> At the first opening; all stand wondering how
> The thing will be, until it is; which hence
> With fresh delight still cheats, still takes the
>   sense;
> The whole design, the shadow, the lights such
> That none can say he shews or hides too much.

The titillating diction of Cartwright's description is given special meaning in light of Brooks's plea for a textual erotics, for both capture the gamesome or sportive quality of romance or tragicomedy.[32]

Narrative progress towards the satisfactions of complete understanding, or closure, is indirect and irregular, and the chief pleasure rests in the delay and the circuitousness of the journey. Romance depends upon suspense, secrets, surprises, discoveries, peripeties, awakenings, revelations. Thus it automatically raises questions of epistemology but almost invariably leaves them open. It is a knowing form, a self-conscious mode reliant upon the audience's familiarity with conventions of tragic and comic storytelling and its willingness to be teased by the playwright's manipulation of generic signals. For similar reasons it is an ironic form in flattering the audience with privileged information; yet it deals in double ironies when it betrays this cosy relationship by a sudden reversal or surprise. Suspense and irony constitute only one pair of several antitheses inherent in tragicomic form (and implicit in its name); these have been described by Philip Edwards as "the pleasure of being kept out of the secret and the pleasure of being let into the secret."[33] Brooks's account of formal erotics is especially pertinent to the gestural narrative style of *The Tempest* and of the mode of romance generally.[34] Although the formal divagations are perhaps not as easy to discern in a compact work such as *The Tempest* as they are in *Cymbeline*, they are present none the less, and they recapitulate on a larger scale the sense of promise and profundity fostered by the texture of the verse.

VI

The sophisticated effects of form and style bespeak a degree of self-consciousness considerably greater than most recent political readings can admit, a self-awareness that comprehends the issues of politics and power central to the colonialist argument. The poetic and structural figures of repetition become directly pertinent to the critical debate over the European colonial impulse when that will to power is regarded as an effort to recreate the self in a new environment. Therefore the episodes and topics political critics have chosen to stress—the proprietary claims of the deceased Sycorax and her legacy to Caliban, Prospero's usurpation of the island from him, the enslavement of Ariel, the dynastic marriages of Claribel and Miranda—all these attest to the play's profound concern with reproduction, in various senses from the biological to the political to the aesthetic. Throughout its narrative *The Tempest* raises disturbing questions about the act of reproduction, not only the genetic possibilities ("Good wombs have borne bad sons") but also the difficulties of recreating society, beginning afresh, repairing in the new world the errors of the old, and it does so in a style that refuses to cease recreating itself.

The opening scene introduces the problem of sovereignty ("What cares these roarers for the name of king?"); Prospero's epilogue begs for remission and release ("let your indulgence set me free"): from beginning to end the playwright gives prominence to the problems of dominion, freedom, political failure, and the repetition of the past. Prospero's expository recital of how he lost control of himself and his dukedom is inflected with multiple variations on political failure and the repetition of past errors. He begins with a consideration of Miranda's memory, her ability to recreate the past imaginatively—"Of anything the image tell me that / Hath kept with thy remembrance" (1.2.43–4)—and the dimness of that memory prompts his rehearsal of the usurpation. Moreover, the daughter's piteous reaction to the tale reproduces emotionally the ordeal of banishment: she "will cry it o'er again" (1.2.134). His lecture reviews Antonio's seizure of power and renovation of the court, and, as Stephen Orgel points out, "this monologue is only the first of a series of repetitions."[35] Antonio encourages Sebastian to repeat the crime of deposing his brother; Prospero seeks to repair political division by arranging the dynastic marriage of Miranda and Ferdinand; Alonso is desperate at the loss of his son, which is the end of the biological line and the forfeiture of his future, Claribel being "lost" to him as well; Stephano, Trinculo, and Caliban seek to establish their own kingdom, taking power from Prospero who has himself seized the island from Caliban; Caliban has tried to reproduce himself by raping Miranda ("I had peopled else / This isle with Calibans" [1.2.353–4]); the masque of Ceres dramatizes the importance of fertility, agriculture, and orderly succession; Prospero has sought by his magical art to remake his kingdom; and Shakespeare has sought by his theatrical art to reconstruct the material world. Looked at from one point of view, colonialism becomes a form of political and cultural reproduction congruent with the effort to transcend time through art, and both of these represent versions of the defence against death.

Considerations of political and artistic recreation lead us back to the poetry of *The Tempest,* for the stylistic and structural repetitions engage the audience textually with the same problems of authority and power that dominate political interpretation. The tendency of words and phrases to repeat themselves is a case of stylistic reproduction that creates, as I have shown, an atmosphere in which control of meaning remains necessarily elusive. The effect of the style throughout is to place the auditor in an intermediate state, and that region of indeterminacy is a version of the various other kinds of liminality associated with this text: the island is located midway between Africa and Europe; it apparently partakes of, or is hospitable to, the natural and supernatural realms; Miranda stands between childhood and maturity, Caliban between demon and human, Prospero between vengeance and mercy; even time seems arrested ("what's past is prologue"). The poetry seduces the audience into a state of stylistic suspension, an intuitive zone between sleep and wake, "a strange repose" like that felt by Sebastian (2.1.218) or that described in Caliban's lyric. It is a marginal condition between expectation and understanding, affirmation and scepticism, comedy and tragedy.

Poetic indeterminacy shows us how to evaluate the appropriation of the play by those who see it as a political act in the colonialist enterprise. It helps to complicate the ideology of *The Tempest,* indicating that the political ideas are more subtle and difficult than recent readings would suggest. Pleas for interpretative caution are often attacked as retrogressive politics, but the recognition that this is one of the most knowing, most self-conscious texts in the canon should warn us about pretensions to ideological certainty. On the very issues that have most deeply concerned materialist critics and their American cousins—power, social and political hierarchy, the theatre as a political instrument, freedom of action, education, and race—*The Tempest* is at its most elusive and complicated. The play valorizes ambiguity and irony, ironizing its own positions and insisting upon the inconclusiveness of its own conclusions. The new orthodoxy, which exalts the colonized, is as narrow as the old, which idealizes and excuses the colonizer.[36]

This stylistic interpretation is not, however, merely another version of New Criticism, a retreat, that is, into the restful shadows of irony and ambiguity. The difference is that this reading of *The Tempest* admits the importance of contextual study and historical location, just as it recognizes the inescapable affiliation of the political and the aesthetic. I acknowledge the capacity of new modes of criticism to identify and promote ideological issues and other points of departure that more traditional forms of criticism have neglected or deliberately suppressed. But I also seek to balance those virtues with a sensitivity to the claims of the text. It needs to be pointed out that as students and teachers of literature we are professionally concerned with political issues not just in themselves but as they are embodied in aesthetic forms. The dismissal of verse is dangerous, especially if the subject of inquiry is verse drama. In reaction to the excesses and orthodoxies of New Criticism, our own critical practice is moving farther and farther away from the text, and in reading this play stylistically I register a mild protest against the implicit cheapening of textuality. The poetry of *The Tempest* alerts us to the delicate relation between literature and ideology.

Which is what, according to Kenneth Burke, art ought to do. In an essay on the fictional uncertainties of Mann and Gide, he identifies the pleasures of the unfixed:

> so long as we feel the need of certitude, the state of doubt is discomforting, and by its very prolongation can make for our hysterical retreat into belief, as Hans Castorp descended from his mountain to the battlefield. But why could one not come to accept his social wilderness without anguish, utilizing for his self-respect either the irony and melancholy of Mann, or the curiosity of Gide? One need not suffer under insecurity any more than an animal suffers from being constantly on the alert for danger. In the unformed there are opportunities which can be invigorating to contemplate. This state of technical apprehension can be a norm, and certainly an athletic norm.[37]

The Tempest promotes in its audience a kind of moral and imaginative athleticism, an intellectual fitness that much recent interpretation, by relaxing—or stiffening—into a single mode of reading, has evaded. The play's epistemological sophistication is inconsistent with the baldness of a single-mindedly ideological interpretation. To listen to its language is to become deeply sceptical about the operation of all kinds of power—poetic, political, and critical too.

Notes

1. " 'Nymphs and reapers heavily vanish': The Discursive Con-texts of *The Tempest*," *Alternative Shakespeares*, ed. John Drakakis (London and New York: Methuen, 1985), pp. 191–205.

2. Recent British readers seem especially unsympathetic to the play, perhaps because, as Walter Cohen suggests, their response to its colonial associations undermines an otherwise unified vision of Shakespeare's political progressivism. See "Political Criticism of Shakespeare," in *Shakespeare Reproduced: The Text in History and Ideology,* ed. Jean E. Howard and Marion F. O'Connor (London: Methuen, 1987), p. 37.

3. Some of the essays that make the topic of colonialism their central theme are the following: Paul E. Brown, " 'This thing of darkness I acknowledge mine': *The Tempest* and the Discourse of Colonialism," in *Political Shakespeare,* ed. Jonathan Dollimore and Alan Sinfield (Ithaca: Cornell University Press, 1985); Paul N. Siegel, "Historical Ironies in *The Tempest,*" *Shakespeare Jahrbuch,* 119 (1983), 104–11; Thomas Cartelli, "Prospero in Africa: *The Tempest* as Colonialist Text and Pretext," in Howard and O'Connor, *Shakespeare Reproduced,* pp. 99–115; Terence Hawkes, "Swisser-Swatter: Making a Man of English Letters," in Drakakis's *Alternative Shakespeares,* pp. 26–46; Stephen Orgel, "Prospero's Wife," *Representations,* 8 (1985), 1–13, and "Shakespeare and the Cannibals," in *Witches, Cannibals, Divorce: Estranging the Renaissance,* Selected Papers from the English Institute, NS II, ed. Marjorie Garber (Baltimore: Johns Hopkins University Press, 1986), pp. 40–66; Stephen Greenblatt, "Martial Law in the Land of Cockaigne," in *Shakespearean Negotiations: The Circulation of Social Energy in Renaissance England* (Berkeley: University of California Press, 1988), pp. 129–63.

4. The essay is printed in *First Images of America: The Impact of the New World on the Old,* ed. Fredi Chiappelli, 2 vols. (Berkeley: University of California Press, 1976), pp. 561–80.

5. (Ithaca: Cornell University Press, 1985), p. 48.

6. *Drama of a Nation: Public Theater in Renaissance England and Spain* (Ithaca: Cornell University Press, 1985), p. 401.

7. "Faithful Servants: Shakespeare's Praise of Disobedience," in *The Historical Renaissance: New Essays on Tudor and Stuart Literature and Culture,* ed. Heather Dubrow and Richard Strier (Chicago: University of Chicago Press, 1988), p. 133 n. 81.

8. *The Tempest,* ed. Frank Kermode (London: Methuen, 1954). Other studies now considered limited for their neglect of political issues would include those of G. Wilson Knight, *The Crown of Life* (Oxford: Clarendon Press, 1947), pp. 203–55; Reuben A. Brower, "The Mirror of Analogy: *The Tempest,*" in *The Fields of Light: An Experiment in Critical Reading* (New York: Oxford, 1951), pp. 95–122; Northrop Frye, Introduction to *The Tempest* in *The Complete Pelican Shakespeare,* gen. ed. Alfred Harbage (Baltimore: Penguin, 1969); D. G. James, *The Dream of Prospero* (Oxford: Clarendon Press, 1967); Harry Levin, "Two Magian Comedies: *The Alchemist* and *The Tempest,*" *Shakespeare Survey,* 22 (1969), 47–58; Derek Traversi, *Shakespeare: The Last Phase* (London: Hollis and Carter, 1954); Harry Berger, "Miraculous Harp: A Reading of Shakespeare's *Tempest,*" *Shakespeare Studies,* 5 (1969), 253–83; Howard Felperin, *Shakespearean Romance* (Princeton: Princeton University Press, 1972); Joseph H. Summers, "The Anger of Prospero," in *Dreams of Love and Power: On Shakespeare's Plays* (Oxford: Clarendon, 1984).

9. For a fascinating commentary on this kind of critical power struggle, see Anthony B. Dawson, "*Tempest* in a Teapot: Critics, Evaluation, Ideology," in *Bad Shakespeare: Revaluations of the Shakespeare Canon,* ed. Maurice Charney (Rutherford, N. J.: Fairleigh Dickinson University Press, 1988), pp. 61–73. Dawson is especially eloquent on "the way 'materialist' critics expose the hidden biases of traditional criticism . . . but fall into some of the same traps, particularly in the vexed area of evaluation and the ideological assumptions that the act of evaluating often makes plain" (71).

10. "Discourse and the Individual: The Case of Colonialism in *The Tempest,*" *Shakespeare Quarterly,* 40 (1989), 47. One of the earliest complaints about the excesses of recent political criticism was Edward Pechter's "The New Historicism and Its Discontents: Politicizing Renaissance Drama," *PMLA,* 102 (1987), 292–303. On the other hand, Carolyn Porter has attacked New Historicists for being insufficiently historical and insufficiently political: see "Are We Being Historical Yet?," *South Atlantic Quarterly,* 87 (1988), 743–86.

11. "Music Does Not Flow," *New York Review of Books,* 17 December 1981, p. 49.

12. Although everyone agrees that the poetry of the last plays is difficult and different from the earlier verse, surprisingly little has been written about it. See F. E. Halliday, *The Poetry of Shakespeare's Plays* (London: Duckworth, 1954); J. M. Nosworthy's Introduction to the Arden edition of *Cymbeline* (London: Methuen, 1955), lxii–lxxiii; N. F. Blake, *Shakespeare's Language: An Introduction* (London: Methuen, 1983); John Porter Houston, *Shakespearean Sentences: A Study in Style and Syntax* (Baton Rouge: Louisiana State University Press, 1987); and George T. Wright, *Shakespeare's Metrical Art* (Berkeley: University of California Press, 1988). In preparing this essay I have also profited from Cyrus Hoy's "The Language of Fletcherian Tragicomedy," in *Mirror up to Shakespeare: Essays in Honour of G. R. Hibbard,* ed. J. C. Gray (Toronto: University of Toronto Press, 1984), pp. 99–113.

13. "*The Tempest,* or Repetition," in *The Bottom Translation: Marlowe and Shakespeare and the Carnival Tradition,* tr. Daniela Miedzyrzecka and Lillian Vallee (Evanston: Northwestern University Press, 1987).

14. For an intelligent discussion of the "abstract" qualities of Shakespeare's late work, see Marion Trousdale, "Style in *The Winter's Tale,*" *Critical Quarterly,* 18 (1976), 25–32.

15. On this and many points of stylistic criticism, I have been aided by the analysis of John Porter Houston in *Shakespearean Sentences.*

16. Introduction to *The Tempest* (Harmondsworth: Penguin, 1968), pp. 13–14.

17. *An Essay on Shakespeare's Sonnets* (New Haven: Yale University Press, 1969), pp. 87–8. Booth's comments on how poetic effects function in individual sonnets are extremely stimulating and applicable beyond their immediate subject. See also the essay by Kenneth Burke, "On Musicality in Verse," in which he demonstrates the complex effects of assonance and consonance in some poems of Coleridge: *The Philosophy of Literary Form* (Berkeley: University of California Press, rpt. 1973), pp. 369–79.

18. Here, as in a few other passages, I have added emphasis to illustrate certain poetic effects.

19. See Anne Barton, "Shakespeare and the Limits of Language," *Shakespeare Survey,* 24 (1971), 19–30.

20. On the expressive possibilities of this tactic, see Wright's *Shakespeare's Metrical Art,* especially chapter 13, "Trochees."

21. On the relative importance of specific and general effects in the last plays, see Anne Barton, "Leontes and the Spider: Language and Speaker in the Last Plays," *Shakespeare's Styles: Essays in Honour of Kenneth Muir,* ed. Philip Edwards, G. K. Hunter, and Inga-Stina Ewbank (Cambridge: Cambridge University Press, 1980), pp. 131–50.

22. See, for example, Joan Hartwig, *Shakespeare's Analogical Scene: Parody as Structural Syntax* (Lincoln: University of Nebraska Press, 1983), chapter 8; Brower's *The Fields of Light;* and Knight's *The Crown of Life.*

23. For an excellent discussion of the densely allusive quality of this scene, see Paul A. Cantor, "Shakespeare's *The Tempest:* The Wise Man as Hero," *Shakespeare Quarterly,* 31 (1980), 64–75.

24. See Ruth Nevo's comments on this metatheatrical device: "The embedding of play within play dissolves representational boundaries so that the audience is required to suspend its attention, to negotiate a constant interchange between fictional reality and fictional illusion." *Shakespeare's Other Language* (London: Methuen, 1987), p. 136. This point of view is consistent with Shakespeare's late attitude toward a device that had served him well from the beginning, as Anne Barton points out: "On the whole, efforts to distinguish the fictional from the 'real,' art from life, tales from truth, come in the Romances to replace the older, moral concern with identifying hypocrisy and deceit." "Leontes and the Spider," p. 147.

25. "Shakespeare and Romance," in *Later Shakespeare,* ed. John Russell Brown and Bernard Harris, Stratford-upon-Avon Studies, 8 (London: Edward Arnold, 1966), p. 75.

26. From time to time aural echoes function as images do, pointing up crucial words and the ideas they raise. Consider the effect of "be" in the following exchange:

ALONSO   Whe'er thou beest he or no,
                Or some enchanted trifle to abuse me,
                As late I have been, I not know: Thy pulse
                Beats, as of flesh and blood; and, since I saw thee
                Th'affliction of my mind amends, with which
                I fear a madness held me. This must crave—
                An if this be at all—a most strange story.
                Thy dukedom I resign, and do entreat
                Thou pardon me my wrongs. But how should
                    Prospero
                Be living and be here?
PROSPERO (*to Gonzalo*)   First, noble friend,
                Let me embrace thine age, whose honour cannot
                Be measured or confined.
                    He embraces Gonzalo
GONZALO   Whether this be,
                Or be not, I'll not swear. (5.1.113–24)

The hammering of the verb underscores the problem that Alonso and finally the audience must confront, the ontological status of what we are witnessing.

      Stanley Fish has written brilliantly on the logical dangers of such interpretation, specifically on the circularity of thematic stylistics: "formal patterns are themselves the products of interpretation and . . . therefore there is no such thing as a formal pattern, at least in the sense necessary for the practice of stylistics: that is, no pattern that one can observe before interpretation is hazarded and which therefore can be used to prefer one interpretation to another." *Is There a Text in This Class?: The Authority of Textual Communities* (Cambridge, Mass.: Harvard University Press, 1980), p. 267. See also John Hollander, "The Metrical Frame," in *The Structure of Verse: Modern Essays on Prosody,* ed. Harvey Gross, rev. ed. (New York: Ecco Press, 1979), pp. 77–101.

    27.   *The Bottom Translation,* p. 97.

    28.   Of the many studies of the oneiric qualities of *The Tempest,* the most recent is found in Ruth Nevo's *Shakespeare's Other Language,* especially pp. 136–43.

    29.   *The White Goddess* (London: Farrar, 1948), p. 425.

    30.   *Two Concepts of Allegory: A Study of Shakespeare's "The Tempest" and the Logic of Allegorical Expression* (New York: Barnes and Noble, 1967), p. 158.

    31.   Peter Brooks, "The Idea of a Psychoanalytic Literary Criticism," *Critical Inquiry,* 13 (1987), p. 339.

    32.   Although I am sensitive to the various differences between the two kinds known as "romance" and "tragicomedy," it will be agreed that the forms share a number of fundamental features, and it is those similarities on which I am concentrating here.

    33.   "The Danger Not the Death: The Art of John Fletcher," in *Jacobean Theatre,* edited John Russell Brown and Bernard Harris (London: Edward Arnold, 1960), p. 164.

    34.   Patricia A. Parker brilliantly develops some of the same ideas as Brooks: "The suspensions which for Barthes become part of an erotics of the text recall not only the constant divagations of romance and its resistance to the demands of closure, but also the frustration in Ariosto of what Barthes calls the teleological form of vulgar readerly pleasure—the desire to penetrate the veil of meaning or to hasten the narrative's gradual striptease—by a continual postponement of revelation which leaves the reader suspended, or even erotically 'hung up.' " *Inescapable Romance: Studies in the Poetics of a Mode* (Princeton: Princeton University Press, 1979), pp. 220–1.

    35.   Introduction to his edition of *The Tempest,* p. 15.

36. See Skura, "The Case of Colonialism," in which she argues that new historicism "is now in danger of fostering blindness of its own. Granted that something was wrong with a commentary that focused on *The Tempest* as a self-contained project of a self-contained individual and that ignored the political situation in 1611. But something seems wrong now also, something more than the rhetorical excesses characteristic of any innovative critical movement" (pp. 46–7).

37. *Counter-statement* (rpt. Berkeley: University of California Press, 1968), p. 106.

"Miranda, Where's Your Sister?":
Reading Shakespeare's *The Tempest*

ANN THOMPSON

These are Prospero's first words in *The Tempest, or The Enchanted Island,* the adaptation of Shakespeare's play created for the most part by William Davenant, with some input from John Dryden, in 1667. They act as a clear signal to a knowing audience or reader that this is not the original. Davenant's Miranda does indeed have a younger sister, Dorinda, and the two are described in the *Dramatis Personae* as "Daughters to Prospero, that never saw Man." Dorinda is balanced, and ultimately partnered, by another new character, Hippolito, heir to the dukedom of Mantua, "one that never saw Woman." In the insistent pattern of parallels and repetitions which characterises Davenant's version, Ariel has a female consort, Milcha, and even Caliban has a twin sister named after their mother, Sycorax, whom he proposes as a bride for Trinculo.[1] This proliferation of female roles can presumably be attributed in part to the need to provide employment for actresses on the Restoration stage.

In contrast, women are notably absent from Shakespeare's *Tempest.* Miranda at one point stresses her isolation and lack of female companionship by saying "I do not know / One of my sex, no woman's face remember, / Save from my glass, mine own" (III.i.48–50),[2] though at the beginning of the play she had claimed at least a vague recollection: "Had I not / Four or five women once that tended me?" (I.ii.46–7). Apart from Miranda herself, the only females mentioned in the First Folio's list of the "Names of the Actors" are Iris, Ceres, Juno and the Nymphs, all of whom are "spirits" explicitly impersonated by Ariel and his "fellows." While Ariel is clearly a male spirit, he is also required to impersonate a "nymph of the sea" (I.ii.301) and a half-female harpy (stage direction at III.ii.52), indicating a degree of ambiguity about his gender. The part has often been performed by women or by androgynous youths. Conversely, the part of Miranda would in actuality have been performed by a boy actor on Shakespeare's stage.

Ann Thompson, " 'Miranda, Where's Your Sister?': Reading Shakespeare's *The Tempest,*" in *Feminist Criticism: Theory and Practice,* ed. Susan Sellers (Hemel Hempstead, U.K.: Harvester Wheatsheaf, 1991), 45–55. Reprinted with permission.

Miranda, in Shakespeare's play, has no sister and apparently no mother. It is odd that she does not even enquire about the fate of the latter, though she might have been prompted to do so by Prospero's reply to her question "Sir, are not you my father?" In his only reference to his wife Prospero says "Thy mother was a piece of virtue, and / She said thou wast my daughter" (I.ii.56–7). This is apparently all that needs to be said about her. Some fifty lines later, Miranda demonstrates that she has fully internalised the patriarchal assumption that a woman's main function is to provide a legitimate succession when asked to comment on the wickedness of Prospero's brother: "I should sin / To think but nobly of my grandmother: / Good wombs have borne bad sons" (I.ii.117–19).

The worldly cynicism of such standard jokes was formerly thought inappropriate to the innocent Miranda and they were often omitted from performances from the late eighteenth century to the early twentieth century; Davenant's Miranda more explicitly denies that she had a mother when she remarks with a coy naïvety to Dorinda that she thinks Prospero "found us when we both were little, and grew within the ground" (I.ii.332–3). In Shakespeare's version, Miranda's destined spouse, Ferdinand, is also motherless, and *his* sister's absence is curiously stressed: although the distance from Naples to North Africa is not enormous, Alonso insists that Claribel is "so far from Italy removed / I ne'er again shall see her" (II.i.108–9), and Antonio expresses her remoteness even more extravagantly:

> She that is Queen of Tunis; she that dwells
> Ten leagues beyond man's life; she that from Naples
> Can have no note unless the sun were post—
> The man i'th' moon's too slow—till newborn chins
> Be rough and razorable;
>
> II.i.244–8.

Claribel had to wait until 1949 for the female poet H. D. to make her visible and give her a voice.[3] Shakespeare's Caliban has no sister and his mother, Sycorax, is long dead by the time the play's events take place. Sycorax also has a North African connection, having been banished by the Algerians who apparently spared her life because she was pregnant. Her power is at least recognised by Prospero, Ariel and Caliban, though she is vilified by the two former characters as a "hag" and a "foul witch." Oddly, Shakespeare draws on the lines Ovid gave another notorious female enchantress, Medea, for Prospero's big "conjuring" speech, "Ye elves of hills, brooks, standing lakes, and groves" (v.i.33ff.), but Medea herself is not mentioned.

The fact that I have chosen nevertheless to discuss *The Tempest* in the context of this book may seem perverse, but my choice is a deliberate one and relates precisely to the *absence* of female characters. I want to ask what feminist criticism can do in the face of a male-authored canonical text which seems to exclude women to this extent. Much early feminist criticism consisted merely in privileging female characters and identifying with their viewpoints, especially if they could be claimed to be in any way subversive or protofeminist. This is clearly impossible in *The Tempest:* even nineteenth-century female critics, who on the whole participated enthusiastically in the trend of aggrandising and romanticising Shakespeare's heroines, could not find a great deal to say for Miranda. Anna Jameson wrote in *Shakespeare's Heroines* (first published in 1833) that in Ophelia and Miranda Shakespeare had created two beings in whom "the feminine character appears resolved into its very elementary principles—as modesty, grace, tenderness," but added that by the same token Miranda "resembles nothing on earth";[4] and Mrs M. L. Elliott remarked in *Shakspeare's Garden of Girls* (1885) that Miranda was too ethereal and thus tended to be more popular with male than with female readers.[5] Anyone who has taught the play recently will know that these seem very moderate views compared to the opinions of twentieth-century female students who find Miranda an extremely feeble heroine and scorn to identify with her. Perhaps, then, *The Tempest* can be used as something of a test case for discovering what else a feminist approach may offer beyond this character-based level.

Faced with a comparable problem in relation to *King Lear,* where modern readers hesitate to identify with either the stereotype of the bad woman represented by Goneril and Regan or with the stereotype of the good woman represented by Cordelia, Kathleen McLuskie writes:

> Feminist criticism need not restrict itself to privileging the woman's part or to special pleading on behalf of female characters. It can be equally well served by making a text reveal the conditions in which a particular ideology of femininity functions and by both revealing and subverting the hold which such an ideology has for readers both female and male.[6]

I shall attempt in the remainder of this essay to explore the "ideology of femininity" at work in *The Tempest,* both through a reading of the play and through a survey of some of the most influential ways in which it is currently being reproduced in literary criticism.

Despite her small and comparatively passive role, the text claims that Miranda is nevertheless crucial to the play. Explaining the storm, Prospero tells her "I have done nothing but in care of thee" (I.ii.16). A feminist critic might ask in what sense this is true, and whether Miranda's gender is significant: would the play have worked in the same way if Prospero had had a son? How does sexuality, and especially female sexuality, function in this narrative? Reading the play with an explicit focus on issues of gender, one is immediately struck by its obsession with themes of chastity and fertility, which occur in its figurative language as well as in its literal events. These themes are often specifically associated with female sexuality. In the first, rather startling metaphor of this kind, Gonzalo imagines the very ship which seems to founder in the opening scene as being "as leaky as an unstanched wench" (I.i.47–8), a phrase interpreted as alluding either to a sexually aroused (insatiable) woman or to one menstruating "without the use of absorbent padding," as the Oxford editor puts it. In his long narrative speech to Miranda in the second scene, Prospero uses a metaphor of birth to describe Antonio's treachery—"my trust, / Like a good parent, did beget of him / A falsehood" (I.ii.93–5), and seems almost to claim that he gave a kind of second birth to Miranda in his sufferings on the voyage to the island:

> When I have decked the sea with drops full salt,
> Under my burden groaned, which raised in me
> An undergoing stomach to bear up
> Against what should ensue.
>
> I.ii.155–8.

This scene also introduces the literal contrast between the chaste Miranda and the "earthy and abhorred" Sycorax who arrived on the island pregnant (by the devil himself, according to Prospero at I.ii.319) and there "littered" or "whelped" her sub-human son. It is notable that the acknowledged, if evil, power of Sycorax is effectively undermined by the bestial stupidity of her son, rather as the power of Tamora is defused in *Titus Andronicus* and that of the Queen in *Cymbeline*. As in the earlier plays, the son of the witch-like woman is a rapist (or would-be rapist); Caliban is accused of attempting to rape Miranda and he does not deny the charge:

> O ho, O ho! Would't had been done!
> Thou didst prevent me—I had peopled else
> This isle with Calibans.
>
> I.ii.348–50.

He later promises Stephano that Miranda, seen as one of the spoils of victory, will "bring thee forth brave brood" (III.ii.103). It is perhaps not surprising therefore that Ferdinand's "prime request" to Miranda on first seeing her is "If you be maid or no" (I.ii.428), a topic to which he returns twenty lines later, ignoring Prospero's intervention in the dialogue.

Miranda's chastity apparently has a quasi-mystical power. She herself swears "by my modesty, / The jewel in my dower" (III.i.53–4) and tells Ferdinand "I am your wife if you will marry me; / If not, I'll die your maid" (III.i.83–4). Prospero warns Ferdinand in what seem to be unnecessarily harsh terms against breaking her "virgin-knot before / All sanctimonious ceremonies" (IV.i.15–16), threatening dire consequences:

> No sweet aspersion shall the heavens let fall
> To make this contract grow; but barren hate,
> Sour-eyed disdain, and discords shall bestrew

> The union of your bed with weeds so loathly
> That you shall hate it both. Therefore take heed,
> As Hymen's lamps shall light you.
>
> IV.i.18–23.

Ferdinand's reply is comparably graphic:

> As I hope
> For quiet days, fair issue, and long life,
> With such love as 'tis now, the murkiest den,
> The most opportune place, the strong'st suggestion
> Our worser genius can, shall never melt
> Mine honour into lust, to take away
> The edge of that day's celebration
> When I shall think or Phoebus' steeds are foundered,
> Or night kept chained below.
>
> IV.i.23–31.

Ostensibly reassuring, such language seems to suggest that the minds of both men are dwelling in morbid detail on the possibilities of completing Caliban's attempted violation: the image of Miranda as a rape victim interferes disturbingly with the image of Miranda as a chaste and fertile wife. The masque which Prospero organises for the entertainment of the young couple in this scene explicitly banishes lust in the form of Venus and Cupid and emphasises the blessed fertility of honourable marriage. And yet, reading as a woman, I continue to get the feeling that the play protests too much on this score.

The speakers in the masque promise rewards for premarital chastity. As Ceres sings,

> Earth's increase, foison plenty,
> Barns and garners never empty,
> Vines with clust'ring bunches growing,
> Plants with goodly burden bowing,
> Spring come to you at the farthest,
> In the very end of harvest!
>
> IV.i.110–15.

This language echoes that of the earlier scene in which Gonzalo speculates on what he would do, "Had I plantation of this isle" (II.i.141), to make nature bring forth "all foison, all abundance" (II.i.161), in a utopian vision which is at the same time colonialist in so far as the "commonwealth" is subject to his royal command. Sebastian jokes that he will "carry this island home in his pocket and give it his son for an apple," to which Antonio replies "And sowing the kernels of it in the sea, bring forth more islands" (II.i.88–91), similarly invoking a picture of benign exploitation and a fantasy of magical male fecundity.

The play at times takes the power of the sea to give birth, or rebirth, quite seriously: later in II.i.249 Antonio refers to all the courtiers as "sea-swallowed, though some cast again," a metaphor repeated by Ariel when, disguised as a harpy, he tells the "men of sin" that Destiny "the never-surfeited sea / Hath caused to belch up you" (III.iii.55–6). These are both parodies of birth: birth from the mouth rather than from the uterus. A cruder version of what the body can throw forth arises at II.ii.101–2 when Stephano sees Trinculo, hiding under Caliban's cloak, as the "seige" or excrement of the "mooncalf." More seriously, in his Medea-inspired speech, Prospero claims the power to resurrect the dead: "Graves at my command / Have waked their sleepers, oped, and let 'em forth" (v.i.48–9), though Ferdinand asserts elsewhere that it is Miranda who "quickens what's dead" (III.i.6). At the end of the play, after Ferdinand's apparent death "mudded in that oozy bed" of the sea (V.i.151), he rhetorically attributes his "second life" to Prospero (V.i.195), although it is Miranda's literal fertility which will, as Gonzalo explains, permit Prospero's "issue" to become kings of Naples (V.i.205–6).

How, then, can a feminist interpret this pattern of references? What is going on in this text which seems, on the one hand, to deny the importance—and even in some cases the presence—of female characters, but which simultaneously attributes enormous power to female chastity and fertility? One noticeable feature of the handling of these themes is the insistence on male control: Prospero must control Miranda's sexuality before he hands her over to Ferdinand. Alonso, her father, formerly controlled Claribel's sexuality, but the play is ambivalent about his decision (a willing version of Desdemona's father Brabantio?) to "lose" or "loose" her to an African rather than to a European suitor (II.i.123),[7] and she herself is said to have been "Weighed between loathness and obedience" in the matter (II.i.128). Men are seen as capable of controlling the fertility of nature, and Prospero even controls Ceres, the goddess of harvests, in so far as the play makes it clear that she is represented in the masque by his servant Ariel (IV.i.167). Recent criticism of *The Tempest* suggests two theoretical frameworks for discussing this question of control, the psychoanalytical and the political, both of which can be utilised in a feminist approach.

The traditional reading of *The Tempest* prevalent in the nineteenth century and earlier twentieth century interpreted Prospero's control of its events and characters as entirely benign; he was often seen as the representative of Art itself, or even identified with Shakespeare as author. Freudian and post-Freudian psychoanalytical studies of the play have undermined this view, exposing the darker side of the "family romance" by suggesting that Prospero's control might be more problematic and that his concern with his daughter's sexuality might indicate an incestuous desire for her. In David Sundelson's essay, " 'So rare a wonder'd father': Prospero's *Tempest*," the play is fraught with anxieties and uncertainties on this level which are only partially resolved by its endorsement of what he calls both Prospero's and the play's "paternal narcissism: the prevailing sense that there is no worthiness like a father's, no accomplishment or power, and that Prospero is the father *par excellence.*"[8] Coppélia Kahn, writing on "The providential tempest and the Shakespearean family," agrees in seeing the play as a "fantasy of omnipotence" in which Prospero, coming from Milan to the island, "went from childlike, self-absorbed dependency to paternal omnipotence, skipping the steps of maturation in between." Miranda, like Marina in *Pericles* and Perdita in *The Winter's Tale,* doubles the roles of mother and daughter, uniting chastity and fertility in a non-threatening way. Yet, in so far as Kahn claims that "Prospero's identity is based entirely on his role as father, and his family is never united or complete"—indeed he is left at the end in a state of social and sexual isolation—the "romance" is still a narrative of imperfect wish-fulfilment representing the universally ambivalent desire we all have both to escape from our families and to continue to be nurtured by them.[9] Both these readings lay stress on the tensions that arise in the play and the sheer struggle involved in asserting the supposedly natural harmony of patriarchal control: it appears that an "unstanched wench" constitutes a serious threat to this order.

Stephen Orgel has pointed out a danger in the tendency of psychoanalytic readings to treat the play as a case-history, either of the author or of the characters, overlooking the extent to which the reader, playing the role of analyst, is a collaborator in the resultant fantasy. He further notices that, while psychoanalysis evokes an unchanging, essential human nature, the theoretical framework does change:

> Recent psychoanalytic theory has replaced Freud's central Oedipal myth with a drama in which the loss of the seducing mother is the crucial trauma. As men, we used to want reassurance that we could successfully compete with or replace or supersede our fathers; now we want to know that our lost mothers will return. (p. 52)[10]

In consequence, his essay, called "Prospero's wife," transfers the centre of interest from the present, dominant father to the absent mother, a strategy comparable to the one employed by Coppélia Kahn in her essay on "The absent mother in *King Lear.*"[11] It is, as Orgel acknowledges, a problematic strategy in so far as it deals not with the text itself but with the gaps and blanks that Shakespeare has chosen not to fill in. Indeed, he begins his study with the defensive statement "This essay is not a reading of *The Tempest,*" and worries about the possible parallels with such currently unfashionable texts as Mary Cowden Clarke's *The Girlhood of Shakespeare's Heroines.* Nevertheless, his work is highly suggestive for feminist critics in its willingness to explore a whole network of feminine allusions and absences, ranging from the obvious one of his title to more obscure issues such as the puzzling references to "widow Dido" at II.i.70–99, Dido being a "model at once of heroic fidelity to a murdered husband and [of] the destructive potential of erotic passion" (p. 51). He also challenges the traditional view of *The Tempest* as a happy courtship comedy, remarking that, while the play does move towards marriage, the relationships are "ignorant at best, characteristically tense, and potentially tragic." He sees this as typical of the author:

> relationships between men and women interest Shakespeare intensely, but not, on the whole, as husbands and wives. The wooing process tends to be what it is here: not so much a prelude to marriage and a family as a process of self-definition. (p. 56)

Current political approaches to *The Tempest* often have links with psychoanalytical approaches. Orgel exemplifies one such link as he moves from his discussion of the missing wife, by way of speculations about Shakespeare's own family experiences, to an analysis of power and authority in the play in terms of the ways these issues were conceived in Jacobean England. He points out that in setting up the contest for the island between Caliban, who claims his inheritance from his mother, and Prospero, whose authority is self-created, Shakespeare is representing positions which were available, indeed normative, at the time. Further, in his edition of *The Tempest,* Orgel goes on to consider the real-life significance of political marriages like the one in the play where Prospero goes to considerable trouble to marry his daughter to the son of his chief enemy, thereby staging a counter-usurpation of Naples by Milan.

The fact that *The Tempest* was performed at court in 1613 during the wedding festivities of King James' daughter Elizabeth and Frederick the Elector Palatine gives a further resonance to such speculations. This historical circumstance is the starting-point for Lorie Jerrell Leininger's feminist reading, "The Miranda trap: sexism and racism in Shakespeare's *Tempest*."[12] She imagines the 16-year-old princess as the real-life equivalent of Miranda: beautiful, loving, chaste and above all obedient to her all-powerful father. Miranda's role as the dependent female is crucial to the play's dynamics of power in so far as Caliban's enslavement is justified by his attempt to rape her: "Prospero needs Miranda as sexual bait, and then needs to protect her from the threat which is inescapable given his hierarchical world" (p. 289). Shakespeare's play allows Miranda no way out of this situation, but Leininger invents an epilogue for a modern Miranda who refuses to participate in the play's assumptions that Prospero is infallible, that Caliban is a "natural" slave, and that a daughter is a "foot" in a family organism of which the father is the head.

Most political readings of *The Tempest,* however, centre on the issue of colonialism. This is the focus of Francis Barker and Peter Hulme's essay " 'Nymphs and reapers heavily vanish': the discursive con-texts of *The Tempest*."[13] and of Paul Brown's essay " 'This thing of darkness I acknowledge mine': *The Tempest* and the discourse of colonialism."[14] Both employ the technique of intertextuality to relate the play to nascent seventeenth-century

European colonialism, reassessing the "sources" in the context of New World voyage materials and arguing that anxiety and ambivalence result from the struggle to create a self-justifying, colonialist discourse. We are encouraged in these readings to be deeply suspicious of Prospero and to sympathise with Caliban as the representative of an exploited Third World. Brown draws on Freudian theory to point out an analogy between the political operations of colonialism and the modes of psychic repression, and he uses the Freudian concept of "dreamwork" to discuss the way in which Prospero's discourse subordinates that of the other inhabitants of the island, as for example when he imposes his memory of earlier events on both Caliban and Ariel in I.ii.

An explicitly feminist version of this kind of reading, and one which is moreover undertaken from a Third World viewpoint, is performed by the Indian critic Ania Loomba as the final chapter of her book, *Gender, Race, Renaissance Drama*.[15] Loomba is critical of the tendency of "alternative" readings of *The Tempest* to seize upon Caliban as a symbol of exploitation and potential rebellion, and points out that some anti-colonialist or anti-racist readings have been unthinkingly sexist: the specific repression of Miranda has been neglected. Setting out to delineate the limits of the text's supposed "radical ambivalence," she discusses the myth of the black rapist, the significance of Sycorax as "Prospero's other," and the contradictory position of Miranda as typical of that of all white women in the colonial adventure: the nature of her participation confirms her subordination to white men.

Both psychoanalytical and political theoretical approaches nevertheless deny some of the pleasures experienced by earlier generations of audiences and readers who were apparently able to identify more readily with the viewpoint of Prospero as white male patriarch and coloniser. Today, white male critics in Britain and the United States understandably feel uncomfortable and guilty about participating in these attitudes. Reading the play as a woman and as a feminist, it is possible to feel good about delineating and rejecting its idealisation of patriarchy, and one can go beyond the play to consider the conscious and unconscious sexism of its critical and stage history. Reading as a white British person, my conscience is less clear: women as well as men benefited (and still benefit) from the kind of colonialism idealised in *The Tempest*.

The current situation as I have sketched it above seems to leave two major questions unanswered (and unanswerable within the scope of this essay): first, is it possible for a staging of *The Tempest* to convey anything approaching a feminist reading of the text (without rewriting it or adding something like Leininger's epilogue), and secondly, what kind of pleasure can a woman and a feminist take in this text beyond the rather grim one of mapping its various patterns of exploitation? Must a feminist reading necessarily be a negative one?

Notes

1. Maximilian E. Novak and George Robert Guffey (eds), *The Works of John Dryden* (vol. X, Berkeley, Cal. and London: University of California Press, 1970). I would like to thank Andrew Gurr for drawing my attention to the line which forms my title.
2. References and quotations from *The Tempest* are from the Oxford Shakespeare text, ed. Stephen Orgel (Oxford and New York: Oxford University Press, 1987).
3. See *By Avon River* (New York: Macmillan, 1949). For a discussion of H. D.'s transformation of *The Tempest* in this experimental work, see Susan Stanford Friedman, "Remembering Shakespeare differently: H. D.'s *By Avon River*," in Marianne Novy (ed.), *Women's Re-Visions of Shakespeare* (Urbana and Chicago: University of Illinois Press, 1990), pp. 143–64.
4. *Shakespeare's Heroines,* 1897 reprint (London: George Bell and Sons), pp. 134, 149.
5. *Shakespeare's Garden of Girls,* published anonymously (London: Remington and Co., 1885), p. 265.
6. "The patriarchal bard: feminist criticism and Shakespeare: *King Lear* and *Measure for Measure*," in Jonathan Dollimore and Alan Sinfield (eds), *Political Shakespeare* (Manchester: Manchester University Press, 1985), pp. 88–108.
7. The First Folio's spelling, "loose," was the normal spelling of "lose," but most modern editors, with the exception of Stephen Orgel, print "loose," presumably because it carries an undertone of greater sensuality.
8. In Murray M. Schwartz and Coppélia Kahn (eds), *Representing Shakespeare: New psychoanalytic essays* (Baltimore and London: Johns Hopkins University Press, 1980), pp. 33–53.
9. In Schwartz and Kahn, *Representing Shakespeare,* pp. 217–43. Passages cited are on p. 238 and p. 240.
10. "Prospero's wife," in Margaret W. Ferguson, Maureen Quilligan and Nancy J. Vickers (eds), *Rewriting the Renaissance: The discourses of sexual difference in early modern Europe* (Chicago and London: University of Chicago Press, 1986), pp. 50–64. This essay was first published in *Representations* 8 (1984), 1–13.
11. In Ferguson, Quilligan and Vickers, *Rewriting the Renaissance,* pp. 33–49.
12. In Carolyn Ruth Swift Lenz, Gayle Greene and Carol Thomas Neely (eds), *The Woman's Part* (Urbana and Chicago: University of Illinois Press, 1980), pp. 285–94.
13. In John Drakakis (ed.), *Alternative Shakespeares* (London and New York: Methuen, 1985), pp. 191–205.
14. In Dollimore and Sinfield, *Political Shakespeare,* pp. 48–71.
15. Manchester: Manchester University Press, 1989, pp. 142–58.

APPROPRIATIONS

◆

Caliban in the "Third World":
Shakespeare's Savage as Sociopolitical Symbol

ALDEN T. VAUGHAN

For nearly four centuries, writers, speakers, and casual commentators have ransacked Shakespeare's works for useful metaphors. Often the purpose has been less literary than ideological—to signify a social or political position by invoking a familiar Shakespearean phrase or character. During the past century, probably the most frequent and malleable Shakespearean sociopolitical symbol has been *The Tempest*'s Caliban, for the "salvage and deformed slave" has played varied metaphoric roles in response to changing national and international ideologies. This essay explores Caliban's adoption by late nineteenth- and twentieth-century writers, especially in Latin America and Africa, as a potent symbol of either Western imperialism or imperialism's victims.

Beginning in the 1890s, and especially since 1950, many writers from Third World nations have contended that *The Tempest* embodies heretofore neglected meanings for their societies and that Caliban conveys a very different message than traditional scholarship has allowed.[1] Such authors—few are Shakespearean scholars but many are distinguished in other fields—argue that Caliban is no mere fish or monster or even, as has often been argued, a North American Indian. His true significance lies instead in emblematic identifications with modern men and women, especially Latin Americans and Africans, no matter how anachronistic those identifications may seem to *Tempest* specialists.

Authors who invoke Caliban as an image of Latin Americans or Africans agree that he is a palpable and poignant symbol, but they disagree, sometimes vehemently, about who or what he symbolizes. Diametrical opposites are proposed: Caliban as exemplar of imperialist oppressors (the prevalent view in the late nineteenth and early twentieth centuries) or Caliban as emblem of oppressed natives (prevalent in recent decades). Advocates of the first approach find Shakespeare's monster a handy image for everything gross and vicious in a domineering nation or social class—Yankee imperialism, for example, or European racism. The second and now almost universal view

Alden T. Vaughan, "Caliban in the 'Third World': Shakespeare's Savage as Sociopolitical Symbol," *The Massachusetts Review* 29 (1988): 289–313. Reprinted, with changes, by permission of the author.

stresses Caliban's implicit virtues—his innate sensitivity, rough dignity, articulateness, and intelligence—rather than his cruder characteristics. Thus recast, Caliban stands for the countless victims of European imperialism and colonization. Like Caliban (so the argument goes), colonized peoples are disinherited, exploited, and subjugated. Like him, they learned a conqueror's language and perhaps his values. Like him, they endured enslavement and contempt by European usurpers and eventually rebelled.

The shift in Caliban's image from symbol of the oppressor to symbol of the oppressed occurred, not surprisingly, when mass movements in both Latin America and Africa brought to prominence a generation of cultural and political spokesmen who stressed indigenous heritages and national independence. Earlier Latin-American intellectuals were tied emotionally and often ethnically to the Iberian peninsula. They wrote in Spanish (or, in the case of Brazilians, in Portuguese) and looked to Europeans, especially French and Iberian intellectuals, for their ethnic identity and cultural heroes. As an Argentinian scholar wrote in 1911, "Despite the [racial and ethnic] mixtures, . . . [o]ur spirit and our culture are Latin. But within our Latinism we belong, and will eternally belong, to the Spanish caste."[2]

For Central and South Americans as a whole, that statement was too broad; for the author's own generation of Latin-American intellectuals it was essentially true. Trained in a European cultural context, they found their symbols in European history and literature. But in recent decades, changing social forces have drastically modified the structure of Latin-American intellectual life. A new breed of scholars and writers, many from non-European ethnic stock and cultural heritage, has inspired new symbols or, at the very least, new interpretations of old symbols, of which Caliban is a prime example. A somewhat similar shift has occurred among African intellectuals. An earlier dependence on European education and European literature is being replaced by an emergent indigenous culture. Along the way, Caliban has witnessed a drastic interpretive change.

Either approach—Caliban as oppressor or Caliban as oppressed—differs fundamentally from traditional interpretive modes. Whereas traditional scholarship is at least partly concerned with the probable prototypes for Shakespeare's characters, most Third World authors who borrow emblems from *The Tempest* ignore, as irrelevant, Shakespeare's sources and intentions. The Third World interpretation of Caliban is symbolic, not historic; it adopts Caliban for what he represents to the observer, not for what Shakespeare may have had in mind. Few Third World authors who apply *Tempest* images contend that Shakespeare expected his audience to see Caliban as a black African, brown mestizo, or white American;[3] instead, they want modern readers to accept Shakespeare's dramatic symbols because, retrospectively, they fit. New situations give the play's characters new meanings. As one exponent of Caliban metaphors explains, "*The Tempest* is a Masque, an art form strongly dependent on symbolism. It presents figures that are suggestive, evocative and allusive; and it often relies on mythopoetic references for full effect. If we accept this, . . . we may . . . come out with applications appropriate for a present cultural dilemma."[4]

Caliban's sociopolitical career has been longer and more diverse in Latin America than in Africa. He first appeared in late nineteenth-century Spanish-American literature as a symbol of the region's political and cultural resentment of the United States. Rubén Darío, a young Nicaraguan nationalist, journalist, and poet (later also a diplomat and Nicaragua's leading intellectual), was probably the first writer to apply images from *The Tempest* to the Western Hemisphere's international rivalries. In 1893 he visited New York City; its crudeness, materialism, and vice convinced him that he was in "the gory, the cyclopean, the monstrous capital of the banknote," where "Caliban soaks up whiskey as he soaked up wine in Shakespeare's play."[5] Five years later, Darío's article "El Triunfo de Calibán" denounced North Americans as "buffaloes with silver teeth"; "red-faced, heavy and gross . . . like animals in their hunt for the dollar."[6] That same year (1898) Paul Groussac, an Argentine writer, dubbed the United States "Calibanesque."[7]

This early casting of Caliban as a greedy, overbearing *yanqui* received major encouragement a few years later from the Uruguayan philosopher/politician, José Enrique Rodó, who had recently published a biographical sketch of Darío. In a long essay entitled *Ariel* (1900), Rodó combined praise for Spanish-American characteristics with sharp but sophisticated criticism of the United States. Rodó structured his book as an impromptu lecture by a master teacher—affectionately called Prospero "after the wise sage of Shakespeare's '*Tempest*' "—to his departing scholars, who have assembled around a bronze statue of Ariel.[8] Prospero urges his disciples to seek art, beauty, virtue, truth, and sensitivity; he warns them against materialism and utilitarianism. Sometimes implicitly, often explicitly, Prospero identifies those virtues with Spanish America or the Spanish "race," the vices with North America or the Anglo-Saxon "race."[9] Nearly a third of *Ariel* is aimed at *yanqui* shortcomings, tempered here and there by grudging praise for American achievements (mostly in the early years of the Republic) and softened a bit by Rodó's affinity for generalizations and abstractions.

Rodó drew symbols from *The Tempest* indirectly. Intermediary were three nineteenth-century French works: two imaginative adaptations of *The Tempest* by Ernest Renan and a long essay by Alfred Fouillée. Both authors implied that metaphors from *The Tempest* fit almost any time and place. Prospero, Caliban, and Ariel are not only specific characters but universal types that an author—playwright, poet, or essayist—may use as he or she chooses. Rodó, writing amid Latin America's modernist movement, found French influences especially congenial. Along with Darío and their contemporaries, Rodó championed a new literary voice and a more nationalistic political stance, yet they could not shake altogether their own cultural heritage; while largely rejecting the Castilian tradition that had long dominated Spanish-American culture, they turned not to truly indigenous sources but to France's creative vitality. The modernists' heroes were Victor Hugo, Baudelaire, Verlaine, and other French authors who flourished in what Latin American intellectuals saw as the era's most free and stimulating cultural environment.[10]

Rodó's *Ariel* is a case in point. It was partly a response to Renan's dramatic epilogues to *The Tempest*. Renan's first play, *Caliban, suite de La Tempête* (1878), ends with Caliban in command of Milan; Prospero is dead; and Ariel, rejecting human machinations, has vanished in the air to be a universal spirit. The workaday world is left to the triumphant mob and an increasingly conservative and manipulative Caliban. The French intellectual community was not wholly sympathetic to Renan's formulation; some critics found it too cynical, too anti-democratic. Fouillée, especially, expressed philosophical dissatisfaction. His *L'idée moderne du droit en Allemagne, en Angleterre et en France* (1878) argued that Ariel should return to the playwright's world as the necessary other dimension of Caliban; anything else, Fouillée contended, would be unjust and illogical. Renan responded with another play, *L'eau de jouvence: suite de Caliban* (1881), but it failed to fulfill Fouillée's suggestion, for in this, Renan's second epilogue to *The Tempest,* Ariel plays no significant role. Again the theme is cynical and elitist.[11]

Nearly two decades later, Rodó's *Ariel* implicitly extended Fouillée's objection to Renan's pejorative dichotomy between refined aristocracy and utilitarian democracy. Like Fouillée, Rodó sought compromise in the idealistic notion that social evolution would eventually improve the human species through natural selection: Caliban's qualities would eventually merge with Ariel's as successive refinements made rough-and-tumble leaders more sensitive and intelligent. Thus Ariel and Caliban, in Rodó's eyes, were complementary; they were concurrent influences in a cultural dialectic that some day would produce an ideal civilization. Rodó hoped, in short, that Spaniards and Anglo-Saxons in America would reach "a higher concord in the future, that will be due not to a one-sided imitation of one race by the other, but to a reciprocity of influences and a skilful harmonizing of those attributes which make the peculiar glory of either race." The gentle Ariel was Rodó's symbol of Spanish-American civilization at its best; and while he refrained from blatant labelling, Rodó implied unmistakably that Caliban represented North-American civilization at its worst. Ariel is "the spirituality of civilization, and the vivacity and grace of the intelligence;—the ideal end to which human selection aspires; that superman in whom has disappeared . . . the last stubborn trace of the *Caliban,* symbol of sensuality and stupidity." Rodó feared that *yanqui* culture might overwhelm Spanish America before an amalgamation could occur. The history of the United States, Rodó presciently complained a year before Theodore Roosevelt acceded to the presidency, "is above all a very paroxysm of virile activity."[12]

Uncle Sam had, to be sure, cast greedy eyes at neighboring territories for almost a century, to the growing unease of Latin-American spokesmen.

Examples of Yankee expansionism abound: the annexation of Texas in 1845; the Mexican War of 1846–48 and, at its conclusion, the acquisition of vast territories from Mexico; frequent, though unfulfilled, demands in the 1850s for the annexation of Cuba; armed encroachments in the 1880s and 90s in Central and South America and the Caribbean.[13] Even before the Spanish-American War of 1898, Latin Americans feared Uncle Sam's imperialist intentions. How could they trust a nation whose Secretary of State, Richard Olney, announced in 1895 that the United States was "practically sovereign on this continent, and its fiat is law upon the subjects to which it confines its interposition." Olney was ready to extend the fiat to the southern continent as well. Senator Henry Cabot Lodge, in his own mind at least, already had. In June 1895 Lodge asserted in the *North American Review* that the United States had "rightful supremacy in the Western Hemisphere."[14]

By its expansionist policy and aggressive rhetoric, the United States unwittingly fostered the pan-Hispanic movement that began in the late nineteenth century. Earlier in the century, Latin Americans had resented Iberian colonial policies even more than North American encroachment. The resulting wars of liberation from Spanish and Portuguese control had drawn some of their inspiration from the United States' struggle for independence from Great Britain; Washington and Jefferson were hailed throughout the hemisphere.[15] But gradually "the Colossus of the North" became too powerful, too expansionist, too dictatorial. Secretary Olney's "doctrine" and Senator Lodge's bombast were prime evidence.

The clash between Spain and the United States in 1898 marked a critical juncture in the evolution of Latin America's attitude toward itself and toward its northern neighbor. Many Latin-American commentators cheered the liberation of Cuba, but most resented Anglo-American intrusion in a Spanish-American affair. Their resentment grew more vociferous when the United States occupied Cuba, annexed Puerto Rico, and embarked on a prolonged war against Philippine insurrectionists. "The disaster of 1898," an American historian argues, "by which the Anglo-Saxon racial foe added several more notches to the stock of his imperialistic gun, aroused sympathy for the ancestral race and praise of its shining virtues."[16] Later the Chilean poetess and pan-Hispanic champion, Gabriela Mistral, advocated "one Spanish-America united by two stupendous factors—the language God gave us and the misery which the United States gives us."[17] It was a continuing misery, exacerbated by Theodore Roosevelt's pseudo-legal acquisition of the Panama Canal Zone in 1903 and his extension of the Monroe Doctrine in 1904. Roosevelt's "corollary" went a giant step further than Secretary Olney's earlier statement by asserting that the United States could intervene anywhere in the Western Hemisphere in cases of "chronic wrongdoing, or an impotence which results in a general loosening of the ties of civilized society."[18] T.R., of course, would be the judge of who was wrong or impotent or uncivilized. In 1904 Rubén Darío's poem "To Roosevelt" vividly expressed Latin-American fears: "The United States is grand and powerful / Whenever it trembles, a profound shudder / Runs down the enormous backbone of the Andes."[19]

Against this backdrop, *Ariel*'s verbal assault on the United States and its ready acceptance by Rodó's contemporaries are not surprising. Rodó denied that his essay was an indictment of the United States, but it quickly acquired that reputation. And Rodó himself grew more critical of the United States in his later years, as continuing Yankee imperialism made Latin Americans increasingly wary of Anglo-America's intentions. Between *Ariel*'s appearance in 1900 and Rodó's death in 1917, the United States intervened often and forcefully in Mexico, Central and South America, and the Caribbean. Each event added fuel to the rhetorical fire that Rodó had ignited, and many disciples carried still further his condemnation of North-American materialism and aggression. By the time of his death, Rodó was a hero throughout Latin America, but the subtle distinctions he had tried to convey had been lost in rampant yankeephobia.[20]

Rodó's death did nothing to dim the popularity or impact of his work. The return of the author's body to Uruguay in 1920 (he died in Italy) occasioned memorials throughout Latin America, and Rodó remains to the present a cultural hero in Spanish-speaking nations of the Western Hemisphere. Through more than thirty editions and countless printings, *Ariel* continues to wield enormous influence on Latin America's self image and, especially, on its image of the United States.[21] "*Ariel*," a prominent Peruvian scholar born in 1900 attested, "we knew by heart."[22] And to know *Ariel* was almost always to subscribe to its thesis. To be sure, a few Latin American authors disagreed with Rodó's position from the outset, and a few more dissenters emerged in the first half of the twentieth century when United States involvement in the World Wars encouraged a kinder view of its idealism and industrial strength. But even then, the Caliban/Ariel dichotomy remained central to Latin American imagery, and Caliban continued to symbolize the United States. During the Second World War, for example, another Peruvian writer couched a more benign view of Uncle Sam in the old metaphor:

> Many [Latin Americans] thought they saw a spiritual antithesis between the United States, representing the vile part of Caliban, and Indo-America, playing the subtle role of Ariel. We now see that this is an exaggeration. There are many Ariels in the lands of the North and among us some Calibans who would shock Shakespeare himself.[23]

Thus the basic identities of Caliban and Ariel persisted, even if their respective spheres became less precise.

Despite Rodó's reputation and his book's popularity, Latin-American writers in the past thirty-five years have repudiated his symbolic strategy while clinging to *Tempest* metaphors. Partly in response to Latin America's turn-of-the-century emphasis on cultural unity, partly as a reaction against a sudden influx of non-Iberian immigrants, and largely, perhaps, in belated recognition that most of the continent's population was not of European background, truly indigenous cultures reemerged throughout Latin America in the 1920s and 30s.[24] In a dramatic and perhaps inevitable transformation, Caliban at the same time became the representative of exploited Latin Americans and Prospero took on the menacing visage of Uncle Sam. Ariel again silently disappeared.

The reasons for the eventual rejection of Rodó's imagery are partly explained by *Ariel* itself. Despite the book's staunch advocacy of Latin-American independence and spiritual superiority, it is palpably Eurocentric, with scarcely a nod toward the Western Hemisphere's cultural achievements. The great heritage to which Rodó appeals throughout the essay is European and classical. His cultural pantheon includes Plato, Aristotle, and Cicero among the ancients; Taine, Bourget, and Comte among the moderns. At bottom, Rodó's vision of the clash between Latin America and the United States pits the Latin branch of the Western tradition against the Anglo-Saxon branch—hardly a compelling vision for those who traced their heritage to American Indian or African roots. Consequently, the image of Caliban that Darío and Rodó used with such success in the late nineteenth and early twentieth centuries collapsed when the old intellectual elite lost its monopoly on Latin American cultural and political leadership. New leaders lauded a different heritage. In the words of a modern Cuban writer, "[O]ur culture—taking this term in its broad historical and anthropological sense—[is] the culture created by the mestizo populace, those descendents of Indians and Blacks and Europeans . . . the culture of the exploited classes. . . ."[25] But if the reversal of Rodó's Ariel/Caliban metaphor was emphatic, it was also respectful. An authority on Rodó epitomized the twentieth-century shift in Latin-American perspective when he observed that "Perhaps Rodó erred in naming the danger [to Latin America], but he did not err in his perception of where it lay."[26]

Caliban's metamorphosis had begun, arguably, in 1928, when Jean Guéhenno's *Caliban Parle* portrayed him more sympathetically than had earlier works. But the influence of Guéhenno, a French writer, on his Latin American contemporaries seems to have been slight on this matter, perhaps because he, like Rodó, was largely concerned with refuting Renan's extension of *The Tempest*.[27] Similarly, Argentinian Aníbal Ponce's *Humanismo burgués y humanismo proletario* (1938) favorably identified Caliban with the exploited masses in partial refutation of Renan; Ponce too had little overt influence on the Caliban metaphor.[28] But in 1950 Caliban's image shifted radically. The impetus was another French contribution: the publication in Paris of Octave Mannoni's *La psychologie de la colonisation,* translated into English in 1956 as *Prospero and Caliban: The Psychology of Colonization.*[29] Because Mannoni wrote about the African island of Madagascar rather than the Americas, consideration of his argument and impact belongs elsewhere in this essay. Suffice it to

say here that Mannoni forcefully and explicitly identified Caliban with colonized and exploited people in general, thereby making Shakespeare's monster
an inappropriate symbol for the European-American population of the
United States but eminently appropriate for most Latin Americans.

In the 1960s and 70s, Latin-American writers, especially Caribbeans,
avidly adopted Mannoni's imagery. In 1969, for example, three Caribbean
writers—each perhaps unaware of the others' work in progress and each writing in a different language—drew on *The Tempest* metaphor. Aimé Césaire of
Martinique published in French an adaptation of *The Tempest* for *un théâtre
nègre;* his Caliban and Ariel are both slaves—the former black, the latter
mulatto.[30] Simultaneously, the Barbadian poet Edward Kamau Brathwaite
wrote in English a collection of poetry entitled *Islands;* one of the poems is
"Caliban."[31] And in Cuba, Roberto Fernández Retamar, writing in Spanish,
identified Caliban with the Cuban people in an essay on Fidel Castro. Two
years later (1970), Fernández Retamar's book *Caliban* explicitly and emphatically rejected José Rodó's formulation:

> Our symbol . . . is not Ariel, as Rodó thought, but Caliban. This is something
> that we, the *mestizo* inhabitants of these same isles where Caliban lived, see
> with particular clarity: Prospero invaded the islands, killed our ancestors,
> enslaved Caliban, and taught him his language to make himself understood.
> What else can Caliban do but use that same language—today he has no
> other—to curse him, to wish that the "red plague" would fall on him? I know
> no other metaphor more expressive of our cultural situation, of our reality. . . .
> [W]hat is our history, what is our culture, if not the history and culture of Cal-
> iban?[32]

Fernández Retamar's declaration, originally in Spanish, reappeared in
English in 1974 in a special issue of *The Massachusetts Review.* The entire issue
is entitled *Caliban* and is devoted to Latin American cultural expression.
Guest editor Robert Márquez described the issue's purpose:

> The stories, poems, play, essays and art work collected in this issue are . . . a
> contemporary echo of the rebellious Antillean slave in Shakespeare's final
> play. . . . [Caliban is a symbol of] a struggle for liberation and cultural authen-
> ticity whose roots must be traced back, from Salvador Allende, Che Guevara,
> and Toussaint L'Overture, to the original revolts of indigenous Indians and
> Black slaves. . . . Against the hegemonic, europocentric, vision of the universe,
> the identity of Caliban is a direct function of his refusal to accept—on any
> level—that hegemony. . . . This, then, . . . a fragment of the world-view of the
> victim, is the world of Caliban.[33]

In the years since that pathmark issue of *The Massachusetts Review,* the
identification of Shakespeare's monster/slave with the dark-skinned peoples of
Latin America has remained firmly entrenched in the region's cultural and

political rhetoric. Recently, Brathwaite has added new dimensions to *The Tempest* metaphor in a history of the 1831–32 Jamaica slave revolt: not only is Prospero the slave owner, Ariel the partially assimilated mulatto, and Caliban the rebel slave, but Alonso now symbolizes the British Parliament and Gonzalo the humanitarian missionaries.[34]

Robert Márquez's 1974 tracing of Caliban's ancestry to Indians and black slaves appeared to limit Caliban's physical sphere to the New World and Caliban's symbolic identity to its exploited inhabitants, whether aboriginal or imported from Africa. But other writers, especially Caribbeans of primarily African descent and native African writers of various nationalities, prescribe no geographical limits to the Prospero/Caliban metaphor. As Fernández Retamar acknowledged more than a decade ago, "The new reading of *The Tempest* has now become a common one throughout the colonial world. . . ."[35] Accordingly, Caliban is as much at home on the African continent as anywhere.

Caliban-as-African, much like Caliban-as-Latin American, endured an early identification with the oppressors rather than the oppressed and then experienced a parallel metamorphosis. In 1930 an English writer, Leonard Barnes, published *Caliban in Africa: An Impression of Colour-Madness*.[36] Barnes's title page carried as epigram a few lines about Caliban from *The Tempest*'s jester, Trinculo:

> What have we here? a man or a fish? dead or alive? A fish: he smells like a fish; a very ancient and fish-like smell; a kind of not the newest Poor-John. A strange fish!

Those insulting lines appear at first glance to be a slur on black Africans; the racist attitudes prevalent throughout England and America in the 1920s and 30s encourage such a reading. Barnes, however, had no such intent. He attacked, virtually slandered, certain Africans, to be sure, but not the blacks. The targets of his wrath were instead the Dutch Afrikaners—the creators and enforcers of apartheid. That system of racial segregation and the white supremacist doctrine on which it is based are, Barnes contended, "worthy of the freckled whelp of Sycorax." In his only other specific reference to Shakespeare's monster, Barnes excoriated "several features in the characteristic Dutch outlook which no civilized person, whatever his nationality, can look on with anything but contempt—for instance, the attitude to animals and persons of colour, and a certain deep intellectual insincerity" which, "like other Calibanesque traits . . . are things which good natures cannot abide to be with."[37]

Barnes drew few other *Tempest* allusions. He apparently assumed that his readers would readily recognize Caliban as a symbol of cruelty, stupidity, and sloth—the qualities he attributed to a major segment of South Africa's white minority.[38] Thus by 1930 Caliban's image had reached its nadir: most metaphorical applications of *The Tempest* identified Caliban with the world's oppressors. Darío's and Rodó's *yanqui* Caliban and Barne's Afrikaner Caliban held sway.

Twenty years later, Mannoni first identified Caliban with *black* Africans. His controversial *Prospero and Caliban* sought no connections between Shakespeare's intentions and Africans; rather he borrowed symbols from *The Tempest* to illustrate what he believed were Madagascan—indeed universal—personality types. Mannoni, a French psychiatrist who in the late 1940s spent several years as a government administrator in Madagascar, was struck by the profound and insidious impact of European imperialism. He concluded that colonial situations produce two basic personality types, which Prospero and Caliban conveniently represent. Colonials (Prosperos) are competitive, crave power, lack patience—else they would have remained at home—and seek an outlet overseas for their energies, their ambitions, and their deep insecurities. They become colonials partly because they are psychologically immature. "[I]f my analysis is correct," Mannoni hypothesized, "no one becomes a real colonial who is not impelled by infantile complexes which were not properly resolved in adolescence." Once in the colonial situation, Prosperos treat the people they rule as objects, as inferiors they can control through the magic of technology, written language, and political authority. Calibans, of course, are the natives who resent colonial rule but have little choice; they become dependent on Prosperos, even grateful to them sometimes, for bringing material and educational "progress."[39]

Initially, Prospero may befriend the native—recall Caliban's plaintive "When thou cam'st first, / Thou strok'st me, and made much of me . . . / and then I lov'd thee . . ." (I.ii.334–38). Soon the mood changes; Prospero becomes an exploiter rather than a benefactor and eventually almost ignores the native. Prospero's rejection of Caliban makes the native dependent, insecure, and in his own eyes inferior. The dependency created during the early years of colonization also leaves Caliban hopelessly enmeshed in a system not of his own making but essential to his survival.[40] Mannoni's characterization of the Malagasies is, admittedly, far more complex than this brief summary suggests, but two points about his paradigm should be apparent: first, Caliban is an African native—or indeed the native of any nation or continent subjugated by European Prosperos—and, second, he is a rather passive, obedient chap. The former conclusion has been widely accepted by Mannoni's admirers and detractors alike; the latter has generally been rejected, or at least modified, especially by black authors in the 1960s and 70s.[41]

If Mannoni's book was a major force in the transformation of Caliban as the oppressor to Caliban as the oppressed, some of the credit must go to Philip Mason, a long-time British civil servant in India and later director of the United Kingdom's Institute of Race Relations. Mason wrote a foreword to the American edition of *Prospero and Caliban* and later, in his own *Prospero's*

Magic: Some Thoughts on Class and Race (1962), devoted considerable attention and praise to Mannoni's metaphor.[42] In some respects, Mason applies *Tempest* symbolism more globally and explicitly than did Mannoni—to India and Asia as well as Africa and America—and gives Shakespeare's characters modern roles. "Ariel is . . . the good native, the moderate nationalist, the gradualist, usually content to wait until it pleases Prospero to give him his freedom; . . . one quite expects Prospero to offer him a knighthood." Caliban, on the other hand, "is the bad native, the nationalist, the extremist—the man who will be Prime Minister after independence. He has to be shut up, . . . not for making seditious speeches but for wanting to violate Miranda." Mason halts his metaphorical flight at that point. "Here I think I must draw the line," he demurs, "and resist any further temptation to make a parlour game of analogies with colonialism; Shakespeare was not gifted with second sight and did not foresee the colonial situation."[43]

Probably not, but the power of Mannoni's adaptation of *The Tempest* has not diminished. Critics continue to address it, although few, including Mason, accept all its implications. Mason, for example, points out that Madagascar is unrepresentative in many ways of colonial situations, particularly in the character of French colonialism and in the nature of Malagasy culture. Still, Mason believes the archetypes in *Prospero and Caliban* are generally valid.[44] So does Frantz Fanon of Martinique, whose *Black Skins, White Masks* (1952) devotes a chapter to "The So-Called Dependency Complex of Colonized Peoples." Fanon objects primarily to Mannoni's minimalization of racism's impact on the Malagasies and to his denial of the economic motives in colonization; Fanon sees the Malagasy dependency complex simply as a product of white colonization, not of any innate or culture-inspired condition. In short, Fanon accepts the Caliban characterization but attributes it to Prospero's tyranny rather than Caliban's nature. Prospero is even more villainous for Fanon than he was for Mannoni.[45]

The shift in the personification of evil from Caliban to Prospero (and, almost unconsciously, the virtual exclusion of Ariel from contemporary symbolism) is, of course, essential to the reversal in Caliban's role from oppressor to oppressed. If Caliban is hero, Prospero must be villain. As Mason pointed out in 1962, "[I]n my country until a generation ago we liked Prospero"; now, however, "some of us are beginning not to like him. . . . [W]e are perhaps moving towards some new conception of authority, in the family, in the state, and in international affairs."[46] That movement was inaugurated, or at least appreciably stimulated, by Aimé Césaire's *Une Tempête*. "To me," Césaire admitted, "Prospero is the complete totalitarian. I am always surprised when others consider him the wise man who forgives. . . . Prospero is the man of cold reason, the man of methodical conquest—in other words, a portrait of the 'enlightened' European." For Césaire, as for most Third World writers who now employ *Tempest* metaphors, the corollary of a totalitarian Prospero is an anti-authoritarian Caliban: "a rebel—the positive hero, in a Hegelian sense. The slave is always more important than his master—for it is the slave who makes history."[47]

The Third World's adoption of Caliban is ironic. Although he readily symbolizes its oppressed and exploited peoples, he is a European artifact—the product of an English imagination. Why, then, does Shakespeare's savage appeal so widely and profoundly to such a variety of non-English ethnic groups and nationalities? Part of the explanation is certainly Shakespeare's international fame: his plays and characters are almost as familiar to people from the Third World as to those from Western nations. An authority on Nigeria reported in 1958 that "it is not uncommon to find a semi-educated Nigerian . . . who can . . . quote the Bible and recite Hamlet."[48] Moreover, for Africans especially, a close knowledge of Shakespeare is often a mark of superior training and wisdom. As one black scholar has suggested, among Africans the ability to quote abundantly from Shakespeare is both a sign of a cultured mind and an eloquent refutation of the white racist assumption that blacks are intellectually inferior.[49] And perhaps, an authority on African literature has suggested, Shakespearean rhythms fit especially well with the cadences and tones of African linguistic traditions and with a widespread affinity for proverbs; Shakespeare is accordingly quoted often in African political and cultural dialogue.[50] Thus African writers readily employ Caliban as an effective rhetorical device, though often—and unlike most Caribbean authors—with ironic undercurrents that suggest ambivalence over an alien symbol.[51]

Perhaps too—and this is more speculative—Caliban is attractive to some authors because of the etymological identification of Shakespeare's monster with Caribbean or African settings through its supposed derivation from cannibal. The evidence for that etymology is unproven at best, but it is widely held and even stated as a truism by scores of Shakespearean specialists.[52] Again, however, the connection is ironic, for the association it calls up is surely pejorative. Third World authors, of course, do not always take that association literally.

But surely the basic reason for the Caliban metaphor's popularity among Africans is its typification of a major phase of their history. If Latin Americans could see in Prospero the embodiment of European and North American imperialism and could see in Caliban a symbol of themselves, Africans were very likely to make similar identifications. The bitter legacy of European colonization, the independence movements of recent decades, and the renewed vitality of indigenous cultures are reasons enough for African writers to employ the same anticolonial metaphor.

For a variety of reasons, then, Caliban has been prominent in African prose and poetry, especially in the third quarter of the twentieth century. For example, Raphael E. G. Armattoe of Ghana includes in his collection of poems, *Deep down the Blackman's Mind,* these lines:

> We have a new freedom, a new mistress,
> Not with lines nor with curves nor symmetry
> Nor with brains nor great talents encumbered:
> She is Africa with her terror and her norms.
> All that in Hades or in Inferno lives
> Which Caliban has made his own beneath the seas
> Plainness beyond despair, folly to the *nth*,
> All these are found in our Hesperides.[53]

A second example: In the early 1970s, Lemuel Johnson of Sierra Leone titled his collected poems *Highlife for Caliban*. Several of the poems have Shakespearean motifs, but they scarcely mention Shakespeare's monster; even "Calipso for Caliban" never uses the name, although it mentions "papa prospero." Johnson clearly expected his readers—Africans and others—to recognize his emblemization of Caliban nonetheless.[54]

A final example: Taban lo Liyong of Uganda, also writing in the early 70s, applied *The Tempest* metaphor explicitly and ironically:

> Bill Shakespeare
> Did create a character called Caliban,
> The unwilling servant of Prospero,
> . . . .
> One thing about Caliban: he was taught language
> And what a potful of curses he contained!
> . . . .
> (By the way,
> I am also called Taban
> Very near to Caliban
> And was taught language
> And what do I do with it
> But to curse, in my own way?)[55]

Taban lo Liyong's final line is, of course, a paraphrase of Caliban's "You taught me language; and my profit on't / Is, I know how to curse. The red plague rid you / For learning me your language" (I.ii.365–67). The irony and poignancy of that passage has intrigued many critics: Prospero's legacy to Caliban is not a glorious new way to express his finest thoughts but merely the means to curse his own fate and his oppressor's power. Civilization's most basic cultural tool is no gift at all. (Some of Caliban's subsequent lines are arguably among Shakespeare's most eloquent. But on balance, Caliban insists, he gained little from Prospero's language.) Until the middle of the twentieth century, most Shakespearean critics implicitly sided with Prospero on this issue, blaming Caliban for his own linguistic limitations: his warped nature was impervious to nurture's lessons.[56] Even the early twentieth-century advocates of the Caliban metaphor at least implied that Caliban was a linguistic boor when they chose him to symbolize imperialistic Anglo-Americans or overbearing Afrikaners.

But language as a key to the special relationship between Prospero and Caliban took a new turn in 1960 when Caribbean writer George Lamming, in keeping with the new view of Caliban as the oppressed, suggested that language was Caliban's "prison." Through language, Prospero controls the monster's present and limits his future—"the first important achievement in the colonising process." "This gift of language meant not English, in particular, but speech and concept as a way, a method, a necessary avenue toward areas of the self which could not be reached in any other way." Language is necessary to expression; expression is essential to change, but it is Prospero's language and therefore largely Prospero's vision of the future that Caliban must accept. Still, language is potentially liberating. As John Pepper Clark put it more recently, Caliban "is as much drunk with his second language [before Prospero's arrival he presumably communicated well enough with Sycorax] . . . as he is with the heady wine Stephano serves him."[57]

The German authority on "neo-African" literature, Janheinz Jahn, interprets Prospero's gift of language quite differently. Jahn, like Philip Mason, is wary of reading too much into an early Jacobean play; he is unwilling "to drag Shakespeare into modern controversies or credit him with ideas some way ahead of his time!" Still, Jahn finds the Prospero-Caliban "parallel" irresistible, and he readily follows the lead of the African writers he studies by applying *Tempest* metaphors to modern conflicts between oppressors and oppressed.[58] Prospero's language, he suggests, provides Caliban with a medium of expression for *Caliban's* culture. Prospero, of course, thinks the monster has no culture, but Caliban possesses

> a culture Prospero did not create and cannot control, which he, Caliban, has recognized as his own. But in the process [of recognition] the language is transformed, acquiring different meanings which Prospero never expected. Caliban becomes "bilingual." That language he shares with Prospero and the language he has minted from it are no longer identical. Caliban breaks out of the prison of Prospero's language.[59]

Jahn even suggests a rough date for Caliban's linguistic jailbreak: between 1934 and 1948 the literature of "Negritude," initiated by Leopold Sedar Senghor of Senegal and others, staged "the successful revolt in which Caliban broke out of the prison of Prospero's language, by converting that language to his own needs for self-expression."[60]

Jahn's analysis elevates Caliban from a symbol of the politically oppressed and culturally stunted native to a symbol of the temporarily inarticulate yet culturally rich native. Whereas Mannoni's Caliban was inferior because Prospero destroyed his culture and never fully replaced it with another, Jahn's Caliban has a valuable heritage that finds expression through Prospero's language even though Prospero is deaf to the message.[61] In sum, Jahn shifts the focus from despair over the deprivation of native culture to pride in its tenacity. In either case, Caliban is a paradigm for the oppressed, not the oppressors. Since 1940 no prominent author—from Europe or America or the Third World—has identified Caliban with the imperialists, as did Darío, Rodó, Barnes, and others in the first half of the century. Rather, as John Wain succinctly summarized the situation in 1964, Caliban represents "exploited peoples everywhere."[62] Caliban's transformation, for the time being at least, is diametric and virtually unanimous.

The universality of the new Caliban metaphor is illustrated by two works that explore current themes: apartheid in South Africa and French nationalism in Canada. Sibnarayan Ray's essay on "Shylock, Othello and Caliban" finds important parallels between certain Shakespearean characters and the victims of "ethnic-cultural superiority"—Ray's universalization of "apartheid." "Broadly speaking, the dominant community holds in arrogant contempt the one that is dominated; the latter, on its part, is driven to reluctant subservience, smouldering hatred and fear, and clandestine schemes of revenge." Thus defined, apartheid appeared in ancient Greece and China as well as in Europe, India, and elsewhere. Not that Shakespeare had any such applications in mind. Rather, because "a work of art, once completed, may communicate meanings which were outside the conscious intentions of the artist," Caliban effectively represents native populations almost everywhere, especially in Africa, the United States, and Australia.[63]

In 1974, Max Dorsinville's *Caliban without Prospero: Essay on Quebec and Black Literature* carried the Caliban metaphor to Canada, one of the few regions of the globe not touched specifically by Ray or his numerous predecessors. Simultaneously, the book gave new emphasis to Caliban's cultural tenacity. As Ronald Sutherland notes in the preface, Dorsinville goes beyond an analysis of the parallels between French Canadian and Black American literature—both are colonial, in a sense, but irrepressible and newly vigorous—to formulate "a new concept [for] . . . the literatures of all emerging national or ethnic groups." In the Caliban-Prospero metaphor, Dorsinville finds readymade "an instrument of insight into the complexities of cultural confrontation in a colonial context." Through a provocative blend of psychoanalytic theory and literary analysis, Dorsinville traces the evolution of two minority literatures in North America from their early dependence on the dominant culture to their recent emergence as literatures in their own right: Caliban *without* Prospero.[64]

Dorsinville is not reluctant, as were Rodó and Barnes much earlier and others more recently, to make *Tempest* metaphors explicit and emphatic. His book bristles with references to "Calibanic literature," "Calibanic culture," "a Calibanic search," "a strictly Calibanic viewpoint," "the Calibanic man," and "the Calibanic writer."[65] All such phrases refer, in Dorsinville's lexicon, to the literature that emerged at various times in various parts of the world where Europeans once settled, imposed their culture, were soon (sometimes not so soon) imitated by their colonial descendants, and eventually were rejected by culturally independent "post-European" authors. Dorsinville's story, in short, is Caliban's cultural emancipation. That Dorsinville invokes not only Québécoise and Afro-American literature but also, at least briefly, the literature of white Americans, English Canadians, Haitians, Argentinians, Brazilians, and Senegalese suggests the remarkable flexibility and versatility of the Caliban metaphor.

Readers of Shakespearean criticism are, of course, accustomed to seeing modern concerns shape interpretations of classical texts. But Caliban is unusual, perhaps unique, in having not only a variety of "lives" on stage and in his readers' minds but still another highly dynamic set of lives in sociopolitical culture. Sometimes Caliban's scholarly and popular worlds overlap (he is often, for example, portrayed in both as a rebellious black), for Caliban's remarkable mutability allows the man-monster to respond to changing fashions of scholarly and theatrical interpretation. He has, at various times, been portrayed on stage as a fish, an ape, an American Indian, or a black rebel, to name but a few of his incarnations.[66] His roles in sociopolitical rhetoric have meanwhile evolved from Renan's corrupt plebeian, to Darío's imperialist boor, to Mannoni's hapless victim, to the resilient native now championed by Márquez and many others.

Because a metaphor's effectiveness on its audiences defies precise measurement, we cannot know Caliban's impact on the Third World's political and cultural consciousness. Yet the frequency and poignancy with which Caliban has been invoked for nearly a century and the variety of authors who have enlisted him in ideological causes are suggestive. Shakespeare's savage and deformed slave must have met exceptionally well the needs of Third World authors and readers for a literary metaphor that was both readily identifiable and emotionally acceptable. That Caliban served so many masters surely reflects Shakespeare's unmatched universality and *The Tempest*'s adaptability to colonial contexts, whether seen from the imperialists' or the natives' perspective. The metaphor's popularity probably reflects too the imprecision of Caliban's shape and character in *The Tempest*'s text. Actors and artists through the centuries have had an almost free hand at portraying Caliban however they pleased, emphasizing his bestiality or humanity, his crudity or rough dignity, his curses or poetic passages. Caliban is malleable enough to fit varied emblematic roles, even contradictory roles, in response to the sociopolitical requirements of changing times and places.

Given the durability and versatility of Caliban's literary career and the volatility of sociopolitical rhetoric, further changes may be in store. Half a century ago, Caliban emblemized white imperialists, an image its adherents probably expected would last indefinitely; it would be foolhardy now to deny that so pliable an image could be reshaped by future events and future ideological perspectives. Yet there is reason to believe that the current Caliban metaphor will stoutly resist revision. Until the 1960s, most metaphoric uses of Caliban had elitist roots and less than universal support. Such intellectual giants as Renan and Rodó faced criticism from the outset to their symbolic strategies for Caliban; Barnes's association of Caliban with Dutch Afrikaners was a cry in the wilderness; and Mannoni, despite the profound influence of his paradigm, aroused vehement rebuttals.

By contrast, Caliban's current role of rebellious and resilient survivor of Western imperialism appears to be widely accepted and deeply felt throughout the Third World and beyond. Despite some concern, especially among African writers, that the literary source is itself the product of an English imperialist, it persists because it has thus far met a palpable social and political need. The *new* Caliban was sired by spokesmen of indigenous Third World cultures and has been nourished by a generation of readers who find in Shakespeare's savage a rich—if sometimes ambivalent—symbol of their own experience and aspirations.

Notes

1. By "Third World" I mean, very loosely, "the developing countries of Asia, Africa, and Latin America not politically aligned with Communist or Western nations" (*American Oxford Dictionary*). Caliban has frequently been used metaphorically by Latin American and African authors, as this essay demonstrates, and occasionally by Asians; writers from other geopolitical areas, moreover, have often applied Caliban metaphors to Third World contexts.

2. Manuel Gálvez, quoted in Harold Eugene Davis, *Latin American Social Thought: The History of Its Development since Independence, with Selected Readings* (Washington, D.C.: University Press of Washington, 1963), p. 424. For the Spanish version see Gálvez, *El solar de la raza* (Buenos Aires: Editorial Tor, [1936]), p. 39.

3. A possible exception is Roberto Fernández Retamar, "Caliban: Notes toward a Discussion of Culture in Our America," *The Massachusetts Review* (Winter-Spring, 1974): 11–16. "There is no doubt," Fernández Retamar contends, ". . . that *The Tempest* alludes to America, that its island is the mystification of one of our islands" (p. 15) and that "Caliban is our Carib" (p. 16). Fernández Retamar thus implies that Shakespeare intended Caliban to be a Caribbean and hence an ancestor of Latin American mestizoes.

4. Max Dorsinville, *Caliban without Prospero: Essay on Quebec and Black Literature* (Erin, Ont.: Press Porcépic, 1974), p. 12.

5. Quoted in John T. Reid, *Spanish American Images of the United States, 1790–1960* (Gainesville, Fla.: University Presses of Florida, 1963), p. 195.

6. Quoted in Reid, p. 195. The Spanish version of Darío's essay is reprinted in *Escritos inéditos de Rubén Darío,* ed. E. K. Mapes (New York: Instituto de las Españas, 1938), p. 160.

7. Quoted in Fernández Retamar, "Caliban," p. 18.

8. All quotations from *Ariel* in this essay are from the English translation by F. J. Stimson (Boston: Houghton Mifflin, 1922). The quotation concerning Prospero is on p. 3.

9. Rodó, *Ariel,* esp. pp. 89–123.

10. For the influence on Rodó of Renan and Fouillée, see especially Gordon Brotherston's introduction to *Ariel* (Cambridge, Eng.: Cambridge University Press, 1967), pp. 3–7. The modernist movement is discussed in Jean Franco, *The Modern Culture of Latin America: Soci-*

ety and the Artist, rev. ed. (Harmondsworth, Eng.: Penguin Books, 1970), pp. 25–51; and Arturo Torres-Ríoseco, *The Epic of Latin American Literature,* rev. ed. (New York: Oxford University Press, 1946), pp. 86–132.

11.   Brotherston, intro. to *Ariel,* pp. 3–7. An English translation of Renan's first play is *Caliban: A Philosophical Drama Continuing "The Tempest" of William Shakespeare,* trans. Eleanor Grant Vickery (New York: The Shakespeare Press, 1896).

12.   Rodó, *Ariel,* pp. 90, 95, 63, 145, 4, 102. For a general discussion of "Arielism" see Franco, *Modern Culture,* pp. 61–70.

13.   The major events in United States' relations with Latin America can be found conveniently in Dexter Perkins, *Hands Off: A History of the Monroe Doctrine* (Boston: Little, Brown, 1941); and Samuel Flagg Bemis, *The Latin American Policy of the United States* (New York: Harcourt, Brace & World, 1943).

14.   Ruhl J. Bartlett, ed., *The Record of American Diplomacy: Documents and Readings in American Foreign Relations* (New York: Alfred A. Knopf, 1948), p. 344; Henry Cabot Lodge, "England, Venezuela, and the Monroe Doctrine," *North American Review,* 160 (1895): 658.

15.   Reid, *Spanish American Images,* pp. 130–31.

16.   Reid, pp. 123 (quotation), 130–31. On the pan-Hispanic movement see also J. Fred Rippy, *Latin America in World Politics: An Outline Survey* (New York: Alfred A. Knopf, 1928), ch. 12.

17.   Quoted in Donald M. Dozer, *Are We Good Neighbors? Three Decades of Inter-American Relations, 1930–1960* (Gainesville, Fla.: University of Florida Press, 1959), p. 318.

18.   Bartlett, ed., *Record of American Diplomacy,* p. 539. The quote is from Roosevelt's annual message to Congress in 1904; a slightly different version appears in Roosevelt's letter to Elihu Root, quoted in Perkins, *Hands Off,* p. 238.

19.   *Selected Poems of Rubén Darío,* trans. Lysander Kemp (Austin, Tex.: University of Texas Press, 1965), p. 69.

20.   Brotherston, intro. to *Ariel,* pp. 9–13; Reid, pp. 131, 192; and Rippy, *Latin America in World Politics,* ch. 15.

21.   Rodó, *Ariel,* p. v; and Brotherston, intro. to *Ariel,* p. 1. Among the many biographies of Rodó are Gonzalo Zaldumbide, *José Enrique Rodó* (Madrid: Editorial America, 1919); Victor Perez Petit, *Rodó, su vida—su obra* (Montevideo: C. Garcia, 1937); Lauxar [Osvaldo Crispo Acosta], *Rubén Darío y José Enrique Rodó* (Montevideo: Agencia General de Libreria y Publicaciones, 1924); and Mario Benedetti, *Genio y figura de José Enrique Rodó* (Buenos Aires: Editorial Universitaria de Buenos Aires, 1966).

22.   Luis Alberto Sánchez, quoted in Reid, *Spanish American Images,* p. 193.

23.   Reid, pp. 192–198, quote at 197 from Manuel Seoane, *El gran vecino: America en la encrucijada,* 2d ed. (Santiago, Chile: Editorial Orbe, 1944), p. [4].

24.   Franco, *Modern Culture of Latin America,* pp. 82–140. In the visual arts, the emergent culture is perhaps best typified by Diego Rivera's murals.

25.   Fernández Retamar, "Caliban," pp. 58–59.

26.   Benedetti, *Genio y figura de Rodó,* p. 95.

27.   Jean Guéhenno, *Caliban Parle* (Paris: Bernard Grasset, 1928), *passim.* Guéhenno returned to this theme in *Caliban et Prospero: suivi d'autres essais* ([Paris]: Gallimard, 1969).

28.   Aníbal Ponce, *Humanismo burgués y humanismo proletario* (Mexico: Editorial America, 1938).

29.   [Dominique] Octave Mannoni, *Prospero and Caliban: The Psychology of Colonization,* 2d ed., trans. Pamela Powesland (New York: Frederick A. Praeger, 1964). The importance of Mannoni and the emergence of *Tempest* metaphors in anti-colonial literature is thoughtfully explored in Rob Nixon, "Caribbean and African Appropriations of *The Tempest,*" *Critical Inquiry,* 13 (1987), which complements the present essay but appeared too late to be incorporated in it.

30.   Aimé Césaire, *Une tempête: d'après "La tempête" de Shakespeare. Adaptation pour un théâtre nègre* (Paris: Editions du Seuil, 1969).

31. Edward Kamau Brathwaite, *Islands* (London: Oxford University Press, 1969).

32. Fernández Retamar first published this statement in his 1971 book *Caliban* and in an article by that title in *Casa de Las Americas*, 68 (Sept.–Oct., 1971); it appears too in an English translation of the essay—with minor variations—in *The Massachusetts Review* 15, 1–2 (Winter–Spring, 1974): 24. For commentary see Marta E. Sánchez, "Caliban: The New Latin-American Protagonist of *The Tempest*," *Diacritics*, 6 (Spring 1976): 54–61; and "Roberto Fernández-Retamar: Caliban y La Literatura de Nuestra America," *ECOS: A Latino Journal of People's Culture*, Series in Cultural and Literary Theory, 1 (Chicago: University of Illinois at Chicago, 1985).

33. Robert Márquez, "Foreword," *Massachusetts Review* (Winter–Spring, 1974): 6.

34. Edward Kamau Brathwaite, "Caliban, Ariel, and Unprospero in the Conflict of Creolization: A Study of the Slave Revolt in Jamaica in 1831–32," in Vera Rubin and Arthur Tuden, eds., *Comparative Perspectives on Slavery in New World Plantation Societies* (New York: New York Academy of Sciences, 1977), pp. 41–62, esp. 46.

35. Fernández Retamar, "Caliban," p. 6.

36. Leonard Barnes, *Caliban in Africa: An Impression of Colour-Madness* (London: Victor Gollancz, 1930).

37. Barnes, *Caliban in Africa*, pp. 118, 54.

38. Barnes's book is discussed briefly in Charlotte H. Bruner, "The Meaning of Caliban in Black Literature Today," *Comparative Literature Studies*, 13 (1976): 240–253. This generally accurate and useful article misinterprets Barnes's use of the Caliban metaphor; contrary to Bruner, Barnes in no way identifies Caliban with black Africans.

39. Mannoni, *Prospero and Caliban*, pp. 97–98, 104–09, quote at 104. Some of the themes developed by Mannoni appear also in Albert Memmi, *The Colonizer and the Colonized*, trans. Howard Greenfeld (Boston: Beacon Press, 1967; orig. pub. 1957), but Memmi does not employ *Tempest* metaphors.

40. Mannoni, *Prospero and Caliban*, pp. 106–09, 128–31.

41. For sharp criticism of Mannoni's interpretation by a "Third World" author, see Aimé Césaire, *Discourse on Colonialism*, trans. Joan Pinkham (New York: Monthly Review Press, 1972), pp. 39–43.

42. Mason, "Foreword" to Mannoni, *Prospero and Caliban*, pp. 9–15; Philip Mason, *Prospero's Magic: Some Thoughts on Class and Race* (London: Oxford Univ. Press, 1962), pp. 78–79.

43. Mason, *Prospero's Magic*, pp. 88–89.

44. Mason, *Prospero's Magic*, pp. 78–81.

45. Frantz Fanon, *Black Skins, White Masks*, trans. Charles Lam Markmann (New York: Grove Press, 1967; orig. pub. Paris, 1952). pp. 83–108, quote at 108.

46. Mason, *Prospero's Magic*, p. 96.

47. S. Belhassen, "Aimé Césaire's *A Tempest*," in Lee Baxandall, ed., *Radical Perspectives in the Arts* (Middlesex, Eng.: Penguin, 1972), p. 176. See also Thomas A. Hale, "Sur *Une Tempête* d'Aimé Césaire," *Études Littéraires*, 6 (1973): 21–34.

48. Ali A. Mazrui, "Some Sociopolitical Functions of English Literature in Africa," in Joshua A. Fishman, Charles A. Ferguson, and Jyotirinda Das Gupta, eds., *Language Problems of Developing Nations* (New York: John Wiley and Sons, 1968), pp. 183–197, esp. 185f., 190 (quotation) and 193. See also Bruner, "Meaning of Caliban," pp. 240–41.

49. Mazrui, "Some Sociopolitical Functions," pp. 185–87.

50. Bruner, "Meaning of Caliban," p. 241; Mazrui, "Some Sociopolitical Functions," pp. 187–90.

51. I am indebted to Lemuel A. Johnson for pointing out the variety of ironies that pervades African uses of Caliban—an aspect of the metaphor that deserves fuller attention than this essay can provide.

52. On Caliban's etymology, see O.E.D. "Caliban"; Frank Kermode, ed., *The Tempest*, Arden Edition of the Works of William Shakespeare, 6th ed. (London: Methuen, 1954; repr.

1977), p. xxxviii; and especially Peter Hulme, *Colonial Encounters: Europe and the Native Caribbean, 1492–1797* (London: Methuen, 1986), pp. 13–43.

53. Raphael E. G. Armattoe, *Deep down the Blackman's Mind: Poems* (North Devon, Eng.: A. H. Stockwell, 1954; repr. Nendeln, Neth.: Kraus, 1973), p. 59.

54. Lemuel Johnson, *Highlife for Caliban* (Ann Arbor, Mich.: Ardis, 1973), pp. 33–35, and an afterword by Sylvia Wynter, pp. 129–56, which underscores the ambiguity of the Caliban symbol in Johnson's poetry. See also Bruner, "Meaning of Caliban," pp. 248–49. Johnson further explicates and undermines the symbol in a manuscript essay entitled "Shoeing the Mule: Caliban as Genderized Response."

55. Taban lo Liyong, *Frantz Fanon's Uneven Ribs: With Poems More and More* (London: Heinemann, 1971), p. 41; another reference to Caliban is on p. 68. For other invocations of Caliban by African writers contemporary with the three quoted here, see Ngugi Wa Thiong'o (of Kenya), *Homecoming: Essays on African and Caribbean Literature, Culture and Politics* (New York: Lawrence Hill, 1973), pp. 7–9; and especially David Wallace (of Zambia), *Do You Love Me Master?* (Lusaka, Zambia: National Education Company, 1977). The latter work, a play that draws extensively on *The Tempest,* was first performed in 1971.

56. See, for example, Edmond Malone, ed., *The Plays and Poems of William Shakespeare,* 15 (London: Rivington, et al., 1821): 13–14.

57. George Lamming, *The Pleasures of Exile* (London: Michael Joseph, 1960), pp. 109–110; John Pepper Clark, *The Example of Shakespeare* (Evanston, Ill: Northwestern University Press, 1970), ch. 1: "The Legacy of Caliban," p. 3, previously published in *Black Orpheus,* 2 (1968): 16–39, quote at p. 17.

58. Janheinz Jahn, *Neo-African Literature: A History of Black Writing,* trans. Oliver Coburn and Ursala Lehrburger (New York: Grove Press, 1968; orig. pub. Düsseldorf-Koln, Ger., 1966), p. 239.

59. Jahn, p. 242.

60. Jahn, p. 242.

61. Jahn, pp. 241–69. See also Bernth Lindfors, "The Rise of African Pornography," *Transition,* 42 (1973): 65–71. Caliban's language is considered from a broader perspective in Stephen Greenblatt, "Learning to Curse: Aspects of Linguistic Colonialism in the Sixteenth Century," in Fredi Chiappelli, ed., *First Images of America: The Impact of the New World on the Old,* 2 vols. (Berkeley and Los Angeles: University of California Press, 1976), 2:561–80, esp. 568–75. See too Houston A. Baker, Jr., "Caliban's Triple Play," in Henry Louis Gates, Jr., ed., *"Race," Writing, and Difference* (Chicago: University of Chicago Press, 1986), pp. 381–395.

62. John Wain, *The Living World of Shakespeare: A Playgoer's Guide* (London: Macmillan, 1964), pp. 226–27.

63. Sibnarayan Ray, "Shylock, Othello and Caliban: Shakespearean Variations on the Theme of Apartheid," in Amalendu Bose, ed., *Calcutta Essays on Shakespeare* (Calcutta: Calcutta University, 1966), pp. 2–3, 10–13.

64. Dorsinville, *Caliban without Prospero,* p. 7.

65. Dorsinville, pp. 15, 33, 78, 206.

66. For Caliban's stage career, see Virginia Mason Vaughan, " 'Something Rich and Strange': Caliban's Theatrical Metamorphoses," *Shakespeare Quarterly,* 36 (1985): 390–405; and Trevor R. Griffiths, "This Island's mine': Caliban and Colonialism," *Yearbook of English Studies,* 13 (1983). On Caliban as an American Indian, see Alden T. Vaughan, "Shakespeare's Indian: The Americanization of Caliban," *Shakespeare Quarterly,* 39 (1988), 137–53.

Index

The Volume Editors

Virginia Mason Vaughan, professor of English and former chair of the English department at Clark University, has published essays on Shakespeare's history plays and three books on Shakespeare's *Othello:* the annotated bibliography in the Garland Shakespeare series, compiled with Margaret Mikesell (New York, 1990); an anthology, *Othello: New Perspectives* (Cranbury, N.J.: Fairleigh Dickinson University Press, 1991), coedited with Kent Cartwright; and *Othello: A Contextual History* (Cambridge: Cambridge University Press, 1994).

Alden T. Vaughan, professor emeritus of history at Columbia University, has published articles on *The Tempest* in *Shakespeare Quarterly* and *The Massachusetts Review*. During more than 30 years on the Columbia faculty, he published widely on England's American colonies in the seventeenth and eighteenth centuries, especially on their racial perceptions and policies. His most recent historical book is *Roots of American Racism* (New York: Oxford University Press, 1995). Earlier titles include *New England Frontier: Puritans and Indians, 1620–1675* (Boston: Little, Brown, 1965; 3d ed., Norman: University of Oklahoma Press, 1995); *American Genesis: Captain John Smith and the Founding of Virginia* (Boston: Little, Brown, 1975); and, coedited with Edward W. Clark, *Puritans among the Indians: Accounts of Captivity and Redemption, 1676–1724* (Cambridge, Mass.: Harvard University Press, 1981).

The Vaughans are coauthors of *Shakespeare's Caliban: A Cultural History* (New York: Cambridge University Press, 1991) and coeditors of *The Tempest* in the Arden Shakespeare, third series (in progress).

The General Editor

Zack Bowen is professor of English at the University of Miami. He holds degrees from the University of Pennsylvania (B.A.), Temple University (M.A.), and the State University of New York at Buffalo (Ph.D.). In addition to being general editor of this G. K. Hall series, he is editor of the James Joyce series for the University of Florida Press and the *James Joyce Literary Supplement.* He is author of six books and editor of three others, all on modern British, Irish, and American literature. He has also published more than 100 monographs, essays, scholarly reviews, and recordings related to literature. He is past president of the James Joyce Society (1977–1986), former chair of the Modern Language Association Lowell Prize Committee, and currently president of the International James Joyce Foundation.